H
O
N
G

K
O
N
G

in Chinese History

HONG KONG

in Chinese History

Community and Social Unrest in the British Colony, 1842–1913

JUNG-FANG TSAI

Columbia University Press
New York

Columbia University Press
New York   Chichester, West Sussex

Copyright © 1993 Columbia University Press
All rights reserved

Maps: Hong Kong and the New Territories 1914: adaptation from *Directory and Chronicle of China, Japan, Corea, Indo-China, Straits Settlements, Malay States, Siam, Netherlands, India, Borneo, The Philippines, etc., For the Year 1914*, Hong Kong: The Hongkong Daily Press Office, 1914.
　　City of Victoria, Hong Kong, 1882 (A, B, and C): adaptation from *Mr. Chadwick's Reports on the Sanitary Condition of Hong Kong*, London: Colonial Office, 1882.
　　City of Victoria, Hong Kong, 1913 (A, B, and C): adaptation from *Directory and Chronicle of China, Japan, Corea, Indo-China, Straits Settlements, Malay States, Siam, Netherlands, India, Borneo, The Philippines, etc., For the Year 1914*, Hong Kong: The Hongkong Daily Press Office, 1914.

Library of Congress Cataloging-in-Publication Data

Tsai, Jung-fang, 1936–
　　Hong Kong in Chinese history : community and social unrest in the British
　　Colony, 1842–1913 / Jung-fang Tsai.
　　　　p.　cm.
　　Includes bibliographical references and index.
　　ISBN 0–231–07932–X
　　1. Hong Kong—History.　2. Hong Kong—Social conditions.
　　I. Title.
　　DS796.H757T77　1993
　　951.25—dc20

92–36866
CIP

Printed in the United States of America

c 10 9 8 7 6 5 4 3 2 1
p 10 9 8 7 6 5 4 3 2 1

To my mother, Ch'ua Ng Luan (Ts'ai Huang Luan),
and in memory of my grandmother, Ch'ua Si K'iugn (1880–1966),
and my father, Ch'ua K'im (Ts'ai Chin, 1906–1963).

Contents

A Note on Romanization   ix

Acknowledgments   xi

Maps   xv

Introduction   1

ONE   Historical Setting: The Making of an Entrepôt   17

TWO   A Frontier Settlement: The Chinese Community   36
Under Alien Rule, 1840s–1860s

THREE   The Chinese Community in a Colonial Situation,   65
the 1870s–1900s

FOUR   Coolies in the British Colony   103

FIVE   Popular Insurrection in 1884 During the   124
Sino-French War

SIX   Coolie Unrest and Elitist Nationalism, 1887–1900   147

SEVEN   The Anti-American Boycott, 1905–6   182

EIGHT   The Anti-Japanese Boycott and Riot in 1908   207

NINE   Hong Kong in the Chinese Revolution, 1911–12   238

T E N   The Boycott of the Hong Kong Tramway, 1912–13   *270*

Conclusion   *288*

Notes   *297*

Character List   *335*

Selected Bibliography   *345*

Index   *363*

A Note on Romanization

In Hong Kong the romanization for Chinese names and terms is primarily based on the Cantonese pronuciation, since most of the Chinese in Hong Kong are Cantonese. Many famous names are known in Cantonese, such as Tung Wah Hospital, Nam Pak Hong, Po Leung Kuk, *kaifong,* Wing Lok Street, Ko Shing Theater, Saiyingpun (Sei Ying Poon), Wanchai, Sze Yap Association, Taikoo Dockyard, Ho Kai, Wei Yuk, Kwok Acheong, Sin Tak Fan, Yuen Fat Hong, and so forth. But the romanization for a few names and terms of Teochiu and Hoklo origins (such as Ko Man Wah, Choa Leep Chee, and Goh Guan Hin) is based on the pronunciation of these respective dialects. An attempt to use standard *kuo-yü* (national language) for all names and terms would render unfamiliar many famous names, institutions, and commercial firms traditionally romanized according to their respective dialects in official documents and historical records. To use *kuo-yü* for all names in Hong Kong is just like singing Cantonese tunes in Mandarin, losing the whole feel of the place and its people, losing the delicate flavor and nuance of a distinctive local culture.

Moreover, the local English newspapers and the colonial police records used for this study abound with persons' names in Cantonese romanization, without providing Chinese written characters— names of fishmongers, hawkers, chair bearers, ricksha pullers, cargo coolies, Triad members, shophands, shopkeepers, and so on. In short, in writing a social history of Hong Kong dealing with large numbers of the ordinary people it is simply impossible to provide a standard *kuo-yü* romanization for all names and terms.

In this book, therefore, names pertaining to China and names rarely romanized or printed in the English historical documents are spelled in *kuo-yü* according to the Wade-Giles system, while those pertaining to Hong Kong are romanized in their respective dialects as they have appeared in official documents, newspapers, and other historical sources.

A character list is provided at the end of the book.

Acknowledgments

Although the idea to write this book was first conceived many years after I left the University of California at Los Angeles, I feel deeply grateful to Dr. Philip C. C. Huang, Dr. Robert A. Wilson, and, especially, the late Dr. David M. Farquhar, from whom I learned a great deal about the craft of the historian and the philosophy of life in ways they might not realize themselves. Professor Farquhar passed away in 1985; his scholarship and selfless devotion as well as the warmth of his friendship had earned him the love and respect of his students, friends, and colleagues.

A number of my friends and colleagues have given me generous help during the course of this study. Peter Yeung, K. C. Fok, Elizabeth Sinn, Rev. Carl Smith, and James Hayes have been most helpful in my acquisition of research materials. I learned a great deal about Hong Kong from pleasant conversations (often over lunch) with them and with Ling-yeong Chiu, Gerald H. Choa, Alan Birch, John D. Young, Lu Yen, Shui Yuen Yim, Lo Hui-min, and Yen Ching-hwang. I wish to express sincere thanks to all of them, particularly for their courtesy and hospitality during my several visits to Hong Kong. I am indebted to Chen Weiming and Ni Junming for assistance in obtaining sources in Guangzhou, and to Sze King Keung of the Hong Kong University Library for photocopy services.

I would also like to thank Hamashita Takeshi, Ikeda On, and my old friend and classmate, Cheng Ching-jen, for their help in facilitating my research at Tôyô Bunka Kenkyûjo at Tokyo University in 1983. I owe a debt of gratitude to the staffs of the last-named institute and to the following—Tôyô Bunko, the National Diet Library, and Gaimushô Gaikô Shiryôkan in Tokyo; the Library of Congress in Washington, D.C.; Academia Sinica in Taipei; Hong Kong University Library and the Public Record Office in Hong Kong; Zhongshan Library in Guangzhou. The staff at the University of Charleston Library have been most gracious and helpful, especially Michael Phillips, Shirley Davidson, and Marlene Barnola.

Generous grants from the American Philosophical Society, the Southern Regional Education Board, and the University of Charleston (which also granted me a sabbatical in the Fall semester of 1986) allowed me to do research and writing on the subject of Hong Kong. Paul A. Cohen, James B. Leavell, Hillel B. Salomon, Malcolm C. Clark, Clarence B. Davis, and Clark Reynolds wrote letters to support my grant applications. My History Department colleagues at the University of Charleston gave me encouragement and moral support. I thank them all.

Clark Reynolds, Malcolm Clark, Nan Woodruff, and Chun-tu Hsueh read some chapters, and Tu-hsun Tsai read the entire manuscript. I am grateful to them for their critiques. I alone, of course, am responsible for all shortcomings that still remain. Several chapters in abbreviated forms were orally presented at the various regional conferences of the Association for Asian Studies; I am indebted to the panelists (Jonathan Porter, Steven I. Levine, and Stephen MacKinnon, among others) and audience for their comments on my papers. Acknowledgments are due to the following journals for permission to draw freely on my two articles, "The Predicament of the Comprador Ideologists: Ho Kai (1859–1914) and Hu Li-yüan (1847–1916)," in *Modern China* 7:2 (April 1981), and "The 1884 Hong Kong Insurrection," in *Bulletin of Concerned Asian Scholars* 16:1 (January–March 1984). Above all, I am very grateful to the anonymous readers at Columbia University Press for their insightful critiques, to Kate Wittenberg, editor in chief, for her advice and guidance, and to Susan Pensak, manuscript editor, for expert editing.

Because of my heavy teaching load most of the research and writing on this book was done during summer vacations. My inadequate knowledge naturally prolonged the writing process. My wife,

Mei-hui, cheerfully helped in research while in Taipei and Hong Kong and rendered valuable assistance while in Tokyo and Washington, D.C. My son, Oliver, now in the sixth grade, has shown great interest in my work. My brothers (Tu-hsün, Tu-hsien, Jung-long, Jung-chung) and sisters (Ts'ai-hsia, Yü-yen, Yü-yun, Ts'ai-yü, Yü-jui) have been waiting for many years, with good humor and great patience, for the completion of this work. I extend my love and gratitude to them all.

This book is dedicated to my mother, Ch'ua Ng Luan (Ts'ai Huang Luan), and in memory of my grandmother, Ch'ua Si K'iugn (1880–1966), and my father Ch'ua K'im (Ts'ai Chin, 1906–1963, landlord and journalist). They taught me a great deal about the values of loving-kindness, social justice, and empathy with the underclasses—values that transcend ethnic and national boundaries. They contributed significantly to the formation of the thoughts that are expressed in the chapters that follow.

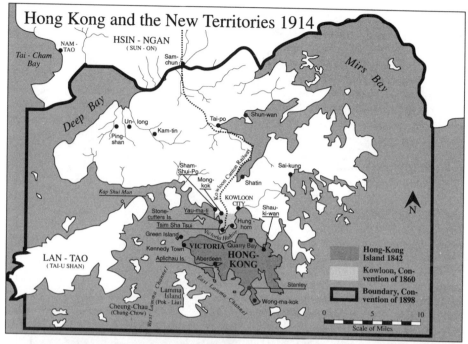

Hong Kong and the New Territories 1914

NAM - TAO

HSIN - NGAN
(SUN - ON)

Tai - Cham Bay

Sam-chun

Mirs Bay

Deep Bay

Un - long

Pingshan

Kam-tin

Tai-po

Shun-wan

Sai-kung

Sham-Shui-Po

Mong-kok

Shatin

Kap Shui Mun

KOWLOON CITY

Stonecutters Is.

Yau-ma-ti

Shau-ki-wan

Tsim Sha Tsui

Green Island

Hung-hom

Victoria Harbor

LAN - TAO
(TAI-U SHAN)

Kennedy Town

Aplichau Is.

VICTORIA

Aberdeen

HONG-KONG

Quarry Bay

N

Hong-Kong Island 1842

Kowloon, Convention of 1860

Boundary, Convention of 1898

Lamma Island
(Pok - Liu)

Stanley

East Lamma Channel

West Lamma Channel

Cheung-Chau
(Chung-Chow)

Wong-ma-kok

0   5   10

Scale of Miles

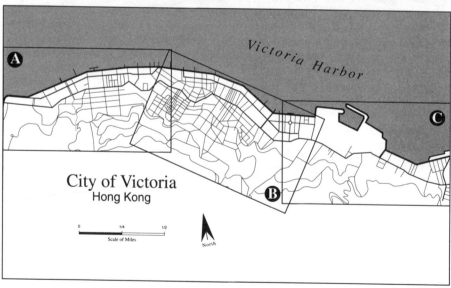

Victoria Harbor

A

C

City of Victoria
Hong Kong

0   1/4   1/2

Scale of Miles

B

North

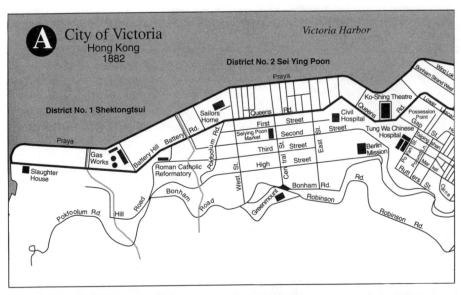

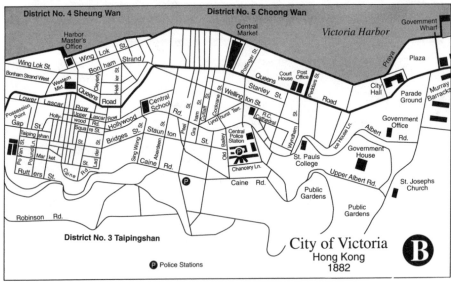

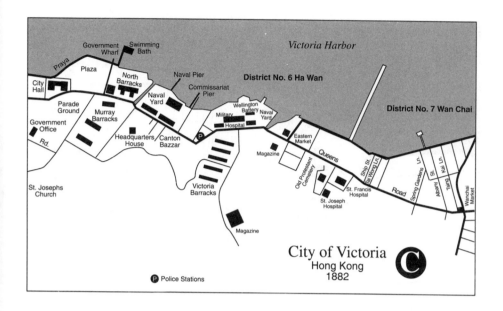

City of Victoria
Hong Kong
1882

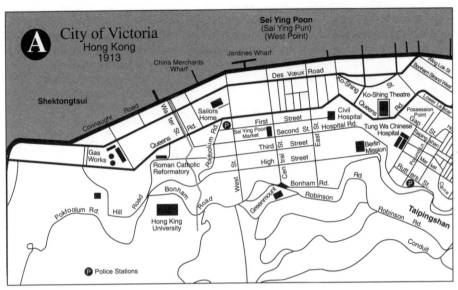

City of Victoria
Hong Kong
1913

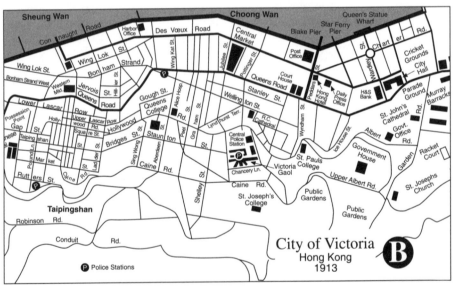

City of Victoria
Hong Kong
1913

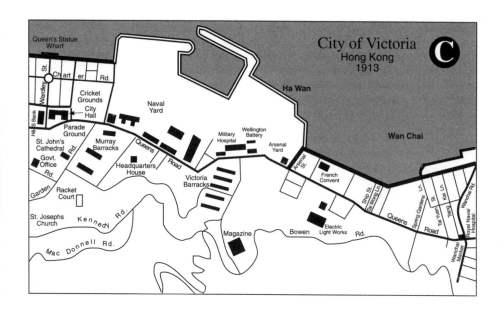

City of Victoria
Hong Kong
1913

C

H
O
N
G
  K
  O
  N
  G *in Chinese History*

Introduction

This book is a study of urban community and social unrest in the British colony of Hong Kong from 1842 to 1913. In it I explore the evolution of a Chinese community under the leadership of a commercial elite and the changing social structure and relations between elite and populace in a society under alien rule. It investigates the relationships between the Chinese community, colonial authorities, and Chinese officials in Canton. Such relationships were often characterized by both harmony and conflict, cooperation and antagonism. This study particularly aims to examine the nature and patterns of social unrest in the colony from its earliest years to the time of the Chinese republican revolution. During this period social unrest took various forms—labor strikes, street riots, boycott movements, rowdyism, and other acts of civil disobedience. Often imbued with antiforeignism, popular unrest gradually acquired a nationalistic overtone in the late nineteenth century. Chinese antiforeignism in Hong Kong was finally transformed into popular nationalism, which found full expression during the republican revolution of 1911.

As a British colony Hong Kong took its own path of historical development, yet Hong Kong remains distinctly Chinese. By exploring Chinese community aspirations and forms of social interaction in the context of alien rule, I hope this book will provide some insights into the enduring structures of Chinese society at home; by examining the intricate relationship between Chinese and foreigners in the colony, I hope that it will shed some light on the complexities and Janus-faced nature of nationalism in China in modern times.

Historiography on Hong Kong Studies

Hong Kong has played important roles in the history of modern China. As an entrepôt Hong Kong has served as a major center of a flourishing commercial network in the Pacific basin that encompasses China, Japan, Southeast Asia, Australia, and America. A meeting place of Eastern and Western cultures, Hong Kong has been China's window to the outside world—from Hong Kong Western culture and techniques have been disseminated to China; during the late Ch'ing period Hong Kong became a major base for the republican revolutionaries conspiring to overthrow the Manchu dynasty; it was also from Hong Kong that Western capital was channeled to the mainland.

Despite the importance of Hong Kong in China's economic and political development in modern times, the history of Hong Kong has until recently been badly neglected by the community of scholars. Monographs on the colony's history have been so rare that some British studies published many decades ago are still considered the authoritative standard works on the subject. For instance, E. J. Eitel's *Europe in China: The History of Hong Kong from the Beginning to the Year 1882,* first published in 1895, was reprinted by Oxford University Press in 1983. This account of the early history of Hong Kong by an old resident, scholar, and official, who observed first-hand many of the events described, remains an indispensable source for historians. But Eitel's basic philosophy of history was informed by racism, imperialism, and colonialism. He asserted, for example, that "the people of Hongkong are inwardly bound together by a steadily developing communion of interests and responsibilities: the destiny of the one race is to rule and the fate of the other to be ruled." Eitel insisted on "the natural process of bringing China into subordination to Europe," whose "destiny is to govern Asia" and to open up China "to the civilizing influences of British power."[1]

James Norton-Kyshe's *History of the Laws and Courts of Hongkong from the Earliest Period to 1898,* first published in 1898, was reissued in Hong Kong in 1971. Compiled by the then registrar of the Supreme Court, this two-volume work is a useful chronology of names and events, but not a work of history. G. R. Sayer's *Hong Kong 1841– 1862: Birth, Adolescence, and Coming of Age* was published in 1937 and reprinted by the Hong Kong University Press in 1980. He wrote another manuscript in 1939 entitled *Hong Kong 1862–1919: Years of Discretion,* posthumously published by the Hong Kong University Press in 1975. Written by an official in Hong Kong with access to some source materials no longer available to researchers, Sayer's books remain useful references. They consist, however, of little more than a chapter-by-chapter account of the various governors' administrations. This approach was largely followed by W. A. Wood[2] and G. B. Endacott.[3]

Most of these works were not only dated but were also written from the British colonists' perspective, which was so "heavily Western-centric"[4] that there was little room even for a discussion of the prominent Chinese who had played important roles in the politics and economy of the Chinese community in Hong Kong. This was ironic because many of these Chinese were business partners of the Europeans and economically tied to Western capital. Due to the colony's proximity to Canton, they were often politically and economically connected with Canton as well. Relying on Western-centric historiography, one would look in vain for adequate treatment of important personalities in the history of Hong Kong such as Ko Man Wah, Li Tak Cheung, Ho Amei, and Sin Tak Fan, to name only a few. If these prominent Chinese did not find a place in the history written from a Western elitist viewpoint, the Chinese populace fared even worse. The common people almost always remained anonymous.

The Eurocentric history of Hong Kong is written in the "colonial" tradition, which portrays the colony "from outside" and "from above," that is, from the perspective of the European elite, and which focuses on British policy and administration. In A. C. Milner's words, this approach "is 'colonial' in the sense that it portrays the British as the principal actors in the period, the initiators of action. The development and execution of British policy are the main concerns of this history."[5] H. J. Lethbridge aptly comments: "The history of Hong

Kong has been written mainly from a European point of view, with the European community in the centre of the stage and the Chinese, when they are heard at all, making confused noises in the wings."[6]

Most scholars in Hong Kong studies today are economists, political scientists, sociologists and anthropologists. They have written about the colony's economic conditions, government administration, political system, social customs and institutions, and cultural values. But the study of the colony's history has until recently been neglected. A comprehensive bibliography of the history of Hong Kong would make a short list.

In recent years there have been witnessed several important contributions such as James Hayes's *Hong Kong Region 1850–1911: Institutions and Leadership in Town and Countryside* (Hamden, Ct.: Shoe String, 1977) and *The Rural Communities of Hong Kong: Studies and Themes* (Oxford University Press, 1983); and David Faure's *The Structure of Chinese Rural Society: Lineage and Village in the Eastern New Territories, Hong Kong,* (Oxford University Press, 1986). But these are largely village studies that hardly deal with urban Hong Kong, where the great majority of the colony's population lived.

Important works on the colony's history also include Carl T. Smith's *Chinese Christians, Elites, Middlemen, and the Church in Hong Kong* (Oxford University Press, 1985), a collection of very informative essays by a scholar and long-time Hong Kong resident who has an unsurpassed knowledge of the colony's elites and history; Frank H. H. King's monumental study on *The History of the Hongkong and Shanghai Banking Corporation* (Cambridge University Press, 1988–1990); H. J. Lethbridge's *Hong Kong: Stability and Change* (Oxford University Press, 1978), a collection of critical and witty interpretative essays on such important historical institutions as the Tung Wah Hospital, Po Leung Kuk, and the District Watch Committee; *From Village to City: Studies in the Traditional Roots of Hong Kong,* edited by David Faure, J. Hayes, and A. Birch (University of Hong Kong Press, 1984); K. C. Fok's *Lectures on Hong Kong History: Hong Kong's Role in Modern Chinese History* (Hong Kong: Commercial Press, 1990), which examines some important themes and documents that deserve scholarly attention; and Elizabeth Sinn's *Power and Charity: The Early History of the Tung Wah Hospital, Hong Kong* (Oxford University Press, 1989), an engrossing study on an important elite institution and the community under its leadership. Wai Kwan Chan's *The Making of Hong Kong Society*

(Oxford: Clarendon Press, 1991) is also informative. These works examine selected aspects of the colony's history, as do some other titles.[7]

This brief list, containing a total of less than three dozen books, almost exhausts the published scholarly monograph studies on the one hundred and fifty-year history of Hong Kong.[8] Most scholars in Hong Kong studies have stressed the colony's growth, development, stability (as illustrated by H. J. Lethbridge's title, *Hong Kong: Stability and Change*), and the alleged political apathy of the Chinese population. In contrast, this book seeks to explore not merely the Chinese community structure but also the social crises, tensions, conflicts, and political activism of coolies, merchants, and intelligentsia in the colony.[9]

Methodology and Contents

Social crises and disturbances often reveal a great deal about the reality of sociopolitical relations between various groups of people in a given society. The French anthropologist George Balandier has observed that social crises enable a student to achieve a comprehensive analysis of the "colonial situation"; since "conflicts expose the totality of relationships between colonial peoples and colonial powers . . . it is precisely at such moments [of crises and conflict that] we can study the colonial society in terms of the concrete colonial situation." Balandier defines the "colonial situation" as

> the domination imposed by a foreign minority, racially (or ethnically) and culturally different, acting in the name of a racial (or ethnic) and cultural superiority dogmatically affirmed, and imposing itself on an indigenous population constituting a numerical majority but inferior to the dominant group from a material point of view; . . . the fundamentally antagonistic character of the relationship between these two [groups and] societies resulting from the subservient role to which the colonial people are subjected as "instruments" of the colonial power; . . . [and] the need, in maintaining this domination, not only to resort to "force," but also to a system of pseudo-justifications and stereotyped behaviors.[10]

With some qualifications, this definition of the "colonial situation" is largely applicable to Hong Kong during the period under study. A major qualification concerns the relationship between the colonizers and the colonized. While Balandier stresses "the fundamentally antagonistic character of the relationship," my study reveals an ambivalent relationship, especially between the British colonists and Chinese merchants—antagonism on the one hand, and partnership on the other—an unequal partnership that caused resentment.

This study is both descriptive and analytical. Description is necessary because many events related to social unrest in Hong Kong in 1842–1913 have not been studied by anyone else before. Detailed description is essential if one wishes to reconstruct a historical event in all its complexities and to reproduce something of people's lives and thoughts of the past. Quantitative statistics do not tell us about the quality of human life. I endeavor to look behind the statistics of trade, shipping and population to see the lives of people at work and at leisure. Of interest to me are not only the wealthy Chinese merchants surrounded by their concubines in their magnificent residences overlooking Victoria harbor but also a sweating sedan chair coolie bitten by a dog owned by a European, the riotous Chinese crowd spitting on the British imperial troops patrolling the streets of Hong Kong, and a ricksha puller spitting blood at the end of a long hard journey. Detailed description of such events is essential if one wishes to recapture the emotions of men and women as they lived their lives.

In contrast to the "colonial" approach and European elitist perspective, I have attempted to explore the social history of Hong Kong from the perspectives of the Chinese people who constituted the overwhelming majority of the colony's population. Such perspectives are greatly needed in Hong Kong studies. While not neglecting the views of the European colonists, my major concerns center on the lives, activities, aspirations and feelings of the great majority of the Chinese population in Hong Kong.

This is a study of "history from below." It seeks to explore the social reality hidden behind a veneer of prosperity, stability, and harmony so often portrayed by the colony's dominant groups and ruling elite. As Barrington Moore justly observes:

> In any society the dominant groups are the ones with the most to hide about the way society works. Very often therefore truthful analyses are bound to have a critical ring, to seem like exposures. . . . For all students of human society, sympathy with the victims

of historical processes and skepticism about the victors' claims provide essential safeguards against being taken in by the dominant mythology. A scholar who tries to be objective needs these feelings as part of his ordinary working equipment.[11]

To use critical language and candid, unadorned words to describe social reality does not preclude the attainment of objectivity.

Economic conditions and social structure contributed significantly to the shaping of social movements. The first three chapters, therefore, discuss the economic conditions and sociopolitical structure of Hong Kong from the 1840s to the 1910s. Chapter 1 examines the historical development of Hong Kong as an entrepôt from the founding of the colony to the 1910s. It discusses Hong Kong as a major center of a thriving commercial network in the Pacific basin. It investigates some Chinese commercial firms in Hong Kong to illustrate the close trade relations among Chinese merchants all around the Pacific commercial network. The Chinese community thrived in Hong Kong under British colonial rule. But how did the community originate? Chapter 2 traces the formation of a Chinese community in a frontier settlement from the 1840s to the 1860s. Aspiring Chinese used all resources available to promote their economic power and social influence in the new settlement. Some emerged as elite to dominate the Chinese community under British rule.

Chapter 3 relates the community structure under the cultural hegemony of a merchant elite from the 1870s to the 1880s, and the emergence of a more heterogeneous society from the mid-1880s to the 1900's as a result of population growth and economic expansion. As the colonial society became more heterogeneous, community consensus became more difficult to obtain. A younger generation of merchants, professionals, and intelligentsia emerged, a generation more Western-oriented than the old elite and more inclined to innovations and new commitments. Most of the events discussed in the subsequent chapters took place during this exciting and creative period in the colony's history. It was a time when laborers also increasingly became more politically activated.

The working people played a vital role in the colony's economy by providing the much needed labor, yet scholarly works on laborers during this period are extremely rare. Chapter 4 examines the wages, cost of living, housing, and general living conditions of the various groups of coolies. They were the most numerous elements among the colony's population, and also the most abused, exploited and neglected. This was a major source of tension in colonial society.

The remaining chapters, 5 through 10, analyze the nature and significance of social unrest in Hong Kong—the 1884 popular insurrection during the Sino-French War; the coolie disturbances in 1888, 1894, and 1895; the reformist and revolutionary movements of the elitist patriots from among the merchants and intelligentsia; the 1905 anti-American boycott; the 1908 anti-Japanese boycott and riots; the nationalistic activities of the colony's Chinese public, politicized by the 1911 Chinese revolution; the labor strike and civil disobedience, inflamed by the Chinese revolution; and the boycott of the Hong Kong Tramway in 1912–13, also inspired by the Chinese revolution.

Unlike most books on Hong Kong that are too Hong Kong–centered, this is a study of Hong Kong in Chinese history. Events in the British colony are studied in the context of the history of China in modern times. Hence the title of this book, *Hong Kong in Chinese History*. Since the very beginning the development of the port of Hong Kong has been closely related to the political and socioeconomic conditions of the Chinese mainland and the Sino-foreign relations. For this reason, Hong Kong cannot be studied in isolation. Constantly subject to the repercussions from the changing political and socioeconomic conditions outside the colony, all major events in Hong Kong have been the results of interactions between local and external forces. In examining the community and social unrest in Hong Kong, this book pursues a number of linkages—between national politics and local interests, between events in Canton and those in Hong Kong, and between elements of the Chinese diaspora throughout the Pacific basin.

Community: How Was It Held Together?

A major theme of this work deals with how the Chinese community was held together under British colonial rule. In some ways the social history of Hong Kong is very similar to that of other large Chinese cities on the mainland. But it is also very different as a result of Hong Kong's experience with alien colonial rule.

Hong Kong belonged to what Paul A. Cohen calls the *littoral*, which in the late nineteenth century included cities like Canton,

Hong Kong, Shanghai, Ningpo, Foochow, and Tientsin. Cohen contends that the littoral acquired a distinctive culture different from the hinterlands. The littoral came under direct Western influence; it was global and outward-looking in orientation; and its economy was geared to Sino-foreign commerce.[12] These certainly applied to Hong Kong. But Cohen's characterization of the littoral society as "dominated by the bourgeois values of its Chinese and Western merchant elites" needs very careful qualification. The littoral in fact retained a great deal of traditional values and institutions. This is of great importance to our understanding of society in Hong Kong.

Although living under alien rule, most of Hong Kong's Chinese residents remained strongly committed to traditional Chinese ideas, religions, language, habits, and customs. The Chinese crowds delighted in religious processions featuring dragon and lion dances celebrating the restoration of the Man Mo Temple. Coolies frequented pugilistic clubs cultivating the art of boxing and fencing; many joined the Triad societies. The Chinese burned incense and paper money for their deceased ancestors at family shrines and in temples worshiping Kwan-ti and T'ien-hou. They believed in *feng-shui* (geomancy) and portents. They consulted fortune-tellers concerning travel, marriage, and business ventures. They took herbal medicine to cure illness. The Chinese remained loyal to their kinsfolk and to their dialect and native district communities. These Chinese traditions were omnipresent in Hong Kong and other "Western beachheads" of the littoral, commanding respect and allegiance of all classes of Chinese, including members of the intelligentsia and merchant class in varying degrees. In fact, the Chinese community in Hong Kong during much of the latter half of the nineteenth century was held together by a commitment to common traditional Chinese values and associations.

In his fascinating study of conflict and community in Hankow from 1796 to 1895, William T. Rowe shows that Chinese cities like Hankow in the nineteenth century had much less disruptive social conflict than occurred in cities like Paris and London in early modern Europe. He attributes this to the cultural hegemony of an activist elite that fostered a social consensus based on Confucian ideals of social harmony and elite paternalism. This consensus was maintained through processes of accommodation and compromise and the mediation of local elite in major conflict situations. Through community service and philanthropy, the elite reconfirmed its claim to social superiority. Yet the "consensus mandated not only recognition of Confucian social hierarchies...but also a deep respect for popular livelihoods."[13]

Rowe's concept of cultural hegemony, in large part derived from Antonio Gramsci and E. P. Thompson, seems also useful in understanding Hong Kong's Chinese community. In this aspect, Hong Kong in the littoral shows remarkable resemblence to Hankow in the hinterland. In Hong Kong during the period from the 1860s to the 1890s the Chinese merchant elite also endeavored to promote social consensus based on Confucian ideas and values; it sought to establish its hegemony over the populace by community service, philanthropy, mediation in conflict situations, and cultivation of loyalties based on vertical ties of occupation, kinship, and native place. The British segregationist policy allowed the Chinese elite to manage the Chinese community affairs, though in the aftermath of the 1884 insurrection the colonial authorities gradually tightened its direct control over the Chinese.

The merchant elite's management of community affairs in Hong Kong paralleled the gentry elite's management of public affairs in late imperial China. Mary B. Rankin clearly demonstrates that the gentry elite steadily increased its public activities to include management of such matters as education, welfare, relief, and taxes.[14] And as Philip Kuhn forcefully shows, this trend greatly accelerated during the Taiping rebellion, bringing about widespread local militarization organized by the elite.[15]

In Hong Kong, however, the merchant elite's public activities were much more constrained by the interventionist colonial authorities; its management of community affairs was not allowed to include taxes and military arms. Colonial experience made it different from elites in China in some important ways. This book will highlight a recurring theme: British colonial rule brought the local elite into a complex, interlocking web of ambivalent relationships between the colonial government, elite, populace, and Chinese officials in Canton.

Social Unrest: Nature, Variations, and Patterns

Another major theme of this work is social unrest, until now a neglected aspect of the colony's history. Unrest took various forms, including strikes, riots, boycotts, and acts of civil disobedience. The boycotts of American goods in 1905, of Japanese goods in 1908, and of the Hong Kong tramway in 1912–13, involving merchants, intelligentsia, and populace, should be perceived as resulting from the interactions of local and external forces, including Chinese and international politics and economy. During the nineteenth century the frequent coolie strikes and riots posed a threat to the colonial order and community peace.

For the working people in Hong Kong their commitment to traditions worked in different directions—it tended to divide the workers, but under certain circumstances it served to bring them together. The traditional dialect group ties prompted coolies of the same dialect to live together in the same house or area. Coolie house fellowship helped in the competition between rival coolie factions for better working conditions. But when confronted with a common foe coolie houses provided the basis of an organization for the promotion of boycotts and strikes. Coolies congregated in coolie houses—from which they rushed out to attack the police and "foreign devils" during street riots—expressing their displeasure against the colonial authorities.

Recent studies of China's labor history find that working-class consciousness often coexisted with workers' vertical loyalties. In his absorbing study of Peking local politics in the 1920s David Strand shows that workers used all strategies available, both traditional and modern, to promote their interests. These strategies included horizontal class solidarities and vertical loyalties associated with the authority of patrons, brokers, and bosses.[16] Emily Honig also clearly demonstrates that for women workers of Shanghai cotton mills prior to 1949 "class consciousness would not transcend, but would at most coexist with, other loyalties." Honig concludes: "Patterns of localism and traditional hierarchical loyalties are perhaps not as antithetical to working-class consciousness as many . . . have assumed."[17] In accordance with changing situations workers used different means and strategies, both traditional and modern, both vertical and horizontal loyalties, to advance and protect their interests. Coolies in Hong Kong conformed to this Chinese labor activity pattern.

E. P. Thompson contends that "class is a relationship, and not a thing," that "class is a cultural as much as an economic formation," and that "class happens when some men, as a result of common experiences (inherited or shared), feel and articulate the identity of their interests as between themselves, and as against other men whose interests are different from (and usually opposed to) theirs."[18] Class relationships were not an eternally fixed entity; they changed according to changing historical situations. Workers sometimes perceived themselves as belonging to a class with common interests against their employers or rulers, but sometimes they did not, depending on situations. Applying Thompson's assumption to her study of the workers of Tientsin in 1900–49, Gail Hershatter concludes that "this perception of interests as structured by class was situational, and therefore transient in the constantly changing political environment of Tientsin."[19]

Thompson's theory is also applicable to coolies in Hong Kong. Traditional dialect group ties often divided coolies into rival groups competing for employment opportunities, but when their interests were threatened by an outside force (usually the colonial government's assertion of power to regulate coolies' lives and work), coolies of different dialect groups often came together to take concerted action in protest. Yet as soon as the threat was over rivalry and tensions between coolie dialect groups resumed. Coolie class consciousness was situational; therefore, it was also transient.

During the period under study the coolies employed in the Chinese enterprises rarely took collective actions against their employers, because vertical, paternalistic relationships were often maintained among them. This was especially true from the 1860s to the 1880s, when the Chinese community was held together under the unchallenged cultural hegemony of a merchant elite. Yet Hong Kong had large numbers of cargo coolies employed by foreign companies, public chair and ricksha coolies, hawkers, and boatmen. It was these laborers who frequently articulated their common interests against the colonial authorities' regulations and assertion of power. When coolie unrest disrupted trade and hurt commercial interests Chinese merchants (with strong economic ties to foreign capital and moral obligations to lower-class coolies) sought to mediate a settlement and cooperate with the authorities to restore law and order. This was a recurring pattern of social relationships in the colony.

Popular Unrest: Imperialism, Antiforeignism, and Nationalism

As class consciousness was situational, so was the effect of imperialism. Again, comparision with situations on the Chinese mainland can be fruitful. Honig's study indicates that women from Su-pei preferred to work in the Japanese mills in Shanghai, which offered better pay and more comfortable working conditions; this in turn increased the Chiang-nan women's contempt for the Su-pei women. Thus, Honig observes, imperialism intensified the division between them rather than bringing them together. This observation is an important corrective to the previously uncritical assessment that "had stressed the cruelty inflicted on Chinese workers by foreign mill owners, and the consequent solidarity and nationalism instilled in the workers."[20]

In Hong Kong, however, the foreign colonial government's assertion of power frequently served to unify Chinese workers against a common foe. This reminds us of the ambiguity of imperialism's effect on the working people; it could be either divisive or cohesive, depending on a wide variety of situations.

Popular unrest in the colony during the nineteenth century was frequently imbued with *antiforeignism,* which is defined as feelings of hostility against foreigners and anything foreign. A word of caution is necessary. Antiforeignism must be carefully distinguished from Chinese *nationalism* or *patriotism,* defined as a sense of collective identity with and loyalty to China as a sovereign nation-state. Antiforeignism did not necessarily entail feelings of patriotic devotion to one's nation-state. It would be grossly uncritical and anachronistic to equate the antiforeignism of the mid-nineteenth century with the Chinese national consciousness that began slowly to develop among the colony's populace in the late nineteenth century. Some signs of popular nationalism began to emerge in Hong Kong in the mid-1880s but did not find full expression until the Chinese republican revolution in 1911.

In much of this study an attempt is made to examine the complex nature of nationalism—to investigate, particularly, the political, cultural, and socioeconomic dimensions of nationalism, the different forms of nationalism, and the paradox of nationalism as a divisive force in history. The elitist nationalism espoused by the merchants and intelligentsia in the late nineteenth century had little appeal to the coolie working people. The workers had their own sense of patriotism, which under certain circumstances took the forms of strikes and riots in the streets. The elitist nationalists, however, refused to accept such popular outbursts as "valid" expressions of patriotism.

During the period under study some social protests were linked to Chinese nationalism and others were not, depending on historical circumstances. Those protests connected to nationalist expressions included the 1884 popular insurrection, the 1895 controversy over the Light and Pass Ordinance, the 1905 anti-American and 1908 anti-Japanese boycotts, the incidents of civil disobedience in 1911–12, and the boycott of the tramway in 1912–13. But in the coolie strikes of 1861, 1863, 1872, 1883, 1888, and 1895, coolies were thinking primarily in terms of how their livelihood was affected by the colonial government regulations, not in terms of Chinese nationalism. Coolies would respond to a nationalist cause when it was fused with an appeal to their immediate interests and mundane social needs. The common people would be more likely to become patriotic if their concerns with local problems and self-interests were fused with national issues. This fusion would provide a powerful incentive to popular nationalism. In other words, the common people were often conditional patriots.

What about the social elites? Nationalism has a cultural and political dimension; it has a socioeconomic dimension too. The responses of the Hong Kong merchants to the antiforeign boycotts, for example, suggested that the merchant patriots were motivated by both a private concern for economic interests and a public concern for China as a nation-state. Even patriotic intellectuals like Ho Kai and Hu Li-yüan did not totally transcend the socioeconomic conditions in which they lived. In fact, their experiences in the highly commercialized city of Hong Kong stimulated them to critically examine the elements implied in traditonal Chinese culture and to advocate commercialism as a means to promote the wealth and power of the Chinese nation-state. Nationalism is Janus-faced, taking many different forms in accordance with the various circumstances of modern Chinese history.

To summarize, in this book I will explore three main themes concerning the history of Hong Kong—the changing urban community structure and relations, the changing nature and patterns of social unrest, and the growth of Chinese nationalism among the merchants, populace, and intelligentsia under British colonial rule. These themes are analyzed in the context of Chinese history during the seven decades between 1842 and 1913.

O
N
E

Historical Setting:
The Making of an Entrepôt

*This Colony . . . commercially is so closely con-
nected with Canton that from that aspect the two
cities may be considered to be one.*
—*Governor F. Henry May*

Although the subject of this study is Hong Kong under British colonial rule, a few words must be said about the Canton delta region
surrounding Hong Kong in precolonial times. The growth of Hong
Kong after 1842 into an entrepôt owed a great deal to the interre-
gional and international trades already developed in the region centuries before the Opium War. In fact, British Hong Kong inherited
these trades, which had long been carried on, with Canton and
Whampoa as a transshipment port for commodities from various
parts of China, Northeast Asia, Southeast Asia, and the Western
world. The historic Nanyang trade figured prominently in the region,
with the Teochiu (Ch'ao-chou), Hoklo (Fu-lao, Hokkien, Amoy), and
Cantonese merchants taking active parts in it.[1] The Nanyang trade
loomed large in the background of the flourishing Teochiu and Hoklo
business circles in colonial Hong Kong. The sojourning Hoklo merchants who had played important roles in Canton had laid the foundation for later creation of a Hoklo business community in British
Hong Kong (which was to gradually replace Canton as the focus of
regional and overseas exports).[2] In short, underlying Hong Kong's
development as an entrepôt was a long history of overseas trade with
Canton as a transshipment port.

Since 1759 Canton had been the only port where foreign trade was legally permitted. The foreign sailing ships were familiar with the anchorages around Hong Kong which had provided refuge for them year after year. The Chinese imperial edict of 1800 prohibiting the import of opium caused the growth of the transshipment services around Hong Kong (including such islands as Lintin, Nine Island, Kap Shui Mun, and Lantao, which are within forty miles to the west of Hong Kong). Thereafter ships carrying opium anchored regularly on these islands where they unloaded their cargo of opium into receiving vessels. The ships then sailed up the Pearl River to carry on legitimate trade. The British East India Company's ships also began to anchor in Hong Kong harbor and other anchorages nearby, where their cargoes including cotton and woolen goods were transshipped to Canton under foreign flags, prominently American.[3] Thus, on the eve of the Opium War (1839–42) some transshipment services had been done in Hong Kong. It was not accidental for the British to select Hong Kong as its colony at the end of the war in 1842.

The Colony in the Early Years: The 1840s

The Chinese population of the island of Hong Kong (29 square miles) in precolonial days numbered only about four thousand. The arrival of the British fleet in June 1839 and the British occupation of the island during the Opium War attracted many boat people, laborers, artisans and adventurers who profited by furnishing provisions and other services, and who defied the Chinese officials' orders not to have any dealings with the *fankwei* (foreign devils).[4] Captain Charles Elliot (British superintendent of trade) proclaimed in 1841 that all inhabitants of Hong Kong would enjoy full security and protection; that the Chinese inhabitants were free to practice their own religious rites, ceremonies, and social customs; and that Hong Kong was a free port in which all vessels were free from import and export duties. This added a powerful incentive to trade.

Conditions in Canton during the Opium War caused a number of European merchants to move their offices from Canton to Hong Kong. Chinese junks from the coast made up their cargoes in Hong Kong rather than going to Canton or Macao. The cargoes consisted of opium, cotton shirtings, woolens, salt, and Straits produce such as pepper, rattans, etc. In February 1842 Sir Henry Pottinger reaffirmed his predecessor Captain Elliot's proclamation of Hong Kong as a free port, and proceeded to remove the whole establishment of the British Superintendency of Trade from Macao to Hong Kong. This further lured some leading British merchants to move their headquarters from Macao and Canton to Hong Kong. Chinese traders, artisans, and laborers flocked to Hong Kong from all neighboring districts. These were mostly from the lowest elements of Chinese society—the outcaste boat population and laborers from the Hakka dialect group. Poverty prompted these adventurers to work for "foreign barbarians" for a few cash, risking the displeasure of the mandarins. In May 1841 the Chinese population on the island was estimated at 5,650, and by March 1842, it had increased to 12,361, the total population (including foreign nationalities) being over 15,000.[5]

At the conclusion of the war the Treaty of Nanking (August 29, 1842) provided for the cession of Hong Kong to Britain in perpetuity. It was widely expected in Hong Kong at the time that the end of war and the opening of five Chinese ports to foreign trade would enhance the commercial prospects of Britain's new colony by attracting Chinese and foreigners alike. Buildings of all kinds were erected— commercial establishments, a post office, a record and land office, a jail, and other government offices, private residences, brick warehouses, hospitals, churches, markets, and schools. By June 1845 the island's population had increased to 23,817.[6] Henceforth the population of Hong Kong continued to increase rapidly. The overwhelming majority came from China's Kwangtung province. What made the Cantonese so receptive to Britain's newly acquired colony? What were the social and economic conditions in Kwangtung?

The Socioeconomic Conditions in Kwangtung

The situation in Hong Kong was closely related to the social and economic conditions in Kwangtung. Several factors must be considered: population pressure, commercialization of the rural economy, the Opium Wars and subsequent unequal treaties, social unrest, and domestic uprisings. These internal and external factors combined to effect social and economic dislocations in Kwangtung, which were greatly to affect the development of Hong Kong.

Since the introduction of American maize, sweet potatoes, Irish potatoes, and peanuts into China in the sixteenth century, the Chinese population had increased rapidly, particularly in the two centuries after 1650, reaching perhaps four hundred and thirty million by 1850. Consequently, China's resources had already become strained by the end of the eighteenth century.[7] Kwangtung was no exception. Its population rose from sixteen million in 1787 to twenty-one million in 1819, twenty-six million in 1841, twenty-eight million in 1850, and twenty-nine million in 1855. The ratio of arable land to population in 1812 was only 1.67 mou (about one-quarter of an acre) per person, making Kwangtung among the most land-hungry provinces in China. The Canton region, though fertile, was densely populated and experienced constant pressure on land and food resources.[8]

The commercialization of agriculture began in the sixteenth century in some areas of south China, particularly Kwangtung and Fukien. Many peasant households abandoned rice planting for cash crops such as sugarcane, fruit, and tobacco. Manufacturing, especially of textiles, had become commercialized during the mid-Ming period, so that cotton and silk cloth manufactured in Kwangtung was "marketed all over the country," and reed and rush matting "all over south China."[9] "In 1819, the mulberry orchards of Shun-te and Nan-hai counties [in Kwangtung] together covered over 15,000 acres, and provided employment for 'several hundred thousand' households." And in Canton in 1841 "sixty-seven thousand men, women, and children wove cottons, silks, and brocades."[10] The commercialization of the rural economy in the nineteenth century made peasants vulnerable to national and international market price fluctuations.

The Treaty of Nanking and subsequent unequal treaties had important social and economic effects on China. To pay the huge indemnities the Manchu government had to increase taxes on the people. In addition, the import of Western manufactured goods hit hard at indigenous handicraft industries located in the treaty port areas. "[A]lthough most of China's peasants continued to wear homespun clothing, many people who were involved in the domestic cloth trade were forced out of business."[11] The importation of foreign products protected by a low tariff brought economic disaster to Kwangtung. Low tariffs on foreign cloth forced half of the women weavers in Shun-te out of work in 1853. A similar situation occurred in P'an-yu county in 1870.[12] The importation of foreign nails and needles also caused a decline in the iron nail and steel needle production in Fatshan (Fo-shan), affecting twenty thousand workers in the iron works.[13] Even though imperialism did not substantially affect the Chinese economy as a whole, it did cause considerable socioeconomic strain and dislocation in the southern provinces, especially in Kwangtung.[14]

After the Treaty of Nanking "free trade" replaced the earlier legally restrictive Cohong system, and Canton's legal monopoly of foreign trade, dating back to 1759, was ended.[15] The newly opened ports of Shanghai, Ningpo, Foochow, and Amoy competed with Canton for China's foreign trade. With the rich Yangtze River valley as its hinterland, Shanghai soon began to fulfill its extraordinary potential as a port of trade. By 1850 the volume of trade in Shanghai had surpassed that of Canton.[16] Much of the tea trade and silk trade was diverted away from Canton to Shanghai, causing over one hundred thousand porters and boatmen in Kwangtung to lose their jobs. Many Cantonese junks were driven out of business by the better armed, swifter foreign vessels that entered the Chinese coastal trade after 1842.[17]

Thus, a large surplus supply of labor was created in the aftermath of the Opium War, consisting of idle weavers, handicraftsmen, iron workers, boatmen, junk crews, and dislocated peasants. Many joined secret societies and bandit gangs; others became pirates along the coast; still others formed urban bands of beggars and thieves.[18] Piracy and social unrest mounted in Kwangtung. Riots broke out in villages near Canton, protesting the importation of foreign cloth that deprived women and child weavers of their livelihood.[19] The Triad secret societies were especially active in the Canton delta counties, committing robberies, plundering, and looting. The Taiping uprising started in 1850 in neighboring Kwangsi province, rapidly spreading to Kwangtung and other southern provinces. The provincial capital of Canton was threatened by an armed revolt, organized by the secret society known as the Red Turbans in 1854–55. In 1856 major fighting broke out in the Sze Yap (Sz-yi) area between Punti (local Cantonese) and Hakkas over land disputes, claiming many thousands of lives in the prolonged feuds that lasted off and on for twelve years. Constant warfare magnified the consequences of natural disasters such as floods and droughts, causing peasants to face famine and starvation in the late 1840s and 1850s.[20]

In sum, social and economic dislocations in South China, particularly Kwangtung, were caused by several concurrent factors—population pressure, commercialization of agriculture and manufacture, foreign invasions, competition from foreign imports, unequal treaties, land disputes, and domestic uprisings—all combined to create economic depression, mass unemployment, social disorder, insecurity, and starvation. The ground was set for the exodus of Chinese from Kwangtung and Fukien in search of economic opportunities overseas. The development of Hong Kong under the British naturally attracted the Chinese from the nearby districts of Kwangtung province.

The 1850s as a Turning Point

During the first ten years of its existence the unsettled conditions in the colony were not conducive to attracting Chinese of substantial means who could strengthen its economy by promoting extensive local and overseas trade. All business in the Chinese community then was in the hands of shopkeepers, compradors, and peddlers whose transactions were on the whole only trifling.[21] They hoped "only to make a fast fortune and then return to their native place to live off the results of their succeess."[22] The great majority of the Chinese in the colony left their families behind in their native land.

The 1850s, however, witnessed important changes in the colony's social and economic structure. Socioeconomic dislocations in Kwangtung, especially after the outbreak of the Taiping uprising, caused an exodus of Cantonese, including wealthy families, to take refuge in Hong Kong. Reflecting on its effect on the colony during his residence there, the Reverend Dr. James Legge (of the London Missionary Society) observed: "It has always seemed to me that this was the turning point in the progress of Hongkong . . . Houses were in demand; rents rose; the streets that had been comparatively deserted assumed a crowded appearance; new commercial Chinese firms were founded; the native trade received an impetus."[23] In 1848 the Chinese population in Hong Kong numbered 22,496. It rose to 28,297 in 1849, and to 37,536 in 1853. It increased dramatically after 1854 and through the long years of unrest in Kwangtung created by the Triads and the Taipings. By 1865 the Chinese population in Hong Kong had risen to 121,497.[24]

The influx of Chinese helped to bring about a period of commercial development in the colony from around 1850. Chinese refugees included wealthy families who brought their capital with them for investment in Hong Kong. Large Chinese commercial establishments (*hongs*) were set up: thirty-five hongs in 1858, and sixty-five in 1859. Some invested in real estate and became large land proprietors. The famous Li Sing family, for instance, acquired much property and diversified the family interests into the money changing business, commercial firms, the opium monopoly, and coolie labor broker-age.[25] Increasing prosperity attracted more Chinese to the colony.

The future of Hong Kong seemed promising. Many other factors contributed to making it an Eastern entrepôt of Western trade. Its geographic position and its deep, spacious, and sheltered harbor, attracted international shipping. Hong Kong provided the only deep-water harbor between Singapore and Shanghai. In fact, with seven-teen square miles of land sheltered water Hong Kong provided one of the world's finest harbors. It gradually superseded Canton as a transshipment port.[26] "British merchants enjoyed the benefits of Brit-ish laws and justice under their own flag, and the principal British firms preferred to establish their headquarters there"; therefore "many ships even if destined for ports further north, called for orders." British liberal economic policies of free trade and laissez-faire admin-istration attracted to the colony merchants of every nationality. Since the treaty ports of China had not developed as expected, cargoes for the less developed ports had to be transshipped at Hong Kong or Shanghai.[27]

Chinese Emigration and the Development of Entrepôt Facilities

Contributing most powerfully to Hong Kong's commercial prosperity was the vast Chinese emigration abroad in the latter half of the nineteenth century, from which the European and Chinese mercan-tile communities in the colony gained great profits. The rapid expan-sion of capitalism in the West in the nineteenth century and the extension of imperialism and colonialism to the rest of the world, created a great demand for labor—laborers to toil on the cotton and sugar plantations in Cuba, Peru and the West Indies; to work in mining industries, railroad constructions, and land reclamations in the American West, Canada, and Australia; and, in Southeast Asia, to work in the tin mine and rubber plantations of Malaya, the spices and sugar plantations of Java, and the tobacco and rubber plantations of Sumatra. The African slave trade, which had supplied labor for plantations in the Americas since the sixteenth century, had been gradually abandoned by Britain after 1834 and France after 1848 for both humanitarian and economic reasons. Slavery was extremely inefficient, and the British economy had come to rest on the sale of cotton goods and not that of men and sugar.[28] The Western powers now turned to India (a colony) and China (a semicolony) for alternative sources of cheap labor, giving rise to the notorious coolie trade.[29]

While emigration to California and Australia involved relatively less coercion due to the popular myth and illusion about the opportunity of getting rich from the gold mines there, Chinese emigrants to other places were more often forcibly abducted or tricked by the agents of Western firms engaged in the coolie trade and by their Chinese accomplices.[30] "Very gross deception was used"—the coolies hired to go to California, for instance, were put on board ships destined for Peru. [31] They were packed crowded together in much the same manner as Africans had been shipped in earlier times. According to an incomplete estimate, the Chinese coolie emigrants from 1851 to 1900 numbered 2,050,000 men.[32] The great majority of them came from Kwangtung and Fukien, which had experienced the greatest social and economic dislocation after the Opium War.

Located on the coast of Kwangtung, Hong Kong became the major center for the vast Chinese emigration abroad. In 1857 alone 17,722 coolies left Hong Kong for Australia. Although their number subsequently decreased due to racial tensions, coolie emigrants departing from Hong Kong for Australia during the period 1860–1874 numbered another 17,052 men. And 29,133 coolie emigrants embarked in Hong Kong for Canada in the years between 1868 and 1900.[33]

Far greater numbers of Chinese departed for the United States, with Hong Kong nearly monopolizing the embarkation of these emigrants. In the period 1860–1874, 112,362 Chinese emigrants (a number of them coolies) left Hong Kong for the United States, not counting the 4,952 women, mostly concubines and prostitutes.[34] According to another estimate, during the years between 1848 and 1882 as many as 300,000 Chinese emigrants arrived in the United States.[35] Between 1855 and 1900, a total of 1,830,572 Chinese emigrants embarked at the port of Hong Kong. In addition, Hong Kong became the major port for the returning Chinese from abroad. Statistics tell part of the story:[36]

YEARS	EMBARKATION IN HONG KONG	DISEMBARKATION HONG KONG
1855–59	81,053	–
1860–69	96,096	75,641
1870–79	317,273	343,881
1880–89	657,479	774,355
1890–99	595,028	1,072,305
1900–09	780,360	1,393,757
1910–19	974,360	1,288,973

Hong Kong had become a very busy port.

The emigration business was extremely lucrative for the shipping firms, brokers, and labor recruiters. Western, especially British, American, and French, shipping firms registered great profits. According to E. J. Eitel, "for San Francisco alone as many as 30,000 Chinese embarked in Hong Kong in the year 1852, paying in Hong Kong, in passage money alone, a sum of $1,500,000."[37] Charles Denby, ex-U.S. minister (1885–98) to China, observed: "To bring a Chinaman from Macao or Hong-Kong would cost less than five dollars, but the steamship companies would charge, as they used to, fifty-five dollars. There would be a clear profit of fifty dollars per head."[38]

In 1860 the average passage money from Hong Kong to San Francisco was fifty dollars; passage money to Central and South America was seventy dollars. Unable to pay the passage money, many "free" coolie emigrants were given "credit tickets" by the labor broker who did the recruitment on behalf of American shipping firms and employers. On arrival in America the coolie under his creditor's control was bound to work many years before he could repay his debt, which consisted of the loan for the passage plus interest. As the credit right could be bought and sold, the indebted coolie could be transferred to work for another master creditor. The "free" emigrant under the "credit-ticket system," then, was not free after all; it was in reality a "veiled slave trade."[39] Thus, the foreign shipping firms and business creditors made large sums of money from the emigration business. During the years 1860–1874, the embarkation in Hong Kong of 112,362 emigrants for the United States involved $5,618,100 in passage money alone, not counting high interests added on loans for large numbers of coolies. The Chinese compradors, crimps, and middlemen also made profits from the emigration business.[40] The emigration of nearly two million Chinese through Hong Kong in the latter half of the nineteenth century contributed significantly to making Hong Kong a major shipping center in South China. Large numbers of emigrant ships were fitted, repaired, and provisioned in Hong Kong, stimulating the colony's general economy.[41] Large shipbuilding companies were established one after another. They were joined by numerous Chinese manufacturers of junks and sampan, numbering 119 by the year 1913.[42]

Meanwhile Hong Kong developed close commercial relations with neighbouring Amoy, Swatow, Macao, Canton, the Pearl River Delta, and the West River valley, from which came the coastal vessels, river boats, and junks carrying cargoes of passengers and provisions. At the same time the China coastal and international shipping service was provided by a number of companies. Professional services such as medical facilities, marine and property insurance, money exchange, and barristers' legal advice and assistance became available. Large international banking institutions were set up one after another. In addition, the Chinese native banks financed trade with China and the Chinese communities overseas. In short, both European and Chinese mercantile communities in Hong Kong prospered by providing commercial, financial and professional services.[43]

Links with Chinese Abroad: The Pacific Basin Commercial Network

The prosperity of Hong Kong was linked to the Chinese communities overseas, which retained close ties with their homeland in China. "Wherever the Chinese goes he retains his national habits, customs, and solidarity," observed Charles Denby.[44] The Chinese communities abroad clung to the Chinese way of life, and Hong Kong became the center of an international trade catering to their needs.[45] The arrival of large numbers of Chinese immigrants in the United States in the latter half of the nineteenth century created a demand for rice, tea, foodstuffs, drugs, and sundries from China. Hong Kong developed a flourishing trade with the United States, where a Chinese merchant class prospered by selling Chinese imports. The American import of rice from China, Hong Kong, and Hawaii rose annually from 18.7 million pounds in 1867 to 59.6 million pounds in 1876, and 61.1 million pounds in 1878. American exports to China included flour, dried fish, and other commodities in exchange. Trade between the United States and China expanded from a value of $11.4 million in 1867 to $26.8 million in 1872.[46] Thereafter, the trade between the two countries grew steadily.

Indeed, Hong Kong became the center of a flourishing commercial network encompassing China, Southeast Asia, Australia, and America. The trade in rice, a staple food of the vast Chinese population, was of great importance to the Chinese both at home and abroad. As the supplies from the rice fields of southern China were often insufficient to meet the demands, rice had to be imported from Burma, Vietnam, and especially Siam. In 1875 about 60 percent (2,420,000 piculs) of Siamese rice exports went to China and Hong Kong and 27 percent (1,140,000 piculs) to Singapore; in 1911–12 43 percent (7,545,000 piculs) went to China and Hong Kong and 34 percent (5,975,000 piculs) to Singapore. A part of Singapore's shipments also went to China. In 1899 three-quarters of the total number of rice mills in Bangkok were in Chinese hands. The Chinese merchants' control of most of the Asian rice trade before 1914 extended from the rice milling in Bangkok to the actual sale of the commodity in Singapore and Hong Kong.[47] Hong Kong became the distributing center of rice for China, Japan, and the United States.

The sugar produced in Indonesia was another important staple for the Chinese. In the years 1890–95, China, Hong Kong, and Japan annually shared an average of 31 percent (122,550 tons) of sugar exports from Java, increasing to 46 percent (327,670 tons) for the years 1905–10. "Sugar . . . was exported from Batavia either direct or via Singapore to Hong Kong where, after refinement, cargoes were transshipped to other Chinese ports and to Japan."[48]

Chinese Merchants in the Pacific Commercial Network

Behind trade figures lie hidden the lives and activities of thriving Chinese merchants in Hong Kong and Canton. A look at some of these men provides insight into the work and leisure of the wealthy in Hong Kong. Choa Chee Bee (Ts'ai Tzu-wei, 1836–1902), a Fukienese merchant from Malacca, was comprador to the China Sugar

Refinery Company, Ltd. He acquired much wealth in the sugar trade and real estate, possessing thirteen houses (two in Malacca, four in Macao, six in Canton, and six in Hong Kong), in addition to other property.[49] In 1898 his nephew Choa Leep Chee (Ts'ai Li-chih, 1859–1909) succeeded him as comprador to the refinery. Choa Leep Chee was also a shareholder in many other companies, and was heavily involved in the sugar trade between Java, Hong Kong, and China. He lived at Burnside, no. 47, Robinson Road, "a house delightfully situated, overlooking the harbor . . . [and] surrounded by a very beautiful garden stocked with some hundreds of varieties of English and European flowers." On his death in 1909, at the young age of fifty, his estate was worth hundreds of thousands of dollars.[50]

Ng Li Hing (Goh Li Hing, Wu Li-ch'ing, 1833–1914) came from Fukien in 1878. He was the founder of Goh Guan Hin, a firm of commission agents, rice, and sugar importers, and exporters of marine edibles. It had "a very large export trade to the Straits Settlements, Java, Philippine Islands, and South China generally."[51] Ng Li Hing was also chairman of the Hongkong and Manila Yuen Shing Exchange and Trading Co., Ltd., a financial company that had branches at Manila, Singapore, Shanghai, Amoy, and Penang. He was the proprietor of a brewery at Wongnaichung and was connected with numerous other enterprises in Hong Kong. On his death at eighty in 1914 his personal estate was equal in value to the sum of $281,639, and consisted of houses, fields and lands in Swatow, Amoy, and Cheng-hai, and of shops, houses, property, businesses, shares, moveable property, and moneies in Hong Kong, Canton, and elsewhere.[52]

This description demonstrates the energy, wealth, and way of life of Chinese merchants in Hong Kong who prospered from the colony's entrepôt trade. It illustrates the close commercial relations between Hong Kong, Canton, and other ports on the China coast as well as the flourishing Pacific commercial network encompassing China, Southeast Asia, Australia, and America.

Large numbers of Chinese emigrants to Southeast Asia were Hoklo (Hokkienese or Fukienese) from Fukien province and from Ch'ao-chou prefecture in northeastern Kwangtung province (with Swatow and Cheng-hai as major cities), where people spoke a version of Fukienese dialect called Teochiu. The Teochiu-speaking Chinese became the dominant elements in the large Chinese community in

Siam.[53] Thus, much of the trade between Hong Kong and Southeast Asia was in the hands of the merchants from Amoy and Swatow, with a close commercial relationship developing between Hong Kong, Amoy, and Swatow. Hong Kong served as the center of transshipments of a large part of merchandise and passengers in the trade and communications between these regions and Southeast Asia.[54]

The famous Yuen Fat Hong was founded in Hong Kong in 1853 by Ko Man Wah (Kao Man-hua), a native of Cheng-hai near Swatow. The firm was chiefly engaged in importing and exporting rice as well as large quantities of native produce. It had branches in all the major East Asian ports, including Singapore. One of the wealthiest Chinese firms in the colony, it owned five rice mills in Bangkok. In 1881 Ko Man Wah was the sixteenth highest rate payer in Hong Kong. When he died in 1882, the value of his estate was estimated at $163,000.[55] Four of Ko Man Wah's nine sons (including Ko Soon Kam) succeeded him as proprietors of the firm of Yuen Fat Hong, engaging in an extensive business with foreign bankers and merchants. For many years, the business acted as agent for the Scottish Oriental Steamship Company and for the Norddeutscher Lloyd's Bangkok-Hong Kong line of steamers. Managing the prosperous Yuen Fat Hong, Ko Soon Kam was a large property owner and leader of the Swatow community in Hong Kong, and chairman of the Man On Insurance Company. Of his nineteen children, one son was sent to Siam and another to Singapore.[56]

The history of Yuen Fat Hong illustrated the importance of Hong Kong in the Nanyang trade between China and Southeast Asia, the tendency of Hong Kong merchants to diversify their commercial interests, the family members' management of businesses, the wealthy merchants' leadership in the Swatow community, and Chinese merchants' economic ties to Western capital.

Although large numbers of Chinese emigrants to Southeast Asia were Hoklos from Fukien and Teochiu from Ch'ao-chou, there were significant numbers of Cantonese emigrants to Southeast Asia. Out of five hundred thousand Chinese in Indonesia in the year 1900, half came from Kwangtung.[57] And there were many Cantonese among the Chinese population in Singapore.[58] They played an important part in the trade with Southeast Asia. For example, Wing Fat Hong was founded in Hong Kong in 1899 by Chan Pek Chun (Ch'en Pi-ch'üan), who came from Canton. As a rice, sugar, and general commission agency, it quickly came into prominence, having by 1917 "a turnover in rice of $2,000,000 and in sugar of $1,500,000." The firm imported produce from Java, Rangoon, Penang, Haiphong, and the Philippines. It also had shipping interests, serving as the agent for a number of steamers. Its office staff numbered forty, and its warehouses employed over a hundred men.[59]

While much of the rice, sugar, and other produce from Southeast Asia was imported to Hong Kong by the colony's Hokkien and Teochiu merchants, the transshipment to America of these products went largely into the hands of the colony's Cantonese and Western businessmen. As the overwhelming majority of Chinese emigrants to America and Australia were Cantonese, Chinese participation in the trade between Hong Kong, Australia, and America, was nearly monopolized by the Cantonese merchants. The *Anglo-Chinese Commercial Directory of Hong Kong* of 1915 listed a total of 239 firms in Hong Kong as "exporters and importers to Melbourne, Sydney, San Francisco and Honolulu" who dealt in a great variety of products.

Among the foodstuffs exported on a large scale from Hong Kong and Canton to America were Chinese delicacies to supply the needs of the Chinese communities and restaurants in the United States. The firm of Cheung Kwong Yuen, founded by Pun Wan Nam (P'an Wan-nan) in 1887, had by 1917 become "one of the most important canning export houses of south China." Lychees, pineapples, ginger, water chestnuts, water lily roots, yuengans, pears, and manis were preserved with sugar syrup. Among the fish exported were the famed flower fish, black fish, eels, and oysters. The firm also exported large amounts of China duck, fried rice birds, and quail. Cheung Kwong Yuen's stores and factories were situated at Canton where the canning, packing, and preparing was done. All the shipping was done at Hong Kong where the firm had a branch.[60]

A considerable amount of ginger was exported from Hong Kong, once again illustrating the close relations between Canton and Hong Kong. The Choy Fong Ginger Factory, dating back to around 1858, obtained ginger from the Canton district, and processed and preserved it in the factory in Hong Kong for export to America, Europe, and Australia. The factory's output during the season in 1908 was about thirty thousand piculs of ginger, a great deal going to the Chinese retail shops in San Francisco. By 1917 there were thirteen preserved ginger factories in Hong Kong with an annual aggregate business turnover of $25 million.[61]

The foregoing discussion of some prominent commercial firms testified to six points: (1) the ingenuity, energy, wealth, and the self-indulgent living of the Chinese merchants; (2) the close relationship between Hong Kong and the Teochiu-speaking area of Swatow and the Hokkien-speaking area of Amoy, with the colony's Teochiu and Hokkien merchants playing a vital role in the trade between these areas and Southeast Asia; (3) the merchant leadership in the Teochiu and Hokkienese communities in Hong Kong; (4) the inseparable economic ties between Hong Kong and Canton, with Hong Kong serving as the entrepôt—importing goods for Canton merchants to distribute to the mainland and exporting goods that Canton had collected from inland. As Governor Sir F. Henry May remarked in 1912, "This Colony . . . commercially is so closely connected with Canton that from that aspect the two cities may be considered to be one";[62] (5) the flourishing commercial network in the Pacific basin, extending from South China through Hong Kong to Southeast Asia, Australia, and America; and (6) the close commercial ties between Chinese merchants and Western business enterprises.

The Number of Chinese Importing and Exporting Firms

The full scope of Hong Kong's economic development up to the early twentieth century still awaits scholarly study. As a free port Hong Kong kept no customs or shipping records. It published no statistics showing the origin of its imports or the destination of its exports.[63] Yet the number of the colony's Chinese firms engaged in international trade in 1915 indicates the degree to which Hong Kong was an entrepôt in the commercial network of the Pacific basin in the early twentieth century.

The Anglo-Chinese Commercial Directory of Hong Hong of 1915 listed the number of Chinese firms in Hong Kong as follows.[64]

Nam Pak Hong (General Exporters and Importers to Southern & Northern Ports, and to Southeast Asian Ports)	84
Kam Shan Chung (Exporters & Importers to Melbourne, Sydney, San Francisco, and Honolulu)	239
Exporters & Importers to Peru	4
Havana	3

Panama			2
Spain &			
Manila	31		
Haiphon	2		
Annam	36		
Cambodia	1		
Siam	19	Southeast Asia	186
Sandakan	4		
Java	5		
Penang	15		
Singapore	73		
Japan			30
Calcutta			1
South Africa			1

Thus, Southeast Asia led the way in its share of trade with Chinese firms in Hong Kong, closely followed by America and Australia. Japan's trade with Hong Kong and China substantially accelerated after 1895, as will be seen in chapter 8.

Hong Kong's position as the commercial center for import and export in South China is illustrated by the number of the colony's Chinese firms trading with Chinese cities and regions (other than Canton, with which Hong Kong formed inseparable commercial ties):[65]

Haikow, Hainan	6
Foochow	11
Peihai, Kwangtung	1
Shantung	3
Yün-nan	24
Tientsin	7
Swatow, Ch'ao-chou	12
Hankow	8
Amoy	22
Shanghai	58

As the two foremost distributing centers of China's foreign trade Hong Kong and Shanghai were closely connected in commercial relations, both dealing in Shanghai silks, piece goods, sundries, leather, fruits, rice, shoes, embroideries, etc. There were, in addition, eighty-six Chinese firms in Hong Kong that dealt in Shanghai silk and European piece goods, and fifty-three firms of Soochow-Hangchow and European goods dealers in the colony in 1915.[66] It must be noted that when a firm was listed as an importer and exporter of certain commodities to various cities or countries it often indicated that the firm was chiefly, rather than exclusively, engaged in trading with a particular city or country.

There were a total of about 1,700 Chinese commercial firms, large and small, listed in the Hong Kong directory of 1915 engaged in the importing and exporting of a wide variety of goods. Many Chinese businessmen tended to diversify their commercial interests, so that they were simultaneously proprietors and partners of several firms in various trades.

In addition to these, there were hundreds of foreign trading companies based in Hong Kong, including the giant Jardine, Matheson & Co.; Butterfield and Swire; Siemssen & Co.; and Gibb, Livingston & Co.; etc. Many foreign companies and Chinese firms were closely tied to each other in a trade relationship. The foreign companies bought from Chinese firms the produce of China which were gathered from the interior and the Chinese firms purchased from foreign companies the foreign commodities for distribution to the mainland.

Each year large volumes of China's imports and exports passed through Hong Kong . The percentage of China's trade with Hong Kong indicated the importance of Hong Kong as an entrepôt. Already in the years 1871–73 Hong Kong handled 32.5 percent in value of China's total import trade and 14.7 percent of China's export trade. The percentages of the subsequent years were as follows:[67]

YEARS	CHINA'S IMPORTS FROM HONG KONG	CHINA'S EXPORTS TO HONG KONG
1881–83	36.2%	25.4%
1891–93	51.2%	39.3%
1901–03	41.6%	40.8%
1909–11	33.9%	28.2%
1919–21	22.4%	23.8%

The decline in the percentage of China's trade with Hong Kong after 1909 indicated the growth of the trade of other ports of northern and central China such as Tientsin, Dairen, and Hankow. Still, Hong Kong maintained its significance as a trading center second only to Shanghai.[68] The colony's Chinese merchants had gained wealth from the expansion of Chinese and overseas trade.

The close business connections between Hong Kong and Shanghai, the two leading trading centers in China, formed a Hong Kong-

Shanghai corridor. The powerful Kuang-tung *pang* (the circle or clique of Cantonese merchants) came to dominate the Shanghai business world. Continuously tapping the Cantonese community in Hong Kong for managerial talents, capital, and overseas connections, the Kuang-tung *pang* rose to a dominant position in rivalry with the Ningpo *pang* and outperforming many other dialect "circles" in Shanghai. While the Kuang-tung *pang* dominated such businesses as department stores, insurance, modern hotel, and the manufacturing of consumer goods, the Teochiu *pang* dominated Shanghai's grocery supplies from Kwangtung and Southeast Asia, via Hong Kong—dried goods such as shark's fin, bird's nests, sea cucumbers and other dried seafood.[69] The Hong Kong–Shanghai corridor had an intellectual and cultural dimension as well; late Ch'ing reformers such as Wang T'ao, Cheng Kuan-ying, Tong King-sing, and Yung Wing spent substantial portions of their careers in or around the two cities, where they were exposed to Western culture and values.[70] Two other reformers, Ho Kai and Hu Li-yüan, were lifelong residents of Hong Kong whose reform program was shaped by the business environment of the highly commercialzed port city.

By the first decade of the twentieth century, some sixty years after 1842, Hong Kong had become an extremely busy entrepôt port. During the year 1907 the total tonnage of shipping, including junks and steam ships (but excluding lighters, cargo boats, passenger boats, fishing crafts, etc.) entered and cleared in Hong Kong (that is, arrivals and departures put together) amounted to 507,634 vessels of 36,028,310 tons. They were as follows:[71]

	NUMBER OF VESSELS	TONNAGE
British ocean-going ships	3,756	7,216,169
Foreign ocean-going ships	4,621	7,720,875
British river steamers	6,828	4,630,364
Foreign river steamers	1,310	743,992
Steamships under 60 tons	1,581	70,021
Junks	29,564	2,651,470
Total foreign trade	47,660	23,032,891
Steamships under 60 tons in local trade	419,202	11,216,532
Junks in local trade	40,772	1,778,887
Grand total	507,634	36,028,310

Thus, during the year 1907 everyday an average of 1,390 large and small vessels of 98,707 tons entered and cleared the Hong Kong port, discounting large numbers of lighters, cargo boats, passenger boats, water boats, and fishing crafts of all kinds. This record exceeded that of any port in the world at the time.

Much of the prosperity of Hong Kong depended on the energy, ingenuity, and hard work of the overwhelming majority of the colony's population, the Chinese laborers and merchants. The Chinese community thrived in the British colony.

How was the Chinese community formed and structured? How did it fare under British colonial rule? How was it related to the European community in Hong Kong and to the Chinese on the mainland? Chapters 2 and 3 examine these questions in historical context.

T
W
O

A Frontier Settlement: The Chinese Community Under Alien Rule, 1840s–1860s

[It is] the common practice of the Chinese of offering seditious resistance to a weak government by combining to strike work in order to mark their sense of irksome or imperfect legislation. —E. J. Eitel

Historians have done considerable research on Hong Kong's rural society, but its urban community structure in the nineteenth and early twentieth centuries is still badly underresearched. Consequently, many aspects of the city's social life and associations (such as craft and trade guilds, secret societies, native place associations, and commercial and labor organizations) are still imperfectly understood. This chapter traces the formation of an urban Chinese community and the emergence and changing character of a community leadership from the 1840s to the 1860s. It examines the pattern of elite dominance and the complex relationship between elite, populace, Hong Kong government, and officials in Canton.

The colony's geographical proximity to the Chinese mainland was a decisive factor shaping its history. Its close social, economic, and demographic connections with China made its Chinese residents liable to the political influence and control of Chinese officialdom. Canton and Hong Kong authorities claimed the Chinese residents' allegiance, putting them in an ambivalent relationship with both governments. This became particularly evident in times of social and political crises.

Since the British occupation of Hong Kong during the Opium War (1839–42) the Chinese had frequently been driven by poverty, hunger, and sociopolitical disturbances on the mainland to take refuge in Hong Kong, which offered relative security and work opportunities. Therefore, it has often been asserted that "[i]nstead of imposing an alien government [on] the natives in the colony, the pattern of alien rule in Hong Kong is just the reverse. The colonized Chinese people came to Hong Kong to subject themselves voluntarily under the rule of an alien colonial administration."[1] In other words "most residents . . . see themselves . . . as willing subjects of a foreign government rather than involuntary slaves of a conquering colonial regime."[2]

This assertion is true, but it tells only part of the story. There was a long tradition of popular animosity toward British colonial rule. This is an important aspect of the colony's history, which has been neglected by most scholars in Hong Kong studies, who have generally emphasized growth, development, stability, and alleged popular apathy, overlooking crises, tensions, and conflicts in the colony.

A Frontier Settlement Under the British in the 1840s

As previously indicated, the Chinese population of Hong Kong prior to the British occupation in 1841 numbered only about four thousand, scattered in a few villages all over the island. In the absence of an established urban population the future city of Victoria was to be built on the northern shore of the island. This was an important fact shaping the development of a Chinese community; for some decades after 1841 urban Hong Kong was a new settlement with little preexisting local power structure. Early Hong Kong was "a frontier outpost"[3] off the coast of south China.

The town grew rapidly as people congregated there seeking employment opportunities. The Chinese migrants from different native places speaking different dialects were all strangers and newcomers in a frontier town, not subject to any established system of social control. They brought with them their religions, customs, prejudices, concepts, and experiences of social organization. Craft and trade guilds were formed. People speaking the same dialect clung together for protection and mutual assistance, in competition with other dialect groups for resources. But in the new environment of a frontier town under foreign colonial rule, Chinese residents of all dialects also experienced common problems that demanded cooperative solutions. Hence they proceeded to organize their community to meet that demand. They gradually formed neighborhood associations (*kaifong*) and temple committees, incorporating various dialect groups and providing public order and a rudimentary self-government. Thus, in the urban Chinese community of Hong Kong under alien rule, conflict and competition did not preclude cooperation among Chinese dialect groups.

Because of the sheer size and diversity of the British empire, the Colonial Office in London could not possibly administer every colony in detail. Decentralization became a hallmark of British imperial organization: each colony was governed according to local conditions. A "crown colony" like Hong Kong had considerable autonomy. A governor representing the crown was assisted by an executive council and a legislative council, which could pass laws and issue ordinances, though requiring Colonial Office approval.[4] Both councils were composed at first of officials, with the subsequent addition of nonofficials appointed by the governor from among the colony's prominent residents.

Britain acquired Hong Kong primarily for the promotion of trade, not for territorial conquest. This primary concern shaped the government attitude toward the Chinese residents. Far from seeking to assimilate them, British rule in its early years left the Chinese to their own devices, so long as public order was maintained and trade enhanced. The British did not have a blueprint for governing Hong Kong. In an empirical manner typical of the English they changed their administrative policy according to changing times and circumstances.

In order to induce the Chinese to settle in Hong Kong, Captain Charles Elliot proclaimed in 1841 that all Chinese inhabitants would be governed "according to the laws, customs, and usages of the Chinese (every description of torture excepted) by the elders of villages, subject to the control of a British magistrate," and all others "according to the customs and usages of British Police Law."[5] Subsequently two separate communities, Chinese and European, were formed, and the town divided into separate Chinese and European quarters. This general pattern of segregation was maintained until the late nineteenth century, when the colonial government accelerated the process of political integration to take more direct control over the Chinese community. During the first few decades of the colony's history, however, British control over Chinese community life was superficial.

The earliest Chinese migrants to Hong Kong were mostly from the poorest elements of society: the outcast Tanka boat people, laborers (a majority of Hakkas, but also Punti Cantonese), artisans, and adventurers who gained profits by furnishing provisions and other services for *fankwei* (foreign devils). They defied Chinese officials' orders not to have any dealings with foreigners. In the aftermath of the Opium War Chinese magistrates still considered Chinese living under the British as traitors. But the prospects for profits were great in Britain's new colony. The construction of commercial establishments, markets, warehouses, and government offices in the new settlement offered opportunities. Chinese from all neighboring districts in the mainland flocked to Hong Kong. By April 1844 the Chinese population on the island had increased to 19,009. These consisted mostly of the lower classes: coolies, boat people, stonecutters, domestic servants, craftsmen, small traders, in addition to Triads, pirates, outlaws, opium smugglers, brothel keepers, gamblers, and like adventurers.[6]

Much concerned about the type of Chinese who came to Hong Kong, in 1844 the colonial treasurer reported to London that the mandarins' policy was to prevent respectable Chinese from settling in the colony: "they encourage and promote the deportation of every thief, pirate and idle or worthless vagabond from the mainland to Hong Kong."[7] Crime was rampant. Burglars even broke into the Government House (April 26, 1843) and attacked three mercantile houses (Dent's, Jardine's, and Gillespie's) in one night (April 28, 1843). Orders were issued in October 1842 and May 1843 prohibiting all Chinese boats from moving about the harbor after gunfire at 9 p.m. and requiring Chinese on shore to carry lanterns after dark and not to go outdoors after 10 p.m.[8]

Ignorant of the native language and customs, the European and Indian police had great difficulty regulating the Chinese population. Therefore, during the first two decades of the colony's history, the colonial government sought to implement the traditional Chinese system of social and political control over its Chinese subjects. In 1844 Governor Sir John Davis adapted the Chinese *pao-chia* system of collective neighborhood responsibility by appointing native officers called *paochang* and *paocheng* to assist the police in such matters as rioting, thefts, robberies, smuggling, illegal assemblies, and registration. G. B. Endacott maintains that these unpaid native officers "had very little power and little incentive to perform their honorary but onerous duties."[9]

As we shall see, the Chinese were developing their own mechanism of social control, but it became clear that the *pao-chia* system adapted by the British did not work. During the 1840s the British exercised minimal direct control over the Chinese community life. An attempt to assume strict control provoked resistance in 1844.

On August 21, 1844, the Legislative Council passed an ordinance intended to control the Chinese population, through registration, and to check the influx of the "scum" of the Chinese into the colony. Government proclamations, posted on October 29, contained an ambiguously worded Chinese translation of the ordinance, giving the impression that the one-dollar poll tax to be levied on the Chinese was monthly and not annual. Thus, Chinese laborers would lose half of their monthly $2–$3 wage. This exacerbated popular opposition to the colonial government. The Chinese hated the poll tax and refused to be individually registered. On October 31 laborers employed by the government and private individuals went on strike. A group of compradors threatened to leave the colony if the ordinance was not abrogated. On November 1 the Chinese went on a general strike. All shops and markets were closed; cargo boats were idle. Construction workers, coolies, and domestic servants were all on strike.[10]

The exorbitant demands of a foreign colonial government presented the Chinese of all dialect groups with a common problem requiring joint action. A sense of Chinese community was gradually being formed, as a deputation of the Chinese traders and compradors claimed to speak for the whole community. They sought to present a petition to the governor but were told that "no petition could be received, until the shops were opened, and the people returned to their labour."[11] In the meantime, an exodus of some three thousand Chinese had brought business to a complete standstill for several days. Eventually, on November 13, the Legislative Council was forced to amend the registration ordinance, abolishing the poll tax and applying registration only to the lowest classes.[12] A local English paper expressed great alarm: "This fatal error of hasty legislation has we fear lowered the English character in the estimation of the Chinese. They will on some future occasion attempt to starve their rulers into a compliance with their wishes, and it will require some wholesome discipline to convince them that government are [*sic*] not always to be intimidated."[13]

Collective action by the Chinese community seemed to have worked. The demands of an interventionist colonial government helped the formation of a sense of Chinese community. Tensions between Chinese and Europeans further enhanced the Chinese community consciousness.

Tensions Between Chinese and Europeans in a Frontier Society

In the aftermath of the Opium War and throughout the 1840s tensions and hostility characterized relations between the Chinese and the British in the whole Canton delta, the homeland of most Hong Kong Chinese. The "Canton city question" (i.e., British insistence on the right to enter the city) caused repeated popular outbursts against the Europeans in Canton. Governor Sir John Davis's naval expedition against Canton in April 1847 to force the opening of the city only aggravated mutual hostility. Foreigners were repeatedly attacked by the Cantonese populace in the delta. Governor Davis himself was assaulted on April 11, 1845, while on a visit to Macao. The Portuguese Governor of Macao, J. M. F. Amaral, was assassinated by the Chinese on August 22, 1849. Tensions in the Canton delta spilled over to Hong Kong. In September 1849 a rumor circulated among the Chinese in Hong Kong that the Chinese government had offered a reward for the assassination of Hong Kong governor Sir S. G. Bonham, whose carriage was henceforth escorted by troops.[14]

Strong antiforeign feelings among the people in the Canton delta were naturally shared by the Cantonese in Hong Kong concerned about the life and safety of their relatives back home. Crime was rife in the colony during Governor Bonham's administration (1848–54). On July 8, 1848, some Chinese attempted to poison twenty-five men of the Royal Artillery. On December 24 another attempt was made to set fire to the Central Market.[15] Piracy on the waters around Hong

Kong remained prevalent, especially from the 1840s through the 1860s, as did the daring robberies and raids in Victoria of armed gangs on stores, shops, and compradors' offices. The sociological significance of piracy and armed robbery in Hong Kong deserves further scholarly investigation.[16]

Eric Hobsbawm wisely cautions against treating all banditry as an expression of social protest or rebellion. He makes a distinction between "social bandits," who formed part of society in the eyes of the peasants, and the criminal underworld which formed an outgroup and was largely recruited from outgroup. Although Hobsbawm also recognizes that "people can readily be recruited from the first into the second [group],"[17] perhaps he distinguishes too sharply between the two groups. In the real world bandits can both help and abuse the poor.[18] As with the Triads in Hong Kong, pirates frequently engaged in nonpolitical criminal actions, but occasionally they also acted politically.

The pirate chiefs Shap-ng-tsai and Chui Apo ravaged South China seaboard villages and shipping, holding them hostage until ransoms were paid.[19] But there were occasions when pirates helped innocent villagers against the *fankwei*, thereby becoming heroes in the eyes of the villagers.

On February 25, 1849, Captain Da Costa and Lieutenant Dwyer strolled into the village of Wong-ma-kok on the southern side of the island of Hong Kong, some ten miles from Victoria. "[I]n a state of intoxication," according to contemporary legal accounts, "they proceeded from house to house inquiring for women until they came to the house of an old man . . . [whose] wife and daughter-in-law were engaged in cooking." One of the British officers began to take liberties with the young girl. And "on being remonstrated with by the old man and his wife, the . . . officer struck them both with his stick with such severity as to draw blood." The old man rushed to the door of the house and cried out to the neighbors for help. When the villagers arrived and attempted to pull the British officers out of the house, the latter resisted and beat them with their sticks. Hearing the commotion, pirate chief Chui Apo and his men "rushed in armed with spears and attacked the officers. . . . The officers upon retreating were hotly pressed by Chui Apo and his spearmen, overpowered, and struck down." They hurled the officers' bodies into the sea.[20]

The following day the Hong Kong police and one hundred British troops scoured the island for the two missing officers. The village of Wong-ma-kok was found deserted, its inhabitants afraid of British retaliation. But the old man whose head was broken by the British officer was unafraid; he did not run away, because he said he "had done nothing wrong." On the evening of February 27 the police found the body of Captain Da Costa in the water. With Chui Apo and his spearmen now wanted by the colonial authorities, the British navy soon destroyed his pirate fleet and used treachery to capture him in 1851. He was tried in the Criminal Court in Hong Kong and sentenced to transportation for life. But Chui Apo sought release through suicide in jail.[21] The pirate chief had defended the villagers of Wong-ma-kok against the *fankwei*'s intrusion.

The Emergence of a Chinese Elite in the 1840s

Chinese adventurers in the new frontier settlement of Hong Kong had a complex and ambiguous character. They were people who took risks in a wide range of activities. They smuggled opium, committed crimes, defended the villagers against foreign devils, or collaborated with foreigners for self-enrichment.

Tensions and hostility were only one side of the relationship between Chinese and Europeans. This did not preclude cooperation and collaboration, a pragmatic side of their relationship. Given material benefit and employment opportunities, the poor boatmen, laborers, artisans as well as traders and compradors were easily coopted by foreign colonists.

In the rough and fluid society of a frontier town in the 1840s, social mobility was great. A daring adventurer who acquired wealth could use his money in worthy causes and acquire social respectability as a community leader.

A leading example was Loo Aqui, originally an outcast *Tanka* bumboatman from Whampoa. During the Opium War he supplied the British fleet with provisions—risking the Chinese officials' displeasure—and was rewarded by the British with a large section of land in Hong Kong. Yet he adeptly played both sides of the game. The Chinese magistrates lured him back to Canton by offering him an official degree, which he accepted. He quickly slipped back to Hong Kong, however, to enjoy the rewards given him by the British. Loo

Aqui operated a gambling establishment and brothels and held the opium monopoly. He built a theater in 1845 and obtained the privilege of operating a market. By 1850 he was collecting rent from more than one hundred houses and shops. He was charged by the colonial authorities with being in league with pirates, though this was not substantiated. Rumor continued to spread that he was the "Sea King," tolling all who passed his squadron.[22]

Such rumors struck fear in people's hearts, but Loo Aqui used his wealth wisely, winning him the Chinese community's respect. The ability to inspire both fear and respect simultaneously was an essential attribute of an elite in a rough frontier society, an elite being defined as individuals who exerted dominance over local society. He was a benefactor "unto whom those who were in distress, in debt, or discontented, resorted [for relief]." He "opened a place for gambling on the hill side along Chung-wan, to which all among the fishing-boat people, who loved gambling, came." He operated a market for the inhabitants. With religion central to the life of the community, in 1847 Loo Aqui and Tam Achoy built the Man Mo Temple on Hollywood Road, where "they 'judged the people' in public assembly."[23]

Tam Achoy, a native of K'ai-p'ing (one of the Sze Yap districts), had been a foreman in the government dockyard in Singapore. He came to Hong Kong in 1841 to serve the British and was granted land and business privileges. He began to buy up property until he had acquired an extensive sea frontage. As a contractor he built a number of pretentious buildings and operated a market. After 1848 he became a leading broker and charterer of emigration ships. He "headed most of the subscription lists for worthy causes with generous donations." He was trustee for the I-Ts'z Temple in Taipingshan in 1851 and the temple in Queen's Road East at Wanchai in 1869.[24]

In a developing entrepôt under alien rule elite individuals like Loo Aqui and Tam Achoy arose from very humble origins. They used various available resources (commercial, social, and religious) to earn and maintain their elite position. Their connections with the British served as a vehicle for social advancement. They collaborated with the British in return for privileges that they used to acquire wealth. Material wealth in turn enabled them to engage in worthy causes for the community. They operated markets to serve the inhabitants and to create greater wealth. Invoking the moral authority of deities, they built the Man Mo Temple where they arbitrated disputes to maintain public order. In these ways a former *Tanka* boatman and a former foreman from a minority Sze Yap dialect group succeeded in becoming community leaders in the frontier town of Victoria.

Native Place–Dialect Groups in Early Hong Kong: Conflict and Cooperation

The origins and background of these adventurers who became community leaders reflected the fluid social conditions of the colony in the early decades of its history. Even the outcast *Tanka* boat people sought to mix with the various dialect groups on shore and merge with the general population. According to E. J. Eitel (resident and official in Hong Kong from 1862 to 1897), the boat people "invaded Hongkong the moment the settlement was started, living at first on boats in the harbour with their numerous families, and gradually settling on shore." Those settled on shore tended to "disavow their Tan-ka extraction in order to mix on equal terms with the mass of the Chinese community." Loo Aqui, who emerged as a community leader, was one of them. Eitel testified to "a process of continuous reabsorption in the mass of the Chinese residents of the Colony" throughout the nineteenth century.[25]

Kwok Acheong was another *Tanka* boatman that supplied the British forces with provisions during the Opium War. He settled on land and was closely associated with Tam Achoy, a Punti Cantonese. He became comprador of the P. and O. Steamship Company. During the 1860s Kwok Acheong developed a fleet of steamships. By then he had become one of the wealthiest Chinese in Hong Kong and was a liberal subscriber to all charities. Until his death in 1880 he remained a community leader with whom the colonial government frequently consulted regarding affairs of the Chinese population [26]

It would seem that a man's native place and dialect background was not a crucial factor in his social advancement at the time. Perhaps it would be anachronistic to perceive early Hong Kong in the light of later regional associations (*t'ung-hsiang hui-kuan*), which only began to appear after the mid-1870s and did not proliferate until around 1911. Although the native place–dialect principle was an important factor in Chinese social and economic life, in the first few decades of the colony's history it was not the most important basis for the Chinese community organization.

Though there has been little research on this subject, a recent article by Elizabeth Sinn confirms my study. She points out that apart from an obscure Hsin-an *hui-kuan*, which had appeared in the late 1840s and fizzled out in 1857, no other associations were organized primarily on a district-dialect basis. "It was common for people from the same districts and villages to engage in a particular trade, so that it was common for guilds to be also *Landesmannschaften*. But in Hong Kong's case most of the larger guilds, e.g., the Nanbei hang guild, the compradore, the rice, opium, piece goods and yard dealers' guilds, for instance, were not district-based." Thus, "until the mid-1870's, district origin had not been an important organizing principle in Hong Kong."[27] By then, as we shall see, some of the most important community organizations, such as the Nam Pak Hong (1868), the District Watch Committee (1866), and the Tung Wah Hospital Committee (1872), had already been formed, cutting across native district lines.

The late appearance of native district associations in Hong Kong was probably due to a combination of reasons. The first could be the absence of a host community in Hong Kong. It was a frontier town in which all Chinese were strangers and newcomers. As Sinn rightly points out, "if district associations were created as a means to maintain identity vis-à-vis the host community, this precondition hardly existed in Hong Kong."[28] Moreover, Hong Kong's ambulatory population and its geographical proximity to the mainland made native district associations rather superfluous. The colony's Chinese had families in Kwangtung and Fukien within a day or two's boat journey. They often moved back and forth between Hong Kong and their home villages. Unlike the Cantonese in Shanghai, nine hundred miles away from home, and unlike the Chinese communities living in isolation in remote foreign countries oveseas, necessitating native district associations for mutual aid,[29] the Cantonese and Fukienese in early Hong Kong did not see the pressing need for such associations.

Though not yet formally organized into native district associations, however, people speaking the same dialect still tended to cling together for protection and mutual assistance, often in competition with other dialect groups for resources and employment opportunities. Pugilistic clubs were formed for practicing the arts of self-defense.[30] But in the rapidly expanding new frontier town of Victoria, where practically all Chinese immigrants were strangers and newcomers, there was also a tendency to congregate and live in huts set up near the sites of new constructions in the port city. They crowded into such districts as Saiyingpun and Taipingshan within the city.

There were both conflicts and cooperations among the dialect groups in urban Hong Kong. As we shall see, fighting broke out in 1894 between coolies of different subethnic groups. But bloody armed feuds (*hsieh-tou*) seemed far less severe or frequent when compared with those that occurred among their brethren in Kwangtung and Fukien on the mainland. This could be attributed to several factors. First, the interventionist British authorities would not tolerate violence in the streets of Hong Kong, as public order was essential for the colony's trade and security. Equally important were the pattern of immigration and social structure in Hong Kong.

Most Chinese immigrants to Hong Kong came as individuals, leaving their families behind in their native villages in the mainland. Even after 1850, when some families started to move in, the majority of immigrants still consisted of individual settlers who went back and forth between the colony and their native villages. In 1848 the population of Hong Kong numbered 21,514; only one-fifth were females. It rose to 39,017 in 1853, with one-third females, and to 125,500 in 1865, of whom sixty-three percent were adult males,[31] still indicating the relative paucity of families in the colony. Nearly two-thirds of the Chinese residents were adult males who left their families behind in their home villages. Whereas dialect groups on the mainland were powerfully reinforced by kinship and lineage ties and by their possession of lands and villages as subethnic power bases, the dialect groups in urban Hong Kong consisted mostly of rootless individual men living together in coolie houses carefully watched by the colonial authorities.

What is more, in a frontier town under alien rule all Chinese were new settlers sharing some common problems that frequently necessitated cooperation and joint actions. They were all concerned with public order, security of life and property, and the often exorbitant demands of their foreign colonial masters whose language, laws, and courts they did not understand. For all of these reasons, tensions and conflicts among Chinese dialect groups in the British colony did not exclude cooperation among them to solve their common problems. The Chinese community could only be formed through the coordination of its subethnic components.

There were variations in customs, beliefs, and social practices among the Chinese of different dialect groups. The *Tanka* boat people in particular had their peculiar ways and taboos. There was a difference in pronunciation of certain words between standard Cantonese and the boat people's Cantonese. Their customs and superstitions reflected their water-borne life-style. When they ate broiled fish they were careful not to break off any of the bones. When they had finished one side of the fish they did not turn it over to eat the other side. And when they drank wine, it was never bottoms-up. All these portended shipweck.[32]

Despite variations in their subcultures, however, the Chinese of all dialect groups under British colonial rule shared much common culture that served to bring them together into a community.[33] They worshipped the same gods—Tin Hau (Ma Tzu), Hung Hsing, Kwun Yum (Kuan-yin), Fuk Tak Kung, Kuan Ti, and so forth. As religion was central to the lives of the Chinese residents, temples served as community centers.

Temples and Community Social Structure

Temples dominated the community social structure in early Hong Kong. James Hayes's essay on temple and shrine organizations in urban British Hong Kong shows that "inter-dialect communities organized to arrange the worship of street shrines" protecting the well-being of their localities. The Chinese settlers of all dialects, including the *Tanka* boat people, came to worship the same gods in shrines and temples because of "their universally desired end—namely, communal good fortune and prosperity under the protection of the gods."[34]

The earth god shrine in the Saiyingpun district of Victoria provides a good example of the unifying force of common beliefs. Local tradition traces the shrine's beginnings to a great epidemic (probably in 1894), which caused many deaths in the district—although it could be even older than that, since the district was already well established by the 1850s. The shrine was dedicated to the earth god Fuk Tak Kung, who in his lifetime was a noted Chinese medical practitioner and in death became the guardian god of a crowded city district. So great was his reputation that people from other districts came regularly to worship at the shrine. A committee consisting of *kaifong* (street neighborhood leaders and prominent shopkeepers of the district) ran the shrine. They arranged for chanting by Taoist priests on the god's birthday in the first moon and at the Yu-lan Hungry Ghosts Festival in the seventh moon. Religious rituals were often accompanied by a puppet show to please the god. Local residents considered the shrine to be of great importance to their well-being.[35]

In the crowded district of Saiyingpun fear of disease posed a common threat to all residents from whatever native places. Epidemics of fever visited the colony each summer, causing much mortality and alarm. Malarial fever and plague knew no dialect differences. The earth god Fuk Tak Kung protected all residents and discriminated against none. In each district of Hong Kong there was at least one shrine dedicated to the earth god, who looked after the district under his jurisdiction. The shrine committee in each district was composed of the *kaifong* of the respective district. As with the committee in Saiyingpun, the shrine committee in the Taipingshan district was concerned with religious matters of that district.[36] But the committee of the Man Mo Temple in Hollywood Road performed the duty of looking after both religious and general civil affairs of the area. Indeed it claimed jurisdiction over the whole Chinese community of Hong Kong as early as the 1850s.

The Man Mo (Wen Wu) Temple was dedicated to two gods: Lord Man Cheong (Wen Ch'ang), who presided over the destinies of civil officials, and the martial god Kuan Ti, who personified loyalty and righteousness. Together, the two gods had the purview of protecting people's well-being and bringing peace and prosperity to the community. The temple originated from a small shrine, probably dating back to the founding of the port colony in 1842. An inscription on a brass bell in the temple records a date of "the 27th Year of Emperor Tao-kuang [1847 A.D.],"[37] the year when Loo Aqui and Tam Achoy built the temple.

The Man Mo Temple was repaired and enlarged in 1851. E. Sinn shows that it was a colonywide project, with support cutting across regional and dialect group divisions and coming from various guilds. Loo Aqui was *Tanka*. Tam Achoy was from K'ai-p'ing, one of the Sze

Yap districts in Kwangtung. Ho Asik, who later succeeded Tam Achoy as the account manager, was from Shun-te. Several people from Panyu donated a couplet, and a mason named Tseng, probably a Hakka, contributed the stone columns at the main entrance. The Pork Dealer's Guild provided the stone lions in the yard, which were to scare away evil spirits. Several tablets were presented by various guilds, including the Shoe Makers' Guild and the Washermen's Guild. The enlarged temple cost nearly a thousand pounds to erect, reflecting the Chinese community's growing wealth. The temple committee, elected in 1851 by shopkeepers of the Sheung-wan district of Victoria, judged all cases of public interest there. The base of the committee was gradually extended, until by 1874 the *kaifong* leaders of all major city districts in Hong Kong were represented.[38] The Man Mo Temple became a focal point of Chinese community life. Coolies and pugilistic clubs of various dialect groups vied with each other in providing lion dance teams for the religious processions organized by the temple committee.

The *kaifong* leaders were prominent merchants and shopkeepers of the street neighborhood. H. J. Lethbridge states that they were "groups of civic-minded, status-seeking and paternalistic citizens in a particular area of the city who set themselves up . . . as a public body" to manage public matters. They were accepted by the Chinese populace because "they commanded the social skills and had . . . much to offer the poor—money, alms and services."[39] The *kaifong* leaders serving on the Man Mo Temple Committee arbitrated disputes and managed community affairs in a "public affairs office" (*kung-so*) built in 1862–63 beside the temple.[40] Thus, the merchant elite acted like China's gentry managers (*shen-tung*),[41] managing public affairs and arbitrating civil and commercial disputes among the Chinese community in Hong Kong. They invoked the moral authority of the temple's two deities: the god of literature, Lord Man Cheong, and the god of war, Kuan Ti, whom the merchants regarded as a god of wealth and fidelity in business transactions.

A matter that concerned the colony's Chinese, regardless of origins, was the urgent need for a common ancestral temple to serve the dead—specifically to receive the deceased persons' tablets awaiting transfer to their native villages. To the colony's growing Chinese community this was a matter of great importance that required the cooperation of all dialect groups. In 1851 Tam Achoy, Lu A-Ling, and twelve others petitioned the government for a grant of land to build such a temple.[42] Given a piece of land in Taipingshan, they raised funds to build the Kwong Fook I-ts'z (wide benevolence common ancestral temple). Like the erection of the Man Mo Temple, this again reflected a growing sense of Chinese community consciousness and the emergence of community leadership.[43]

The Chinese and European communities remained segregated. The Chinese were allowed to manage their own affairs as long as public order was maintained and trade carried on. But when order and security were at stake the British colonial authorities were quick to resort to force. This became evident in the crises of the 1850s.

Tensions and Crises in the 1850s

Paradoxically, this was a decade of rapid economic growth and socio-political crises. As stated in chapter 1, during the Taiping uprising (1850–64) tens of thousands of Chinese, including wealthy merchant families, fled the disorder on the mainland for the relative order and security of Hong Kong. The influx of people and capital stimulated trade and brought about commercial prosperity. But disorder on the mainland also caused tensions and crises in Hong Kong.

The Taiping rebels were active in and around the British colony, where they made common cause with pirates, brigands, and the Triads. From late September 1854 Kowloon City, across from Victoria Harbor, was contested between the Taipings and the Chinese impe-rial forces. Armed Taiping bands occasionally paraded the streets of Hong Kong. On December 21, 1854, the Hong Kong police arrested several hundred armed rebels who were about to embark on an attack on Kowloon City. On January 23, 1855 a fleet of Taiping war junks came to the brink of a naval battle with the Chinese imperial war junks in Victoria Harbor but were ordered away by the British colonial authorities. Officers of the Taiping war junks fraternized with the Hong Kong Chinese Christians and some missionaries.[44] In Hong Kong the Taiping leaders' friends and relatives, such as Hung Jen-kan and Li Cheng-kao (Li Tsin-kau), formed close relations with missionaries such as Theodore Hamberg, James Legge (of the Lon-don Missionary Society), and Rudolph Lechler (of the Basel Mission-ary Society), who wished to use such relations to exert influence on the Taiping movement.[45]

Tensions in the colony were compounded by the Arrow War. The Arrow Incident on October 8, 1856, involved a lorcha named *Arrow* that was owned by some Hong Kong Chinese. Anchored off Canton, it was registered with the British colonial government, flying a British flag. With the excuse of searching for pirates Chinese officials arrested its twelve Chinese crew members and hauled down the British flag. Britain used this incident as a pretext to press for the opening of Canton and for more concessions from China. Failing this, the British started the Arrow War (1856–60) against China. In response to the British bombardment of Canton in October and November of 1856, Viceroy Yeh Ming-ch'en put a price of one hundred taels of silver on each English head and called upon the Chinese in Hong Kong to leave the colony immediately. Under his instruction placards were posted in the streets of Hong Kong and Canton inciting people to fight the British enemy by any means.[46] The placards also offered rewards for the heads of compradors collaborating with the foreign enemy.[47] The police quickly pulled down the placards.

The British bombardment of Canton, their blockade of the Canton river, and other war acts naturally aroused anti-British sentiments among the Chinese in Hong Kong, who worried about the safety of their families, relatives, and homeland property. Indeed, the ambulatory Hong Kong Chinese themselves were threatened by the British war actions. Apprehensive of an uprising, a British gunboat named *Acorn* was anchored near the Central Market on December 30, 1856, to overawe the Chinese "rowdies" congregating there. The police force was strengthened and night pass regulations strictly enforced.[48]

On the morning of January 15, 1857, the European community in Hong Kong was seized by a panic because their bread had been poisoned. About two or three hundred Europeans who had partaken of the bread supplied by the E-sing Bakery suffered, more or less, from arsenic poisoning. Some became seriously ill, including the governor's wife, Lady Bowring. Cheong Ah-lum, the bakery's owner and a well-known comprador, had left that morning for Macao with his father, wife, and children, but they themselves were also poisoned. Cheong Ah-lum was arrested in Macao. The police also arrested fifty-one of his workmen, who were detained until February 3 in a tiny room measuring only fifteen-feet-square at a police station. Finally a doctor urged the authorities to remove them to the jail. It was believed that the poisoning was ordered from Canton, but neither proof nor the culprits could be found. At the trial the attorney-general asserted: "Better to hang the wrong men than confess that British sagacity and activity have failed to discover the real criminals."[49]

As there was no evidence incriminating the suspects, they were acquitted by a British jury. But they were quickly rearrested as "suspicious characters." What did the Chinese elite do on behalf of the bakery owner and fifty-one workmen who were acquitted and rearrested? The leading Chinese merchants petitioned the governor against their retention and recommended "voluntary banishment" instead. The Chinese elite could do no more than this when the colonial authorities were determined to use force to keep public order and ensure the security of the European community. Fifty-one European residents memorialized the governor to urge forceful deportation of the prisoners to Formosa. Fourteen others petitioned the governor to express their concern that prisoners, once acquitted, "cannot be twice called in question for the same offence," and that their rearrest would "throw discredit on our system of administrating justice in the eyes of the Chinese population." Nevertheless, the petitioners recommended that each prisoner "should be compelled to absent himself from the Colony." In other words, the European petitioners thought that the acquitted Chinese could not be legally expelled but must nevertheless be expelled from the colony. Eventually the crowded conditions of the jail induced the governor to release the rearrested prisoners, who were ordered never to return to Hong Kong.[50]

Meanwhile, indiscriminate mass arrests occurred. Some five hundred or six-hundred men were rounded up and 167 deported to Hainan; 204 "suspicious looking characters" were arrested in Bonham Strand, and 46 others imprisoned. A further 146 men were apprehended.[51] The Chinese community elite remained subdued during the whole operation.

As no culprits could be found, a local English paper subsequently speculated that the bread poisoning might have been caused by a mere accident: flour could have been contaminated on board a cargo ship also carrying arsenopyrite.[52] Whatever the real cause of the bread poisoning, it revealed a great social tension in the colony. The damage to racial relations had been done by the colonial government's arbitrary measures and indiscriminate mass arrests and deportation. Among the Hong Kong Chinese the incident had left a legacy of bitterness and anticolonialism. It also magnified the Europeans' fear and defensiveness, widening the divisions existing between them and the Chinese community.

The bread poisoning incident was significant in still another way. It revealed the dilemma of the Hong Kong Chinese resident caught between the conflicting demands of the Chinese and British authorities. During the Arrow War mandarin intimidation caused some Hong Kong Chinese merchants, who had been providing provisions for the British, to close their businesses and return to the mainland. Cheong Ah-lum, the comprador and the bakery's owner, had been warned many times by the Chinese residents in Hong Kong about his dealings with the British, and his shop in Canton had been set on fire. But he ignored all warnings. He continued to provide bread and other provisions for the Europeans, making big profits until the bread poisoning case broke out. Expelled by the colonial government, Cheong Ah-lum dared not return to China. He boarded a ship for Saigon.[53]

This incident served to highlight the predicament of the Chinese residents in Hong Kong. Both Canton and Hong Kong authorities claimed their allegiance, putting them in an ambivalent relationship with both governments. This became particularly evident in times of crises such as the 1856 *Arrow* incident and the 1857 bread poisoning case. And it would be evident again in the 1858 exodus and the conflicting responses of the colony's Chinese to foreign intrusion during the Second Opium War.

Tensions continued throughout the war. Incendiarism was prevalent in the colony. George Duddwell's bakery, which had taken over from Cheong Ah-lum the supplying of bread to the European community, was burned on February 28, 1857. It was then discovered in April 1857 that a vast conspiracy in Canton was organized to make war against British lives and property in Hong Kong. British shipping and even gunboats were frequently attacked. On December 28, 1857, the Anglo-French forces commenced a bombardment of Canton, which fell on January 5, 1858. Vicerory Yeh Ming-ch'en was captured and sent to Hong Kong en route to Calcutta. Canton was occupied by the Anglo-French forces and governed by the Allied Commissioners from January 5, 1858, to October 21, 1861. Rural militia under the gentry and loyalist officials offered vain opposition to the occupation forces.[54]

The Chinese magistrates of the neighboring districts had repeatedly called on the Chinese residents of Hong Kong to fight with any means against the foreign invaders. The magistrates now moved the rural militia "to compel all village elders to cut off the market supplies of the Colony and to send word to their respective clansmen in Hongkong to leave the Colony immediately on pain of their relatives in the country being treated as rebels." This resulted in an exodus in July 1858 of over twenty thousand Chinese—mostly laborers—from the colony back to their homeland. They boycotted the European community by staying away and stopping the food suplies. No work of any kind could be accomplished, since tailors, shoemakers, carpenters, and artisans of every kind had departed from Hong Kong.[55] Governor Bowring issued a proclamation calling on the Chinese magistrates and gentry to help end the boycott. When a British crew was fired upon by the braves of Namtao, a walled town in Hsin-an district, Bowring sent a naval force to take Namtao and to coerce the magistrates to restore the market supplies to the colony.[56] This represented another instance of large-scale hostile confrontation between the Chinese and the British colonists.

Some Chinese historians are quick to claim that the 1858 exodus reflected popular nationalism against foreign imperialism, meaning that the Chinese laborers who left the colony were motivated by a sense of collective identity with and loyalty to China as a nation-state.[57] But anti-British feelings did not necessarily entail Chinese national consciousness. The historian should not magnify the exodus into an incident of popular nationalism. Until solid evidence is found to support the Chinese historians' claim, perhaps it is better to regard the exodus as a response of the Hong Kong populace to the Chinese magistrates' coercion. Nevertheless, the hostile confrontation had exacerbated tensions and mutual suspicion already existing between Chinese and Europeans in the British colony.

Conflicting Responses to Foreign Intrusion

Dr. E. J. Eitel (who was a missionary in Hong Kong from 1862, acting Chinese secretary to Governor Hennessy, and inspector of schools, 1879–97) admitted that "from the first advent of the British and all through the wars with China, the Puntis [Cantonese] as a rule were the enemies and the Hakkas the friends, purveyors, commissariat and transport coolies of the foreigners, while the fishing population provided boatmen and pilots for the foreign trade."[58] This was a frank admission by a high colonial official that the Punti Cantonese, the majority of Hong Kong's population, were the enemies of the British colonists.

In fact, however, the Punti Cantonese merchants were also easily coopted by the British. The brothers Li Sing and Li Leong, for instance, had diversified their investments in the money changing business, shipbuilding, trade, opium monopoly, gambling, and coolie labor brokerage. With so much investment in Hong Kong, they identified their interests with the British when China was at war with Britain and France. They "gave contributions to foreigners to the extent of over a lakh of ready money and recruited native braves who went to the front at Tientsin. When peace was declared they shared in the War Indemnity as well as in the Imperial effects and curios of the Yuen-ming-yuen [Summer Palace]."[59] A Chinese coolie corps of seven hundred and fifty Hakkas was organized to work for the Anglo-French forces in 1857.[60] Again, two thousand Hakka coolies were easily recruited in 1860 to serve as porters for the Anglo-French expedition forces against Tientsin.

Thus, given material benefit, the poor boat people and Hakka laborers as well as the Punti Cantonese merchants were easily coopted by the foreign invaders. The majority of the Hong Kong Chinese, however, remained suspicious of and hostile to the British invaders, whose acts of war had directly threatened the lives and safety of many people. The Chinese residents of Hong Kong found themselves in a dilemma. Forced by poverty and disturbances on the mainland to move to Hong Kong, which offered relative security and job opportunities, they submitted themselves to foreign colonial rule, which they hated. This predicament helped to explain their conflicting responses to the progress of the war between China and the Anglo-French forces. Eitel observed:

> The defeat of the British fleet at the Peiho (January 25, 1859), while it depressed the foreign community of Hong Kong, appeared to evoke no feeling of any sort among the Chinese population. Indeed, those Chinese who gave any thought to the matter, seemed rather to regret this temporary success of Mandarin treachery. But the capture of Peking in 1860 and particularly the flight of the Emperor was felt by all but the Triad Society partisans as a national disgrace.[61]

If this was true, it indicated a faint beginning of national awareness on the part of some Chinese residents in Hong Kong in 1860.
They seemed to realize that their fate was tied to events in Peking,
China's national capital. In a colonial situation where the Chinese
were a subject people, ruled, dominated, and discriminated against
by the British masters, it was probably easier for them to acquire a
sense of identity with the Chinese nation than it was for their countrymen in the interior of China.

Primary Concern with Livelihood, Not with Nationalism

But one must not exaggerate the extent of Chinese national consciousness in the British colony at that early date. In their daily
struggle to make a living, the issue of national awareness was only
incidental to the Chinese in Hong Kong, especially after the war was
over and peace restored. Of primary importance to the common
people was one's daily means of subsistence. Whenever an employment opportunity working for the foreign colonist became available,
it was quickly seized upon. When livelihood was threatened, either
by employers or by the colonial government, the Chinese rose in
resistance, both individually and collectively. Their primary concerns
were with local issues affecting their daily existence. Issues of national or international import, if not related to the realities of their
daily experience, and if not fused with concern about their livelihood, had limited appeal to the ordinary people.

Hence, in the aftermath of the Arrow War, the cession of Kowloon
to Britain in the Peking Convention (October 24, 1860), and the
British takeover of the peninsula on January 19, 1861, evoked no
Chinese resistance.[62] On the other hand, when the colonial government sought to regulate the lives and work of the Chinese, they rose
in protest. Eitel affirmed that it was "the common practice of the
Chinese of offering seditious resistance to a weak government by
combining to strike work in order to mark their sense of irksome or
imperfect legislation."[63] In January 1853, for instance, pawnbrokers
"complain[ed] against the action of the Police in occasionally intrud-
ing upon their premises in search of stolen property." Then, in July
1858, they closed their shops in protest against the exorbitant licence
rate. And again, in 1860, they struck in protest against the Pawnbro-

kers' Ordinance regulating their business.[64] The government made no concession on either occasion.

Detailed discussions of the lives, work, and collective actions of the laborers are provided in subsequent chapters. Suffice it here to note two labor strikes to illustrate the workers' major concerns in Hong Kong in the 1860s. A strike of the cargo boat people took place in 1861 in protest against an ordinance requiring the registration and regulation of those employed on cargo boats. But the firmness of the government brought them to submit to registration.[65] The chair coolies also staged a strike in 1863 in opposition to an ordinance regulating and licensing public vehicles. They too had to yield after nearly three months of passive resistance.[66]

While most chair coolies came from the Hoklo and Tieochiu dialect groups, both cargo boat people and cargo-carrying coolies consisted of Chinese of different dialect groups and native place origins. Despite rivalry and tensions between the dialect groups, they took common actions in resistance when their livelihood was threatened by the colonial government regulations. As we shall see, in the process of their repeated confrontations with the colonial government, they came to feel the identity of interests among themselves against a common foe.

Many Hong Kong Chinese had originally come from the villages of the surrounding regions where they were accustomed to managing their own affairs. The Chinese government generally governed by proxy. Absentee gentry landlords were concerned only with the collection of rents or other levies on land, making no attempt to control routine local affairs.[67] The Chinese villagers moved to Hong Kong to make a living, expecting to be left alone. When the British colonial government sought to regulate their lives and work, they rose in resistance. Much of the coolie unrest in Hong Kong in the nineteenth century took the form of "reactive collective actions," to use Charles Tilly's term, which consisted of "group efforts to reassert established claims when someone else challenge[d] or violate[d] them."[68] Many incidents of labor unrest in Hong Kong in the nineteenth century were provoked by the modern European interventionist state's assertion of power to accelerate political integration and to impose direct government control on a community accustomed to self-management of its own affairs. When coolie unrest occurred, the elite played an important role mediating the disputes.

The Elite and Its Organizations, the 1850s-1860s

The British colonial policy of segregation allowed the elite members to manage public affairs pertaining to the Chinese community. They arbitrated civil and commercial disputes among the Chinese. So far as they assumed the role of civil arbiters to help maintain public order, the British tolerated it. But that was also the limit of British tolerance, which allowed no room for the Chinese elite to possess private armed power.

In a recent volume of essays on local elites and patterns of dominance Joseph W. Esherick and Mary B. Rankin rightly affirm that "different environments and resources available to elites in different areas of China and different periods of Chinese history . . . [have] produce[d] different types of elite."[69] There were also variations even within the type of "frontier elites" on the edge of Chinese society. The local arena of Hong Kong as a British colony limited the power of its Chinese elite. Loo Aqui and Tam Achoy were not the frontier strongmen commanding militia and armed followers that Johanna M. Meskill finds in Taiwan in Ch'ing times,[70] nor the militia leaders and military governor that Edward A. McCord finds in Kwei-chou from the mid-nineteenth century through the early twentieth.[71] The suspicious colonial authorities charged Loo Aqui with being in league with pirates, though it was not substantiated. And when Tam Achoy became involved in the use of armed force, he was quickly brought to court.

In 1860 Tam Achoy's home district of K'ai-p'ing in Kwangtung was ravaged by the Hakka armed bands. Several of his relatives, including his mother, were killed. In response to the mandarin's request for assistance, Tam Achoy engaged an armed corps of about a hundred Punti Cantonese, officered by some American and European sailors whom he despatched on a chartered steamer, flying the British flag, to attack a Hakka village near Macao. Three Europeans and several others were killed in the expedition. The Hong Kong police arrested Tam Achoy and charged him with piracy and murder. However, before sending off the expedition, Tam Achoy had notified a government officer of his intentions and received no warning of the illegality of his actions. Tam Achoy pleaded guilty of misdemeanor and threw himself upon the mercy of the court. He was, thereupon, discharged with a reprimand.[72]

According to Max Weber, the effective monopoly of the legitimate use of violent coercive force within a given territory is an essential attribute of a modern state.[73] Britain would not tolerate the Chinese elite's use of armed force in the colony under her jurisdiction. But the Chinese government's connivance at the local elite's assumption of military power in other frontier societies like Taiwan and Kweichou was born of necessity, for they laid largely beyond the reach of Chinese state power. Thus the power of the local elite was conditioned by the local social context.

The composition of Chinese elite in Hong Kong began to change with the changing social context in the 1850s and 1860s.[74] New elements were added to the elite group. The turbulent conditions on the mainland created by the Taiping uprising led to the influx of Chinese families and capital into Hong Kong. This changed somewhat the characteristics of the Chinese population in the colony. "It acquired more stability, respectability and economic strength," as Carl Smith puts it. The elite who emerged in the 1850s and 1860s included more respectable wealthy merchants. Large merchant establishments known as *hongs* were set up in Hong Kong. In 1858 there were thirty-five and in the following year sixty-five *hongs* owned by merchants of different dialect groups, including Punti Cantonese, Teochiu, and Fukienese.[75]

Aspiring Chinese used all resources available to promote their power and influence. In Hong Kong connections with the British served as an important vehicle for social advancement. Chinese contractors, merchants, and compradors formed business connections with the British colonists. Resources for the aspiring Chinese also included the native place–dialect ties as well as the transregional associations. These two were not perceived as mutually exclusive.

"In Hong Kong, . . . the Chinese were not divided to any great extent by dialect or provincial hostilities, only by differences in wealth and status," observes H. J. Lethbridge.[76] This was true of the merchants, though not quite true of the lower class Chinese who had no other resources but dialect group ties to rely on. Merchants of the same dialect and native place often joined together in business partnership, yet in the commercialized city of Hong Kong it was also common for merchants of different dialects to gather for social and business purposes. Moreover, commercial guilds in Hong Kong were organized on a transregional basis.

The colony's historical experience and social context helped to bring together merchants of various dialects. For several decades after 1841 Hong Kong was an entirely new settlement. The earliest pioneer merchants from different regions and dialect groups arrived in the 1850s and 1860s to set up their firms, clustering around a few narrow streets named Bonham Strand and Wing Lok Street. In a new settlement under alien rule they confronted common problems that demanded coordinated actions. To build an environment conducive to trade, they had to cooperate to promote market prosperity and assist the police in maintaining law and order. Among the small group of Teochiu pioneer merchants "business deals were sealed by the lips only. . . . Written contracts were unheard of and highly unnecessary."[77] In fact, in such a new settlement under foreign colonial rule, the small community of pioneer merchants from various native districts could more easily establish personal relations with one another and cooperate to build an environment conducive to trade.[78]

Merchants used all resources available that would enhance their business and social influence. They retained their separate native place loyalties and used such loyalties for social and commercial purposes. But they also joined together to found transregional institutions to promote their common interests and community welfare.

The District Watch Committee was such an institution. The Chinese residents of all dialects and native places in Hong Kong were faced with the common problem of maintaining public order and protecting life and property. The colony had a regular police force whose main duty, however, was to protect the central business district where most of the European firms clustered. The European officers and Indian policemen spoke no Chinese; the Chinese constables were recruited from the dregs of society. The regular police were corrupt and inefficient. Therefore, the Chinese trade houses and neighborhoods were compelled to employ their own guards and watchmen.[79]

On February 1, 1866, a meeting of the *kaifong* leaders of all city districts in Hong Kong decided to petition the government for permision to create a District Watch Force, to be supported by subscriptions from the Chinese community. Sanctioned by the government, it was an amalgamation of private watchmen and guards already employed by merchants and shopkeepers. Supervised by a committee of Chinese merchants, and under the ultimate control of the Hong Kong Registrar General, the district watchmen assisted the police in keeping law and order in the Chinese quarters.[80]

The famed Nam Pak Hong guild was also founded on a transregional basis. It was established in 1868 by some leading merchants of various dialect groups in Hong Kong "to promote members' welfare and market prosperity, to assist the police in the maintenance of law and order in the neighbourhood and to formulate plans for the prevention of fires and alleviation of disasters."[81] Within the Nam Pak Hong guild were many Teochiu merchants who dominated trade with Southeast Asia, but Punti Cantonese merchants also played an important role in that trade. At first, the Nam Pak Hong (*Nan-pei-hang* literally means south-north firms) consisted of a few firms engaged in the trading of native produce between regions south of the Yangtze and Northern China. In a few years its membership came to include dozens of trading firms run by merchants of various dialect groups and native districts. These merchants included the Punti Cantonese (e.g., Chiu Yue-tin, Lo Chor-san, Lau Lo-tak), the Teochiu merchants (e.g., Ko Man-wah, Chan Chun-chuen, Choi Si-kit), and the Hokkienese (e.g., Ng Li-hing, Wu Ting-sam, Wong Ting-ming). Also included in its membership were trading firms run by merchants of Shantung origin.

The directors and managers of the Nam Pak Hong guild were mutually elected. For the first term Chiu Yue-tin served as the chairman of the Board of Directors, and Lau Lo-tak as the manager. Both were Punti Cantonese. The power and influence of the Nam Pak Hong came from its wealth and its connections with various trades in the Pacific commercial network. The Nam Pak Hong exporting and importing business stretched as far as Peking and Tientsin in North China to the distant countries in Southeast Asia. It later extended its scope to cover America and Europe as well.

Besides acting as a medium for trade, the Nam Pak Hong firms also served as banking institutes through which overseas Chinese remitted money home. In addition, the Nam Pak Hong guild provided important social services for the community, organizing a fire brigade, a street watch force, and religious celebrations.[82] The wealthy Nam Pak Hong merchants came to dominate the Man Mo Temple Committee, which "secretly controlled native affairs, acted as commercial arbitrators, arranged for the due reception of mandarins passing through the Colony, negotiated the sale of official titles, and formed an unofficial link between the Chinese residents of Hongkong and the Canton Authorities."[83] And as we shall see, in times of social unrest in the colony, the Nam Pak Hong merchants often played an important role mediating between the populace and the colonial authorities.

Though living under alien rule, the Nam Pak Hong merchants had to deal with the Canton government, which exerted some measures of political influence and control over the colony's Chinese residents. A number of wealthy merchants purchased the Chinese official degrees in order to protect their relatives and property in China, and also to enhance their position and prestige among the Chinese residents in Hong Kong.

The earliest Chinese community leaders in the 1840s and 1850s such as Loo Aqui, Tam Achoy, and Kwok Acheong, had originated from the marginal groups of society. Having acquired wealth, they sought to become "gentrified" in order to justify and rationalize their new social position and to promote their prestige in the eyes of the Chinese public. Kwok Acheong purchased Chinese official ranks. Loo Aqui acquired an official degree of the sixth rank. And Tam Achoy rendered services to his home district by supplying its militia with Western-made armaments, and thereby earned Chinese official recognition and a biographical notice in the K'ai-p'ing gazetteer.[84]

The Nam Pak Hong merchants, too, became gentrified, seeking to assert their "cultural hegemony" over the Chinese populace. As Mary Rankin and Joseph Esherick aptly observe, "a clear consciousness of class and status existed both among elites and between elites and masses. . . . Superiority was demonstrated through life-styles, honor, and cultural display."[85] The following description of the nineteenth-century Nam Pak Hong merchants is most revealing:

> With wealth came the desire for honour, and it was quite common that most of the better-off members held official sinecures which were bought from the Chinese government. This entitled them to don colourful official robe during the ceremonies and important festivals. It was a spectacular sight to see these celebrities moving around, impressively attired during the Chinese New Year when European executives from leading shipping and insurance companies called to present their greetings. These were usually carried out amidst highly decorated surroundings, coupled with theatrical

performances and lavish receptions which lasted for weeks. Class distinctions were obvious, and only the privileged few had the right of access to particular installations ranging from private clubs to public tea houses. An employee who was caught by his employer sneaking into one of these would be dismissed almost instantly.[86]

Chinese official sinecures, colorful official robes during the ceremonies and festivals, greetings from European business executives, theatrical performances, and lavish receptions all conveyed images of wealth, power, and authority, intended to induce popular subordination. These had "much of the studied self-consciousness of public theatre . . . designed to exhibit authority to the plebs and to exact from them deference," to use E. P. Thompson's words in his description of the gentry's elaborate hegemonic style in eighteenth-century England.[87]

With the creation of a unified District Watch Force in 1866 and the powerful Nam Pak Hong guild in 1868, a sense of Chinese community dominated by a merchant elite in Hong Kong was greatly enhanced. And it was to be further strengthened by the founding of a renowned institution, the Tung Wah Hospital, in 1872.

The Chinese Community in a
Colonial Situation, the 1870s–1900s

Much credit is due to the influential Chinese residents who co-operated so cordially with the Government officials to bring about a proper understanding with the hawkers, who have now resumed their avocations, and at the same time recognised the sovereignty of the law.

—Hongkong Daily Press, *May 24, 1883*

The mighty spirit of free trade . . . fused the interests of European and Chinese merchants into indissoluble unity.

—E. J. Eitel

I condemn the [Light and Pass] Ordinance simply because it is against the Chinese only. —Ho Tung

Like the gentry elite in late imperial China, the merchant elite in Hong Kong sought to foster a social consensus based upon Confucian ideals of social harmony and elite paternalism. But colonial experience made it different from elites in China in some ways. British colonial rule brought the local elite into a complex, interlocking web of ambivalent relationships between elite, government, populace, and mandarins in Canton. Chapter 3 examines how the Chinese community in Hong Kong was held together under the dominance of this merchant elite and how the scope of elite dominance changed according to the changing social milieu in the years between 1870 and 1900.

The Founding of the Tung Wah Hospital, 1872

As previously noted, the I-ts'z common ancestral temple was built in 1851 by the Chinese community to receive the deceased persons' tablets awaiting transfer to their native villages. Soon afterward it began to house coffins awaiting shipment and even dying persons from among the colony's poor. Because of cultural prejudice and a strong aversion to Western medical practices (particularly abhoring surgical operation), the Chinese would rather die than enter the Government Civil Hospital. The I-ts'z increasingly looked like what was called the "city of the dead" in Canton; it became a "great nuisance" to the European community. Reports in 1869 by the acting registrar general and the inspectors of nuisances revealed the appalling "filth and wretchedness of the place" and "the horrible indifference" to the dying inmates. This caused an outcry among the Europeans. The Chinese elite then came forward with liberal subscriptions for the erection of a Chinese hospital to be managed by the Chinese and to provide Chinese medical treatment. Subsidized by the government grants of a site and $15,000, it cost about $45,000 to build the Tung Wah Hospital.[1]

The opening ceremony on February 14, 1872, was "the grandest ever witnessed in Hongkong," reported the local newspapers. At an early hour over seventy leading Chinese serving on the hospital committee assembled at the *kung-so* adjoining the Man Mo Temple on Hollywood Road. They were "all dressed in the mandarin costume, some even with a peacock's feather attached to their buttons," displaying symbols of wealth, power and status designed to impress the general public and to enhance their social hegemony over the community. The elite joined a long and gorgeous procession that paraded the streets of the Chinese section of town leading to the hospital amid the din of gongs and drums. The concourse of spectators was so great that the district watchmen and Sikh and Indian police were despatched to preserve order. Leong On (chairman of the committee, and comprador of Messrs. Gibb, Livingston & Co.) played a prominent role in the ceremony, offering sacrifice and performing kowtows to the altar dedicated to the deity Shen Nung (a mythical sage-emperor and discoverer of medicines). Accompanied by fireworks and the booming of guns, "the ceremony produced a profound impression" on the Chinese crowds.[2]

Governor Sir Richard MacDonnell honored the proceedings by his presence. Arriving at 2:30 p.m. at the hospital, his excellency took up his position in the center of the reception hall "amid the respectful salutes of the Chinese present." He praised the committee for undertaking "a great and responsible task to give shelter, medical assistance, and comfort to all indigent persons . . . without charge." While "not interfering with the Chinese arrangement of details," the governor reminded the Chinese, the government reserved for itself the "great power" to inspect and supervise the hospital. The governor acknowledged "the cordial co-operation . . . from the respectable members of the Chinese community in promoting law and order, and protecting life and property in the Colony."[3] Promising a government fund of one hundred thousand dollars, MacDonnell declared the formal opening of the Tung Wah Hospital, which was henceforth managed by the Chinese and supported by voluntary contributions from the Chinese community.

As Sinn has demonstrated, the hospital was managed by a general committee consisting of managers, assistant directors, and directors. Central to the management system was a board of directors composed of twelve members. The board was annually nominated by the major commercial guilds and elected by the hospital subscribers and the *kaifong* street neighborhood leaders. It usually consisted of three compradors, two Nam Pak Hong merchants, and one merchant each from the rice, piecegoods, opium, California trade, yarn dealers', and pawn brokers' guilds, in addition to one or two merchants from unspecified trades. These guilds made yearly contributions to the hospital's funds. As most of the guilds included both employers and employees, the guild-based structure of the Tung Wah Board of Directors allowed it to influence and find support from the Chinese lower classes. And the election process served both to legitimize its claim to represent the community and to inspire among the people "a sense of community, commitment, and participation."[4]

The Tung Wah's claim to represent the whole Chinese community was reinforced by a management structure that incorporated leadership from various dialect groups. The Tung Wah directors and committee members included prominent merchants and businessmen of different dialects and native origins.[5] Wealthy Chinese, from whatever geographical and social background, served on its prestigious committee and directorate.[6] In the highly commercialized and fluid society of Hong Kong, commercial wealth was a major resource for Chinese aspiring to an elite status. By performing public service on the hospital committee, they won respect and gratitude from the community residents.

Charity, Social Service, and Management of Public Affairs

In addition to medical care, the Tung Wah Hospital rendered important social service. It housed the poor and sick and provided coffins and free burials for the dead. It repatriated shipwreck victims, coolie-emigrants abducted abroad, and women kidnapped for prostitution. To prevent the kidnapping of girls for sale, prostitution, and other immoral purposes, the Tung Wah elite organized the Po Leung Kuk (society for the protection of women and children) in 1878, giving shelter to destitute women and children and handling their repatriation.[7] The Po Leung Kuk board of directors, composed of Chinese merchants from different dialect groups, performed charitable work and advised the government on various issues concerning the welfare of the Chinese. Closely linked to the Tung Wah Hospital, the Po Leung Kuk worked as its "junior association."[8]

The Tung Wah Hospital also provided free vaccinations both in Hong Kong and Kwangtung. Its charitable work was extended beyond Hong Kong to the Chinese mainland. To help raise relief funds during the 1877 North China famine caused by floods in Shansi, the governor of Fukien, Ting Jih-ch'ang, appointed Ko Man Wah and O Chun-chit—two Teochiu merchants in the Hong Kong Nam Pak Hong guild, who had served as the Tung Wah directors, and who had purchased Chinese official ranks. A large sum was raised by the Tung Wah Hospital, which in return received honors and awards of a plaque from the governor of Shansi, Tseng Kuo-ch'üan, and a tablet scroll from Emperor Kuang-hsü. A matter of pride for the Chinese community in Hong Kong, it greatly enhanced the power and prestige of the Tung Wah elite in the eyes of the Chinese public. For many years thereafter the Tung Wah continued to raise large amounts for relief in China. Its fame spread throughout the Chinese empire. In fact, the Tung Wah also served the overseas Chinese communities, throughout the Pacific commercial network, which often sent money, letters, and other personal effects to the Tung Wah for distribution to their native villages on the Chinese mainland. Such services explain why the Chinese communities both at home and overseas subscribed readily and generously to its fund-raising campaigns.[9]

Possessing wealth, moral authority, and prestige, the Tung Wah Committee extended its scope of activities beyond charitable work to include management of Chinese public affairs in Hong Kong. At the top of the Chinese social hierarchy, its authority was supported by the Po Leung Kuk, the District Watch Committee, the Man Mo Temple Committee, and the *kaifong* associations, all of which continued to function at their own levels. The Tung Wah Hospital became the most important civic center for the Chinese, where members of the community could bring forth any matters of public interest for discussion. On important occasions, as we shall see, several hundred people attended the meetings where the public voted on resolutions. As Sinn rightly contends, the Tung Wah Committee was "extremely responsive to public opinion," seeking to run community affairs by consensus.[10]

The committee arbitrated civil and commercial disputes among the Chinese. Ever since the founding of the colony in the early 1840s, Chinese social customs had generally been tolerated or respected except where they conflicted with government ordinances. Wherever possible, the ordinary Chinese sought to avoid the British magistrate's court, whose laws and language they did not understand. They preferred the Tung Wah arbitration. For example, men whose wives or concubines had deserted them, craft masters whose apprentices had run away, and creditors claiming repayment from debtors would come to the hospital committee for justice. The committee used its social influence and moral authority to persuade and arbitrate. Where it failed to resolve disputes, it was willing to appeal to the legal, coercive power of the colonial government as a last resort.[11]

To assert cultural hegemony over the populace, the Tung Wah committeemen consciously played the role of the elite. Periodic rituals reconfirmed hierarchical social relations in the community. Wang T'ao, who spent most of the period from 1862 to 1884 in Hong Kong, observed: "Since the founding of the Tung Wah Hospital, the members of its board of directors have begun to hold an annual gathering to celebrate the lunar new year. For the occasion they don all sorts of fine headgear and gowns, as if they were illustrious officials having an audience with the emperor."[12] On the occasion of a visit to the hospital by Governor Hennessy in 1878, nearly three hundred influential Chinese were present, of whom "some 50 or 60 were in their Mandarin costumes, some with blue buttons, some with crystal, and some with gold buttons, while a few had the additional honour of wearing the peacock's feather."[13]

The imposing hospital compound was designed to impress the public, as the traveler Isabella Bird recorded in 1879:

> The Tung-Wah hospital consists of several two-storied buildings of granite, with large windows on each side, and the lofty central building which contains the directors' hall, the accommodation for six resident physicians, and the business offices. The whole is surrounded by a well-kept garden, bounded by a very high wall. . . . It was a charming Oriental sight, the grand, open-fronted room with its stone floor and many pillars, the superbly dressed directors and their blue-robed attendants, and the immense costumed crowd outside the gate in the sunshine, kept back by crimson-turbaned Sikh orderlies.[14]

The display of cultural symbols of wealth, power and authority rivaled those at the official *yamen* compounds in China.

A Parallel to Elite Management of Public Affairs in Late Imperial China

The elite management of public affairs in Hong Kong paralled a similar development in late imperial China. The generalist county magistrate, representing the Chinese bureaucratic state, exercised formal and superficial control over local society, leaving much of the governance to local elites outside the bureaucracy. As Mary Rankin forcefully observes, the local elite's management of public affairs can be traced back to late Ming times, when gentry joined officials in managing public works like water control projects, using hired workers rather than corvée labor. Commercialization and population growth from the sixteenth century had gradually brought about an increase in the numbers of market centers and an expansion in social mobility and organization. These changes enlarged the amount of nonofficial elite management of public affairs in the eighteenth century, as the

Ch'ing state proved unable to finance and expand local government, and could no longer intervine vigorously in such matters as grain distribution and population movement. This trend continued into the first half of the nineteenth century, when local elite management augmented to include extensive educational, welfare, relief activities.[15]

The trend greatly accelerated during the Taiping rebellion, bringing about widespread local militarization organized by the gentry elite. As Philip Kuhn shows, a *t'uan-chia* system emerged, in which *pao-chia* (collective responsibility) and *t'uan-lien* (militia) had merged. The supremacy of gentry managers (*shen-tung*) became the "cornerstone of local order." They played ever greater roles in local security, tax collection, and public works.[16] Postrebellion reconstruction, accompanied by augmented commercialization and foreign trade, opened up career opportunities for activist gentry and merchants and encouraged their fusion into a vigorous elite known as *shen-shang* (gentry merchants) or *shen-tung*. Rankin refers to them generally as "elite managers," because "they did not necessarily have formal gentry qualifications or engage in such gentry occupations as scholarship, teaching, or estate management." Their power "rested on varying combinations of landownership, trade, usury, and degree holding."[17]

These developments in China had important impacts on Hong Kong. The turbulent conditions on the mainland created by the Taipings led to the influx of wealthy Chinese families into Hong Kong. The elite that emerged in the 1850s and 1860s included more respectable, wealthy merchants. Aspiring Chinese used all resources available to promote their power and influence—these included business connections with the British, the native place–dialect ties, the transregional guild and social associations, the charitable works, the purchase of Chinese official degrees and ranks, and the display of cultural symbols of power, wealth, and status.

In the post-Taiping era and thereafter throughout the Ch'ing period, more of the colony's merchants became gentrified. The Tung Wah elite gained honor and official titles from the Chinese imperial court by raising relief funds for natural disasters such as the famine in North China in 1877. To raise revenue for reconstruction, the Chinese government expanded the sale of honors among the Chinese communities in Hong Kong and Southeast Asia.[18] The Tung Wah elite vied with each other in acquiring Chinese official ranks and degrees, many by purchase and some by regular examinations. From then on, the mandarins and local people addressed these gentlemen respectfully as the aforementioned gentry merchants and gentry managers. The Chinese community in Hong Kong had matured. Its elite now consisted of respectable and gentrified merchants, not the type of rough frontier adventurers of the 1840s and 1850s like Lu Aqui, who operated local markets, brothels, and gambling houses, or Tam Achoy, who was charged with piracy and murder in connection with an expedition to attack a village near Macao.

Regarding the patterns of elite dominance in China Esherick and Rankin affirm: "[T]o maintain their position, local elites often seek influence at higher levels of the administrative hierarchy or rely on external social connections and economic resources, but they focus their activity and purpose on the local arena"; and to maintain their dominance they must control certain resources: material, social, personal, and symbolic.[19] The history of the Ko family provides much information about how a Hong Kong merchant family used various resources to attain and maintain its elite status. It also provides interesting insights on three generations of an elite family, reflecting both changes and continuities in elite composition and commitment.

Gentrification of the Ko Family

Ko Man Wah (founder of the famed Yuen Fat Hong firm in 1853) was originally from a poor peasant family at Cheng-hai, Kwangtung, where he had learned how to read at a village temple, but he was still "hardly able to write a simple letter." During his teens he went to Siam, working as a cook and a rice cargo coolie for some years until he accumulated enough savings to start a rice mill. Later on he began to engage in a shipping business between Siam and Ch'ao-chou, reaping a high profit. In 1853 he commenced operating the Yuen Fat Hong, one of the earliest Nam Pak Hong firms in Hong Kong.[20]

Business obliged Ko Man Wah to travel between Bangkok, Singapore, Hong Kong, and Swatow. On one occasion, when he returned to Cheng-hai in 1856, he was arrested by mandarins for "collaborating with barbarians." Obliged to pay eight hundred silver taels to absolve the charge, he learned a hard lesson about the importance of official connections for self-protection. Subsequently he purchased a fifth rank official title to protect his family and property in China. To change his own self-image and enhance his respectability in the community, he acquired a new name, T'ing-k'ai, an honorable style (*tzu*), Tsung-shih, and a courtesy name (*hao*), Ch'u-hsiang, thus adding more symbols of elite status. Having gained much wealth, Ko Man Wah became a leader of the Teochiu community in Hong Kong and one of the founders of the Tung Wah Hospital in 1872. During the North China famine of 1877 mandarins enlisted his support in raising relief funds in Hong Kong and Southeast Asia. In return, he gained more Chinese official ranks and recognition.

Ko Man Wah's impressive life-style became the admiration of the town; he had five wives (the first wife in his ancestral home at Cheng-hai, the other four in Hong Kong and Bangkok) who bore him nineteen children. He was certainly a rich and capable man, as the Chinese would say. Some of his nine sons assisted him in the family's business in various ports overseas. To maintain the family's elite status he encouraged his sons to study for Chinese civil service examinations. His filial second son Ko Soon Kam (Kao Shun-ch'in) developed a genuine fondness for scholarship, which delighted the semiliterate father who had acquired official ranks—not in the orthodox way of taking examinations, but by purchase. Ko Man Wah died in 1882, leaving his offspring two thousand mu of land and the family business in Swatow, Hong Kong, Bangkok, and Singapore. The Yuen Fat Hong in Hong Kong came under the management of his favorite second son.

With an older cousin's able assistance the young scholarly merchant Ko Soon Kam managed to run the family business and pursue classical learning at the same time, winning much respect and trust in the community. He was elected in 1882 to serve on the prestigious Tung Wah Board of Directors, quite a feat for a young man of twenty-six at the time. Then, in 1888, he earned a "real" *chü-jen* degree by examination, fulfilling his deceased father's life long dream for the family. Inspiring even greater respect and admiration, he was elected chairman of the Tung Wah directorate in 1892, reflecting the changing quality of elite in Hong Kong. Moreover, as a leader of the Teochiu minority group in the colony, where the great majority of the population was the Punti Cantonese, his election to the position of Tung Wah chairman served to highlight the transregional charactor of the elite organization.

Significantly, Ko Soon Kam earned the degree in order to continue his merchant profession, not to start an official career. With its proprietor-manager so honored, the Yuen Fat Hong "entered its golden age." Merchants and traders vied with one another to contract with the *hong* for imports and exports. The firm in Hong Kong alone (not counting overseas extensions) made a net profit of over two hundred and fifty thousand silver taels each year during the period 1883–1889. Business expanded to include extensive transactions with foreign bankers and merchants as well. It acted as agent for the Scottish Oriental Steamship Company and for the Norddeutscher Lloyd's Bangkok-Hong Kong line of steamers. In addition, Ko Soon Kam also opened a commercial firm in Canton and another in Kobe, dealing in produce from China and Southeast Asia.

All over town, the admiring people began to wonder about the secret of the Yuen Fat Hong's prosperity. Some people said: It must be the auspicious *feng-shui* wind and water. The geomantic site of the Yuen Fat Hong is right, facing just the right direction! Others said: It must be Ko Soon Kam's *pa-tzu*, the cyclic characters for the year, month, day, and hour of his birth that brought him such good luck. Still others said: His father Ko Man Wah had done a great many good deeds in charitable works, founding the Tung Wah Hospital, bringing relief to the sick and poor, and saving the lives of tens of thousands of drought and famine victims in North China. According to Confucian and Buddhist teachings, the accumulated ancestoral virtue and deeds protected and rewarded the offspring. That must be it! Besides, through hard work Ko Man Wah had established a great family reputation and a solid business foundation for his offspring. "Early arrivers plant the trees, late comers enjoy the breeze," went one Chinese proverb. More important, Ko Soon Kam was, after all, no ordinary merchant, but a reputable scholar-merchant, honest and trustworthy, with official ranks and good connections, and so forth. So, the talk of the town went on and on.

The scholarly tradition was passed down to the third generation. Ko Sing Tze (or Kao Sheng-chih, Ko Soon Kam's oldest son, Ko Man Wah's grandson) earned a *chü-jen* degree by examination. As a scholar-merchant, he closely followed the footsteps of his father who, alas, suddenly passed away at the prime age of forty-three on a business trip to Kôbe in 1909. Ko Sing Tze took over the Yuan Fat Hong management. In fact, he further diversified the family interests by launching new industrial enterprises such as a textile factory at Chenghai and waterworks in Swatow. Though an extremely busy man, Ko Sing Tze secretly joined the republican revolutionaries in their conspiracy to overthrow the Manchu dynasty. Thus, while maintaining the family business and gentry status, he also launched modern industrial enterprises and made a new commitment to republicanism and nationalism. Unfortunately, his untimely death in 1913 proved ominous for the business decline of the Yuen Fat Hong, which eventually closed its doors in 1933, partly due to poor management.

The history of the Ko family illustrates how merchants in Hong Kong used various resources to enhance and maintain their elite status: material (commercial and industrial wealth, foreign business connections, land property); social (kinship, native place–dialect ties, transregional associations such as the charitable Tung Wah Hospital and Nam Pak Hong guild); personal (leadership and organizational abilities, personal qualities); and symbolic (honor, official ranks and titles, life-style). Particularly important among these resources was a set of cultural values and traditions shared by both elite and commoners up to the 1890s. Such values and traditions included beliefs and practices like *feng-shui*, religious worship, superstitions about *pa-tzu* and omens, veneration of ancestors, filial piety, family loyalty, and Confucian ideology. It was these shared values that bound the Chinese community together and that distinguished it from the European community in the colony.

Confucianism as the Hegemonic Ideology

Like the gentry elite in China, the merchant elite in Hong Kong sought to foster social consensus based on Confucian ideals of social harmony and elite paternalism. The consensus was maintained through compromise and elite mediation in conflict situations. The Tung Wah elite arbitrated in civil and commercial disputes. Through community service and philanthropy, the elite affirmed its claim to social superiority. It used all available social and economic resources to cultivate loyalties based on vertical ties of occupation, kinship, and ethnicity. Such loyalties reinforced Confucian ideals of social order, harmony, and a sense of hierarchy. The elite sought to propagate Confucianism as the hegemonic ideology. Each year the Tung Wah directors performed the Spring and Autumn Sacrifices to Confucius at the Man Mo Temple. They espoused the cult of Confucius by founding Confucian schools, encouraging veneration of the sage, and acting in Confucian ways.[21]

The colony's socioeconomic structure provided a fertile ground for the Confucian ideology. Chinese merchants often hired their trusted kinsmen and fellow provincials as assistants, office coolies, and domestic servants. Vertical, paternalistic relationships were usually maintained among them. This was also true of the commercial guilds, most of which included both employers and employees. Prior to the 1880s workers employed in the Chinese enterprises rarely took collective actions against their employers. Labor unrest throughout much of the nineteenth century generally involved the relatively rootless coolies whose actions were directed against the colonial government's assertion of power to regulate their lives and work. The elite often interceded in labor unrest to restore peace and order and to fulfil its moral commitment to the lower classes.

Urban Hong Kong was in large part a city of small shopkeepers. Though there were some large-scale enterprises, mostly owned and operated by foreign capitalists, the small business with only a few employees was the predominant type of business operation among the Chinese during the nineteenth century. Paternalistic relationships easily developed between employers and employees, who often belonged to the same native place–dialect groups. In fact, there were large numbers of small shops owned and operated by family members and relatives. In much of the Chinese quarter of the town, commercial and residential areas were combined. These neighorhood shopkeepers were upholders of traditional Chinese way of life and sustainers of Confucian culture. As we have seen, the more prosperous among the shopkeepers became leaders of the *kaifong* association who participated in the election of the Tung Wah Committee. Merchants, shopkeepers, shophands, coolies, and servants shared a common culture.

Confucianism sanctioned social hierarchy and inequality but it also stressed reciprocity and elite paternalism. The elite and populace were bound together in a community in a close relationship with reciprocal rights and obligations. The elite used all resources available to induce popular deference and subordination; at the same time it was obliged to fulfil its moral commitments to the populace, providing community services and philanthropy, representing the community in its dealings with the colonial authorities, and resolving conflicts. The Tung Wah directors were extremely sensitive to public opinion. They often felt strong pressure from the subordinated groups for fulfillment of the elite's moral obligations. As we shall see, tensions even developed between the elite and the general public during the 1890s.

The Chinese merchant elite acted as self-proclaimed leaders of the community, managing public affairs in the colony. But why did the British authorities tolerate the elite's assumption of such power? There were several reasons. First, the elite management of public affairs was carefully watched by the colonial government. Unlike elites in late imperial China who played a prominent role in tax collections and military forces, the Hong Kong elite exercised no such power. Second, the elite provided important community services at no government expense. The charitable institutions were set up with the government's blessing, which in turn enhanced the elite's prestige. Third, the colonial government had always looked favorably on the elite's espousal of Confucianism, a conservative ideology calling for peace, order, harmony, and social hierarchy. And fourth, the British needed elite support, which enhanced the government's prestige and legitimacy in the eyes of the Chinese public. The elite also provided the government with advice and information concerning the governance of the Chinese and the maintenance of law and order in the colony. Whenever coolie strikes broke out, elite mediation became indispensable to the colonial authorities.

During the nineteenth century labor unrest was mostly directed at the government's attempt to regulate workers' lives and work. But popular unrest threatened not only the government but also community peace and Chinese commercial interests. Moreover, the elite also had moral obligations to the lower classes in conveying their grievances to the government. Therefore, the elite sought to mediate to restore peace and order.

The Cargo Coolie Strike, 1872

The entrepôt of Hong Kong had large numbers of cargo-carrying workers living in coolies houses that provided the basis for labor organization and collective action. The colonial government sought to control coolie lodging houses by imposing on the coolie house-keeper a license fee of five dollars per annum for every ten men boarded. Unwilling to pay such fees, the coolie housekeepers incited the coolies to strike, saying that the government intended to levy a poll tax of fifty cents on each coolie. Coolies hated poll taxes. A general strike of cargo coolies broke out on July 25, 1872. The police arrested about sixty agitators and ringleaders, of whom twenty-three were coolie housekeepers. Some were discharged but others were fined for obstruction or creating a disturbance. On July 29 ten coolie housekeepers who did not take out licenses were sent to jail for fourteen days and one month at hard labor.[22]

All cargo coolies joined the strike. They numbered nearly nineteen thousand men. The loading and unloading at the harbor came to a standstill. Both Chinese and European business suffered. The Chinese trade was nearly paralyzed. Thereupon the *kaifong* leaders met with the coolie delegates in the Nam Pak Hong guild hall, urging coolies to end the strike and promising to exert themselves on behalf of the coolies. The cargo coolies resumed work on July 30, when they were given to understand that the government would consider repealing the license law. Meanwhile, a deputation of the leading Chinese waited on the registrar general, the Honorable C. C. Smith, request-ing him to reconsider the license law. Smith intimated that the li-cense fee could be changed, though those coolies imprisoned for intimidating other workers would have to serve their jail terms.[23]

Thus threatened by the government housing regulation, the cargo coolies of different dialect groups and native origins grew to perceive their common interests and purpose. They came together to join the strike, which seriously affected the entrepôt trade and commercial interests. Eager to restore law and order, the Chinese merchant elite served as intermediaries between coolies and colonial authorities to end the strike. In so doing the merchants were motivated by both their commercial interest and a sense of moral obligation as a social elite.

The workers' resistance to colonial government regulations was often organized along preexisting, traditional dialect and occupa-tional lines. Coolies were organized on the basis of native place and dialect groups. The carrying work was largely controlled by either Tung-kuan or Sze Yap coolies. The Tung-kuan coolies lived in the coolie houses run by Tung-kuan housekeepers and Sze Yap coolies in those run by Sze Yap housekeepers. These rival dialect groups fought over employment opportunities and the right to work at certain docks and wharves. The coolie houses provided the basis of an organization for boycotts and strikes.[24] Rivalry and hostility between cargo coolies of different dialects, however, did not prevent them from coming together to protest government regulations threatening their common interests. Similarly, chair coolies and ricksha pullers of different dialect groups also "combine to make common cause"; as the police chief observed, "the [chair] coolies of Chiu Chau [Ch'ao-chou, Teochiu] combine with the Punti coolies."[25] This was also true of the hawkers, who were regarded as a "nuisance" by the colonial authorities.

Hawkers' and Rickshamen's Disturbances, 1883

In the 1880s there were several thousand hawkers (*hsiao-fan*), licensed and unlicensed. Hawkers from the same native district speaking the same dialect tended to group together at work and to live together in the same dwellings or area. The ground floors of a block of buildings in Taipingshan district were mainly tenanted by vegetable hawkers who washed their wares in the alley, making the whole place "continually damp and offensive."[26] Among the various kinds of hawkers, the colonial authorities regarded the fruit and vegetable hawkers as "the greatest obstructionists" and "most insanitary." Many of them thronged the approaches to the markets. The peddlars were "the most harmless and cleanest," and hardware hawkers also "caused little trouble." But the congee hawkers were "a great nuisance"; they "congregated mostly above the water side and streets adjacent." Finally, there were hawkers of miscellaneous goods, from live fowls, ducks and geese to toy lizards.[27]

Shopkeepers often rented the footpath or side channel in front of their shops to hawkers for the accommodation of their stalls. These stationary hawkers were much better off than large numbers of poor ambulatory hawkers who often obstructed the approaches to the shops and who "go and come with the arrival and departure of the police," much to the annoyance of the shopkeepers.[28] European businessmen were "constantly annoyed by the discordant yells of street hawkers, worse when they take the form of howls by Chinese urchins."[29] The Europeans' annoyance with hawkers led to the proclamation of an ordinance in 1872 forbidding hawkers to cry out on the Praya and the Queen's Road and in Chung-wan, the central (European) part of the town.[30] To satisfy the annoyed Europeans, the magistrate imposed a fine of two dollars for street crying to stop the "nuisance."[31] The police made frequent raids on hawkers.

In January 1883 "an influential Chinese deputation" waited on the administrator W. H. Marsh to advise him on the issues of gambling, sly (unregistered) brothels, and "the hawker nuisance." Speaking on behalf of the shopkeepers, the deputation asserted that "hawkers in many cases occupied positions to the detriment of the shopkeepers, who as householders paid high rents and taxes and required protection." As the approaches to the shops were often blocked by hawkers' stalls, the government sought to bring hawkers under control. A new government regulation prohibited the licensed hawkers from maintaining stationary positions. When the police attempted to enforce it, many hawkers felt that the government meant to deny them the right to make a living.[32]

Hawkers fought back. Rumors circulated that the Chinese were contemplating an uprising against the Europeans. "Highly inflammatory placards have been posted about Taipingshan fixing the 23rd May as the date for a rising against the Governor and the European community," according to the local press. The disaffection was believed to have originated among the hawkers. A few evicted squatters and the jinricksha coolies lately thrown out of employment (due to the government's suddenly reducing the number of licenses from 898 to 500) helped to swell the outcry. "The Chinese higher class have been somewhat perturbed in mind as to the state of affairs." One or two days earlier, "a body of the [coolie] malcontents" had gone to the Tung Wah Hospital to lay their grievances before its directors, but the latter "shut the gates of the Hospital in its face." "The crowd," according to the press, "palavered for some time, and it probably occurred to one of its number to write and stick up the ridiculous placards."[33]

Thus hawkers, unemployed ricksha pullers, and a few evicted squatters came together to express their displeasure with the colonial government regulations. But the Tung Wah directors had arbitrated in favor of the shopkeepers who were annoyed by the hawkers and ricksha coolies obstructing the approaches to their shops. *Hau-tzu jih-pao*, a local Chinese paper, defended the shopkeepers against the lower class "stupid" hawkers who were "ignorant of the established laws of a well regulated state."[34]

Yet once the disturbance was created by hawkers the Tung Wah directors, eager to soothe the hawkers and to restore law and order, prevailed upon Governor G. F. Bowen to publish a proclamation on May 23, conceding that the removal of the hawkers' stalls from the major thoroughfares had not been "carried out in all cases with the necessary discretion and forebearance," and that "in the future, no summons shall be taken out against Chinese accused of infringements of Sanitary or Police Regulations without previous consultation with the Registrar General."[35] In matters affecting the Chinese the governor was to obtain the elite's opinions through the registrar general, also known as the "protector of the Chinese."[36] Appeased by the merchant elite's intercession and the governor's proclamation, hawkers resumed work on May 24. The *Hongkong Daily Press* commented: "Much credit is due to the influential Chinese residents who co-operated so cordially with the Government officials to bring about a proper understanding with the hawkers, who have now resumed their avocations, and at the same time recognised the sovereignty of the law."[37]

The government needed Chinese leaders' cooperation in maintaining law and order in the colony but it also looked upon them with a watchful, suspicious eye, particularly when they were politically motivated and became closely connected with the Canton Chinese officials.

The Triangular Government-Elite-Mandarin Relationship

The colonial situation brought the local elite into a complex, interlocking web of ambivalent relationships. The geographical proximity of Hong Kong to the Chinese mainland, and their close social, economic, and demographic connections, made the colony's Chinese residents vulnerable to mandarin's political influence and control. Both Canton and Hong Kong authorities claimed their allegiance; the local elite therefore served two masters, frequently finding itself in a difficult situation but seeking to manipulate them to its own advantage.[38]

To protect their families and property in China and to enhance their local elite status, elite members actively sought Chinese official degrees and ranks. But gentrification brought them not merely honors and status but also obligations to the Chinese officialdom, which made various demands on them (such as assistance in fund-raising for reliefs in China) and treated them as Chinese subjects under Chinese jurisdiction. This in turn incurred the displeasure of the colonial government, which insisted on its sole jurisdiction over all Chinese in Hong Kong. Thus, gentrification paradoxically brought elite members under mandarin control, which they resented; they therefore turned to the colonial government for protection against exessive mandarin demands. The colonial government needed the elite's cooperation in the maintenance of local community order, but the government also looked with a suspicious eye on the elite's connections with the mandarin in Canton. These complex relationships were often revealed in crisis situations.

In 1884 the Sino-French War provoked a major social crisis in Hong Kong, an event discussed at length in a separate chapter. Suffice it here to note that the European community suspected some leading Chinese who had close connections with mandarins to be instigators of the unrest. Canton officials issued patriotic proclamations exhorting all Chinese along the coast to use all means to do harm to the French enemy. The Hong Kong gentry merchants Ho Amei and Li Tak Cheung became involved with the circulation of mandarin proclamations in the colony supporting China's war against France.[39] Moreover, Ho Amei despatched several telegrams to Viceroy Chang Chih-tung reporting on French movements around Hong Kong.[40] When a riot broke out (unintended by elite and mandarin) the colonial government sent British troops to the scene to be quartered in the great hall of the Tung Wah Hospital.[41] In addition to pacifying the crowd the military occupation of the Tung Wah (the colony's Chinese civic center and power headquarters) was symbolic of the British authorities' determination and readiness to use forceful means to exert control wherever necessary. In reporting to Viceroy Chang Chih-tung on French movements in the colony, Ho Amei and Li Tak Cheung were motivated by Chinese patriotism while also fulfilling their gentry obligations to the mandarin. In so doing, they incurred British displeasure.

Yet, there were occasions when the local elite appealed to the British colonial government for protection against excessive mandarin demands; one such instance occurred during a controversy over a relief fund in 1886. When Kwangtung was devastated by floods in the spring of 1885 the Tung Wah Committee quickly sent foodstuff to the victims and helped to raise funds locally and overseas. Money began to pour in from the Chinese communities in Hong Kong, Singapore, America, and Australia, until a sum of $100,000 was collected, again reflecting the power and influence of the Tung Wah Hospital. Under the Tung Wah supervision most of the fund was expended on relieving the distressed, leaving a balance of $31,000, which was held by the Tung Wah Chairman Kwan Hoi Chun for safekeeping in the bank for use in the event of future distress. The Canton Board of Reorganization dispatched an instruction to the hospital ordering that the remaining fund be sent to the board to be used for repairing the embankments. However, the Tung Wah directors thought that any arbitrary use of the fund could subject the hospital to the fund subscribers' prosecution. This was another indication of the elite being extremely sensitive to public opinion. When acting registrar general J. Stewart Lockhart found out about the board's demand, he told Kwan Hoi Chun that the Chinese officials had no control over Chinese residents in Hong Kong. Kwan Hoi Chun therefore ignored the board's instruction.[42]

But the mandarins repeatedly sent letters to the Tung Wah directors demanding payment. Running out of patience, they wrote in a threatening tone:

> As you, gentlemen, belong to the ranks of the Gentry, it was naturally supposed that you would be sure to desire to help and relieve the distressed; and accordingly an official communication was addressed to you, speaking of you in the highest terms of praise, and ordering you to at once forward the balance of the funds to Canton. . . . But you have not only delayed to send the money as commanded, but have not yet petitioned a single word in reply. . . . This despatch of orders is therefore addressed to you, again urging you (to forward the money). On arrival of these orders, you must immediately obey them. . . . Do not try to shirk the matter by making excuses and let there not be the least neglect or delay, lest such conduct involve you in trouble.[43]

Thus, the mandarins treated the Tung Wah directors in the same manner that they treated gentry in China, reminding them of both their honors and obligations and disregarding British sovereignty over Hong Kong.

The Tung Wah chairmen Kwan Hoi Chun was three times summoned to appear before the Canton Provincial Treasurer, but he was too terrified to comply. Alarmed that his wife, children, and property in Canton might suddenly be ruined, he felt compelled to tender his resignation as the Tung Wah chairman. But the hospital committee refused to accept his resignation. He finally petitioned the colonial authorities for protection. Under British protestation the Tsung-li Yamen in Peking telegraphed Canton to prevent further mandarin interference in the matter.[44] In seeking the foreign colonial power's protection, the Tung Wah elite incurred the mandarin's displeasure.

The 1884 social crisis and the 1886 controversy over the relief fund illustrated the dilemma of the local elite in Hong Kong and the ways it sought to manupulate the situation to its own advantage. The colonial government frowned on the elite's close connections with the mandarins and on its pretension to political power and influence over the Chinese in the colony. Henceforth, the government sought to assume direct control over the elite organizations and to restrict their activities to only philanthropy. At the same time, new avenues for social advancement were created for the aspiring Chinese, including younger and Westernized Chinese.

New Channels for Social Advancement and Reorganization of the Elite-Sponsored Institutions, the Mid-1880s–1900s

As Sinn's study clearly shows, "the grace period" (1869–1882) in which the Tung Wah Hospital had received on the whole friendly and sympathetic support from the governors (especially the "pro-Chinese" John P. Hennessey) was over. Governor George Bowen (r. 1883–85) upgraded the office of the registrar general, through whom the elite's views regarding the Chinese affairs would be communicated to the governor. Gradually more Chinese were able to understand and appreciate the British way of government, and the number of naturalizations increased. The colonial government created other avenues for political participation, appointing the naturalized Chinese to serve on various official bodies such as the legislative council, the sanitary board, and the commission of peace. As these government-created channels to power and status evolved, the relative position of the Tung Wah Committee declined.[45]

After consulting the "wealthy and better Chinese" Governor Hennessey nominated Wu T'ing-fang (Ng Choy, barrister, one of the Tung Wah founders) in 1880 to represent the Chinese on the legislative council. But it was a temporary position, which ended in 1882, when Wu resigned to join Viceroy Li Hung-chang's staff in Tientsin. The next Chinese to be given a seat on the legislative council was Wong Shing (one of the Tung Wah founders), who served from 1884 to 1890. Governor George F. Bowen described him as a man of property, "much travelled, speaking good English," and "fully qualified to look at Chinese affairs with English and at English affairs with Chinese eyes." The prominent Chinese in Hong Kong endorsed Wong Shing's appointment.[46] In 1890 Wong Shing's place was taken by Ho Kai (barrister, unaffiliated with the Tung Wah, a Westernized Chinese of a younger generation) who served on the legislative council until 1914. Meanwhile a second Chinese member was added to the council when Wei Yuk (comprador, a Tung Wah committeeman) was nominated in 1896. Then Lau Chu Pak (a comprador) was appointed to serve on the Council from 1913 to 1922.[47]

In 1886 Dr. Ho Kai (a doctor and barrister at the age of twenty-seven) became the first Chinese appointed to serve on the sanitary board. Subsequently other prominent Chinese appointed to the board included at one time or another Wong Shing, Wei Yuk, Woo Lin Yuen (a Hokkienese), Lau Wai Chuen (comprador), Lau Chu Pak, and Fung Wah Chuen (comprador). The government also appointed the naturalized Chinese to serve as justices of the peace. Of the sixty unofficial justices in 1884, seven were Chinese. In 1893, twelve out of a total of eighty-four unofficial justices were Chinese.[48] These were the colonial government's trusted agents and advisors to help maintain law and order in the colony.

Although many of these men were also members of the Tung Wah committee, they were government appointees directly dependent on the government's favor for their new positions. At the same time, such positions greatly enhanced their social status in the Chinese community. Of all elite members these coopted Chinese leaders enjoyed the most influence with the government. Thus, after the mid-1880s connections with the colonial government became the most important ladder to the top elite status in Hong Kong.

Meanwhile, the government also sought to reorganize the old elite-sponsored institutions to bring them under direct government control. In 1891 the District Watch Committee was reconstructed to include twelve appointed members to advise the government on important issues concerning the Chinese. Further reorganized in 1899 on the recommandations of J. H. Stewart Lockhardt (registrar general and colonial secretary) and Wei Yuk (legislative councillor), the committee was strengthened to include not mere *kaifong* leaders but the wealthiest and most prominent Chinese who could better cooperate with the registrar general.[49] Similarly, the Po Leung Kuk was also reconstituted in 1893. In addition to an annually elected committee, a permanent board of directors was nominated by the governor, including the registrar general as ex-officio president and the Chinese legislative councillor as ex-officio vice-president. Its autonomy severely curtailed, the Po Leung Kuk became something like a self-funding department of government. Sinn aptly calls these developments a process towards "political integration" and a departure from "segregationism typical of the first four decades of British rule in Hong Kong."[50]

In this process, a number of wealthy, prominent Chinese were coopted by the colonial government. It must not be assumed, however, that the leading Chinese were given actual political power in the government. Most of the time, the sanitary board deliberated on such politically irrelevant matters as the disposal of city refuse and night soil.[51] Even members of the legislative council in fact served only as advisors to the colonial government, since the official members always commanded a majority in the council, meaning government executive control of the legislature. Hence the *legislative council* was in fact merely a consultative council.

Moreover, in a colonial situation most Chinese appointees were docile and subservient to the British colonial authorities. Governor Hennessey thought that Wu T'ing-fang was "a cipher on the Legislative Council." Wong Shing was satisfactory to the government because he "was content to adopt a co-operative attitude which at least had the merit of demonstrating that no hazard was likely to result from having a Chinese representative permanently on the Legislative Council."[52] Ho Kai took an active part in the business of the legislative council from 1890 to 1914. He identified himself with the European unofficial members in a policy of "loyal opposition" to the government. In recognition of his cooperation and loyal service, the British Crown named him in 1892 a Companion of the Order of St. Michael and St. George (C.M.G.) and bestowed a knighthood upon him in 1912. Wei Yuk received the same honors in 1918 and 1919.

Such hononary titles and official recognition greatly enhanced the coopted Chinese elite's social status and prestige, adding an important asset to the elite's business and professions. Most wealthy compradors, businessmen, and professionals were therefore eager to cooperate with the colonial government, which in turn gained in some important ways from the elite's cooperation. Elite support enhanced the government's prestige and legitimacy in the eyes of the Chinese public. Elite also provided government with advice and information concerning the governance of the Chinese and the maintenance of law and order in the colony.[53] The elite's cooperation with the government was reinforced by its economic ties to foreign capitalism in the colony.

The Elite's Economic Ties to Foreign Capitalism

E. J. Eitel observed in 1895: "[T]he mighty spirit of free trade . . . fused the interests of European and Chinese merchants into indissoluble unity. . . . [T]he tendency . . . was the inchoative union of Europe and China, by the subordination of the latter to the former."[54] The numerous foreign firms in Hong Kong employed Chinese merchants as compradors and assistant compradors, who at the same time diversified their own interests in various enterprises. Compradors were among the wealthiest and most prominent Chinese in the colony, including such famous names as Ho Tung, Ho Fuk, Ho Kam Tong, Wei Yuk, Fung Wah Chuen, Lau Chu Pak, and Lo Koon Ting.[55] All these gentlemen had at one time or another served on the Tung Wah Committee.

According to Governor G. W. Des Vaeux's report, in October 1889, the Chinese had began to make considerable subscriptions in common with Europeans to the joint-stock enterprises undertaken almost entirely with local capital. Thirty-five joint-stock companies had been formed since the beginning of 1888, "with capital already paid-up aggregating $9,508,475, for land investment, manufacture, and trade in Hong Kong and for mining and for planting enterprises in the Malay Peninsula, Borneo, and Tonking." In addition, there were ten other joint-stock companies registered in Hong Kong, making a total of forty-five.[56] European business enterprises attracted a number of

Chinese investors. Ho Kai, Wong Shing, Leung Pui Chee, and Fung Wah Chuen were among the shareholders of the Green Island Cement Company.[57] Li Tak Cheung and Fung Tang worked with W. Reiners, E. R. Belilios, and H. Foss as directors of the Chinese Insurance Company, Ltd.[58] In the shareholders' meetings, Chinese merchants sat side by side with their European colleagues and partners to discuss their common business interests.

Chinese barristers and solicitors also went into partnership with foreign firms of solicitors. Tso Seen-wan, after passing his law examination in 1896, practiced in Hong Kong as a partner of the Tso and Hodgson.[59] The solicitor H. K. Woo (Hu Chiung-t'ang, second son of the reformer-writer Hu Li-yüan) worked in partnership with Geo. K. Hall Brutton. Sinn Tak Fan (a prominent Chinese to chair the Tung Wah Board of Directors in 1908) worked as the managing clerk and chief interpreter to Messrs. Ewens and Needham, solicitors. And more than a dozen Chinese architects, surveyors, and civil engineers also worked in partnership with Europeans.[60]

The predominance of Western (especially British) commercial, financial, and industrial establishments in China meant that Chinese merchants were to a large extent dependent on Western capitalism in such services as shipping, banking, insurance, and industrial equipment supplies.[61] Kwong Hip Lung & Company, Ltd. (an engineering and shipbuilding firm in Hong Kong), for instance, had a capital of two hundred thousand dollars in 1890. Its managing director Chan Wan Chi had learned his craft in the European-operated Hong Kong Dock Company as an apprentice for eight years before founding his own in 1877.[62] Chinese engineers and shipbuilders had to rely on foreign firms for the supply of equipment and machines.

In banking, in addition to large foreign banks, there were at the end of the nineteenth century several dozen Chinese native banks in Hong Kong serving the colony and overseas Chinese communities. But the native banks had to rely on foreign banks in business transactions. According to Wang Ching-yü, the "compradorization" (*maipan hua*) of Chinese native banks had occurred since the late 1860s when a close connection was established between them and foreign banks in China. Foreigners used native banks as a tool of economic penetration, while native banks depended on foreign banks for loans and for honoring native bank orders.[63] The foreign merchants' acceptance of the native bank promissory notes enabled them to sell more goods than if they insisted on cash payments. At the same time the native banks, strengthened by their ties to foreign capital, now "turned to exports like silks and tea and imports like cotton textile"; the native banks also engaged in business with compradors and brokers who acted on behalf of foreign firms. The investors in native banks came to include compradors and "compradorized" merchants.[64] In short, native banks became "compradorized," acquired some "modern" elements, established economic ties to foreign capital, and invested in the import and export business.

The Merchant Elite's Ambivalent Relations with Colonial Authorities and Foreign Capitalism

Such close and extensive economic ties to foreign capitalist interests prompted the Chinese merchants in Hong Kong to support British colonial rule. This was especially true of the wealthy compradors, businessmen, and bankers who occupied a strategic position in Hong Kong's entrepôt trade, involving large-scale importing and exporting businesses. They were eager to cooperate with the foreign colonial authorities to maintain peace and order in Hong Kong. As the Reverend Dr. James Legge had remarked as early as 1872: "There is a large body of Chinese merchants who have as great a stake in the colony as the British and merchants of other nationalities have."[65] Wealthy Chinese merchants, like their European colleagues and partners, had a great stake in maintaining the colony's status quo.

Economic ties prompted Chinese merchants to support and cooperate with their foreign colonial rulers. However, the relationship was characterized by both harmony and conflict, as Chinese merchants sought constantly to gratify their economic and political aspirations. Their economic dependence on foreign capitalism did not preclude political protest against it, though such protests were ultimately ineffective and self-destructive for the Chinese merchants.[66] The status of economic dependency nurtured among them political resentment against foreign capitalist domination and control. Even compradors who collaborated directly with foreign capitalism as junior partners were not always subservient to it.[67] Seeking to assert their independence, the Chinese merchants had to compete rigorously with foreign capitalists in the colony who enjoyed the privileged status of being the ruling class with political and economic power to influence the colonial government's action and policies.

To illustrate, one can cite the experience of Ho Amei and Li Tak Cheung (prominent merchants who chaired the Tung Wah Board of Directors in 1882 and 1883 respectively). In 1882 the colonial government rejected on ethnic grounds their application on behalf of the Chinese-financed Wa Hop Telegraph Company for permission to lay a cable from Kowloon to Hong Kong. The government argued that a Chinese company controlling the telegraphic communication "might under certain circumstances be a source of serious danger."[68] Significantly, this action was taken by the government under the supposedly "pro-Chinese" Governor Hennessy. In the meantime, however, Li Tak Cheung and Ho Amei had other important commercial interests in the colony such as insurance companies that were closely tied to Western capital.

Thus, to Chinese merchants the foreign businessmen were simultaneously partners and rivals, friends and enemies. This relationship of both cooperation and competition created a major contradiction in the Chinese merchants—their cooperation with and dependence on the foreign capitalists on the one hand, and their resentment and political protest against them on the other. The Chinese elite's relation with the colonial government was therefore equally ambivalent, producing simultaneously collaboration and resentment. This relationship was rendered more complex by Hong Kong's colonial situation. It became part of a triangular relationship between government, elite, and populace.

The Triangular Government-Elite-Populace Relationship

The colonial government subsidized and supervised the operations of elite-sponsored institutions such as the Tung Wah Hospital and the Po Leung Kuk, which the suspicious government insisted must remain purely philanthropic, not political organizations. Ironically, it was through these organizations that the elite exerted sociopolitical influence over the populace, thereby cooperating with the government. The government relied on the elite for advice on the governance of the Chinese, but it also looked upon the elite with a watchful, suspicious eye. The elite in turn relied on the government's grace and blessing to promote their social position and to pursue their commercial interests; so they cooperated with the government while also resenting its domination and jealous control over them.

In order to enhance their legitimate position as community leaders, the elite had to demonstrate their concern for the people's welfare. The Tung Wah Hospital and the Po Leung Kuk were intended to promote popular welfare and also to facilitate social control by alleviating social problems caused by coolie poverty. Coolies resented their subsistence living. The colonial government encouraged and subsidized these charitable organizations because it also had a stake in social control and in promoting welfare to enhance its legitimacy in the eyes of the public. Due to racial tensions, however, the government sought to supervise and control the operation of these organizations, preventing them from becoming independent political power bases of the Chinese elite. Within the framework of government supervision the Tung Wah Hospital and the Po Leung Kuk became vehicles with which the elite reached out to the people and exerted sociopolitical influence over them.

Poverty of the coolie working class was a source of tension in the colonial society. Each year the Tung Wah Hospital gave asylum and free medical treatment to hundreds of sick destitute and coolies. In the fourteen years from 1893 to 1907 the Po Leung Kuk recorded a total of 6,471 men, women, and children kidnapped from their homes in Hong Kong, Macao, and the adjoining districts on the mainland. Of this number, the Po Leung Kuk redeemed 929 victims and sent them back to their homes.[69] The elite used charity to ease social tensions resulting from poverty, unemployment, and street crimes.

E. P. Thompson observes that " 'liberality' and 'charity' may be seen as calculated acts of class appeasement in times of dearth and calculated extortions (under the threat of riot) by the crowd: what is (from above) an 'act of giving' is (from below) an 'act of getting.' "[70] And as the anthropologist Kani Hiroaki contends, the colonial government and wealthy Chinese merchants had a mutual interest in seeking to use charity as a means to divert the direction of the lower class's anger and frustration away from them. They sought to use charity to ease social tensions, thereby helping to maintain political stability and perpetuate the existing system of commercial capitalism under British colonial rule.[71] Where charity did not suffice, they resorted to coercion.

Crime thrived on poverty. The Victoria Jail in Hong Kong became overcrowded in the early 1890s, prompting the colonial government to build a new jail. However, all unofficial members of the legislative council representing the tax-paying commercial interests in the colony opposed the vote for a new jail. Ho Kai argued that solitary confinement and nourishing food would hardly be a punishment for the criminals among the lower class Chinese. The acting registrar general asserted that three methods would make the jail more of a deterrent: depriving the prisoners of food, increasing hard labor, and solitary confinement.[72] A local English paper voiced support:

> [The Chinese] are a stolid, nerveless race; and it is this stolidity which make them so indefatigable as workers and enabled them to support an amount of seclusion which would be insufferable to a European. . . . It is our opinion that if "bamboo chow chow" [the lashing with bamboo stick] were more frequently administered. . . . the present accommodation in the Gaol, with perhaps some structural improvement, would be found ample for the needs of the colony.[73]

Similarly, the wealthy Chinese merchants petitioned the colonial government in 1893:

> The prisoners have more space allowed them than they have ever had when not in prison. In a word, they are far better off in the gaol than out of it. Because the gaol is already looked upon as a paradise by many a rascal . . . , any extension of the gaol will certainly lead to an influx of bad characters from China. . . . [T]he most efficacious way to prevent persons from committing crimes in the colony is . . . to use more freely the power of banishment and the rattan.[74]

In short, Chinese merchant elite advised the British colonial authorities that the best ways to prevent the lower-class Chinese from committing crimes were flogging, banishment, and making prison conditions more miserable.

During the 1890s tensions surfaced from time to time between the lower class Chinese and the merchant elite who collaborated with the colonial government to keep them in line. There was a case of a rice warehouse coolie who sustained a fractured leg and was taken to the Tung Wah Hospital. A European doctor came to look at his leg and ordered him to be sent to the Government Civil Hospital, and before the relatives or the Tung Wah Directors could interfere the coolie's leg was amputated. Said a contemporary report, "The man's relatives and children go frequently to the [Tung Wah] Hospital now and give trouble to the Directors and say they had no right to amputate the man's leg without his consent and that he could not get his living to support his family."[75] The elite had not been able to fulfill its obligations to protect the coolie, which caused coolie resentment.

In May 1894 an epidemic plague broke out in Hong Kong. To contain the disease the colonial government took certain sanitary measures, including house-to-house visits to search for infected persons and the removal of such persons for isolation on board the *Hygeria,* a hospital ship attended by Western doctors. These measures caused mass resistance because of the deep-rooted Chinese bias against Western medicine and doctors. The Chinese complained that the privacy of women's quarters was invaded by the daily visits of the military and police; they suspected that the foreign devils "had sinister and unspeakable designs on the women and children."[76] The crisis split the Tung Wah Committee. Hospital chairman Lau Wai Chuen (a naturalized British subject, justice of the peace, and member of the sanitary board) "lent the government his hearty cooperation." In the words of the local English press, he had "an intelligence which unfortunately does not belong to all his countrymen."[77] Some of his colleagues resisted the government policy, causing European suspicion that they were creating a strong opposition among the native population to the authorities.[78]

In a mass hysteria, wild rumors began to spread that Western doctors cut open pregnant women and scooped out the children's eyes in order to make medicines for the treatment of plague-stricken patients.[79] Resentful of forcible removal of patients, the crowd blockaded houses to be visited and stoned sanitary officers on May 19. Aggravated by the Chinese elite's inability to protect patients from Western doctors, a mob gathered at the Po Leung Kuk and broke its windows, but was dispersed by the police before doing further damage.[80]

The following day a community meeting chaired by Lau Wai Chuen was held at the Tung Wah Hospital, attended by some seventy members of the leading firms and four hundred others. Captain Superintendent of Police F. H. May sought to explain the government sanitary measures. While the meeting was in progress news arrived that Lau Wai Chuen's shop in Bonham Strand was attacked by a mob, which complained that Mr. Lau as a member of the sanitary board had not protected the interests of his countrymen. He at once left the meeting, which then broke up, but no sooner had he got into his sedan chair than he was surrounded by a howling mob which turned his chair upside down and stoned him. He quickly got out of the chair and ran back into the hospital. Captain F. H. May at once sent a mounted contingent of armed Sikhs to the scene to prevent further disturbances. Mr. Lau had to be escorted by police to his residence. Two coolies were arrested in the incident and were each subsequently fined fifty dollars.[81]

Mr. Lau's collaboration with the colonial authorities incurred popular indignation. This was a great humiliation for the Tung Wah Hospital and its chairman, the result of the elite's inability to fulfill its moral obligation to protect the populace from the hated government sanitary measures.

The plague of 1894 provided an occasion for the government to interfere in the operation of the Tung Wah Hospital. In 1896 Governor Robinson appointed a commission to investigate its operation and organization.[82] Despite the resistance of some of its committeemen, the governor appointed for the hospital a Chinese doctor trained in Western medicine in 1896, and in the following year a Chinese steward was appointed to supervise the sanitary maintenence of the building. By these appointments the Tung Wah ceased to be the Chinese hospital offering purely Chinese treatment. The hospital's autonomy had been the basis of its claim to community leadership. The curtailment of its autonomy marked the decline of the hospital's community leadership and the acceleration of political integration underway ever since the mid-1880s. The British assumed more direct rule over the Chinese community, a departure from the government's segregationist policy of earlier decades.[83] All these events took place in a new social milieu.

Changing Social Milieu: A More Heterogeneous Society, the Mid-1880s–1900s

What was political integration from the government's view point was in fact a tendency toward community disintegration from the Chinese standpoint. The mob attack on the Tung Wah chairman would have been inconceivable during the 1870s and early 1880s, when the elite exerted an unchallenged cultural hegemony over an integrated Chinese community. The fact that the mob attack happened in 1894 reflected not merely the panic situation during the plague but also the changing social milieu at the time.

Several factors contributed to create a new milieu. First, the colony's Chinese population increased from 130,168 in 1876 to 171,290 in 1886, to 237,670 in 1895, and to 359,873 in 1905.[84] The colony's entrepôt trade also rapidly expanded. In the years 1871–73 Hong Kong handled 32.5 percent in value of China's total import and 14.7 percent of China's export. By 1891–93 these figures jumped to 51.2 percent and 39.3 percent respectively.[85] With population growth and economic development society became more complex and heterogeneous, and a community consensus became increasingly more difficult to obtain. To provide mutual aid and social service for the new immigrants from the Chinese mainland, native place associations began to appear from the latter half of the 1870s until the 1890s, when several of them could be identified.[86] But it was not until 1911 that such regional associations started to flourish and proliferate owing to the influx of the Chinese and the unsettled conditions on the mainland. And as we shall see, the Sze Yap (Four District) Association was to become particularly active in the politics of the Chinese community in the years 1911–13.

Second, economic development also contributed to the beginning of labor consciousness. During the 1880s and 1890s some employees' guilds reminiscent of trade unions began to appear. The Artisan Tailors' Guild called for a strike in 1883, and the Carpenters' Guild also staged a strike in 1891 to demand wage raises. In 1889 the Masons' Guild protested against the inferior quality of rice supplied by masters. The Rattan Chairs' Guild struck work in 1891 to demand shortened hours of labor. And in 1894–95 the Coopers' Guild took collective actions four times to protest against the dismissal of members and employment of outsiders. The consciousness of different interests of capital and labor was beginning to emerge in the 1880s and 1890s. And during the 1900s labor strikes for better wages and working conditions sporadically took place among the brass smiths, painters, rattan splitters, bricklayers, coopers, dyers, and sandalwood workers.[87]

Yet, the paucity of material on labor strikes is perhaps an indication that labor disputes had not yet become very serious. According to A. E. Wood's report in 1912, strikes were "usually settled by the Registrar General, with the assistance of Chinese gentlemen, by means of compromise." Wood observed: "On the whole, masters and employees are remarkably willing to listen to reason, and serious strikes have been few."[88] Serious labor strikes against employers were indeed few until the compositors' strike of late 1911, to be discussed in a later chapter.

The third factor contributing to the creation of a heterogeneous society from the mid-1880s to the 1900s was the emergence of a young generation of businessmen, professionals, and new intelligentsia who were more inclined to innovate and more Western-oriented than the old elite members. Many of these businessmen invested in foreign enterprises, entered into partnership with foreign merchants, and sat on the boards of directors with their European colleagues. Lau Chu Pak, for instance, invested in many Western-operated enterprises and worked in partnership with European colleagues as a director of the Hong Kong Tramway Company, Ltd., the Gold Mine Company of Manila, and the Shanghai Insurance Company. He was also a member of the Consulting Committee of A. S. Watson & Company, Ltd., and a managing director of the Hong Kong Mercantile Company.[89]

Inspired by the models of Western enterprises, Chinese entrepreneurs in Hong Kong began to introduce innovations in management and operations. For example, the Kwong Hip Lung & Company (an engineering and shipbuilding firm founded in 1877) was reorganized into a limited liability company in 1890 with a capital of two hundred thousand dollars, with Chan Wan Chi as the managing director assisted by a consulting committee. Its engineering works, managed by To Li Ting, employed three hundred workers in 1908. Similarly, the managers of another engineering and shipbuilding firm, the Tung Tai Tseung Kee & Company (founded in 1897), had received their education in Hong Kong and learned their techniques in the European-operated enterprises. Employing five hundred workers in 1908, the company built about a hundred steam launches for Malina; it also held contracts from the French government in Saigon.[90] Some Chinese enterprises in Hong Kong were growing in size and capital investment. Unlike small enterprises characterized by paternalistic relationship between masters and employees, the developing capitalist enterprise with large number of workers was conducive to the growing consciousness of different interests of capital and labor.

Innovative managerial techniques in organization and operation were introduced by Ma Ying-piao, who founded the Sincere Company—the first modern department store in Hong Kong—in 1900, and by Kwok Lok (Kuo Lo) and Kwok Chuen (Kuo Ch'üan), who founded another in 1907, the famed Wing On Company.[91] And as we have seen, the gentry merchant Ko Sing Tze (third generation of the Ko family from Teochiu) launched new industrial enterprises, such as a modern textile factory at Cheng-hai and a water works in Swatow, in addition to managing the Yuen Fat Hong in Hong Kong. His secret involvement in the Chinese republican revolution epitomized the new commitments to republicanism and nationalism on the part of a number of merchants from the younger generation.

The development of service facilities in the entrepôt of Hong Kong produced a group of professionals. Just as compradors were experienced in modern Western business methods, so doctors, barristers, solicitors, journalists, teachers, architects, engineers, and insurance company managers were well versed in modern Western professional services. Chinese barristers admitted to practice before the Hong Kong Supreme Court included Ng Choy (Lincoln's Inn 1877), Ho Kai (Lincoln's Inn 1882), and Wei Piu (Middle Temple 1888); solicitors included Ho Wyson (1887), Tso Seen Wan (1897), Wei Wah On (1897), and H. K. Woo. The barrister Ho Kai was also trained in Western medicine at Aberdeen University. The graduates of the College of Medicine who practiced in Hong Kong included Kwan Sun Yin (1893), Ho Nai Hop (1894), U I-kai (1895), To Ying Fan (1899), Ma Luk, and S. F. Lee (further study at Edinburgh University, 1911). Two graduates of the Tientsin Government [Medical] College also practiced in Hong Kong during the 1890s: Chung King-ue and Wan Tun-mo.[92] Some Chinese were learning to accept Western medicine in the 1890s.

In sum, during the years from the mid-1880s to the 1900s a younger generation of merchants, businessmen, professionals, and new intelligentsia emerged in Hong Kong, a generation more Western-oriented than the old elite and more inclined to innovations and new commitments. It was a generation progressively politicized by such events in China as the Sino-French War (1884–85), the Sino-Japanese War (1894–95), the Boxers' uprising (1900), the boycott movement of

1905–08, and the Republican revolution of 1911. Many people of this rising generation were to take part in the social and political movements connected with the Chinese mainland.

Although still bound to many Chinese ideas, values, and customs, the new intelligentsia was also ready to challenge some parts of Chinese culture and tradition. Tse Tsan Tai (1872–1938), for example, described himself as "a staunch supporter of Confucius and his teachings," yet Tse also strongly supported "all that is wise and good in other religions," being a baptized Christian himself. During his school days at Queen's College in Hong Kong in the late 1880s he had sixteen friends who were in his confidence; and it began to dawn upon him that the time was ripe for planning "a movement for the reformation of China's millions" and for the overthrow of the Manchus in China. Tse and his sixteen close friends, including Yeung Ku-wan (Yang Ch'ü-yün), Huang Yung-shang (Wong Shing's son), and Wen Tsung-yao, founded a revolutionary society called Fu-jen wen-she in 1892. From 1895 these men became involved in Sun Yat-sen's revolutionary movement in Hong Kong.[93]

These members of the new intelligentsia were iconoclasts, ready to attack some time-honored beliefs and values. Tse Tsan Tai launched attacks on such practices as *feng-shui*, foot-binding, opium-smoking, and *mui-tsai* (bonded maid servant system).[94] In a heterogeneous community after the mid-1880s social consensus was increasingly more difficult to achieve. Some old cultural values and practices shared by the old elite and populace came under attack. During the 1894 plague Tse Tsan Tai openly questioned the wisdom of some Tung Wah elite members who insisted on petitioning the government to stop the house-to-house sanitary inspection, "in order to please and appease the angry, ignorant, and riotous mobs composed of the coolie classes."[95]

The split of elite into factions reflected the tendency toward community disintegration after the mid-1880s. Some new elite members found themselves alienated from the old values and practices that had bound the old elite and populace together. Ho Kai (barrister, medical doctor, legislative councillor) complained about the performance of old rituals at the founding of the Chinese Chamber of Commerce on January 17, 1896.

On that auspicious day, Colonel Ch'en K'un-shan, commander of the Chinese garrison at Kowloon City, was invited to perform the opening ceremony of the chamber of commerce, conducted in a purely Chinese way, including the installment of god of war Kwan-ti in the building. Although Ho Kai and Wei Yuk had been elected as the chamber's secretary and vice-chairman respectively, they did not attend the ceremony, because of their disagreement with the chamber chairman Ho Amei on the ceremony proceedings. The *China Mail* called this incident a "public scandal" in which the "ultra-Chinese faction" of the community had calculated to impress the Chinese inhabitants with the idea that Hong Kong was a mere appendage of the Chinese Empire.[96]

Under British protestation, the viceroy of Canton had to issue a proclamation reprimanding Colonel Ch'en for taking part in the ceremony.[97] What is relevant to us here is that Ho Kai admitted in public that he "had never learned how to go through properly a regular Chinese ceremony of that kind and was never one of the worshippers of the God of War."[98] The new elite members coopted by the colonial government were alienated from the old elite and the populace. It was difficult to reach community consensus. Soon afterward, the chamber of commerce was closed, probably due to internal discord among elite members. Yet, reopened in 1900, it took over many of the extraneous functions of the Tung Wah Hospital Committee.[99] The split of the elite into factions was again revealed in a heated controversy over the Light and Pass Ordinance in 1895. Some elite members organized a protest movement against the ordinance, which reflected the government's racial discrimination against the Chinese in the colony. On this occasion the Tung Wah Hospital became a forum for some elite members to denounce others.

Protest Against the Light and Pass Ordinance in 1895

European racism provoked strong Chinese feelings. The colonial government had attempted to fight crimes by strictly enforcing the Light and Pass Ordinance, requiring only the Chinese to carry a lamp and pass at night. The requirement of carrying a lamp had been in force since 1870 and was considered by the Chinese reformer K'ang Yu-wei as a stigma of national humiliation.[100] The leading Chinese businessmen and local Chinese press pleaded in vain against the ordinance.[101]

The community held a public meeting at the Tung Wah Hospital on December 22, 1895, attended by over four hundred Chinese. A number of prominent merchants, compradors, and businessmen were present. But Ho Kai and Wei Yuk were conspicuously absent. Ho Amei, nominated to chair the meeting, denounced the ordinance, insisting that carrying a lamp was not necessary because the streets were well lighted. He deplored police brutality in the enforcement of the ordinance—people were tied together by their queues and marched to the police station. Moreover, the ordinance adversely affected the Chinese business interests, for fewer people visited the eating houses at night, reducing the demand for foodstuffs supplied by the Nam Pak Hong merchants. In his long speech, Ho Amei's inflammatory language drew repeated applauses from the audience: "Some Chinese have said, 'We should have a Light and Pass Ordinance.' I say those persons are not Chinese (Applause); . . . they ought to be condemned (Applause). . . . Some of the Chinese do not respect themselves (Applause). We object to being stopped in the streets by Sikh policemen."[102] The Tung Wah Hospital, supposedly the consensus-building center for the community, became a forum for one faction of elite to denounce the other.

The Chinese elite was divided in its views on the ordinance. Wei Yuk and the majority of the District Watch Committee saw the relationship between the enforcement of the ordinance and the decrease in crime: "Between 7 and 9 p.m. the wealthier Chinese shops and places of business are closing. These hours are, therefore, the best hours for robberies."[103] But Ho Amei and his friends believed that the streets were well lighted, making the carrying of lamps unnecessary.

Another speaker in the Chinese public meeting, Robert Ho Tung, complained that the Chinese theater had to be closed at 11:00 p.m. "In the City Hall, however, they [Europeans] are allowed to go on until one in the morning. . . . We pay more taxes than the Europeans," he charged, "and derive the least advantage . . . I condemn the Ordinance simply because it is against the Chinese only. I advocate an increase in the police force, and this would have a far wider effect than the Ordinance."[104] The meeting concluded with unanimous approval of another petition to the colonial government for the abolition of the ordinance.

The following day, December 23, 1895, a deputation of seven Chinese merchants—mostly Tung Wah directors led by Ku Fai Shan—

called on Governor William Robinson. Ho Kai acted as an interpreter. The governor, in a bad mood, gave them a lecture: "You Chinese know that there is no place in your own country where you can live so quietly, so free from disturbance or interference, as Hong Kong; or if there is, it only surprises me that you do not go and live there. Is it not as I say, Dr. Ho Kai?" Ho Kai said yes. The governor threatened to take action against the agitators. At the end of the lecture, the docile Chinese deputation announced their decision to "think it over."[105]

The local English press condemned the Chinese agitators: "Ho Amei ought to be taught a stern lesson," and "Ho Tung's speech should remove him from the Roster of Justices of the Peace," for it could have the effect of "inciting his hearers to defy any law in the Colony."[106] The local Chinese press fought back, praising the courage and wisdom of Ho Amei and Ho Tung. It declared that the Chinese in Hong Kong had been peaceful and law-abiding, docile and subservient, that they had been victimized by foreigners, and that this could no longer be tolerated.[107]

Thus, moral indignation against racial discrimination and concerns about the ordinance's adverse effect on business, prompted the Chinese to agitate for the abolition of the ordinance. When Chinese businesses were adversely affected the colony's economy and foreign businesses were also hurt. Eventually, in June 1897, the system of the night pass was abolished; henceforth, night passes were to be required only as ordered by the governor. The number of Chinese arrested for breach of light and pass regulations was 2,196 in 1895, increased to 3,477 in 1896, and then dropped to 150 in 1897.[108]

The controversy over the ordinance revealed the split of Chinese elite into rival factions, Ho Amei and Ho Tung versus Ho Kai and Wei Yuk. The latter two gentlemen (appointed to serve on the sanitary board and the legislative council) were coopted into the government power structure and hence more inclined than other elite members to collaborate with the colonial authorities. In a more heterogeneous society after the mid-1880s what was political integration from the colonial government's view point was community disintegration from the Chinese standpoint.

Meanwhile, the new generation of Chinese merchants and intelligentsia in the colony became increasingly politicized by the main currents of events in China, from the Sino-French War in 1884–85 to the Revolution of 1911. The subsequent chapters of this study will show how the Chinese in Hong Kong took part in the social and political movements connected with the Chinese mainland from 1884 to 1913. During these years both elite and common people became activated socially and politically.

The working people, generally labeled *coolies*, constituted the great majority of the colony's population. The following chapter examines the lives, work, and organizations of these coolies under British colonial rule.

F
O
U
R

Coolies in the British Colony

The coolie does not possess civic rights . . . yet—he is happy. Work and toil are to him second nature.
—Hongkong Daily Press, *October 10, 1906*

Bran is what a rickshaw puller gets to eat and blood is what bursts out of him.   —Lao She, *Rickshaw*

Scholarly publications on the working people in Hong Kong during the period from 1842 to 1913 have been extremely rare. Perhaps this is partly because of the scarcity of materials about them. By putting together bits and pieces of information from scattered sources, this chapter provides a glimpse of the lives, work, and organizations of coolies under British colonial rule.

It is important to note that different segments of the working people had different degrees of attachment to the merchant elite. Members of the elite assumed leadership in the communities of their fellow provincials in Hong Kong. The wealthy Teochiu merchants Ko Soon Kam and Chan Tin San were prominent leaders in the colony's Teochiu community. The Hokkienese businessmen Yip Oi Shan and Ng Li Hing were leaders in the Hokkienese community. Vertical relationship among the community members cut across class lines, although this did not preclude transregional cooperation among the wealthy merchants. Committed to their kinsfolk and regional communities, merchants often employed their trusted relatives to help in their business and hired their fellow provincials as shophands, doorkeepers, domestic servants, private chair bearers and ricksha pullers.

Hong Kong had large numbers of these working people, who often developed paternal relations with their merchant employers and rarely engaged in organized strikes.

But Hong Kong also had large numbers of other workers relatively unattached to the merchant elite. These included cargo-carrying coolies (employed in large numbers by such establishments as the Hong Kong and Kowloon Wharf and Godown Company), public chair coolies, public ricksha coolies, hawkers, sampan people, and boatmen. In discussing social unrest in Hong Kong, it is important to differentiate these two general categories of coolies. During much of the nineteenth century, it was the latter that frequently engaged in organized strikes against government regulations affecting their livelihood. Popular unrest threatened both community peace and commercial interests. To protect commercial interests and to fulfill its moral obligation to the lower classes, the elite sought to mediate between the striking coolies and the colonial government to help restore law and order. These coolies are the main focus of this chapter.

Labor Groups

Judging from the censuses of 1881 and 1901, the people who relied chiefly on manual labor for a living consisted of about 80 percent of the colony's gainfully employed Chinese population. The work of shipping, loading, unloading, and transshipping cargoes that were brought into the port by junks and steamers required a large pool of workers. Those working afloat in the harbor consisted mainly of three groups—sampan people, cargo boatpeople, and operators of steam launches. They worked on the transference of goods from steamer to steamer, from steamer to shore, and vice versa. In 1876 there were only 8 steam launches operated by about 40 engineers. By 1881 thirty-seven steam launches were operated by 186 engineers. But there were many more cargo boats used for transshipping and landing cargo. Although they varied in size, an average of 8 persons (including children) worked on board each cargo boat. In 1876 there were 494 cargo boats worked by about 2,700 men and women (a total of about 4,000 persons, counting children). By 1881 as many as 656 cargo boats were worked by 3,628 boatmen and women (a total of 5,319 persons, counting children).[1]

Sampans were hired to transship and land cargo. A sampan carried a family averaging 5 persons. The number of sampans increased from 1,357 in 1876 to 2,088 in 1881, involving 7,200 and 11,218 persons respectively. In addition, in 1881 there were 370 pullaway boats for passengers in Victoria and Kowloon worked by 2,314 persons, and a larger fleet of 775 fishing boats engaging a population of 7,128 anchored and plied in harbor and bays.[2]

Working on shore were cargo-carrying coolies, who formed a large proportion of the laboring class in Hong Kong. In 1872 there were nineteen thousand cargo coolies, and in 1891 there were about twenty thousand. They loaded and discharged cargo on board ship and handled it on shore. Half of the cargo coolies were *ch'ang-kung*, regularly employed and paid by the month. The remaining ten thousand cargo coolies worked as temporaries and were paid by the job, unable to secure employment every day.[3]

The population census of 1881 registered 2,118 licensed hawkers, but there were many more unlicensed hawkers in Hong Kong. Different kinds of hawkers plied their wares in the city—vegetable hawkers, pedlars, hardware hawkers, congee sellers, and fruit sellers.[4] Although considered by Europeans and "better-class" Chinese as a "nuisance," hawkers performed important service to the colony's population.

Another group of laborers who rendered important service to the public were sedan chair bearers and jinricksha pullers. There were 859 licensed chair coolies in 1876, and 980 in 1881.[5] Jinricksha was first introduced in 1880 into the colony from Japan. It supplemented, rather than superseded the sedan chair, as jinricksha could only ply on the level streets and the hilly areas of Hong Kong still requiring sedan chairs as a means of transportation. In 1883 the government issued 898 jinricksha licenses.[6] In 1897 a total of 7,164 public ricksha pullers and chair bearers were licensed. Their numbers were increased to 8,252 in 1898, to 8,923 in 1899, and 9,984 in 1900.[7]

An even larger group of laborers were domestic servants, who numbered 21,957 in 1881—of whom 5,529 were servants to a small population of 3,040 resident Europeans and Americans. [8] Twenty years later, in 1901, the number of servants swelled to 49,476 persons (43,410 males and 6,066 females). Well-to-do Europeans employed large staffs of Chinese servants—a cook with one or two assistants; a house boy acting as a butler answering the door and waiting at tables; one or more house coolies to sweep and clean the house and carry water for baths; amahs (maids) and a washerwoman for children; a sewing woman; gardeners; a ricksha coolie or four chair coolies.[9] So, the well-to-do European family employed twelve to fifteen Chinese servants.

The 1881 census returns also listed other laborers: 1,439 stone cutters, 1,083 rice pounders, 560 mat bag makers, 448 rattan workers, 439 washermen, 1,198 barbers, 1,857 tailors, 864 braziers, 708 blacksmiths, 2,923 carpenters, 2,082 seamen, 542 masons, 508 painters, and 1,315 brothel keepers and inmates.

Wages

Labor was cheap since the earliest days of the colony. During the Opium War in 1841 "coolies were plentiful. Five dollars a month each would provide for as many as one could employ."[10] More often wages were much lower; in 1844 coolies' wages ranged from two dollars to three dollars per month.[11] The situation did not improve much for the coolies. In 1872 women employed at the sugar refinery were paid thirty cents a day, and house coolies received a monthly six dollars. In 1872 the legalized fares for certain groups of laborers were set by the colonial authorities as follows:[12]

Chairs (with two bearers) & Ordinary Pullaway Boats:
    Half hour   10 cents;   Hour   20 cents.
    Three hours 50 cents;   Six hours 70 cents.
    Day (12 hours, 6 a.m.-6 p.m.) $1.00.

Licensed Chair Bearers (each):
    Hour 10 cents;   Half day 35 cents;   Day 50 cents.

Cargo Boats:
    First class boat of 8 or 900 piculs:
        per day $3.00;   per load $2.00.
    Second class boat of 600 piculs:
        per day $2.50;   per load $1.75
    Third class boat or Ha-kau boat of 800 piculs:
        per day $1.50;   per load $1.00;   Half day 50 cents.

Sampans or Pullaway Boats:
    Half hour   10 cents;   One hour 20 cents.
    After 6 p.m. 10 cents extra;   Per day $1.00.

Street Coolies:

Half hour	3 cents;	One hour	5 cents.
Three hours	12 cents;	Half day	20 cents.
One day	33 cents.		

Two decades later, in 1893, the legalized fares for these laborers remained practically unchanged.[13] Due to an ample supply of laborers from the mainland, wages were constantly maintained at a subsistence level. In 1895 cargo coolies still earned only six dollars or seven dollars a month.[14] It was not until 1901 that they started to make a little more, between eight dollars and ten dollars a month. But as late as 1901 the earth coolies received only thirty cents for a long day's work, the ordinary coolies receiving forty cents.[15]

According to the government statistics, the average rate of wages for laborers in 1901 was as follows:[16]

Praedial	paid in kind.
Domestic servants employed by Chinese	$12 to $48 per annum (i.e., $1 to $4 per month) with board & lodging.
Chinese employed by foreigners	$48 to $180 per annum (i.e., $4 to $15 per month).
Trades, Chinese workmen	$36 to $72 per annum (i.e., $3 to $6 per month) with board & lodging.
Ordinary Competent Mechanics:	
Blacksmiths & Fitters	30 cents to $1.50 per day.
Laborers	20 cents to $1.00 per day.
Carpenters & Joiners	20 cents to 75 cents per day with board & lodging.
Masons & Bricklayers	20 cents to 50 cents per day with board & lodging.

Thus, skilled laborers fared little better than unskilled coolies. Suppose the average coolie's monthly earning in 1901 was $9, his yearly income would be $108. The European community considered white persons in Hong Kong with incomes of less than $80 per month (or, $960 per annum) as very poor: "Their lot is cruelly hard. It is a disgrace that such incomes should exist."[17] But the average Chinese worker was ten times worse than the "poor" Europeans in the colony. Among the Europeans, those who were employed in the government service earned a yearly average of $1,892, not counting the colonial secretary and the governor, who earned $10,800 and $35,000, respectively.[18]

Cost of Living

While wages were kept low, since 1881 the cost of living had steadily risen. John W. Hanson, chief detective inspector, testified in 1901 that a dollar could buy only sixteen bundles of firewood, whereas "a few years" previously it was thirty-three bundles; that a jar of lamp oil was charged $2.50, while formerly it was only $1.50; and that the price of rice had increased by 80 percent. Ngan Wing Chi, a head coolie and labor contractor, confirmed that food had formerly cost $2 or $3 a month for a coolie, though now in 1901 it cost at least $5.[19] Even the more prosperous European community complained about the high cost of staple foods, for there was a great rise in prices between 1895 and 1900. The price of bread had increased by 22 percent, rice by 23 percent, beef by 33 percent, mutton by 45 percent, fish by 50 percent, eggs by 80 percent, and peanut oil by 100 percent.[20]

As manual laborers, coolies ate a great deal of rice each meal. Ng A Tong, a headman of public chairs at the Peak, said that coolies were great eaters; it cost them in 1901 a monthly $5 or $6 each for food. In that year the Hong Kong and Kowloon Wharf and Godown Company employed about five hundred warehouse coolies through the labor contractor who paid coolies $8, $9, or $10 per month, according to the amount of work they were capable of performing. "If he is lazy, he only gets eight dollars. If he works hard, he will get nine and ten," said one contractor who sent half of the coolies' wages to their parents on the mainland. But the "lazy" coolie paid $8 would have only $4 in his pocket to pay back the contractor for house and food, all costing more than $5 or $6. So, each month the "lazy" coolie was about $2 short. He had to do extra night work to make up his losses. If he worked five hours overtime, from 7 to 12 of a night, he got 20 cents extra (that is, 4 cents an hour). Most of the Kowloon warehouse coolies worked this overtime, twenty days out of the thirty each month. Similarly, Jardine's Sugar Refinery emloyed in 1901 through contractor one thousand coolies who were paid between $8 and $12 per month. The dockyard cargo coolies received a similar amount.[21]

The chair and ricksha coolies employed by the private Chinese and European residents fared no better. In 1876 the private chair coolies were usually paid about $6 a month plus lodging. In 1891 they still received the same wage, despite the increase in the cost of living. In 1896 monthly wages paid to private chair and ricksha coolies ranged from $6 to $8.50; and in 1901, from $8 to $12 according to circumstances. Wages paid by some prominent Chinese were as follows: Wei Yuk (comprador, on the legislative council) paid his chair and ricksha coolies $5.50 each per month in 1896 in addition to giving them board and lodging; in 1901 he paid them $8 and gave them oil, firewood, and lodging but no food. Fung Wah Chuen (comprador, on the sanitary board) had four chair coolies in 1901; two old hands who acted as chair coolies and house coolies got free board and lodging and $9 each per month; the other two, newer hands, got $9 and free lodging, but no board. Lau Chu Pak (comprador, on the sanitary board) paid his two ricksha coolies $7 each in 1896 and $9 each in 1901 without providing lodging. In 1906 private employers still paid a monthly wage of no more than $10 to the ricksha, chair, punkah, and house coolies.[22]

Ku Kiu, a Hakka, had been a chair bearer for over twenty years. In 1896 he paid 30 cents for house rent and $4 for food per month. Five years later, in 1901, he had to pay 70 cents for rent and $6 for food. Making a total income of about $12 a month, Ku Kiu had $5.30 left for clothing and other expenditures. Ku Kiu and his partner owned their chair.[23]

Yan Ping Hup, public ricksha puller, earned a gross income of $12 or $13 per month after paying about 20 cents (200 cash) each day for the hire of a ricksha. Food cost him $5 or $6 and lodging rent was $1 per month. He earned a net monthly income of $7 or $8. He had to pay a man $30 as tea money (swindled) to get the license for him. Besides, he managed every now and then to send some money to support his family on the mainland. Like the large majority of coolies in Hong Kong, he could not afford to bring his family to live in Hong Kong because of the higher cost of living.[24] Still, Yan Ping Hup was doing well in comparison with other ricksha coolies who were not so lucky.

Pulling ricksha was hard work—especially in Hong Kong, with its oppressive, hot, and humid climate that lasted nearly half the year, from May to October. The traveler Henry Norman described in 1895 his experience with the summer heat in Hong Kong:

> The damp is indescribable. Moisture pours down the walls; any-
> thing left alone for a couple of days—cloths, boots, hats, portman-
> teaus—is covered with mould. Twenty steps in the open air and
> you are soaked with perspiration. Then there are the cockroaches,
> to say nothing of the agile centipede whose bite may lay you up for

a month . . . It does happen, too, that men die in summer in Hongkong between sunrise and sunset without rhyme or reason.[25]

Manual labor in such a trying climate was hard, and it usually took younger and stronger men to pull ricksha. When asked before a commission: "How long do these coolies last, only a few years? It kills them doesn't it?," the police chief, Mr. F. Henry May (later to become governor of Hong Kong in 1912), replied: "I don't know that. I never enquired." Ngan Wing Chi, headman of the Kowloon licensed ricksha coolies, knew that it was tough. He had difficulty getting coolies to pull rickshas. He still had ten rickshas that he could not get men for. "Over ten men have died because they had a long journey to run from Kowloon to Shatin. The journey over the new road kills them, and when they get home, they spit blood."[26]

District and Dialect Groups

A great many chair and ricksha coolies were Teochiu (Chiu Chau, Ch'ao-chou) men and Hoklos (Hokkienese) from Amoy and Foochow; some were Hai-feng men, and others were Punti Cantonese.[27] "Hok-los are very clanny"; "being strangers in Hongkong, speaking a different language," "they stick together very closely. . . . Living in the same coolie house."[28] In a report on sanitary conditions of Hong Kong in 1882, twenty-five chair coolies were listed as lodged in the upper floor of a house in Market Street, having erected bunks to sleep on; the lower floor was occupied by seven chairmakers who used it as a workshop and dwelling.[29] The five hundred warehouse workers employed by the Hong Kong and Kowloon Wharf and Godown Company and the one thousand coolies working at Jardine's Sugar Refinery in 1901 all came from Ch'ao-chou and Swatow and spoke the Teochiu dialect.[30]

The parochialism of the working people in Hong Kong found expression in the rivalry and hostility between different district and dialect groups. Sir Henry A. Blake (governor of Hong Kong, 1898–1903) noted that "the junks from Swatow land their cargoes in Hong Kong at a wharf where Swatow coolies are employed; did they land it at a wharf worked by Cantonese, there would certainly be disorder, and possibly fighting, before the discharge of the cargo."[31]

Why were the Hoklos and Teochiu coolies particularly "parochial" and "clanny"? Because traditional kinship ties and dialect group cohesion were important to these minority groups in their competition for resources and employment opportunities with larger and more powerful dialect groups of Punti Cantonese. Unlike merchants who had acquired considerable economic and social resources to promote their interests, coolies had only kinship ties and dialect group cohesion to rely upon in their daily struggle to compete with one another to make a living. Dialect group cohesion gave members protection and enhanced mutual assistance. Rivalry and tensions existed not only between the Hoklo, Teochiu, Hakka, and Punti Canotonese coolies but also between Cantonese coolies from Tung-kuan and those from Sze Yap.

Coolie Houses

The Tung-kuan coolies lived in the coolie houses operated by Tung-kuan housekeepers, and the Sze Yap coolies lived in those run by Sze Yap housekeepers. Some housekeepers were landlords themselves, but many others rented the houses from absentee landlords. As a labor broker and head of the house of a dialect group of coolies living together for mutual aid and protection, the housekeeper exercised great power over his coolie boarders, who relied on him for finding employment at various jobs at the docks and wharves, in competition with coolies of other dialect groups. The coolie houses varied in size—all very crowded. In one instance, 428 people lived in a row of eight small houses, having but two hundred and thirty cubic feet of space per head. It was not unusual for over one hundred coolies to crowd into a lodging house.[32]

While some larger employers provided housing accommodations near their works, most laborers could not afford transport expenses and were compelled to live in proximity to their place of employment.[33] This explains why coolie houses were mostly concentrated at the West Point of the city of Victoria. Poverty forced coolies to live in crowded, unsanitary conditions.

Ngan Wing Chi was a labor contractor and head coolie to Jardine's Sugar Refinery while renting houses from absentee landlords for the company's coolies. He paid the rent for his coolies, collecting later the rents from them. Both Ngan and his coolies came from Ch'ao-chou. But not all coolie housekeepers were labor contractors or head coolies. For example, Lo Sz was a coolie housekeeper who considered himself a sort of coolie. He went to Yaumati daily to obtain some earth work to do. In addition, he did some private trading business of his own. For about twenty years he had kept a small coolie house at Gough Street. The majority of his tenants were street coolies, with a few ricksha pullers, all from Swatow and Ch'ao-chou.[34]

Housing accommodations were of great importance to coolies. They would not come to Hong Kong from Swatow, Hai-feng, or anywhere else unless they could find accommodation with some friends at a minimal cost. Nor were there enough houses in the colony to admit them. The housing shortage allowed coolie house keepers to exercise power over their coolie tenants. Many coolies who had already found private employment with free quarters, continued to subscribe some fee towards the rent of their coolie house for fear that should they lose their job or fall ill, they would have no place to live.[35]

Coolie houses often served certain "guild" functions. Since each accommodated coolies from the same dialect district on the mainland, the coolie house keeper acted as collector of an annual subscription for religious purposes connected with their native district. Also, if coolies left an employer and had a grievance against him, they could return to their lodging house, urging their fellow coolies to boycott the employer. Coolie houses provided the basis of an organization for the promotion of boycott and strikes when necessary. When individual coolies were fined by the magistrate for any reasons, coolies of their dialect groups often combined to pay the fines. Coolie house fellowship also helped in the constant fights between coolie factions for the best vehicle stands in town or for their right to work at certain docks and wharves.[36]

Triad Society

Another important association of the working people in Hong Kong was the Triad Society, which was organized along dialect and native place principles. In some lodges the members were chiefly Punti Cantonese, and in others, Hoklos or Hakkas. Their aim was to promote their members' interests and to provide them with assistance and protection in competition with other groups. The Triads in Hong Kong came mostly from the lower classes of the Chinese population—coolies, boat people, hawkers, and artisans.[37] The Triads rarely made connections with the wealthier classes in the colony. Political stability, general peace, and relative security rendered it unnecessary for the wealthier Chinese of Hong Kong to seek protection and enhancement of their interests under the banner of the Triad society. As the police inspector William Quincy pointed out, there was no reason to believe that rich members of the Chinese community were connected with the Triad society.[38]

The number of Triads was variously estimated at between ten thousand and twenty thousand out of a total population of 181,529 in 1884. A special committee report of 1886 allows for a list by occupation of about five thousand Triad members in Hong Kong as follows: 1,540 coolies, 900 boatmen, 660 hawkers, 400 rice pounders, 310 gamblers, 300 stone cutters, 200 coal coolies, 150 barbers, 50 earth carriers and barbers from the Hakka ethnic group, 100 tailors, 100 chair carriers, 40 copper smiths, 40 washermen, 40 lodging house keepers, and 120 "bad characters." Triads were also found among boiler makers, soy dealers, chandlers, seamen, pirates, head coolie of emigration agency, and fishing boatmen. A Buddhist priest and two herb medicine practitioners were also known to be Triad members. About one hundred to two hundred Triads were said to have penetrated the Hong Kong government services as policemen, detectives, district watchmen, and in the surveyor general's department, harbor master's office and the registrar general's office.[39]

The Triads in Hong Kong had no unified command; rather, they split into various independent branches and factions, frequently opposing each other in fighting and litigation.[40] The Triads set up pugilistic clubs, promoting the cultivation of the art of boxing and fencing. The clubs were frequented by all of the "low characters" in the colony as well as by the ordinary workers. Club members often became active in times of popular disturbances.[41] The Triads could do a wide variety of things, ranging from petty crimes to political revolution; they constantly threatened the Chinese government and reacted strongly to foreign imperialism. The Hoklo Triad Society in Hong Kong, for instance, "took the colloquial name of Ghee Hin, the Hokkien equivalent of 'Let Patriotism Flourish' "; it appealed to patriotic motives and sought to "protect its members against the law itself."[42] The Triads wished to revolt against the Hong Kong government or Chinese government, should an opportunity arise.[43] While their criminal actions alienated them from the populace, on other occasions their patriotic motivation gave them popular support.[44] They took an active part in the popular insurrection in Hong Kong in 1884, and subsequently a number of Triads joined the revolutionaries in 1911 against the Manchus.

Coolies Under British Justice

How did workers fare under British justice? Choi Atim, chair coolie, was attacked by a dog in the street and bitten in the left thigh. At the police court on May 28, 1883, the dog's owner Mr. Linde paid one dollar to Choi Atim as compensation and the case was dismissed.[45]

At the police court on May 29, 1883, Chan Acheung, house coolie, was charged by Mr. A. Millar, plumber, with leaving his employment without notice. In defense Chan Acheung said that Mr. Millar had beaten him and that he had told his master to get another servant. Still, he was fined five dollars—nearly the amount of his monthly earning. Unable to pay the fine, Chan Acheung was sent to jail for a fortnight.[46]

These random bits of local news items on the obscure pages of the Hong Kong press may seem "trivial," but they were in fact politically significant. Ordering a European dog owner to pay only one dollar to a chair coolie as compensation for being attacked and bitten by his dog, and imposing a fine of five dollars on a Chinese servant for leaving an abusive European employer demonstrated how the judicial system worked for the coolies in Hong Kong.

There were, of course, important judicial cases in the history of Hong Kong that served to illustrate the capability of the British judges to administer impartial justice on some occasions. In 1854 two Europeans who had murdered a Chinese boy on the ship *Mastiff* were brought to justice by execution. This "greatly impressed the Chinese residents with the equality of justice dealt out by British tribunals." And in 1871 there was the case of the *Nouvelle Penelope*, a French coolie ship from Macao seized on the sea by Kwok Asing and his fellow coolies, who murdered the captain and crew and fled to Hong Kong. Chief Justice Sir J. Smale ruled that the offense was against a French slave ship, and that "the murders committed with the object of regaining liberty were no crime."[47]

Yet numerous "trivial" cases imposed on many coolies summary and unjust punishment. Experience with the police magistrate and with the judges contributed to the formation of the coolies' view of British colonial rule. To the masses of coolies, the "foreign devil's" rule in Hong Kong often seemed arbitrary and unjust. The judicial system was frequently biased against the Chinese lower classes. Coolies were brought to trial often without benefit of counsel. They were consequently found guilty, and were either fined or sentenced to imprisonment. The court assumed that "most Chinese prisoners would do well to avoid the witness box, in view of consequent cross-examination," implying that the Chinese mentality was such that they would help their case more by being silent than by trying to defend themselves.[48]

Numerous court cases were reported in the local press, showing that lower-class Chinese when charged were most likely to be found guilty. Tsang Fung was accused of larceny and forgery. He was not represented by counsel and had entered a plea of not guilty. Still, the European jurors and chief justice found him guilty. When the verdict was given, Tsang Fung told his lordship not to be so hasty, he had something to say. The chief justice would not hear him and ordered him to be removed. Tsang Fung refused to leave the dock, and was pulled out, dragged from the court shrieking and yelling.[49]

In some ways British justice did protect coolies, fining those European sailors who refused to pay the ricksha coolie, or ordering reluctant employers at times to pay back wages.[50] Yet British justice often ruled harshly and unjustly against coolies. Coolies and Europeans who were charged for the same kinds of crimes were treated in a different manner. Often, in addition to jail terms, the coolies suffered the added insult of public exposure in the stocks.[51]

The colonial government stood behind the employers, using the judicial system to keep the working class in line. A group of coolies employed on the Naval Yard works demanded a wage increase from thirty-five cents per day to forty cents. When the employers refused to grant a raise, the laborers went on strike in February 1904. A new group of coolies were engaged but were prevented from working by the strikers. One of the ringleaders was arrested by the police and sentenced to three months' imprisonment and three hours' stocks. The strike was thus ended.[52] The judicial system was constantly used in the colony as a force of labor control. Coolies were expected to be quiet and obedient. Mr. McEven's servants were punished for making too much noise. The Europeans loathed the noisy coolies at the Peak station as a "great nuisance."[53]

Every year large numbers of coolies were tried and convicted in the police magistrate's court and the supreme court. In the magistrate's court alone during a period of ten years from 1897 to 1906, a total of 135,460 cases were heard involving 162,945 defendants, of whom 136,899 persons were convicted and punished. That is to say, each year an average of 13,689 persons were given summary punishment. In 1900 only one police magistrate was charged with the responsibility of hearing the cases. In that year Acting Police Magistrate Mr. F. A. Hazeland alone handled a total of 14,081 cases involving 16,696 defendants, of whom 13,650 persons were convicted and punished. In other words, each month Mr. Hazeland handled an average of 1,173 cases; that is, an average of 47 cases each day. He felt obliged to request the colonial secretary to appoint an assistant magistrate to help him hear the cases, because he said it was absolutely impossible for him to handle the cases alone.[54]

Summary "justice" brought anguish to numerous men, women, and children. Testimony was given by Lai Wing Sheng, shroff to the police magistracy for more than twelve years, from 1895 to 1908 (at a salary of seventy dollars per month). Highly regarded by his supervisor as "a good man and doing his work well," he nevertheless wrote a letter to the police magistrate on February 22, 1908, applying for his transfer to the harbor department: "The reason why I apply for transfer is because I do not like seeing defendants cry and weep who have not sufficient or no money to pay fine and also because I cannot bear the harsh treatment I received on occasions from the Police."[55]

Flogging of Prisoners

Chinese prisoners in Hong Kong were frequently subjected to corporal punishment. Ordered by the magistrate or judge, the half-naked prisoner was marched from the Victoria jail through several crowded streets to the public whipping post located near the harbor master's office, the busiest thoroughfare of the colony. A crowd of spectators, including children, often gathered to see "the public exhibition of an English turnkey flogging with a vigorous arm the speedily bleeding body of a Chinaman, tied to the whipping post."[56]

There were three kinds of instruments employed in flogging the prisoners: the regulation cat, the naval cat, and rattan. The regulation cat had nine tails, with knots on each tail, while the naval cat had no knots. The rattan was generally forty-seven inches in length and two inches in circumference; a heavy weapon, its effects were "very likely to go deep into the cellular and muscular tissues, . . . and thus for a long time delaying the healing of the wounds." In one case, a prisoner who was punished with thirty-six strokes of the rattan on the breech in March 1878 received wounds that were not yet completely healed in September, a period of six months. Flogging with a "cat" on the prisoner's back not merely caused external injury of the skin but also involved a risk of injury to the internal organs, such as congestion of the lungs.[57]

From April 1871 to July 1876 the number of floggings of prisoners in Hong Kong was 1,149. As some prisoners received two or three floggings, the actual number of prisoners flogged was 902. Compared with Britain, the number of floggings in Hong Kong was exceedingly high, far out of proportion to its population:[58]

	NUMBER OF FLOGGINGS (APRIL 1871–JULY 1876)	POPULATION
England	4,988	24,000,000
Scotland	679	3,400,000
Ireland	34	5,250,000
Hong Kong	1,149	140,000

To justify the penal system in the colony, Lord Carnarvon, the secretary of state for the colonies in London, argued in 1878: "The barbarity of Chinese punishments is notorious, and no flogging inflicted in Hong Kong is able to compare with them in severity."[59] Whatever the rationalization, the British colonial government did not commend itself to the masses of Chinese coolies in Hong Kong by freely resorting to flogging their brethren.

The Victoria jail superintendent often "inflicted the punishment of flogging without authority" on prisoners for "breach of regulation or discipline." Mok A Kwai was four times "illegally flogged." On August 4, 1873, "for making a noise" he received six strokes of the "regulation cat" on the back. On October 6, he received the same punishment, again for "making a noise." On December 13 he received still another three strokes of the "cat" for "making a noise."

Mok A Kwai "died of phthisis" in the Gaol Hospital on September 28, 1877, aged twenty-four. Cases similar to this took place in 1874 and 1876.[60]

Sir John Pope Hennessy arrived in April 1877 to hold the reins of government in Hong Kong. Moved by humanitarianism, the new governor soon proceeded to reform the prison. He got rid of the worst of the foreign turnkeys who were "brutalized by having to administer excessive floggings."[61] Branding of criminals and "public" flogging were declared permanently abolished in 1880, although "private" flogging of prisoners still took place within the walls of the jail.[62] But Governor Hennessy was exceptional among the British colonists in insisting on humane treatment of Chinese prisoners. By pursuing such a policy, he made himself immensely unpopular among the colony's European residents, who looked upon him as a man of "peculiar" temperament bent on "creating trouble" for the colony. They blamed him for the increase of crimes and the lack of order and discipline among the Chinese of the lower classes. But the governor, in fact, desired order and discipline no less than they, only he doubted the deterrent effect of brutal treatment of prisoners.[63]

Sir John Pope Hennessy departed from the colony in March 1882. In June the new governor, Sir George Bowen, approved the flogging of prisoner Li A On, aged twelve, for stealing an umbrella. Corporal punishment of both adults and children quickly and quietly returned to the Victoria Gaol.[64]

The Destitute

A thin line separated a working coolie from a mendicant. A few days out of work, a worker became vagabond in the street. In the rugged capitalist society under British colonial rule there were always numerous destitutes and vagabonds roaming the streets of Hong Kong. Under British justice poverty and destitution was considered a crime. Mr. Evans, the "protector of Chinese" in Singapore, suggested some measures to deal with beggars—two or four months in prison, with compulsory cleanliness, should be enough to convert most beggars into decent members of society! The *China Mail* commented that this recommendation was worthy of consideration in Hong Kong. An European resident in the colony published a letter in a local English paper, wishing to call the authorities' attention to "the importunate beggars who infested Wyndham Street. . . . Surely something ought to be done to remove these pests."[65] In fact, a series of ordinances in 1845, 1858, 1866, and 1876 subjected paupers to fine, imprisonment, whipping and deportation at the magistrate's discretion.[66]

There was no poor law in Hong Kong. Although the Tung Wah Hospital directors provided relief for destitute Chinese, they were so afraid of being burdened with permanent pauper patients that they admitted into the hospital only those who had recommendation of influential subscribers.[67] In 1879 the hospital admitted 1,614 poor Chinese, provided 221 burials, and sent 123 destitutes back to the mainland.[68] Still, there were always hundreds of Chinese destitutes roaming the streets.

The humanitarian governor Sir John Pope Hennessy (r. 1877–82) became concerned about the abuses under the system of deporting Chinese mendicants—"old men and women who had worked a good many years in Hong Kong, but who, on getting feeble from age, were deported to the opposite shore of China to die." Chan Foon, a widow eighty-two years of age, who had resided in Hong Kong for thirty-two years, was arrested by the police for begging in the street. E. J. Eitel, the acting Chinese secretary under Governor Hennessy, admitted: "The unusual number of suicides constantly occurring in Hong Kong, and of cases of persons found dead, is to be laid at the door of this brute deterrent policy in dealing with destitution." This "barbaric policy of brute repression" was "anything but creditable to a Christian Government or a civilized community."[69]

In expressing sympathy and humanitarian concern for the down-trodden Chinese both Governor Hennessy and his protégé, E. J. Eitel, were exceptional among the European community in Hong Kong. The scholarly Eitel was a German missionary and was made a naturalized British subject by the governor's special ordinance only in September 1880. Both men were heartily disliked by the British community in the colony.[70]

But the community could not conceal the fact that every year hundreds of paupers and vagabonds were arrested, fined, impris-oned with hard labor, put in the stocks, and deported. Around 3:30 a.m. Sergent Hedge discovered twelve coolies sleeping peacefully under a verandah in Des Voeux Road Central. Upon being awakened they admitted that they had no place of abode and were compelled to sleep in the street. They were all marched off to the police station.

The magistrate sentenced them to four days' jail with hard labor.[71] A cripple who had been a "nuisance" to the passers-by in Charter Road was sent to jail for fourteen days.[72] A one-armed Chinese and a blind Chinese were charged by Police Constable John Clarke with begging for alms. The magistrate imposed a fine of five dollars on each of them.[73]

In short, the police sought to round up the unfortunate poor and destitute for whom the colonial government provided no relief. The judicial system, supposedly society's instrument of justice, served in Hong Kong as a tool for the repression and control of the coolie working class.

Coolie-Fankwei Relations

The coolies' plight and their experience with the police magistrate and colonial justice shaped their attitude towards British colonial rule. They were suspicious of the *fankwei* and hostile to the colonial government. Sensitive to popular antipathy, an official report of 1874 warned: "At Hong-Kong where 30,000 Chinese are regularly employed, they would not hesitate, at a given signal, to massacre all the Europeans."[74]

But what had attracted the coolies to the *fankwei*'s colony in the first place? The entrepôt of Hong Kong offered job opportunities and a relatively higher wage, though still a subsistence one. Moreover, in contrast with their homeland, which frequently suffered from political and social unrest, the *fankwei*'s government in Hong Kong offered political stability, even though its police magistrates and judges were often harsh and arbitrary in their dealings with the coolies. Poverty drove coolies into working under harsh terms. Just as Chinese merchants were easily coopted by the colonial authorities, coolies were as easily bought off by the foreign colonists. While merchants cooperated with their foreign business partners, coolies worked for their foreign employers to make a living. They worked for *fankwei* whom they disliked. Concerning the laboring people in Hong Kong, in 1892 a French author made this observation: "They crowd round the Europeans, because money can be made, but they display no affection or esteem, and remain strangers to their [European] civilisation."[75]

Coolies played a vitally important role in the colony's economy by providing the much needed labor. Without them, the loading and unloading of ocean steamships would cease, the harbor would come to a standstill, and the traffic in Victoria City would halt. They contributed significantly towards Hong Kong's growth and development into a prosperous entrepôt in return for a bare subsistence wage. They comprised the most numerous elements among the colony's population as well as the most abused, exploited, and neglected. This was a major source of tensions in colonial society.

Coolies and Queen Victoria's Diamond Jubilee, 1897

In appearance, all seemed well about the flourishing port city. On June 20, 1887, the colony celebrated Queen Victoria's Golden Jubilee. John A. Turner, a Wesleyan missionary, observed that "in addition to the demonstration made by Europeans, the Chinese themselves spent $100,000 [correctly, $10,000] in triumphal arches, processions, and shows, to express their satisfaction with the good government under which they lived. Thousands went from Canton to see what was done, and at their return, all the river steamers were densely crowded."[76]

In 1897, again, Queen Victoria's Diamond Jubilee was celebrated with much fanfare in Hong Kong. At a ceremony in the Government House on June 22, Ho Kai presented a Chinese tablet to Governor Sir William Robinson "in token of the profound respect and great admiration" for the queen and the governor. Ho Kai's speech drew repeated applause from the audience:

> For over half a century the Chinese in Hong Kong have enjoyed the fruits of strong, righteous and benevolent government, and in the prosperity of this port they have shared largely. Under the British flag they have found perfect protection and liberty and from the Government they have received equal justice and consideration (applause).[77]

Ho Kai's flattering eulogy of the British Empire was characteristic of the "leading Chinese" from the wealthy merchant class on such state occasions. The Chinese mercantile community subscribed thirty-five thousand dollars (of which ten thousand was actually spent) for the jubilee celebration, which lasted for several days and nights.[78]

Why were Britain's Chinese subjects so enthusiastic about the

Queen's jubilee? Many of them heartily welcomed the celebration for a pragmatic reason. Merchants, businessmen, traders, shopkeepers, and owners of restaurants, eating houses, and tea shops were lured by material gains; they desired to use the grand occasion to attract tourists and customers. The city of Victoria was "crowded with visitors from all the southern provinces of China and elsewhere, giving 'the place an unusually animated appearance.' "[79] As an old resident recollected, "the guilds of various trades sought to use the great celebration of the colony's golden jubilee in 1891 as an excuse for promoting their trades and business." In fact, Chinese businessmen and traders eagerly petitioned the colonial authorities for permission to sponsor theater performances, dragon dances, religious festivities, popular assemblages, and street processions "to attract their countrymen from Kwangtung to do sightseeing in Hong Kong" and thereby to promote their trades and business.[80] They used many such occasions to advertise their businesses.[81]

Coolies, too, were delighted about the jubilee celebrations. Preparations for religious festivities and processions gave employment to large numbers of artisans, coolies, and boatmen. Street hawkers, ricksha pullers, and sedan chair bearers could earn a few extra cash from serving the great crowds of tourists. Pickpockets and beggars were also delighted over the jubilee as it offered gainful opportunities. However, they had no interest in the ritual and ceremonial purporting to honor the queen and glorify the British empire.

In short, all classes of Chinese rejoiced at the queen's jubilee because it was useful to them in varying degrees, depending on their position in the colony's social hierarchy. Ho Kai's eulogy of the British empire truly reflected one aspect of the wealthy Chinese merchants—a general complacency about their position in the colony. But for the coolies, the great majority of the queen's subjects, the colony provided no more than political stability and an opportunity to sell their hard labor for a subsistence living.

The jubilee celebration concealed the reality of social tensions in the British colony. The working people disliked *fankwei*, who in return frequently complained about the "insolent coolies." The governor was officially known in Chinese as Tu-hsien, but the Hong Kong Cantonese had a rather disrespectful nickname for him. They called him *Ping Tau* (military boss), and the botanical garden adjoining the Government House was known as *Ping Tau Fa Yuen* (the military boss's flower garden). St. John's Cathedral was officially known in Cantonese as Tai-Lai-Pai-Tong (the Great Worship Hall), but the street coolies referred to it instead as *Hung-Mo-Miu* (the Red Hair Temple), meaning the temple of the red-haired foreign devils. On the day after Queen Victoria's golden jubilee, an Englishman wrote a letter to the local English press to express his indignation at hearing the chair coolies using this nickname:

> I felt a little disconcerted on that glorious jubilee morning by hearing a nick-name applied to the British people as represented by the august assembly gathering in the Cathedral. . . . How can Her Gracious Majesty's authorities in this great Colony allow such disrespectful terms to be applied to themselves and us all?[82]

Later on, the Chinese in Hong Kong had a nickname for Governor Sir Reginald E. Stubbs (r. 1919–25). They called him *Si-Tap-Si*, that is, shit Stubbs, not a very polite nickname for his excellency.[83] In 1886 young Charles S. Addis (of the Hong Kong and Shanghai Banking Corporation) wrote to his sister back home in England that the Chinese in the colony hated the "foreign devils." "They tell a crying child as I pass that if he does not be quiet the 'foreign devil' will come to him."[84]

On his visit to Hong Kong in 1895 the traveler Henry Norman sensed the danger of popular hostility toward *fankwei*. He predicted a revolt of the Chinese masses. "I never ceased to prophesy two things about Hong Kong, one of which, the epidemic [of bubonic plague, 1894], has come true indeed. The other waits, and as it is rather alarmist it is perhaps better left out of print."[85] In fact, Hong Kong had a long history of popular resistance to British colonial rule. As will be seen in chapter 5, the Sino-French War in 1884–85 provided an occasion for a popular insurrection in Hong Kong.

F
I
V
E

Popular Insurrection in 1884
During the Sino-French War

Canton and Hong Kong are conterminous; they
share each other's peace and peril.
—Governor General Chang Chih-tung (1884)

What the Chinese authorities wish these men
[Triads] to do is to set fire to French ships and to
find out what houses are supplying the French
with provisions. . . . Many of the boat-people are
members of the Triad Society and are much en-
raged against the French for attacking their coun-
try without reason.
—Hong Kong Police Intelligence

During the Sino-French War (1884–85) a wave of antiforeignism swept the southern provinces of China from Chieh-kiang to Yün-nan.[1] Hong Kong was not immune to it. In 1884 a popular protest movement broke out in Hong Kong involving large numbers of laborers in a nearly general strike and acquiring a nationalistic overtone. What were the circumstances leading to the insurrection? How did the crisis reveal the complex social relations and community structure in the colony? This chapter addresses these issues.

The Impact of the Sino-French War

Since the times of Louis Napoleon Bonaparte (r. 1848–71), the French had harbored an ambition to build a French Indo-Chinese empire in the East. Two military campaigns, in 1858–59 and 1861–62, forced Vietnam (Annam) to cede three provinces in Cochin China to France. A Franco-Vietnamese treaty in 1874 in effect reduced Vietnam into a French protectorate. But as Vietnam had historically been a Chinese dependency, China refused to recognize the treaty. To counter the French advance the Vietnamese sought assistance from the Chinese. By 1882 the irregular Chinese Black Flag army, under Liu Yung-fu, had begun to engage the French troops along the ill-defined Annam-China border. In late 1883 the Chinese and French troops began to fight open battles in Tongking, though negotiations for peaceful settlement went on.[2]

The French aggressions had profound impacts on China. It was an important stage in the evolution of bureaucratic public opinion leading to a nationalist, reformist movement in the bureaucracy in the 1880s and 1890s. The war stimulated *ch'ing-i* (pure discussion), that is, critical and theoretically disinterested discussion of national affairs. A coterie of young officials in Peking, including Chang Chih-tung, Chang P'ei-lun, Ch'en Pao-ch'en, and others, assembled to form a militant and patriotic group called *ch'ing-liu* (pure group), which expressed moral indignation against Li Hung-chang's appeasement position and advocated war to defend China's honor and its tributary state.[3] To strengthen the defense of China's southern front, the imperial court appointed P'eng Yü-lin (president of the board of war) as commissioner for the coastal defence in Kwangtung and Chang Chih-tung as governor general of Kwangtung and Kwangsi.

On August 5, 1884, the French fleet attacked Taiwan. And on August 23 Admiral Amede Courbet led a French fleet to bombard Foochow, destoying its shipyard and sinking eleven Chinese warships. The French threat of attack on Canton incurred alarm and strong anti-French feelings among the Cantonese in both Canton and Hong Kong. Located only eighty miles from Canton, the colony lay middle way between the war theaters of Hanoi to the south and Foochow and Keelung to the north. The harbor of Hong Kong would have provided an ideal shelter for French vessels and warships to obtain repairs and supplies of food and ammunitions. But the Chinese in Hong Kong would not cooperate, and the officials in Canton did not stand idly by. The Chinese officials issued proclamations on August 30, offering awards for the lives of French soldiers. The arrival of French ships in Hong Kong gave rise to disturbances.

A description of the disturbances is first in order, to be followed by analysis and assessment. The fury and excitement of the crowds and the complex nature of the strikes and riots can be comprehended through detailed description of some major incidents that occurred.

The Strike and Riots in September and October, 1884

On September 3, 1884, the French frigate *La Galissoniere* arrived in Hong Kong, with Admiral Courbet on board, saluted by British guns in the harbor. But Chinese dockworkers in Hong Kong refused to repair French vessels. The Chinese residents had petitioned the colonial authorities against allowing French vessels to dock in the Hong Kong harbor. But the British authorities disregarded their Chinese subjects' feelings, again extending a warm welcome to the visiting French rear-admiral Lespes.[4] The Canton officials issued more proclamations on September 5 and 15, calling on the Chinese to "show a devoted regard for [their] fatherland" and warning them against working for the French. On September 18 a strike broke out in the shipyards in protest against the presence in Hong Kong of *La Galissonniere*, the French warship that had taken part in the attack on Foochow, now anchored for repairs in Hong Kong.[5] On September 25 the cargo boat people joined the strike. A French merchant named Francis Vincenot had four cattle to send on board a French warship, but tried in vain to engage cargo boats to do the work. Two boatwomen were fined five dollars each by the Hong Kong magistrate for refusing to accept employment. Eight more cargo boat people were fined five dollars each on September 29 for refusing to unload a steamer of the French Messageries Maritime Company.[6]

Infuriated by the fines, nearly all cargo boat people staged a strike on September 30, and all work of loading and unloading cargo in the harbor came to a halt. Cargo-carrying coolies on shore also joined the strike. Most boat people went away with their boats to Yau-ma-ti in Kowloon. In the afternoon a crowd of nearly one thousand assembled on the Praya; they began to stone and drive away the few remaining cargo boats and the passenger boats. Although the police soon arrived to restore order, the harbor came to a standstill. A night meeting of the boating community was held at Yau-ma-ti to decide their future action. And a Chinese notice was posted on the wall of the French merchant Francis Vincenot's store on the Praya Central intimating that the premises would be blown up with gunpowder and warning the Chinese employees to leave.[7]

The strike continued on October 1 and 2. The boat people demanded the right to refuse working for the French without penalty. Forced by the necessity of earning a living, many cargo boat people returned to Praya West early on the morning of October 3, intending to resume working (though still not for the French vessels). But an angry crowd of coolies showered them with stones and bricks. The police rushed to restore order, but shortly before 8 a.m. cargo coolies went to the principal thoroughfares in the Western or Chinese part of the town to prevent the jinrickisha and chair coolies from working for foreigners. The crowd attacked British officers and other Westerners in the streets[8] because it was obvious to the crowd that they were all sympathetic with the French invaders. "They are cats of the same hill," says a Chinese proverb. The Sikh constables fired into the crowd. Ngu Ayow, a street coolie, was found dead, lying in blood in the street in front of the Civil Hospital with his brains protruding from his skull. There were most likely a good many wounded, probably carried off by their friends.[9]

The excitement, exacerbated by the police shooting the crowd, spread until the whole district from Central Street to East Street was in a state of turmoil. "All the shops were closed, and coolies from all points flocked together to join in the revolutionary movement," reported the local English press. Strong police reinforcements were sent to the scene, including Sikh and Chinese police and some mounted Indian troopers. The huge mass of people that gathered on the Chinese Recreation Ground threw stones at the police, who fired revolvers into the crowd. No killed or wounded persons were seen, again as friends probably carried them away. No sooner had the riot subsided in one direction than it broke out in another. A number of wounded policemen were sent to the Civil Hospital. The police made a number of arrests, and by noon the riots had ended.[10]

Meanwhile, the British military authorities had sent two companies of troops to the scene of the disturbance. With fixed bayonets, their presence did much to overawe the dispersed crowd. At 4 p.m. thirty persons were brought to the police court. A number of placards posted by the crowd announced that the town was to be set on fire at night in three places. The police, taking precaution, seized all dynamite and other explosives that they could find in the hands of the Chinese shopkeepers in Queen's Road West. A hundred troops marched to the Tung Wah Hospital, to be quartered in its buildings, which was situated in a district densely inhabited by the Chinese.

The streets were patrolled by police and troops at night, and the harbor by the launches and water police.[11]

Early next morning, October 4, the "rowdies" were astir. Six cargo boats that came back to the Praya intending to start work were immediately stoned away. Some stone throwers were arrested, but almost all business afloat remained suspended. By then street coolies, artisans, and workmen of all descriptions had generally ceased working. Waiters at the Hong Kong Hotel and the crew of the hotel launch refused to serve the former French consul from Shanghai.[12] The rice pounders and coal men also joined the strike. The butchers, having been threatened while driving their bullocks to the slaughterhouse, intended to join in the strike, but when assured of police protection they returned to work. The chair and jinricksha coolies resumed working in all but the most disturbed parts in the western district. Many of them, however, encountered violent interference. Sporadic pelting of Europeans in the streets continued. The feeling against foreigners, particularly the police, was very strong. The French convent had the greatest difficulty in getting food, the Chinese being unwilling or afraid to supply them.[13]

At noon the following day, October 5, Chinese employees of Messrs. Butterfield and Swire visited Yau-ma-ti and asked their own boat people to return to work. With assurance of police and troop protection, large numbers of cargo boats and sampans returned shortly after noon to the Praya to work. After six or seven stone throwers were arrested, things remained quiet along the Praya West, although the cargo coolies ashore remained on strike. Meanwhile, about five hundred coolies, some armed with bamboos, gathered in Ship Street in Wanchai to intimidate the coal and cargo coolies working for Wing Kee, a ship comprador providing coal for foreign vessels. The policemen quickly arrived to disperse the crowd; two men were arrested. The coal coolies seemed delighted to work again, for they were "a very poor class, living from hand to mouth." By then the boat people were also glad to resume work. On strike for about a week since September 30, many of them were beginning to "feel the pangs of hunger."[14]

But a large crowd assembled on the recreation ground around 8 p.m. Jeering and shouting, they threw stones at the police. The Nam Pak Hong merchant guild had drawn up a notice and posted it all over the town, "advising the people to refrain from lawless acts, and warning them that if they continued riotous proceedings, the military would probably fire into them."[15] By October 6 the strike and riots were practically over, although the cargo boat people still refused to work for the French. Order had been restored for the time being, though sporadic attacks on Europeans continued to occur after that date.[16]

Thus, unlike prior labor strikes involving only certain occupational groups of workers, the strike in 1884 spread beyond earlier parochial boundaries, cutting across both occupational and dialect lines to include most sectors of Hong Kong's working population. This was a significant difference. Why did it happen?

Circumstances of the Strike and Riots

The disturbances in 1884 were complex in nature. A number of causes and circumstances converged to bring about the strike and riots. The Canton officials' proclamations exhorted people along the coast to patriotism (i.e., to help defend their homes, relatives, and country against a foreign enemy) and warned them against working for the French enemy. As most Chinese in the colony had homes, relatives, or property on the mainland, fear of mandarin retaliation was an important factor that initially caused many people in Hong Kong to refuse to work for the French.

But other factors were also at work. The French attacks and threats of attacks on various points along the coast had provoked an anti-French patriotic feeling among all classes in Hong Kong. Disregarding the Chinese feelings, however, the colonial government prosecuted the local Chinese newspaper editors for publishing mandarins' patriotic proclamations; it also imposed fines on ten boat people who refused to work for the French enemy. This was an important factor that set off the labor strike. It occurred in a social context of general poverty and misery among the working people. The strike then spread to most sectors of the working population because many of them faced the threat of a five dollar fine and the loss of a whole month's earnings. Concerned about their livelihood and morally indignant at the fines, the coolies became politically activated. By late September many workers had not only refused to work for the French but had also gone on strike to protest against the colonial authorities' repressive measures. In fact, such measures had inflamed the peo-

ple's initial anti-French sentiment into a popular anticolonial movement with a nationalistic overtone. A confluence of moral indignation and material concern provoked the patriotic social protest movement.

However, the strike soon split the colony's working class. While
many laborers quit work due to fear of mandarin retaliation or patriotic feelings against the French or resentment against the colonial
government's repressive measures or a combination of all these,
many other laborers would rather have stayed at their work to make
a living. To enforce labor solidarity the striking coolies had to use
force to coerce the refractory coolies to join the strike. Among those
intimidated were Hakka sampan people, Hoklo ricksha coolies, as
well as Punti Cantonese butchers and coal coolies. When the police
intervened, riots broke out against Westerners in the streets and
especially against the colonial police. The police shooting into the
crowd causing death and injuries further incensed the angry crowd
against the colonial government.

The strike and riots were led by occupational guild associations
(directed by head boatmen, head cargo coolies, and coolie housekeepers) as well as the Triad societies. The Triads engaged in a wide
variety of acts ranging from frequent petty crimes to occasional patriotic actions against foreign intruders. The Canton authorities sought
to enlist the Triads to fight against France by promising them material rewards and by appealing to their antiforeign patriotism. But not
all actions of the Triad activists were sanctioned by the Canton authorities.

Anti-French patriotic sentiment was prevalent among all classes of
Hong Kong Chinese. However, the Chinese merchants did not lead
the popular protest movement. Though sympathetic with the boat
people who were unjustly fined, the Chinese merchant elite did not
approve of riots in the streets. With strong economic ties to Western
capital, they desired law and order in the colony. When riots broke
out, the merchant elite was eager to cooperate with the colonial
authorities and to serve as mediators to restore law and order.

To adequately explain the origins and significance of the 1884
insurrection, we must take all these causes and circumstances into
consideration.

Chinese Officials' Patriotic Proclamations

The Canton magistrates' proclamations exhorted the Chinese people to "comprehend the distinction between China and a foreign country, and show a devoted regard for your fatherland." The magistrates promised the forgiveness of past offenses and the reward of official ranks to the Chinese who would secretly kill any French commander or destroy French munitions of war. The proclamations threatened death penalty for traitors and punishment for their relatives.[17]

These proclamations were directed particularly at the Chinese "traitors" from the coastal provinces and Southeast Asia who worked for the French for material gains. Some served as spies and informers for the French in Kwangtung, Taiwan, and even Peking. Lured by monetary gains, poor Hoklo fishermen secretly supplied the French vessels off the Fukien coast with rice and other grains. Some Shanghai merchants, using foreign firms as fronts, profitted from providing the French vessels with meat, flour, chicken, eggs, and other provisions. In early 1885 the French recruited in Singapore five or six hundred unemployed Chinese as soldiers, promising each a monthly salary of eighteen dollars. But most of the Chinese working for the French during the war were forced laborers—sampan boat people, fishermen, soldiers, merchants, and others captured by the French fleet on its way to Taiwan. The French enslaved a large number of black people, Vietnamese, and Chinese during the war.[18]

When a French mail steamer visited Yokohama, Japan, in October 1884, twenty-one Chinese workers, "unwilling to serve the enemy," jumped ship to desert; and all Chinese employees of a French warship did the same. The French vessels *Menzaleh* and *Volga* were forced to hire Japanese replacements. Another group of over thirty Chinese enslaved by the French in Keelung, Taiwan, escaped from the French encampment after killing seven overseers. Also in Keelung twenty-five Chinese, suspected of giving information about French troops to the Chinese army, were shot to death by the French.[19] Thus, the Canton newspaper *Shu-pao* reported such incidents concerning both "patriots" and "traitors" among the Chinese. Those who voluntarily worked for the French for material gains were a tiny minority in comparison with the masses in China's southern provinces who rose to attack the French and other foreigners and burned down their churches.

The patriotic mandarin proclamations repeatedly sought to promote popular national awareness of the distinction and hostilities
between China and the French enemy. In ordinary times, the concepts of "Chinese nation" and "patriotism" (i.e., a sense of collective
identity with and loyalty to one's country) were probably quite remote from the coolies' mind in Hong Kong. But in 1884 the French
war acts directly threatened coolies' lives and work. The people's
anti-French patriotic sentiment was aroused by the French threats of
attack on Canton and the Chinese coast where the Hong Kong Chinese
had their homes and families. The French warship interfered with
the junk trade in Hong Kong. On September 14 the French crew
threw overboard eight guns and ammunition of a Chinese trading
junk when it was passing the Chung Chow island bound for Hong
Kong. Chinese junks in Hong Kong were afraid to go out of the
harbor.[20] Wartime hostility caused a "considerable amount of feeling
and enmity" against the French.[21]

Fighting a war against France, the Chinese officials sought to
explore all possible means to defeat the enemy, including an attempt
to coopt the Triads by promising them material rewards and by
appealing to their antiforeign feelings. The Triads came to play an
important role in the Hong Kong strike and riots, which, however,
were unintended by the Chinese officials.

Chinese Magistrates and Triads

There were thousands of Triads in Hong Kong in 1884, mostly confined to the lower class Chinese population. In August, 1884, an
expectant Taotai named Chan Kwai Sze came to Hong Kong to
recruit volunteers for service in the Chinese army. About eight hundred
men consisting mostly of "pirates, robbers, and outlaws" were enlisted, "promised a pardon," and despatched to Canton.[22] According
to Hong Kong police intelligence, about a hundred more Triads were
recruited to Canton on October 6. Some Triad leaders became directors of the disturbances in the colony.[23]

A Chinese detective sergeant working for the Hong Kong police
testified as follows: through the arrangement of Aha and Ayik (two
informers secretly serving the Hong Kong police), the Chinese imperial commissioner of war P'eng Yü-lin interviewed thirteen Triad

members, including some leaders named You Put-in (Pit-yin) and Li A-un (nicknamed Ngan Nga-un). The detective further testified:

> What the Chinese authorities wish these men to do is to set fire to French ships and to find out what houses are supplying the French with provisions. The Chinese government does not wish to harm Hong Kong. But the Triads wish to stir up trouble in the Colony in order to enrich themselves. They stirred up the boat-people in order that they might benefit themselves. . . . The strike arose on account of the fines. . . . Many of the boat-people are members of the Triad Society and are much enraged against the French for attacking their country without reason. They consulted together, and agreed to strike. Ngan Nga-un gave the order.[24]

This testimony gave several factors that combined to cause the unrest. The Triads cooperated with the Chinese officials to discourage the Hong Kong Chinese from working for the French; the Triads wished to stir up trouble, hoping to profit from it; many boat people were Triad members and were "much enraged against the French for attacking their country without reason"; so, they refused to work for the French, and this led to their being fined, which infuriated them and led to strike.

The Hong Kong police received a report that the Canton government plotted to use three thousand dollars to employ some Triads to blow up a French mail steamer in Hong Kong harbor.[25] Pressed by British protestation, the Tsungli Yamen in Peking telegrammed Canton to inquire about the plot. In response, Governor General Chang Chih-tung denied it as a false report, but he confided to the Yamen that a "secret arrangement" was made against French war vessels rather than mail steamers. Chang Chih-tung added that he attempted to "strictly forbid causing disturbances in Hong Kong."[26] While some Triads were in league with Chinese officialdom against France, they remained quite independent and not all of their actions were sanctioned by the Canton authorities.

In fact, the Chinese officials had a number of reasons to desire peace and order in the colony. First, Chang Chih-tung had received foreign newspaper reports on the easing of tensions between France and Germany and on German chancellor Otto von Bismarck's visit to Paris. Chang feared a French coalition with Germany against China. Feeling that China was already diplomatically isolated, Chang would not be eager to stir up turmoil in Hong Kong to antagonize the British.[27] Second, the Chinese officials heavily relied on Hong Kong banking institutions for loans to finance the war against France—a total of 9,144,762 taels from 1883 to 1885.[28] Third, they also relied on Hong Kong for importing a large amount of weapons and munitions ordered from abroad.[29] It was, therefore, most unlikely that the mandarins would incite strikes and riots in Hong Kong at the risk of antagonizing the British and disturbing peaceful trade in the colony.

In fact the Canton authorities feared that turmoil in Hong Kong could adversely affect Kwangtung province. Chang Chih-tung stated most emphatically:

> Canton and Hong Kong are conterminous; they share each other's peace and peril. If coal, rice and flour from Hong Kong do not arrive for ten days, Canton suffers. If cattle, pig and vegetable supplies from the province do not go to Hong Kong for a day, people in Hong Kong become restless. When Hong Kong is in turmoil, the trade routes in the province are blocked. When the province is in disorder, bandits in Hong Kong rise up from all sides. During the Sino-French War, the province was on the alert day and night, and Hong Kong too hurriedly made preparations, water police being constantly vigilant. When Hong Kong is in trouble, we [in Canton] become anxious. If we have problems, neither can Hong Kong rest in peace.[30]

There is no reason to doubt the sincerity of Chang Chih-tung's hope that peace and order would prevail in Hong Kong.

While seeking to enlist some Triads against the French, the Canton officials also feared domestic Triad uprisings. They were apprehensive that the "Triad bandits" in Hong Kong and Hui-chou areas might scheme to join with the French against the Chinese government.[31] In short, the Canton officials were in league with some Triads against the French, but they had no control over the Triad activities in the colony and were on the alert against possible Triad uprisings.

Although the Triads played important roles in instigating the disturbances in Hong Kong, one should not be tempted to attribute the strike and riots solely to the "criminal" Triads. The reality was considerably more complex. It was only when there was already a solid social basis of popular animosity to the colonial authorities that the Triads could successfully instigate a disturbance. Another major source of popular discontent was the poverty and misery of the coolie class.

As the Hong Kong English press admitted, coolies were forced by poverty to live "in places where you would not stable horses in England. . . . Cathedrals, Churches, Chapels, Missions, are a mockery in the midst of the squalid, filthy, crowded houses and narrow streets of this Colony"; it was "a disgrace to humanity."[32] Poverty and misery spawned social discontent and provided a general social context conducive to the unrest.

Again, it is important to note that the Triads were capable of a wide variety of acts, ranging from petty crimes to political revolution. While their criminal actions alienated them from the populace, on other occasions their patriotic motivation gave them popular support.[33] They took an active part in the strike and riots of 1884, gaining popular support in Hong Kong, although the colonial authorities were subsequently able to arrest some of them for deportation.[34]

The Chinese Merchant Elite

Due to racial tensions, many Europeans suspected that some "leading Chinese residents" were directing the rioters. But the Hong Kong administrator W. H. Marsh pointed out that this was very unlikely, as the elite Chinese had "themselves been considerable sufferers from the general interruption to work."[35] In fact, with economic ties to foreign capital, the Chinese elite members were eager to cooperate with the colony's government to end the disturbances. On the day of riots, October 3, when the government decided that British troops should be called, "the Tung Wah Committee at once placed their large hall at the disposal of the troops."[36] Quartering British troops in the Tung Wah buildings was particularly significant, for it showed the readiness of the elite to cooperate with the British authorities in resorting to force in time of crisis. But the following day, as soon as the situation was under control, some elite members began to propose the removal of troops from the Tung Wah buildings. One can imagine the ambivalent feelings of the elite regarding the British military occupation of the Tung Wah, the Chinese civic center and elite power headquarters.

The Chinese elite would much prefer a peaceful settlement of the issue, since they sympathized with and felt moral obligations to the coolies, who were fined by the colonial authorities. By mediating between coolies and government, the elite endeavored to exert their influence to terminate the strike and riots. On October 4 Li Tak Cheung and Ho Amei "summoned" the heads of the boat people and coolies to attend a meeting of the Nam Pak Hong merchants. They also invited acting colonial secretary Frederick Stewart to attend. Li Tak Cheung suggested that he would have been glad if Stewart would give coolies and boat people an assurance that they would not be called on by the government to work for the French. Stewart refused to attend and to give such assurance, because his compliance would have meant giving official recognition to the Chinese merchants' assumption of political and governmental power. The meeting was held without Stewart.[37] About twenty merchants were present who promised the striking coolies and boat people that they would endeavor to induce the colonial government to forgive them and remit the fines. The heads of the coolie houses in return promised to end the strike.[38]

Such was an effort made by some elite Chinese to terminate the strike. But the elite was divided into factions. When the acting registrar general, S. Lockhart, called a meeting on October 4 of the native justices of the peace and naturalized British subjects to discuss how to restore law and order, arrangement was also made for Li Tak Cheung and his friends to attend. The native justices suggested that the government administrator should issue another proclamation. Leung On (comprador) was deputed to draft the proclamation, which would state that "the government, on the intercession of the merchants," had pardoned the rioters, who should therefore resume work. Acting colonial secretary Frederick Stewart objected to these words, because they would imply official recognition of Chinese merchants' political power and influence.[39]

The next point they discussed was the need to arrest and banish the "bad characters" who had instigated the riots. While this subject was under consideration, Li Tak Cheung and a number of his friends arrived. To the British officials' surprise, the native justices and their associates almost immediately left the council chamber. Leung On, who remained, proposed that troops should be removed from the Tung Wah Hospital hall, that the Tung Wah directors and their friends should hold a public meeting after which someone would address the crowd to be assembled at the hospital gates to induce them to end the strike. Again, Frederick Stewart objected, saying that political matters did not in any way concern the Tung Wah

Directors, and that the collecting of a crowd in time of disturbances was undesirable. When it was proposed to issue a proclamation in the name of the Tung Wah directorate, Stewart strongly objected, stating that it "would amount to an abdication on the part of the government and the assumption of governmental power by the Corporation."[40]

Then, Un Sing-ts'un (a merchant of the Tsun Ch'eung Hong) made a speech that made sense to the British officials. He said, "It was the duty of all loyal citizens to cooperate with the government in restoring order and terminating the strike," and that "each person present in his ware-house, his shop, or his household should individually do his utmost to assist the efforts of the government." It was agreed to issue street notices to induce the people back to work.[41]

The two meetings revealed a great deal about sociopolitical relations in the colony. First, when the lower-class Chinese were in revolt, the ambivalence of the British attitude toward the Chinese elite became all the more apparent. The British authorities desired the advice and cooperation of the elite in restoring law and order, yet because of racial tensions they were also apprehensive of the elite's pretension to political power and influence over the Chinese community. Second, while cooperating with the colonial government, the Chinese elite also wished to play the role of community leaders by requesting the government to proclaim that the rioters were pardoned as a result of the elite's representations. But the British authorities were sure of one thing—it was the British, and not the Chinese elite, that ruled the colony.

The vacillation of the Chinese elite in its relations with the colonial government is not difficult to understand. It reflected the predicament of those who served as intermediaries between the populace and colonial government. In order to win the confidence of the colonial government and to end the disturbances hurting their commercial interest the elite had to collaborate with the government, giving it advice regarding the arrest of "bad charactors" and the stationing of troops in the Tung Wah buildings.[42] On the other hand, in order to obtain the trust of the populace and retain their "legitimate" position as community leaders, the elite were obliged to demonstrate their concern for the desires of the populace and to convey these desires to the government. If they succeeded in persuading the government to proclaim that the rioters were pardoned because of the elite's representations, the elite's political influence as community leaders would be greatly enhanced. It was precisely this political influence that the suspicious colonial government tried to discourage and avert while at the same time it paradoxically sought to ask elite groups to use their influence to help end the unrest. Thus, the events of 1884 reveal most vividly the ambivalent relations between the Chinese elite and the colonial government.

Rivalry Between Elite Factions

The elite's meetings described above also revealed the rivalry and tensions between different factions of the Chinese elite: Li Tak Cheung, Ho Amei, and their friends versus some Chinese justices of the peace.[43] All Chinese justices were naturalized British subjects from the commercial elite with close ties to foreign commercial interests; four out of the seven justices were compradors to foreign companies. Their appointment by the colonial government as justices to help maintain peace and order in the colony indicated that they were the Chinese gentlemen most trusted and favored by the British authorities. Two of them were Hoklo (Fukienese), who, together with their Punti (Cantonese) colleagues, cooperated with the British authorities to help keep law and order, which was essential for their business interests. The Chinese merchants' concern with social order and economic interests was a major factor conditioning their actions in times of popular unrest. Chinese commercial firms posted a street notice calling upon the striking workmen to resume work, and expressing grave concern about "the general loss and damage done to every branch of trade by the stoppage of labour."[44] In the meantime, racial and national consciousness remained an important factor of life among the Chinese merchants, and the degree of ethnic feeling among them generally varied according to the individual's social relations with the colonial officials.

Among the elite faction surrounding Li Tak Cheung and Ho Amei, ethnic feeling was strong. Ho Amei condemned the French war vessel's harassment of Chinese trading junks around Hong Kong waters as "an act of piracy."[45] The Chinese elite was also sympathetic with the Chinese boat people, who were unjustly fined by the colonial government for refusing to work for the French. The elite felt moral obligation to intercede with the government on behalf of the boat people, but it disapproved of popular outbursts of strike and riots. Members of the elite faction surrounding Li Tak-cheung also had close economic ties to Western capital, and they too sought to cooperate with the British authorities to restore law and order in the colony. Ho Amei was the manager of the On Tai Insurance Co., Ltd., with offices in Praya West, the scene of riots on October 3. Li Tak Cheung served on the board of directors of the Chinese Insurance Company, Ltd., which included William Reiners, E.R. Belilios, and H. Foss, with J. B. Smith as the company's secretary.[46] Thus, like his rivals among the Chinese justices, Li Tak Cheung was closely tied to foreign capitalist interests in the colony. As a businessman and a director of an insurance company in partnership with prominent European merchants, Li Tak Cheung naturally desired law and order in Hong Kong.

Essentially the two rival elite factions were competing with each other for political influence with the Chinese community and with the colonial authorities. In comparison with Ho Kai and other naturalized British subjects who were appointed as justices, Li Tak Cheung and Ho Amei did not find as much personal favor with the colonial government. They had not forgotten that their application on behalf of the Wa Hop Telegraph Company for permission to lay a cable from Kowloon to Hong Kong was rejected in 1882 by the government on ethnic grounds—a Chinese company controlling the telegraphic communication "might under certain circumstances be a source of serious danger."[47] Consequently, Li Tak Cheung and Ho Amei could not help bearing a grudge against the British authorities.

The European community, in return, was suspicious of Li Tak Cheung and Ho Amei because of their connection with the Chinese officialdom in Kwangtung. They had been involved with the circulation of mandarin proclamations in the colony in support of the war against France.[48] Ho Amei had sent several telegrams to the Canton authorities to report on French movements around Hong Kong.[49] As we have seen, Viceroy Chang Chih-tung desired peace and order in Hong Kong; hence he sent a telegram to the Hong Kong gentry merchants asking them to exhort the striking workers "to stop within the limit of what is appropriate,"[50] implying that some measure of unrest such as a strike against the French was alright but that street riot was inappropriate.

Li Tak Cheung's and Ho Amei's ties with the Chinese authorities were based not merely on ethnic and patriotic considerations but also on economic interests. Hong Kong merchants often sought Chinese official connections to protect their business and property in China. Ho Amei was the owner and manager of the Tam Chow [Silver] Mine near Canton (whose European staff had to be withdrawn during the war time due to Chinese ill-feeling against the French and other Europeans).[51] Li Tak Cheung and Ho Amei's Wa Hop Telegraph Company had been sanctioned by the Kwangtung government, with an initial capital of three hundred thousand dollars in 1882. All its promoters were Chinese, including Hong Kong and Canton merchants and Kwangtung officials.[52] When popular disturbances broke out in Hong Kong, Kwangtung officials naturally became concerned. Viceroy Chang Chih-tung asked Li Tak-cheung and Ho Amei to ensure that the Hong Kong populace would "stop within the limit of what was appropriate." This coincided with Li Tak Cheung's and Ho Amei's wishes. Both men had other important commercial interests in Hong Kong, such as insurance companies that were closely tied to Western capital, so they too desired peace and order in the colony.

Incipient Popular Patriotism: Its Scope and Limitations

The Hong Kong working people had been divided by rivalry and hostility between dialect groups. Yet when their common interest was threatened by an outside force (e.g., colonial government, and foreign intruders), many of them would come together to take common actions.

In ordinary times, in their daily struggle to earn a living, the concepts of "imperialism," "patriotism," and "Chinese nationalism" were probably quite remote from the workers' mind. But in 1884 several factors combined to arouse an elementary sense of Chinese patriotism among the populace in the colony: the French threats of attack on Canton and the Chinese coast where the Hong Kong Chinese had their homes and families; the French war acts and the colonial government's repressive measures threatening the laborers' lives and work; the mandarin proclamations exhorting people to patriotism; and the colony's merchant elite circulating such proclamations that were also published in the Chinese popular press. All these combined to arouse among the working people a vague sense of collective identity with the Chinese nation against the French enemy.

In his report to the Colonial Office in London, Governor George Bowen testified to the emergence of "popular nationalism" in the colony. He stated that at the time of Britain's previous war with China in 1858 the southern Chinese cared little for Peking in the north, so that there was no difficulty in raising at Hong Kong a corps of more than two thousand coolies to act as porters to the allied English and French expedition against Peking. "But now all is changed. The Chinese artisans, coolies, and boatmen refused all offers of pay to do any work whatsoever for the French ships at Hong Kong." Governor Bowen attributed this change to the establishment of a vernacular press, the opening up of rapid communication between the north and south of China by steamers and telegraphs, and, above all, the irritating and yet indecisive hostilities of the French at various points along the coast. All these had combined with "other causes" to awaken a common national spirit among the Chinese people.[53]

The Canton officials worked hard to enhance patriotism by exhorting the Chinese to "comprehend the distinction between China and a foreign country, and show a devoted regard for [their] fatherland" by helping to defeat the enemy and protect their homes and relatives. The "other causes," which Governor Bowen did not specify, included precisely those measures adopted by the colonial authorities to suppress that patriotic feeling—measures such as the prosecution of Chinese newspaper editors who published mandarin proclamations, the imposition of fines on the boat people who refused to work for the French, and the police shooting the crowd causing death and injury.

The vernacular press indeed began to play an important role in promoting popular national awareness. Chinese newspapers published in Hong Kong and Canton had avidly carried battlefield reports and propagated the cause of patriotism. News of French attacks on Foochow and Formosa and of the valor of the Chinese Black Flag forces helped to rouse national awareness among the populace. On August 25 a report was widely circulated and credited among the Chinese in Hong Kong that the French steamer *Nam Vian* had been captured by a Chinese gunboat. The destruction of the Foochow arsenal by the French was at first believed by many Chinese to be a foreign invention, for it contradicted their will to believe in the Chinese officials' announcement that the French fleet had been ignominiously thrashed. Indeed, a broadsheet illustrating the alleged disaster inflicted upon the French ships was offered for sale in Hong Kong streets.[54] A pictorial from Shanghai, *Tien-shih-chai hua-pao*, published pictures of battle scenes that appealed to the illiterate and semiliterate.[55] Sun Yat-sen, then a student at the Hong Kong Government Central School, "heard stories told in the rice- and tea-shops of the great success of Chinese arms." And "the populace embraced these delusions joyfully."[56]

The war evoked a sense of patriotism among all classes of Chinese overseas. The Hong Kong Chinese community subscribed to a fund for purchasing two big cannons from England reportedly costing over forty thousand dollars to help strengthen coastal defense in Kwangtung. Patriotic Chinese residents in Osaka and Kōbe also raised five thousand dollars to help China's coastal defense.[57] Chinese merchants in Singapore opened a subscription for the same purpose. And a party of French officers was attacked by "the Chinese of lower order" in Singapore.[58]

The Hong Kong people's lives were affected by the war. For a few days in late August and early September the river steamers on their trips down from Canton were crowded with "terror-stricken natives" fleeing to Hong Kong for fear of a French attack on Canton. A large number of what the English press called "rowdy characters, strangers and refugees" who had been evicted from Foochow, Canton, and other cities, flocked to the colony.[59] Their presence in Hong Kong increased the people's awareness that their own well-being depended on the well-being of the Chinese nation. An eyewitness to the events, young Sun Yat-sen felt encouraged by the patriotism of the Hong Kong dock workers who refused to repair the damaged French vessels, docked in Hong Kong from campaigns in Foochow and Formosa.

Under these circumstances the colonial government's imposition of fines on ten boat people served to bring large numbers of the working people together in opposition. To a working coolie in Hong Kong in 1884 a fine of five dollars was equal to his earnings for a whole month. Any coolie who refused to work for the French could suffer the same fate. The confluence of moral indignation and concern with livelihood prompted coolies to action. The excitement was further exasperated by the police shooting the Chinese crowd, causing death and injuries.

The convergence of all these factors provoked a labor strike with a nationalistic overtone. National awareness was fused with local concerns with family safety and livelihood to propel popular action. The boat people were infuriated by the fines and "much enraged against the French for attacking their country without reason."[60] They posted a proclamation in Queen's Road protesting the fines and imploring the Chinese merchant elite to "be good enough to assist us with the strength of one arm in order that we may not be laughed at by the French."[61] Self-interest was fused with patriotism in the coolie labor strike. To the English police constable Denis Delargy, a Chinese butcher named Wong Aleung said in pidgin English: "Hei Yah!—you thinkee Fan Kwai [foreign devils] can fight Chinaman?" Turning to the admiring crowd of "Chinamen" on the Recreation Ground, Wong Aleung incited them to *ta fan kwei* (strike the foreign devil).[62]

Patriotic protest against foreign invasions was not confined to the working people, although they constituted the major force in the strike and riots. The rioters arrested by the police consisted mostly of the lower classes, including a carpenter, a servant, a coolie, an earth coolie, a butcher, a boy, an unlicensed hawker, a coal coolie, a restaurant waiter, a tailor, fishmongers, and two shopmen. A shopkeeper named Leong Ahung was charged with throwing stones at a European riding in a ricksha along Queen's Road West.[63] Viceroy Chang Chih-tung's informers in Hong Kong reported to him that shopkeepers and their employees in the Western district of the town closed their shops to join the strike.[64] But after three days of riots, many shopkeepers, merchants and property owners were getting impatient with the tumult. A meeting of the *kaifong* (street neighborhood) leaders resolved to post notices all along the Praya on October 5 calling on the striking coolies to resume work and create no more disturbances.[65] The strike and riots were largely a working people's movement.

But labor solidarity had its limitations, for the activists had to use force to coerce many reluctant and refractory workers to join and continue the strike. Those who were intimidated included the Hoklo chair coolies and ricksha coolies, the Hakka sampan people, as well as the Punti Cantonese coolies. While large numbers of workers joined the strike and riots, many others remained passive and reluctant participants in the event. Nevertheless, for the large numbers of workers who engaged in the strike and riots and who attacked the police and Europeans in the streets, the differences of dialect or occupation had largely, though only temporarily, faded into the background.

It is significant that neither looting nor wanton destruction of property took place during the riots.[66] Rather, the excited crowd directed their anger at specifically selected targets—the French merchant Vincenot's store and the *fankwei*. Also selected for attack was the store of Wing Kee, a ship comprador providing coal for foreign vessels. Chinese Christians were "afraid to come out of their dwellings on account of the threats and insults addressed to them."[67] Notices were circulated among the Chinese employees of foreign residents calling on them to cease work or face penalties.[68] The Triads wanted to attack the government office, the Hong Kong and Shanghai Banking Corporation, and the Victoria jail where about one hundred Triad members were held prisoners; but the planned attack was not carried out because of a lack of arms.[69]

The people's hostility towards the French was extended toward the British colonial authorities, which attempted to suppress the expression of anti-French sentiment. The Chinese crowd spit upon the British troops patrolling in the streets of Hong Kong and threw stones at them. Such indignities to the British imperial forces were something hitherto unheard of in China, the British military commander complained.[70]

Antagonism against the French persisted among the working people in Hong Kong after the riots had subsided. As late as November, when order had been restored, riot ringleaders had been banished, and hundreds of Triads had left the colony as a result of the proclamation of the Peace Preservation Ordinance,[71] they still refused to work for the French Messageries Maritime Company. The cargo brought on by the steamer *Saghalien* a month earlier could not be landed.[72] The strikers and rioters had attained their purpose—the right to refuse to work for the French.

The strike and riots were largely a working people's movement, led by head coolies, head boatmen, coolie housekeepers and Triads. These coolie leaders subsequently organized a legal defense for those arrested, engaging four lawyers (Ho Kai and three Europeans) for the defense of the arrested coolies in law court.[73] Coolie leaders had promised to end the strike if the Chinese elite (who served as intermediaries) would induce the colonial authorities to forgive the arrested coolies and remit the fines.[74] However, their request was denied. Eager to end the disturbances affecting the Chinese merchant elite's commercial interest, and eager to fulfill its moral obligation to the lower class coolies, the Tung Wah directorate reportedly repaid the fines inflicted on the cargo boat people.[75] At the same time, the elite sought to strengthen the District Watch patrol of the Praya to help maintain law and order.[76]

It is important to note that cooperation with the British authorities to terminate popular unrest in Hong Kong did not necessarily mean a lack of Chinese "patriotism" on the part of the Chinese merchant elite. Patriotism could be expressed in different ways. As long as there were different views regarding what was in the best interest of the nation, there would be different kinds of patriots and nationalists, including "populist nationalists," "elitist nationalists," and what might be paradoxically called "collaborationist patriots" (that is, those who collaborated with and rendered service to imperialism under certain historical circumstances in the hope of eventually building a strong nation to resist imperialism).[77] As we shall see in chapter 6, collaborationist patriotism was prevalent in Hong Kong during the period under study. With strong economic ties to Western capitalism, the Chinese merchants in Hong Kong in 1884 did not regard the popular outbursts of strikes and riots as "valid" expressions of Chinese patriotism.

The lower-class Triads took an important part in the anticolonial movement in 1884.[78] Yet, the Triads could engage in both political revolt and nonpolitical criminal actions, often blurring the distinction between the two. In fact, in ordinary times, the Triads' criminal actions were frequently directed against members of the working people.[79] Hence the Triads could not organize the workers into a solidarity group to act politically in pursuing and defending their common interests on a constant and permanent basis.

The events of 1884 in Hong Kong are significant, not only for what they revealed about the nature of British rule and social tensions in the colony but for what they also demonstrated about the capacity of the Hong Kong people to become politically activated. The popular insurrection in 1884 left a lasting impression on the colonial government, which was now determined to impose more direct political control over the Chinese community. The interventionist government sought to accelarate political integration in the aftermath of these events.

In 1884 popular nationalism was in its incipient stage of development: the people of Hong Kong had just begun to show some vague awareness of China as a nation-state at war with the French, who had the sympathy of the British and other *fankwei*. When that awareness was fused with their concern about the colonial government's repressive measures threatening their livelihood, the people were aroused to action.

Incipient popular nationalism aroused in 1884 proved ephemeral, however. Local issues affecting the working people's livelihood remained of primary importance to them. Issues of national import, if not aligned with local issues, had little appeal to the common people and were merely incidental to their lives. From the aftermath of the Sino-French War to the end of the nineteenth century, the elitist nationalists from among the merchants and intelligentsia could hardly win over the colony's working people to the nationalist causes under their auspices.

Coolie Unrest and Elitist Nationalism, 1887–1900

> *If England suffers, the greatest volume of our trade being with that country, we shall be sufferers to the same extent. . . . China's army should be organized under the English.*   —Ho Tung, comprador
>
> *The existence of a body of 20,000 coolies—lusty coolies—in Hong Kong, disaffected and armed with their formidable bamboo poles . . . is a direct menace to the Colony.*
> —Granville Sharp, an English merchant

Nationalism: Its Complex Nature, Manifestations, and Historiography

Nationalism is a powerful force in the history of the modern world. Its manifestations are sometimes beneficial and constructive and sometimes malignant and destructive to humanity—particularly in the twentieth century when advanced science and technology produce dreadful tools and weapons for the assertion of power by the government of one nation against another, and even against its own dissident citizens. As a powerful sociopolitical force, nationalism can sometimes inspire loving care for one's neighbors and benign patriotic feelings for the nation. But it can also provoke wars among nations, and create in belligerent countries an intellectually stifling war climate, with thousands of mindless flag-waving crowds clamoring for violence and more violence, as in the recent war between Iraq and the United States. With such awesome power for both construction and destruction, it is not surprising that nationalism has been subject to voluminous studies for many decades by scholars in various fields and disciplines, including Hans Kohn, Carlton Hayes, Karl Deutsch, and Eric J. Hobsbawm, among many others.[1]

Nationalism is extremely complex in nature. When fused with different concerns and ideologies it takes different forms, such as liberal nationalism, conservative nationalism, totalitarian nationalism, cultural nationalism, economic nationalism, elitist nationalism, populist nationalism, and so forth.[2] "My country, right or wrong!"— this assertion reflects only one kind of nationalism, a conservative and irrational one. But there are many other kinds contradicting it.

In this study nationalism is defined as a sense of collective identity with and loyalty to one's nation-state. National consciousness means that members of a given nationality become aware of their interrelationship with their conationals who together constitute a social group distinct from all others. Nationalism often presumes some prior community of territory, language, ethnicity, and culture, which may be called the "objective" basis for the existence of nationality. But more important, nationalism as a state of mind also involves "subjective" and conscious human effort and creation. In other word, the emergence of national consciousness is not an automatic result of some objective static elements that compose a nation. Rather, "creative political action is required to transform a segmented and disunited population into a coherent nationality," as Geoff Eley asserts. "Nationality is best conceived as a complex, uneven and unpredictable *process*, forged from an interaction of cultural coalescence and specific political intervention, which cannot be reduced to static criteria of language, territory, ethnicity or culture."[3]

Just as nationalism in early nineteenth-century Europe "was very much a movement of intellectuals rather than masses,"[4] so nationalism in China during the latter half of the nineteenth century was at first a movement of literati-officials and other members of the intelligentsia (i.e., educated persons aspiring to independent thinking and capable of forming public opinion, such as professionals, businessmen, journalists, teachers, students, etc.). In the creative process of transforming segmented and disunited population into a coherent nationality, members of the intelligentsia often played a leading role, for they were the first to become politicized by the crises China confronted.

In the historiography of Chinese nationalism a very influential interpretation stresses the dichotomy of culturalism (loyalty to traditional Chinese culture symbolized by the dynastic emperor) versus modern nationalism (loyalty to the nation-state), which is said to have emerged during the 1890s. In his classic work, entitled *Modern China and Its Confucian Past*, Joseph Levenson maintains that nationalism emerged "when the Chinese nation began to supersede Chinese culture as the focal point of loyalty."[5] Benjamin Schwartz aptly points out that Chinese cultural tradition was not a monolithic entity; nevertheless, he asserts that one had to make a choice of priority "between the preservation of the state and the preservation of basic Confucian values" before one became a nationalist.[6] This definition of a nationalist is so demanding and restrictive that it excludes large numbers of Chinese, during the latter half of the nineteenth century, who developed some sense of patriotism and national consciousness while still remained loyal to the dynasty and committed to many traditional values.

Foreign war was an important agency in provoking patriotism and national consciousness. Mary Rankin's point is well taken: "Resting upon people's impulses to defend their territory, possessions, social power, or political structure against foreign attack, it [patriotism] did not require any fundamental change in values" or "unambiguously transferring their loyalty from the dynasty to a Chinese nation-state."[7] To illustrate, Liu Kwang-ching portrays Li Hung-chang as a "Confucian patriot," loyal to the Manchu dynasty, concerned with both the maintenance of his own power and the security and independence of China as a country.[8] David Pong also characterizes Governor General Shen Pao-chen as a "Confucian patriot."[9] Daniel Bays depicts Chang Chih-tung as a "bureaucratic nationalist" who always identified himself "as part of the central dynastic apparatus of government," and "was actually rather effective in dealing with foreigners and promoting China's interests."[10] John Schrecker demonstrates how at the turn of the twentieth century the governors of Shantung Yüan Shih-k'ai, Chow Fu, and Yang Shih-hsiang successively labored to defend the territorial integrity of the province against German imperialism, and how a new nationalistic foreign policy was adopted by the Ch'ing imperial court after 1900 to defend China's sovereignty.[11]

Foreign intrusion politicized not only the Chinese officials but also the literati outside the bureaucracy, including the gentry merchants and gentry managers on the Chinese mainland and merchants and intelligentsia in Hong Kong and the treaty ports. The Sino-French War (1884–85) and the Sino-Japanese War (1894–95) prompted them to advocate Westernizing reforms to strengthen China to resist foreign imperialism. Most of them were "elitist nationalists," who basically distrusted the common people and had no faith in the mass mobilization for national reconstruction envisioned by the twentieth-century "populist nationalists" like Li Ta-chao and Mao Tse-tung. The Sino-French war provided an occasion for the outbreak of a popular insurrection in Hong Kong that acquired a nationalistic overtone: the riotous populace showed some vague awareness of China as a sovereign nation-state at war with the French enemy. But the merchant elite disapproved of the social unrest and did not regard street riots as a "valid" expression of patriotism.

My purpose here is to illustrate the very complex nature of nationalism, which historically manifested itself in different ways and took many different forms. To a large extent, nationalism reflected the subjective human consciousness of nationality. As long as there were different views regarding what was in the best interest of the nation, there would be different kinds of patriots and nationalists: "liberal nationalists," who advocated liberal reforms to strengthen the nation; "conservative nationalists," who wished to use authoritarian means to strengthen the country; "Confucian cultural nationalists," who sought to use Confucian cultural tradition for national regeneration; what I shall call "collaborationist nationalists," who collaborated with the imperialists at the sacrifice of some sovereign rights in the hope of eventually building a strong nation to resist imperialist aggression.

The paradoxical nature of the collaborationist nationalists is quite obvious. Let us look at some examples. To the Kuomintang nationalists Yüan Shih-k'ai was a "traitor" to the Chinese nation. But as Ernest P. Young shows, Yüan was a genuine "nationalist" in his own way, adopting "a strategy of selling out some part of his country's sovereignty in order, ultimately, to defend that same sovereignty."[12] Similarly, Wang Ching-wei collaborated with the Japanese invaders in 1940–45, partly out of "patriotic" intentions. Concerned about the welfare of the Chinese people in the Japanese-occupied areas, and driven by defeatism to conclude that China could never win the war, he set up a puppet government in Nanking, hoping that China would be better off as a member of the "new order in East Asia" under the wing of a modernizing Japan. To the Japanese, Wang Ching-wei made the following proclamation:

What I ask the Japanese people to understand is that for the Chinese, the argument for peace [with Japan] is an expression of patriotic spirit and the argument for resisting Japan is also an expression of patriotic spirit. Anyone who has either of these beliefs loves his country and desires the prosperity of the people. Therefore the difference between these two theories of peace and resistance to Japan is caused by diferences in understanding of Sino-Japanese relations in the Far East. It is impossible for Japan to correct, by using military power alone, the understanding of those who believe in resisting Japan. I want you to understand that the best means for the Japanese to change their policies is through changing their [Japanese] own policies.[13]

In a wartime situation peace advocates who vote their conscience against war are not necessarily less "patriotic" than those who hold an opposing view. This was true during the *ch'ing-i* (pure discussion) debate over the Sino-French War (1884–85), and during the two Sino-Japanese wars. No one had a monopoly over patriotism, which could be expressed in different ways. Patriotism could be a divisive as well as a mobilizing force.

Thus, both Yüan Shih-k'ai and Wang Ching-wei were collaborationist nationalists. Similarly, as we shall see, a number of merchants and professionals in Hong Kong became collaborationist nationalists in the late nineteenth and early twentieth centuries, although under different historical circumstances and with different visions for the Chinese nation-state.

Nationalism did not merely have political and cultural dimensions; it also had a socioeconomic one. It is important to examine the social basis of nationalism's appeal. In his essay on nationalism and social history, Geoff Eley forcefully argues for "the need to re-situate the historiography of nationalism in a strong context of socioeconomic analysis."[14] This study is an attempt to do so.

Nationalism took many different forms. But why did some people subscribe to liberal nationalism, while others turned to conservative nationalism? Why did prominent merchants in Hong Kong become collaborationist nationalists? And why did elitist nationalism appeal more to the social elite and less to the masses? A socioeconomic analysis may help to answer these questions. Chinese elitist nationalists in modern times often demanded that a citizen must put his or her priority on devotion to the state above all other concerns, and that he or she must be "selfless" and "disinterested," transcending and even sacrificing self-interests for the common good of the nation. Were these elitist nationalists themselves always "disinterested"? Would a disinterested and transcendental concept of nationalism appeal to the ordinary people? This chapter attempts to answer some of these questions.

As indicated in our discussion of the Chinese community in chapter 3, because of population growth and economic expansion during the period from the mid-1880s to the 1900s the colonial society became more heterogeneous and community consensus became more difficult to obtain. A new generation of merchants, businessmen, professionals, and intelligentsia emerged in Hong Kong, a generation more Western-oriented and more closely tied to Western capital than the old elite, and more inclined to innovations and new commitments. It was a generation progressively politicized by main currents of affairs in China.

During the last two decades of the nineteenth century, a series of important events occurred in China—the Sino-French War (1884–85), the Sino-Japanese War (1894–95), the Hundred Days' Reform of 1898, the imperialist powers' "scramble for concessions," the British occupation of the New Territories in 1899, and the Boxer uprising in 1900. These events aroused nationalistic responses from the new generation of Chinese merchants, professionals, and intelligentsia in Hong Kong. Ho Kai and Hu Li-yüan established their fame as advocates of reforms in China. With strong economic ties to foreign capital in the colony, some prominent merchants in Hong Kong expressed collaborationist patriotism in reaction to the "scramble for concessions" in China. Some members of the Westernized intelligentsia, inspired by nationalism and republicanism, organized the Hsing-Chung-hui revolutionary society, seeking to use the British colony as a base for revolution against the Manchus.

This chapter seeks to explain why the elitist nationalists in Hong Kong won little support from the colony's working people for the nationalist causes in 1887–1900. These years witnessed three incidents of coolie unrest—the 1888 boatmen's strike, the 1894 coolie feud, and the 1895 coolie strike. In these instances the coolies' primary concerns were local issues relating to their livelihood. The immediate economic interest and mundane needs were of primary importance to the laborers in their daily struggle to earn a living. But the elitist nationalists from among the merchants and intelligentsia often failed to address the local issues relating to the workers' pressing social needs and economic problems. A large gap separated the elitist patriots from coolies. I will first examine the elitist nationalist responses to the events in China in 1887–1900.

Nationalist Responses to the Sino-French War and the Sino-Japanese War

The Sino-French War (1884–85) roused a wave of popular antiforeignism in the southern provinces of China from Chekiang to Fukien, Taiwan, Kwangtung, and Yün-nan. It also aroused nationalist responses from the Chinese literati and officials. For about two decades prior to the war a handful of the Chinese literati (such as Feng Kuei-fen, Kuo Sung-tao, Ma Chien-chung, Cheng Kuan-ying, Wang T'ao, and Chang Tzu-mu) had become critical of China's "self-strengthening" policy for its narrow focus on Western techniques and had advocated institutional reforms to strengthen China. But prior to the Sino-French War such criticism was faint and sporadic. The Sino-French War was a turning point for the reform movement in China. The war stimulated *ch'ing-i* (pure discussion), that is, critical and theoretically disinterested discussion of national affairs. It marked an important stage in the formation and evolution of public opinion leading to a nationalistic, reformist movement.

The Canton newspaper *Shu-pao* abounded with articles calling for reforms to strengthen the country against foreign aggressions. In January 1885 one such article advocated in most unequivocal terms the adoption of Western style parliamentary government and freedom of the press.[15] The year 1887 saw the publication of Ho Kai's and Hu Li-yüan's reformist essays as well as Wang T'ao's essay "On Foreign Armaments and Techniques." They advocated reforms of governmental institutions, and forcefully challenged the Ch'ing government's "self-strengthening" policy. In 1888 the reformer K'ang Yu-wei presented his "First Memorial to the Emperor," calling for sweeping reforms of government.[16]

Some of these reform advocates came from Hong Kong. Wang T'ao (1828–97) was cofounder and editor-in-chief of *Hsun-huan jih-pao* in Hong Kong from 1874 until 1884.[17] Hu Li-yüan (1847–1916) was a scholar from a merchant family in the colony. In 1887 Hu and Ho Kai jointly published an essay criticizing Tseng Chi-tse (China's minister to England and France 1878–86) for his espousal of the "self-strengthening" policy.[18] Ho and Hu argued that the real cause of China's troubles lay not so much in its military weakness as in its "loose morality and evil habits, both social and political." The true foundation of every truly great nation was "equitable rule and right government."[19] "The government which is accepted by the public opinion will flourish, and that which is rejected by the public opinion will soon see disorder."[20] Ho and Hu used the Mencian idea of the "primacy of the people" to justify institutional reforms at a time when China's power holders were preoccupied with ships, guns, and military defense. Thus, in 1887 Ho and Hu pioneered a line of thought to be loudly espoused in the late 1890s by other reformers such as Yen Fu, K'ang Yu-wei, and Liang Ch'i-ch'ao.

The futility of the "self-strengthening" movement predicted by Ho and Hu in 1887 was fully exposed during the Sino-Japanese War (1894–95), a landmark in the evolution of Chinese public opinion supporting a nationalist, reformist movement. The dictated peace at Shimonoseki was considered by many literati both within and outside the official bureaucracy as a national humiliation. A nationally conscious public opinion developed, demanding continuation of war with Japan and institutional reforms to save China. Patriotic scholars like K'ang Yu-wei, Liang Ch'i-ch'ao, and Yen Fu began to organize "study societies" (*hsüeh-hui*) and publish journals and newspapers advocating governmental reforms and reevaluation of traditional ideas and values to strengthen the country. The two Hong Kong reformist writers Ho Kai and Hu Li-yüan, again, joined the Chinese nationalist reformist movement.

Hu Li-yüan had been in Kôbe and Osaka, Japan, since July 1893, probably on a business trip in connection with a coal shop owned by his brother in Hong Kong. He stayed in Japan for two years, until the end of the Sino-Japanese war. While in Japan, he witnessed a strong sense of nationalism and chauvinism among the Japanese populace aroused by the war. He reported that almost the entire nation was united behind their government in the war effort. This made very strong impression on him. He also witnessed the Meiji constitution and parliament at work and became convinced that Japan was strengthened by her parliamentary government. Corresponding with Ho Kai in Hong Kong, Hu Li-yüan discussed the crisis confronting China. The two men observed the progress of the war with dismay, for China suffered one defeat after another in battles, both on land and at sea.[21] They jointly produced a pamphlet titled "Discourse on the New Government." Its fame "is so widespread in China that the first edition is exhausted and a fresh edition is being put through the press as rapidly as possible," reported The *China Mail*.[22] This reflected the sense of crisis and urgency prevalent among the Chinese literary public at the time.

Ho Kai and Hu Li-yüan observed that in wartime Japan, "the military and civilians are in concerted harmony," and "the sovereign and people with one heart"—"thanks to the effects of the parliament."[23] The parliament opened the "channel of expression" through which the people's views and opinions could reach the sovereign. Herein lay the secret of unity and strength of the Japanese nation.[24] Although Cheng Kuan-ying (c. 1841–1923) and Ch'en Chih (d. 1899) were the first well-known reformers in China to advocate representative institutions, their thoughts about this were fragmentary.[25] In comparison, Ho and Hu's "Discourse" in 1894–95 presented the most elaborated reform proposal for representative institutions up to that date; and it was also more "advanced,"[26] as it called for a thorough reorganization of government, including the creation of a "responsible cabinet."[27] To make their views respectable in the eyes of China's scholar-officials, they couched their reform ideas in Confucian terms. The Mencian doctrine of "the primacy of the people," with its emphasis on the people as the most important element of the state, reinforced their belief in the Lockeian theories of social contract and popular sovereignty, resulting in an intellectual synthesis of their ideas.[28]

Ho and Hu's reformist thought was shaped not merely by wartime crisis and Hu's experience in Japan but also by their social backgrounds and personal experiences in the British colony of Hong Kong. Their backgrounds were similar in a number of ways, so that they came to hold many identical or virtually identical political views. Both were inspired by Western classical liberalism as formulated by the liberal thinker John Locke, Enlightenment *philosophes* Adam Smith and Montesquieu, and Utilitarians Jeremy Bentham and John Stuart Mill. Ho Kai went to Britain for studies in 1873, when the bourgeois ethos of the mid-Victorian era still permeated the island nation, and he left England in 1882 (with medical and law degrees), just before laissez-faire liberalism began to face the serious challenge of trade unions and socialist movements. Impressed by Britain's wealth and power, Ho Kai came to value Britain's liberal tradition, which stressed individual rights, free trade, industrialism, and constitutionalism.

Hu Li-yüan, a bicultural scholar-merchant, was inspired by the same tradition of Western classical liberalism. Though he did not go to England, he acquired a mastery of the English language in Hong Kong, writing excellent English.[29] He served from 1879 to 1881 on the translating staff of Wang T'ao's newspaper *Hsun-huan jih-pao*. In 1885 he assisted the comprador Lo Hok Pang to found the journal *Yüeh-pao*. In his Chinese writings we find references to Western personalities like Francis Bacon, René Descartes, Isaac Newton, Montesquieu, Immanuel Kant, Queen Victoria, and "eminent Victorians" such as Charles Darwin, Thomas Huxley, J. S. Mill, Herbert Spencer, and William Gladstone.[30]

In short, both Ho Kai and Hu Li-yüan found inspiration in classical liberalism, which was believed to be the foundation of Britain's wealth and power. Another scholar steeped in the British tradition of classical liberalism was Yen Fu, who expressed similar liberal reformist thought. Yen Fu had studied in England, had access to British political writings, and was able to come up with similar views about the "people's rights" and parliamentary government. Yet, Ho Kai and Hu Li-yüan, living in Hong Kong, had opportunities to experience liberal political philosophy in action, which made liberal government more real in Hong Kong than in China. As a legislative councillor for fourteen years, Ho Kai had a singular opportunity to actively participate in the free discussion and debate on numerous issues presented before the "law-making" legislative council. With business experience in Hong Kong, the Chinese businessmen tended to conceive of the polity of an organized state as something similar to a joint-stock company, in which important decisions were made by shareholders in a democratic way. All these deepened the Hong Kong liberal reformers' conviction about the soundness of the liberal democratic principle.

In the late Ch'ing period the intellectuals who had lived in Hong

Kong were among the first Chinese to acquire new Western knowledge. Personal experiences in Hong Kong provided the shock of self-discovery that made Wang T'ao, Cheng Kuan-ying, Ho Kai, and Hu Li-yüan pioneers of modern Chinese thinking. Their contact with modern Western culture stimulated them to critically reexamine some elements of Chinese culture and traditions. They provided much information about Western learning for other Chinese reformers like K'ang Yu-wei and Liang Ch'i-ch'ao who had scant knowledge of the English language.

Life-long residence in Hong Kong made Ho Kai's and Hu Li-yüan's reformist thought representative of a Hong Kong commercial perspective. Classical liberalism appealed to Ho and Hu not only because of its intrinsic value. It was also congenial to their commercial and professional interests and aspirations. Living in the bourgeoning city of Hong Kong, the Westernized barrister and doctor Ho Kai and the scholar-merchant Hu Li-yüan fared well under the protection of British colonial government. They came to admire and advocate British liberal political institutions and capitalist economic system as models for China. They found Lockeian liberal thought (with its emphasis on man's "natural rights" to life, liberty, and property) particularly congenial to their tastes and interests.

Ho Kai and Hu Li-yüan as Spokesmen for Patriotic Merchants in Hong Kong and Overseas

During the eventful years of 1898–1900, Ho and Hu coauthored seven more reformist essays. In 1901 their collected works were reprinted in Shanghai, entitled *Hsin-cheng chen-ch'üan* (The true meaning of the new government). The two essayists from Hong Kong helped to promote the Chinese reform movement. They exposed the corruption, inefficiency, and oppression of China's gentry-dominated ruling bureaucracy. They insisted that merchants and businessmen were the backbone of the nation, commercialism the road to the nation's wealth and power, and capitalist private enterprise the best way to develop China's economy. Thus, they equated the merchants' interest with the nation's interest—what was best for the merchants was best for the state. They advocated a thorough reorganization of China's government, with a ministry of commerce taking the leading position. They demanded that merchants and overseas Chinese businessmen should have the right to serve as government officials and the people's representatives.[31]

Ho and Hu's essays represented a commercial perspective from Hong Kong. In expressing the merchants' political demands, Ho's and Hu's reformist ideas were more explicit and undisguised than Cheng Kuan-ying's, which similarly "reflected the views of the newly emerged merchants in the treaty ports."[32] It was characteristic of the Western-oriented intelligentsia from the commercial background in late Ch'ing times to assert the merchants' social and political demands in the name of patriotism. In advocating parliamentary democracy and commercial capitalism, they were motivated by both a public, nationalist concern for China's wealth and power, and a private concern for the merchants' interests. They wished to change the existing sociopolitical order dominated by the gentry-scholar-officials who represented the bureaucratic state, and to promote simultaneously the national interests and merchants' interests.

Ho and Hu had to contend with Governor General Chang Chih-tung, who, in his famous work *Ch'üan-hsüeh p'ien* (Exhortation to learning, 1898), denounced the "people's rights" as incompatible with the Confucian ethics of "three bonds" and "five constant virtues."[33] The radical doctrine of the people's rights and parliamentary government challenged the existing social and political order dominated by the established gentry-scholar-officials who held a privileged position sanctioned by classics and history. Chang Chih-tung and other members of the established elite (such as the famous classicist Wang Hsien-ch'ien, 1842–1918, and his disciple Yeh Te-hui), sought to defend the Confucian "three bonds" and "five constant virtues"; these ethics served to prop up the existing order, thereby safeguarding their established interests, which they, too, equated with the nation's interests.[34] "The old [Chinese] learning as the foundation, the new [Western] learning for practical use." This famous maxim proposed by Chang Chih-tung served as an ideological basis of the "self-strengthening" and moderate reform movement, which aimed at strengthening China while preserving the existing Confucian order dominated by the established bureaucratic elite.

The Chinese patriots from Hong Kong, Ho Kai and Hu Li-yüan, wrote a "Review of *Ch'üan-hsüeh p'ien*" in 1899, to refute Chang Chih-tung's ideological assumptions. They argued: "Where the people's rights flourish, the country is strong; where the people's rights decline, the country is weak." People valued their "natural" and "inalienable" rights to life, liberty and property; if the state allowed them to exercise their rights, they would rise with one heart to protect the state; and if the state should deny them their rights, "the people would rise in anger to destroy the state."[35] The people's "natural rights" took precedence over the state. This reflected the Western liberal nationalism that inspired Ho and Hu. As Hans Kohn has observed, in Western Europe since the eighteenth century individual freedom had "activated the people, giving them a new interest and stake in their government, and giving the government a new vitality"; the authority of government had gained a new and stronger legitimacy as the nation's servant.[36] According to Ho and Hu, Chang Chih-tung's fear that the people's rights would diminish the government's power was unfounded. They asserted that Chang's defense of the "old [Chinese] learning" was basically flawed.

It is important to note that what Ho and Hu referred to as the "people's rights" basically meant the "merchants' rights." Rarely were they concerned about the rights of the peasants who constituted the great majority of the people in China. Despite their talk about the people's rights, Ho and Hu's program remained basically an elitist political thought.

The distinctiveness of Ho and Hu as spokesmen of the Hong Kong Chinese merchants became more evident when compared with other reformers of their day like K'ang Yu-wei and Liang Ch'i-ch'ao. Although they all shared some general reformist ideas (such as the "people's rights" and parliamentary government), Ho and Hu scorned K'ang Yu-wei and his associates for their lack of knowledge of foreign languages, their reliance on Chinese translations of Western works, and hence their superficial understanding of Western culture and traditions. Ho and Hu believed that an important reason for the failure of the Hundred Days' Reform in 1898 was the reformers' unfamiliarity with Western learning; for reform to succeed, "those who had mastered the Western learning" and "foreign specialists of good reputation" must be placed in responsible positions in government.[37] Ironically, Ho and Hu's reformist essays "were read with avidity by K'ang Yu-wei and his disciples."[38]

A striking characteristic of Ho's and Hu's reform program was its equation of the merchants' interests with the nation's interests, its strong emphasis on the development of commercial capitalism as the road to the nation's wealth and power, and its demands of political power for the merchants and overseas Chinese businessmen. This has led one Marxist historian to conclude that if K'ang Yu-wei's ideas could be regarded as the "reformist thought of the 'national essence' and bureaucratism," Ho's and Hu's ideas could be called the "reformist thought of comprador commercialism," for "their ultimate goal was to reorganize the bureaucratic system with the commercial capitalist class as its core, and to protect the interests of that class." [39] Their ultimate goal was a rich and strong Chinese nation under the hegemony of the merchants.

Another striking characteristic of Ho and Hu's reform program was its collaborationist thought. Patriotism and collaboration with foreign power were not necessarily mutually exclusive. A patriot could collaborate with the imperialists at the sacrifice of some sovereign rights in the hope of eventually building a strong nation to resist imperialist aggression. Collaborationist patriotism of the Chinese merchants in Hong Kong was clearly revealed in their enthusiastic support for the "open door" policy advocated by the British statesman Lord Charles Beresford.

"Open Door" Policy: Lord Charles Beresford and the Chinese Merchants' "Collaborationist Patriotism"

In 1898–99 Lord Beresford was touring the major Chinese cities and Hong Kong on behalf of Britain's Associated Chambers of Commerce, propagating the "open door" policy. During his stay in Hong Kong a meeting was held at the Chinese Chamber of Commerce, January 22, 1899, attended by fifteen hundred Chinese compradors, merchants, financiers, businessmen, traders, and other residents in the colony interested in trade. [40] Eight prominent Chinese addressed the meeting, including Ho Tung (a comprador), Ho Kai (a barrister), and Ho Amei (an insurance company manager). All speakers emphasized the development of commerce as a means to strengthen China against foreign powers; all acclaimed the "open door" policy, the "friendship" between China and Britain, and the "identical interests" of the two countries. Five speakers specifically stressed the need to ask Britain to help reorganize China's army and navy in order to better protect Chinese merchants and strengthen China against the incursion of other powers such as Russia and France. [41]

In his speech Robert Ho Tung warned that the Russians "have approached within dangerous proximity to Peking, and the completion of their great Trans-Siberian Railroad may augur the advent of many evils political and commercial. The integrity of the Chinese empire may be imperilled." Robert Ho Tung, a collaborationist patriot in Hong Kong, stressed the "identical interests" of England and China:

> If England suffers, the greatest volume of our trade being with that country, we shall be sufferers to the same extent. Now is our opportunity . . . to ward off the impending evil. We know from all these years of our residence in Hong Kong what the benefits of an unrestricted and unhampered trade means. It means profit with safety to those engaged in it; it means occupation and the means of livelihood to the people, and its inevitable result—happiness to the masses. [42]

This was exactly what Ho Kai and Hu Li-yüan had asserted in their reformist essays: commercial capitalism was the road to develop China's economy; it would bring prosperity to the merchants and happiness to the whole nation. Robert Ho Tung continued:

> We must admit, however reluctantly, the weakness and inability of China by herself to reorganize her fragmentary army. . . . In suggesting therefore that China's army should be organized under the English, I think that it will be seen that, apart from the nation's friendliness, they have furnished examples both of India and Egypt that should have satisfied even the most sceptic minds . . . [This is] for China's good, for the good of the country and its people. [43]

Here is a classic case of collaborationist patriotism.

At the end of the public meeting at the Chinese Chamber of Commerce resolutions were passed by acclamation expressing full confidence in Lord Beresford and enthusiastic support for the "open door" policy, and urging "the reorganization of the Chinese army under the British." The local English press was delighted that the Chinese had "resolved to join hands with the British commercial classes in an effort to bring about a Chinese Millennium." [44]

On his return to England, Lord Beresford received a long letter

written by Ho Kai and Wei Yuk (two legislative councillors appointed
by the governor), which read in part:

> Great Britain requires in China the "Open Door" and not a "Sphere
> of Influence," and China needs radical reform and not absorption
> by any foreign Power or Powers. But it is quite apparent immediate
> reformation must be inaugurated. Without reformation the admin-
> istration of the Chinese Empire will speedily become impossible;
> partition will become inevitable; and Great Britain will have no
> choice but to join the international scramble for "Sphere of Influ-
> ence." It is also clear that without external aid or pressure China is
> unable to effect her own regeneration. For obvious reasons—per-
> sonal gain and aggrandizement—those who hold high office, those
> who constitute her ruling class, do not desire Reform; those in
> humble life, forming her masses, wish Reform, but are powerless
> to attain it. In this predicament, we venture to think that England,
> having the predominant interest in China, and being the country
> most looked up to and trusted by the Chinese, should come for-
> ward and furnish the assistance and apply the requisite pressure.
> . . . When we recall the magnificent successes achieved in India,
> and in Egypt, and other parts of the world, we are confident that
> even greater successes will crown British effort and energy in China.[45]

Thus, as Chinese "patriots," Ho Kai and Wei Yuk were worried
about the possible partition of China and her "absorption by any
foreign Power or Powers"; so they wished for reform in China. But,
as members of the marginal intelligentsia and merchant class in Hong
Kong on the periphery of China, they were "powerless to attain it."
Therefore, they turned to Great Britain, the predominant imperialist
power that had joined in the scramble for concessions, for help to
"regenerate" China.[46] This was a great paradox of collaborationist
patriotism.

Ho Kai and Wei Yuk recall Dr. Veraswami of George Orwell's
Burmese Days. The Indian doctor "had a passionate admiration for
the English, which a thousand snubs from Englishmen had not
shaken," believing that the British brought modern civilization and
progress to India.[47]

Different historical circumstances produced different collaborationist patriots. In 1940–45 Wang Ching-wei was forced by circumstances of Japanese invasion of China to collaborate reluctantly with
the invaders, hoping to mitigate the suffering of the Chinese in the

areas under Japanese occupation. In contrast, a number of Hong Kong Chinese merchants and professionals in the late nineteenth and early twentieth centuries positively pushed for collaboration with Britain to help "regenerate" China. They conceived of Britain as a "benign," liberal imperialist power interested only in promoting international trade that would benefit both the British and Chinese. As Ho Tung clearly stated, "We know from all these years of our residence in Hong Kong what the benefits of an unrestricted and unhampered trade means," emphasizing the "identical interests" of England and China. But many other Chinese patriots would dispute this peculiar collaborationist patriotism. K'ang Yu-wei, for one, scorned the Westernized Hong Kong Chinese for their servile attitude toward the British.

British Acquisition of the New Territories

In fact, Britain had forced the Chinese government to sign the Convention of Peking, on June 6, 1898, by which 356 square miles of land to be known as the New Territories were leased to Britain for ninety-nine years and added to the colony of Hong Kong. The two Chinese members of the legislative council, Ho Kai and Wei Yuk, approved of the British acquisition of that land. They looked forward to the day when it would "become enlightened and prosperous like Hong Kong."[48] Meanwhile, Robert Ho Tung helped the colonial authorities to collect information about the situations in the New Territories to facilitate the British takeover. A Hong Kong land investment company sent agents to the New Territories to buy up title deeds at low prices at selected places that might appreciate in value under British jurisdiction. To persuade the reluctant owners to sell their land, they allegedly used unscrupulous methods, such as spreading rumors about the Hong Kong government's intention to impose high taxes and to expropriate privately owned land. It was said that the leaders of the land company were none other than the Honorable Dr. Ho Kai and the Honorable Mr. Wei Yuk.[49]

Such rumors spread by the "land jobbers" aggravated the local inhabitants' fear that the British government might interfere with their established rights and customs. The gentry and lineage leaders also feared for their positions of power and privilege. And the peasants dreaded the foreign rulers' interference with their traditional ways of livelihood and with *feng-shui*. Rumors spread that "cattle and swine would be taxed," "women would be violated," and "fishing and wood cutting would be prohibited."[50] Therefore, when the British forces sought to take over the New Territories in late March 1899 they encountered popular resistance under the leadership of the gentry and lineage leaders. Organized resistance, however, was subdued by April 18. The British proceeded to occupy and set up an administration over the New Territories.[51] Assured that local interest and customs would be respected, the gentry and village leaders submitted themselves to the foreign rule, their petitions couched in respectful Confucian terms.[52] These events in the rural New Territories had little direct effect on the populace in the city of Victoria and Kowloon, preoccupied as they were with their everyday struggle to make a living.

But during these years of wars and foreign incursions some young men from the intelligentsia had become revolutionaries, using Hong Kong as a base to conspire and plot for uprisings on mainland China.

Hong Kong as a Revolutionary Base

The Hong Kong Hsing-Chung-hui (society to restore China's prosperity) was founded on February 21, 1895, by about a dozen revolutionaries, including Sun Yat-sen, Yang Ch'ü-yün, Tse Tsan Tai, Ch'en Shao-pai, Cheng Shih-liang, Lu Hao-tung, Huang Yung-shang, and others. Most of them had received a Western-style education in Hong Kong. They immediately sought to take advantage of the social unrest in Kwangtung in a plot to seize power in Canton. They readily won Ho Kai's support. Sun Yat-sen was a former student of Dr. Ho Kai's at the Hong Kong Medical College for the Chinese, and was much inspired by the Westernized doctor's liberal ideas. The revolutionaries also won the sympathy of some British journalists in the colony. Ho Kai and Thomas H. Reid (editor of the *China Mail*) worked closely in 1895 to help the revolutionaries, hoping that a new China would adopt a more pro-Western stand in the future. The Hsing-Chung-hui proclamation to foreign powers on the eve of the Canton plot scheduled for October 1895 was reportedly drafted by Thomas Reid and T. Gowen (*Hong Kong Telegraph* subeditor) and then revised by Ho Kai and Tse Tsan Tai. But the conspiracy was discovered by Hong Kong officials, who notified the Canton government. Poor coordination led to the suppression of the Canton plot, dealing a severe blow to the Hsing-Chung-hui in Hong Kong. Most of its leaders including Sun Yat-sen were banished from the colony.[53]

The revolutionaries had attempted to align themselves with K'ang Yu-wei's group of constitutional monarchists. But the scholar-gentry K'ang Yu-wei rejected the idea, looking with disdain and incomprehension at the Westernized Hsing-Chung-hui revolutionaries; he scorned the servile attitude of Britain's Chinese subjects in Hong Kong. With the abrupt end in September 1898 of his Hundred Days' Reform, however, he had to flee to Hong Kong with the help of the British authorities, ironically as a guest of the wealthy comprador and collaborationist patriot Robert Ho Tung.[54] In October K'ang started on a tour of Japan, Canada, and America, and founded a society to protect the emperor (Pao-huang-hui), competing with the revolutionaries for financial and moral support from the Chinese communities overseas. In October 1899 K'ang returned to Hong Kong, where he stayed until January 30, 1900, leaving at that time for Singapore. Meanwhile, the Hsing-Chung-hui revolutionary organization was reactivated in Hong Kong with the founding of the *China Daily News* (*Chung-kuo jih-pao*) in January 1900 by Ch'en Shao-pai, to propagate revolution and to counter the influence of K'ang's Pao-huang-hui group of contitutional monarchists.

In 1900 eight foreign powers sent expeditions to North China to suppress the Boxer uprising. The revolutionaries in Hong Kong sought to take advantage of this opportunity to stage a coup d'etat in south China. Sun Yat-sen had been in contact with Liu Hsüeh-hsün (a subordinate of Governor General Li Hung-chang of Kwangtung and Kwanghsi) about the possibility of declaring the independence of the two provinces with Sun's cooperation and British protection. The Imperial Court, in flight at Sian, had asked Li Hung-chang to go to Peking to negotiate with the expedition powers, and Li was to pass through Hong Kong on July 16 on his way to the capital. Ho Kai became involved in the revolutionaries' attempt to use the good offices of Governor Henry Blake of Hong Kong to persuade Li to declare the independence of the two provinces in the south. Concerned that Li's departure might bring chaos to the south, Governor Blake was eager to cooperate with the revolutionaries in their plan for the negotiated seizure of the southern provinces, but instructions from London were cautious, forbidding the use of any forcible means to prevent Li from going north. In the end the plan did not material-ize.[55]

Still hoping to use the crisis in North China to their advantage, the revolutionaries sought to obtain the friendly support of Britain and the foreign powers for their cause. Acting as their spokesman, Ho Kai drafted, on July 24, 1900, a proclamation to foreign countries entitled the "Regulations for Peaceful Rule," which was signed by Sun Yat-sen, Yang Ch'ü-yün, Tse Tsan Tai, and other revolutionary leaders, to be presented to Governor Blake. The proclamation was expressly designed to win the approval of foreign powers, especially Britain. It condemned the Manchu government for its corruption and inefficiency, its inability to fulfill the treaty obligations in protecting foreign merchants in China, its attempt to seize the foreign legations in violation of international law, and its ingratitude to Britain, which had helped to prevent China's partition by other powers. The proc-lamation besought Britain's help to reconstruct China for the mutual benefit of the Chinese and foreigners. Specifically, it outlined a pro-gram to set up a parliamentary government under a constitution, and to request foreign ambassadors to form a temporary advisory body to the central government, and foreign consuls general to form an advisory body to the provincial governments. Under such a gov-ernment foreign missionaries would be protected; China would be opened to foreign commercial and industrial interests; foreign coun-tries would be consulted in matters concerning any change in cus-toms duties; a new school system would be set up, and a Western-ized code of law adopted.[56]

What characterized this Hsing-Chung-hui program drafted by Ho Kai was its pro-Western stand, its subservience to Western powers, and its reliance on foreign tutelage to remake China in the image of the West. What was Governor Blake's response to this program? He seemed sympathetic, but again instructions from London ordered him to clamp down on agitators like Sun Yat-sen and K'ang Yu-wei, who might bring violence to the south. Thus, the negotiations of July and August 1900 for foreign support to "reconstruct" China failed.

Ho Kai's Open Letter to John Bull

As it has been justly stated, Ho Kai "was essentially a conditional revolutionary, who could not conceive of activism except when supported by British gunboats."[57] While Sun Yat-sen proceeded with his war plan for the Waichow (Hui-chou) uprising, Ho Kai still insisted on collaborating with foreign powers to "regenerate" China. He thought that the foreign powers' military occupation of Peking in the wake of the Boxer uprising was a golden opportunity to introduce reforms to China, an opportunity to be seized with both hands. In a remarkable "Open Letter on the Situation" published in The *China Mail* on August 22, 1900, he addressed "John Bull" as follows.

> [Y]ou must capture not only Peking, but also the lawless band of mandarins and their confederates the leading Boxers. . . . I take it that you are well agreed upon the principles so fearlessly propounded by your Under-Secretary for Foreign Affairs that China shall be for the Chinese, and there will be no partition of the Middle Kingdom by the Foreign Powers. The Indianising of China you will not have, but then you must not go to the other extreme to leave China severely alone and permit her to get along as before. . . . The present rotten and corrupt system of government must go and radical reforms should be introduced. . . . Pray remember that Manchus are not Chinese, and it will only be fair to leave China for the Chinese and Manchuria for the Manchus. All the enlightened sons of China are earnestly looking to . . . Great Britain and the United States of America for deliverance from the yoke of an oppressive and corrupt Government.

Ho Kai reminded John Bull that China's regeneration would benefit both the Chinese and the British, for the British trade with China "could only be materially developed by increasing the prosperity and welfare of the Chinese people." Ho Kai asserted that Britain had the moral obligation to help the Chinese. He assured the imperialist powers that they could count on the collaboration of many "intelligent and gifted" Chinese to carry out the "much desired reformation."[58]

Thus, Ho Kai wished the imperialist powers to "dictate" the government of China, "at the point of the bayonet,"[59] to carry out reforms along Western lines in order to make China in the image of the West even at the price of compromising China's sovereignty. But the expedition powers, beset with mutual suspicion and confronted with a sea of hostile Chinese masses, would disappoint Ho Kai. They did what he entreated them not to do—leaving the Manchu government as it was, after suppressing the Boxers and exacting a huge indemnity of four hundred and fifty million taels.

A Gap Between Elitist Nationalists and Coolies

So far we have discussed the nationalist responses of the Hong Kong Chinese merchants and intelligentsia to the important events that took place in China from 1887 to 1900. What about the responses of the colony's populace? During the Sino-Japanese War of 1894–95 the *Hua-tzu jih-pao* offices were "wrecked by an infuriated mass of Chinese, because the paper published the first-hand information about the loss of the Chinese fleet in the China Sea, the surrender of Port Arthur, and the defeat of the Chinese army near Korea."[60] I cannot find detailed sources about this incident in Hong Kong beyond this cursory reference.

There was probably little coordinated nationalist popular response in Hong Kong to the major events that occurred in China in 1887–1900. Had there been, the local English press and the colonial government, extremely sensitive to law and order, would have reported it. The Sino-Japanese War, the Hundred Days' Reform, the Boxer uprising, and the foreign expedition to China, all occurred in North China and hence did not directly affect the livelihood of the populace in Hong Kong. Even British occupation of the New Territories in 1899 and the Chinese villagers' resistance to it did not have direct impact on workers in the city of Victoria and Kowloon, preoccupied as they were with their daily struggle to make a living.

Nationalism did not merely have political and cultural dimensions; it had economic dimensions as well. A nationalist program that sought to enhance people's livelihood would be better able to win popular support. But Chinese elitist nationalists in modern times often demanded that a citizen must put his top priority on devotion to the state above all other concerns, and that he must be "selfless" and "disinterested," transcending and even sacrificing his self-interest for the common good of the nation. Such a disinterested and transcendental concept of nationalism had little appeal to the common people. In fact, it was a "mystification" of nationalism, to use Peter Worsley's term. "All nationalisms are mystifications in that they postulate the immanent and absolute priority of the interests of the whole, usually defined by those who dominate society, over any merely sectional interest."[61] Ho Kai and Hu Li-yüan mystified nationalism by equating merchants' interest with the nation's interest, seeking to advance merchants' interest in a society dominated by the gentry-scholar-officials. Ho's and Hu's ultimate ideal was a strong and prosperous China under the hegemony of a merchant elite.

The elitist nationalists themselves were not always "disinterested." In her study of class and national consciousness in Georgian Britain from 1750 to 1830 Linda Colley reveals that "almost all sectional interest groups in Britain resorted to nationalist language and activism to advance their claims to wider civic recognition" and that "patriotic initiatives were ideal vehicles for sectional self-assertion."[62] Such a marriage of patriotism and self-interest was also prevalent in China. Conservative gentry-scholars like Wang Hsien-ch'ien and Yeh Te-hui; "self-strengtheners" like Li Hung-chang and Shen Pao-chen; bureaucratic nationalists like Chang Chih-tung; Confucian cultural nationalists like K'ang Yu-wei; and collaborationist nationalists like Ho Kai, Wei Yuk, Ho Tung, and Hu Li-yüan—all were elitists and all resorted to nationalist language and activism to advance their sectional group interests.

Purporting to bring about national unity and promote national well-being, nationalism was ironically often a divisive force in history causing conflict and dissensions. Patriotism could be expressed in different ways; nationalism took many different forms. As long as there were different views regarding what was in the best interest of the nation, there would be different kinds of patriots and nationalists. The most dramatic illustration of nationalism as a divisive force in Chinese history was the war between the right-wing Kuomintang nationalists and the left-wing Communist nationalists (despite their theoretical commitment to internationalism), each side claiming to be the "genuine" nationalists, and each accused the other of attempting to project the "false image" of being nationalists.

At the turn of the twentieth century elitist nationalism as propagated by the Hong Kong merchants and intelligentsia (like Ho Kai, Hu Li-yüan, Wei Yuk, Robert Ho Tung) and the Hsing-Chung-hui revolutionaries had little appeal to the lower-class working people in Hong Kong, because it was built on a sectional foundation and seldom sought to advance the laborer's interest. Members of the new intelligentsia like Ho Kai and Tse Tsan Tai were alienated from the working coolies in the colony. Ho Kai admitted in public that he "had never learned how to go through properly a regular Chinese ceremony" worshipping the god of war Kwan-ti.

The leading Hsing-Chung-hui revolutionaries came mostly from the Westernized intelligentsia, and a number of them were baptized Christians. Rejecting some traditional values and religious customs that had bound the old elite and populace together prior to the mid-1880s in an integrated Chinese community life, the English-educated new intelligentsia—in a more heterogeneous society after the 1890s—was alienated from the populace. To win over the working people, one had to burn incense with them at the Man Mo Temple and join them in traditional religious processions, but the new intelligentsia looked down upon such old religious customs with disdain. It would take several more years before some republican revolutionaries came to realize that it was necessary for them to "stoop" to work with coolies in order to win them over to the revolutinonary camp.

To do the fighting in their organized uprisings against the Manchus, the revolutionaries did seek to recruit antidynastic secret society members, who, however, were not easily converted into dedicated republican nationalists. In the abortive Canton uprising of October 27, 1895, some six hundred coolies from Hong Kong, "all of the poorest class," were hired at ten dollars a month by the revolutionaries, but the coolies thought that they were engaged as soldiers for the Manchu government! They had no interest in the revolutionary uprising.[63] A large gap separated the elitist nationalists from the coolies in the British colony.

The years of elitist nationalists' activism in 1887–1900 witnessed several incidents of coolie unrest, which reflected coolies' own pressing concerns and problems, all related to local issues, not nationalism. Coolies were primarily concerned with local issues affecting their daily subsistence, work processes, and religious beliefs. The colony's elitist nationalists, insensitive to coolies' mundane needs, were unable to enlist them for the nationalist causes under their auspices in those years.

The Strike of Cargo Boatmen, 1888

On April 17, 1888, the cargo boat people, who numbered some four thousand, went on strike to protest the government regulations requiring a license with a photograph and a license fee of twenty-five cents per annum for each boatman.[64] The government required each license applicant to be photographed, because the practice of personation was very common among the cargo boat people, by which means licenses were passed from hand to hand and were largely held by people without licenses. The license with a photograph would be useful for the police to check the thefts of cargo that frequently occurred on the cargo boats.

For eleven days, from April 17 through 27, all the cargo boats withdrew into the Chinese waters, bringing almost to a standstill the business of the port of Hong Kong. The loss suffered by the mercantile community was very great, estimated at not less than fifty thousand dollars a day. The boat people petitioned the government for the cancellation of the photograph requirement. A similar petition was presented by a number of Chinese merchants who suffered from the strike and sought to smooth things over. Unwilling to yield to pressure which would mean weakness in the eyes of the public, the government posted notices all over the colony urging boat people to return to work first before their petition could be considered.

The boat people, on the other hand, sought to put pressure on the government by calling on other laborers in the colony to join the strike. The cargo boat guild "paid $400 to another guild of labourers to induce them to join in the strike." "Whether from that or some other cause a large number of the dock-labourers had struck, while many others were threatening to do so," reported Governor Des Voeux. On April 25 "a great mob collected on two of the principal streets was stopping all the traffic, and was by threat, and in one or two cases by actual violence, preventing the jinricksha coolies and other labourers from following their occupations." "The concerted cessation from work" of thousands of laborers "constituted a direct coercive measure and a menace to the Government."[65]

Governor Des Voeux took actions. He proclaimed the Peace Preservation Ordinance, stationed a gunboat off the Harbor Office, and sent two companies of troops to parade the Western District of the town. The sight of the troops had "a salutary deterrent effect upon the excited crowds." By the night (of April 25) the crowds had dispersed and the troops returned to their barracks. The excitement calmed down a little the following day. "The traffic was allowed to pass through the streets as usual." By this time, the old rivalry and tensions between Tung-kuan coolies and Sze Yap coolies surfaced again, as the colonial government showed no sign of yielding to the boat people's demand and as coolies faced economic hardship after nine days on strike. The striking coolies began to split. The Tung-kuan coolies, numbering some thousands, petitioned the government for protection, saying that "they wished to return to work but were in fear of the cargo coolies." Economic hardship forced the coolies back to work. On the morning of April 28, after eleven days on strike, the boat people went back to work, though scarcely any licenses with photographs had been taken out as required by the government regulations.[66]

Displeased with the cargo boat people's persistent defiance of the regulations, Governor Des Voeux summoned the leading Chinese merchants to a meeting in the Government House to consult their views on the matter. As their business was hurt by the coolie strike, the merchants tried to mediate and to smooth things over by suggesting that the boatmen's "delay in taking out licences was simply due to a feeling of uncertainty as to the final decision of the Government on their representations." Although the governor was somewhat doubtful as to this view, he deemed it expedient to decide on a compromise solution. The license fee on the ordinary boat people was abolished, and the license with a photograph was to be imposed only on the head in charge of each boat.[67]

Such a confrontation with the colonial government was an education for the laborers. They came to see that by combination they could achieve their common purpose to defend their common interests against the threat of an outside force. The striking cargo boat people used various means (including money payment, intimidation, threat of violence, and appeal to common interests) to induce other coolies to take common actions. And they succeeded in inducing large numbers of coolies to join in the strike. There was a long tradition of coolie resistance to the colonial government's regulations. But throughout the nineteenth century rivalry and tensions between coolies of different districts and dialect groups were strong, as shown in the coolie feud of 1894; nevertheless, when confronted with the threat of a common foe, many of them would join force again as in the coolie strike of 1895. Let us first look at the 1894 coolie feud.

Coolie Feud in March 1894

The Chinese delighted in religious processions. On such occasions, many coolies were employed to prepare for the carnival; many others joined in it. The great three-day procession in connection with the restoration of the Man Mo Temple started on March 2, 1894. The streets in the Chinese quarters of the city of Victoria were very crowded; forty thousand visitors arrived from Canton and nearby villages to witness the procession. Police interference with the course of the procession almost gave rise to a riot. Europeans complained about the noisy Chinese crowd in the business quarters.[68]

The festivity occasioned a collision between coolies of different dialect groups from Tung Kuan and Sze Yap. They had established certain clubs in the colony. "Some of these called Hung Shing Clubs promote the cultivation of the art of boxing, fencing, etc. They are frequented by all the low characters in the Colony as well as by the ordinary working coolies," reported the Police Chief F. Henry May.[69] Fencing masters and pugilistic club brothers often played big roles in religious processions by providing dragon and lion dance teams. On March 4 a fight took place in Hollywood Road between Tung Kuan men and Sze Yap men from the Hung Shing Club over the issue of a prize given for the "lions" in the processions. The fight was quickly quelled by the police; five men were arrested and fined four dollars each.

The quarrel was aggravated by a small incident on March 9. Two gangs of the belligerent coolies were employed in unloading a vessel at a wharf. While a man was carrying his load to a warehouse, an oppositon man either accidentally or intentionally knocked the sack from his back. Tension mounted between the two dialect groups of cargo coolies. A fight at Praya West on March 10 and another on the following day were speedily stopped by the police. Extra police patrolled the streets from 4 to 9 p.m. On March 12 the police arrested seven men (unemployed pugilistic club members) in possesion of deadly weapons such as revolvers, swords, and iron bars. Although there was no rioting or fighting, a series of terrorist, murderous assaults on individauls resulted in two deaths and several injuries.[70]

On the following day, March 13, a meeting at Tung Wah Hospital was called by the registrar general, Stewart Lockhart. Present were the police chief, F. Henry May, the Chinese justices of the peace, some leading Chinese merchants, and sixty coolie representatives, including the heads of the Tung Kuan and Sze Yap coolie houses. These head coolies were urged to state their grievances against each other with a view to arriving at a settlement of the matter in dispute. From the long discussion "it appeared that neither party had had any particular grievance against the other." During the meeting, the sound of sniper gunshots and police whistles was heard outside. It became apparent that by this time "the principal actors in the disturbances were not the coolies who had originally quarrelled but certain members of the pugilistic and other low-class clubs."[71]

The quarrel had passed out of the coolies' hands into those of the unemployed "professional ruffians." In fact, coolies were afraid to go into the streets, for they did not know who was fighting for them or against them. [72] Coolies of both dialect groups had not turned out as usual for work since March 12. They were "anxious to go back to work, but were deterred from doing so by the fear of being made the objects of attacks by ruffians who had constituted themselves [as] their champions."[73] Here is another instance of how "social bandits" could both help and abuse the poor at the same time.

The police chief was determined "to break up the worst of these [pugilistic] clubs." Police raids at night and in the early hours of the morning resulted in the arrest of seventeen "ruffians" for deportation. Nine more were arrested for carrying arms on March 14. These had the effect of closing down "some of the worst of the clubs," and the disappearance from the colony of some sixty other members of the clubs. Police search of the clubs found a large quantity of ammunition on March 15. Under police protection, all coolies went back to work on March 16. For the four days from March 12 to 15, it was estimated that twelve thousand coolies were out of work daily, seriously affecting business in the harbor.[74]

After the restoration of order, Registrar General Stewart Lockhart and Police Chief F. Henry May each received "A Respectful Letter from the [Chinese] Justices of the Peace and Merchants of Hong Kong" signed by seventy-two leading Chinese, which read in part:

> You displayed great resource in the measures you adopted for quieting the recent local disturbances. On that occasion, the rioters spread a rumour that the disturbance was created by Tung Kun and Sz Yap coolies with intent to throw Hong Kong into confusion. But for your earnest efforts and your co-operation with the Justices

of the Peace in suppressing disorder and restoring peace, there would not have been so speedy an end to the crisis. Now, we Justices and others . . . are grateful and cannot allow this occasion to pass without expressing our united thanks and hope that in case of any future disturbance in Hong Kong, you will again co-operate with us in suppressing the rioters.[75]

A very informative letter, it showed the Chinese elite's readiness to call on the government to use coercion to suppress the coolie riot, revealing the extent of community disintegration in 1894. In a progressively heterogeneous society in the 1890s, the elite found it increasingly difficult to control the lower class Chinese.

It is significant that in the long meeting at the Tung Wah Hospital, the representatives of the two dialect groups of coolies found that "neither party had had any particular grievance against the other." They were rival groups of coolies competing with each other for work opportunities, for better stations in the street, warehouse, and dockyard. Their differences did not go much beyond this. In fact, they had much in common, participating in the same religious processions, frequenting the same kind of pugilistic clubs, and occupying the same lowly position in the relations of production, selling their manual labor to earn a living. Confronted with the threat of an outside force, they could forget their differences and combine to take collective actions to defend their common interest, as in the coolie strike of 1895.

Coolie Strike of 1895

In March 1895 the Hong Kong legislative council passed the lodging house regulations, imposing a number of new restrictions on the coolie houses: at least seven cubic feet must be given to each inhabitant of the house; certain lavatories must be provided; the keeper of the lodging house "shall cause the windows of each room to be kept open for four hours each day"; he "shall not permit males and females above ten years of age respectively to occupy the same sleeping compartment except in the case of husband and wife"; he "shall not knowingly permit persons of bad character to lodge in his house, and shall also keep a registration of the names of each lodger."[76]

This was a well-intentioned piece of legislation by the colonial government to improve sanitary conditions and also to safeguard law and order in the colony. But coolies were always suspicious of the colonial authorities. They hated government regulation of their lives and work. What concerned the coolies most in the sanitary regulation was the stipulation of seven cubic feet for each coolie tenant of the house; this meant that coolies could no longer crowd fifteen people into a room designed for five, which in turn meant rent increases for coolies.

On March 23, 1895, hundreds of dockyard workers, led by coolie housekeepers, went on strike, protesting the lodging house regulations. Rumors soon spread that the government would impose on coolies a poll tax and registration fees. The strike spread rapidly within two days, when coal workers and several thousand carrying coolies and stevedore's coolies all joined the strike. Significantly, almost the entire Chinese staff at the Taikoo Sugar Refinery at Quarry Bay (fitters and other Chinese employees), though themselves not affected by the lodging house regulations, came out on a "sympathetic strike." The laborers at the East Point and Lee Yuen Sugar Refineries also joined the strike, as many cargo boatmen also did. But the street coolies, chair bearers, and ricksha pullers (many of whom were Hoklo and Teochiu people) did not join the movement, nor did the laborers employed by the building contractors.[77] The Swatow coolies did not join the strike, being "under police protection."[78]

Nevertheless, a large proportion of coolies of different occupations and dialect groups joined the movement. By March 29 more than twenty thousand people, including both the Tung Kuan and Sze Yap dialect groups, were on strike. The European and Chinese business interests, especially the shipping trade, were badly hurt. The British naval and civilian authorities could only put about three thousand laborers (sailors, soldiers and convicts) to work as emergency substitutes. The merchants themselves attempted to telegraph to Amoy, Swatow and Japan for new laborers.[79]

In the meeting of the legislative council on March 26 Governor William Robinson expressed his surprise and disgust at "the obstinacy, stupidity and ignorance of the Chinese labourers." He believed that either they were willfully misled by the coolie house keepers, or else they wilfully misunderstood the object of the regulations, which were intended to improve sanitary conditions and not to pave the way for a poll tax. The governor saw the possible effect of the regulations causing a rent increase. But he believed that labor wages could be "easily adjusted by the employers." The governor hoped that Ho Kai, who represented the Chinese in the legislative council, "would take the opportunity of conferring with respectable Chinese merchants and would endeavour to persuade the coolies to abandon the foolish and shortsighted policy they have chosen to adopt." The acting attorney general, Mr. Leach, reported to the council that many coolie house keepers had bolted to Canton to avoid prosecution for neglecting to register their houses. He complained that the lower-class Chinese were too much in the habit of thinking that they could coerce the government: "the time has come for the Government to put down its foot and to put it down firmly, and if the coolies do not like the law, the sooner they leave the Colony the better."[80]

In response, Ho Kai said that he and many other Chinese leaders including Wei Yuk, had for a long time been reasoning with the coolies, and had explained to their headmen that the government had no intention of imposing a poll tax on them. Ho Kai assured the governor and the council:

> We, as the leaders of the Chinese and their representatives, will not cease our efforts to bring them [coolies] to reason (applause). We regret they are so pig-headed at this time. . . . Your Excellency can rely upon those Chinese who have come to the help of the Government hitherto giving the Government their strong support on the present occasion (applause).[81]

But the strike went on.

The Hong Kong [European] Chamber of Commerce called an urgent public meeting, attended largely by the Europeans, in the City Hall on March 28 to discuss the matter. The speakers urged the government to stand firm against the Chinese, and called upon every European in the colony to support the government. Because of racial tensions, two speakers expressed their suspicion that the "leading Chinese" were "answerable for a great deal of our trouble here." "If the Government did not do what certain Chinese in the Colony wished, they intended to bring out first the carrying coolies, then the rice coolies, then the market coolies, and then the house servants and the ricksha coolies and everything else."[82] The Europeans were suspicious of a coalition of the Chinese of all classes to stage a coolie strike in the colony. But this suspicion was unfounded; commercial ties between the Chinese merchants and Europeans proved to be too strong and their commercial loses too heavy for the Chinese merchants to ignore.

Granville Sharp, another speaker in the European public meeting, complained: "When I first came to Hong Kong, the Chinese did not behave as they do now. Every Chinese coolie who met you in the street doffed his hat and stood on one side to allow you to pass. When do you see a coolie do that now?"[83] Indeed, through a long series of confrontations with the British authorities and European employers, large numbers of coolies had learned to combine their forces in collective actions to defend their common interests. Gone were the days when the Chinese coolie "doffed his hat and stood on one side to allow you to pass." Much annoyed by the coolie strike, Granville Sharp insisted that a disobedient coolie ought to be "caned without his clothes, and then . . . sent into the street showing his blue and red back." Englishmen must recognize and enforce their "undoubted superiority"; "we must rule by power. . . . It is by power we have ruled the Great Empire of India."[84]

The speaker was given a loud applause by the excited European audience. Granville Sharp was representative of the British colonists in the non-Western world. He resembled P. W. Ellis in George Orwell's *Burmese Days*. "Living twenty years in the country without learning a word of the language," Ellis insisted that the natives understood only brute force.[85]

The Hong Kong European merchants' meeting concluded with the appointment of a committee of six members to meet with their Chinese colleagues and partners, the leading Chinese merchants, to discuss the labor crisis. The committee included Mr. J. J. Keswick (director of the Hong Kong and Shanghai Banking Corporation) and other European businessmen representing powerful firms such as Jardine, Matheson & Co. and the Butterfield & Swire Co.[86]

Meanwhile, the Chinese mercantile community held their own meetings to discuss the labor strike. The compradors met on March 28 in Robert Ho Tung's office at Jardine, Matheson & Co. After a conference with other Chinese merchants they decided to meet their European colleagues and partners. Thus, confronting the coolie strike that threatened the colony's business interests, the Chinese merchants got together with the European merchants to discuss how to deal with the labor crisis. The meeting took place on March 29, with more than a hundred Chinese merchants present. Appealing to their common interests, hurt by the labor strike, Robert Ho Tung repudiated the English merchants' allegation about certain influential Chinese backing up the coolies. To end the labor strike the Chinese merchants asked the European merchants' committee to guarantee that there would be no imposition of a poll tax. The Europeans readily agreed to issue placards giving coolies "the strongest guarantees" that the government had absolutely no intention of imposing a poll tax or registration fees.[87]

The following day, March 30, the committee of the European merchants, accompanied by Ho Kai, waited on the governor to make recommendations concerning the guarantee given to the coolies. Governor Robinson was still uncertain about the best policy to follow, indicating that any concession to the strikers would be interpreted as a sign of weakness on the part of the government. Referring to the European merchants' guarantee to coolies, the governor added: "Your action has placed me in considerable difficulty."[88]

Impatient about the labor strike, the European merchant community held another public meeting on April 1 in the City Hall to discuss the crisis. Robert Ho Tung came to give a long talk, saying that he strongly condemned the strikers and strongly admired the government for being firm about the lodging house regulations. He repudiated the allegation that the leading Chinese were supporting the strike: "I appeal to you, as successful business men to think what benefit or what good leading Chinese derive from this strike considering the very heavy losses which they have already sustained. . . . So far we have lost if not more, at least as much as the Europeans." Ho Tung reminded the Europeans that the leading Chinese had given the government the most loyal support whenever they were called upon to do so. He expressed his eagerness to assist the government or any gentlemen who would form a committee to end the strike.[89]

Listening to Ho Tung's appeal to their common economic interest, the English merchant Granville Sharp was readily convinced. Sharp's aversion to the labor problem was typical of the British merchants in Hong Kong; he warned in graphic terms:

> The present position is . . . one of rebellion; it is war. The existence of a body of 20,000 coolies—lusty coolies—in Hong Kong, disaf-

fected and armed with their formidable bamboo poles . . . is a
direct menace to the Colony (laugh and applause). . . . I think we
must . . . stand shoulder to shoulder and present an uncompromis-
ing front (applause).[90]

To induce the coolies back to work, the colonial government finally followed the Chinese and European merchants' advice in issu-
ing a proclamation on April 1, affirming that no poll tax or registration fees were to be imposed; it also offered a reward of one thousand
dollars to anyone who gave information leading to the arrest of strike
agitators.[91] Three days later, on April 4, many coolies returned to
work, ending the twelve-day labor strike.

Several factors helped to terminate the strike. First, the government had arrested a few strikers and agitators and had denied the
rumor about the poll tax and registration fees. Second, over a hundred
head coolies had fled Hong Kong, leaving their followers without
leadership. Third, thousands of cheap laborers could be recruited
easily from Amoy, Swatow, and elsewhere on the mainland.[92] Fourth,
the Chinese authorities at Kowloon City cooperated with the British
colonial government in driving the head coolies out of the city that
had been their place of refuge. Finally, coolies had to work to make a
living. A prolonged strike would cause them economic hardship.
Many coolies demanded an increase in wages before returning to
duty. The demand was not only refused; in many cases their daily
wages were reduced from one dollar a day to seventy-five cents.[93]

The coolie strike of 1895 revealed the social relations and political
structure in the colony of Hong Kong. Once again it was demonstrated that when their common interest was threatened by government regulations, large numbers of coolies of different occupations
and dialect groups joined forces in collective resistance. Dockyard
workers, coal workers, carrying coolies, stevedore's coolies, cargo
boatpeople and fitters, all came to feel the identity of interest among
themselves against a common foe. Workers of the rival dialect groups
from Tung Kuan and Sze Yap joined the strike, though the minority
groups of Hoklo and Teochiu coolies did not.

Whenever laborers went on strike, the Chinese and European
mercantile communities suffered economic losses. Chinese merchants sustained a loss of over two hundred thousand dollars during
the first week alone in the 1895 coolie strike.[94] The labor strike brought

together Chinese and European merchants in a cooperative common effort to resolve their common problem. They supported the colonial government, advising it on how to end the labor unrest. While cooperating with the British, the Chinese elite also sought to convey to the government the coolies' apprehension about the rumored poll tax. The Chinese and European merchants, together, pursuaded the colonial government to guarantee against the imposition of such tax on coolies.

The coolie strike took place at the time of the Sino-Japanese War (1894–95), but it had nothing to do with the war. It was the colonial government's housing regulations (threatening laborers' interests) that aroused the strike. Coolies' concern with a rent increase, a poll tax, and registration fees prompted them to take collective actions. Local issues affecting their daily subsistence were of primary importance to the poor laboring class. Living on a bare subsistence wage, coolies had to guard constantly their immediate interest and mundane needs for food, clothing, and shelter.

The working people would be more inclined to respond to a nationalist appeal if it were fused with an appeal to the enhancement of their livelihood. The elitist nationalism advocated by Ho Kai, Hu Li-yüan, Wei Yuk, Robert Ho Tung, and the Westernized Hsing-Chung-hui revolutionaries held little appeal for the lower-class working people because it was built on a sectional foundation. The Chinese patriots from among the merchants and Westernized intelligentsia often failed to address local issues relating to the coolies' pressing social concerns and economic problems. A gap separated the coolies from the Chinese intelligentsia and revolutionaries. So long as the gap remained formidable, the scope and appeal of the social and national movements promoted by the intelligentsia would remain sectional and limited. This helps to explain the limited participation of the Hong Kong coolies in the anti-American boycott of 1905–6.

S
E
V
E
N

The Anti-American Boycott, 1905–6

*A new corporate life is being awakened and fostered among the
more intelligent of the maritime and riverine population.*
— *China Mail*, July 24, 1905

*Though living in a land under foreign rule, we shall use the
traitors' and public enemies' skulls as wine vessels in libation.*
— *Ch'en Ch'ing-ch'en, journalist*

In the history of modern China the Chinese frequently resorted to
boycott as a means of passive resistance to foreign imperialist en-
croachment. Although the boycott of American goods in 1905–6 has
been subject to several studies, many aspects of the boycott in Hong
Kong have so far remained uninvestigated. This chapter examines
the origins and nature of the boycott and discusses the roles played
by the colony's Chinese community in the boycott movement.

Origins and Nature of the Boycott

By a series of exclusion acts—in 1882, 1884, 1888, 1892, and 1894—
the American government had prohibited the Chinese laborers from
entering the United States. This prohibition was extended to include
Hawaii in 1898 and the Philippines in 1900. Racial discrimination
against the Chinese in America involved not merely a ban on the
immigration of Chinese laborers; the "exempted" groups of officials,

teachers, students, journalists, merchants, and travelers were all subjected to abuses and mob violence. Numerous racial incidents involved Chinese of all classes. In one incident, on October 11, 1902, about two hundred and fifty Chinese were arrested by the Boston immigration officers without warrant; only five among the arrested were found to be unlawful residents. One of the innocent victims of the unwarranted raid was Feng Hsia-wei, who later returned to China in distress and wrote a book about his unhappy experience. His feeling against America was so strong that he committed suicide in front of the American consulate in Shanghai on July 16, 1905, and thus became a martyr in the anti-American boycott.[1] Outraged by such mistreatment and activated by patriotism, the Chinese of all classes were to join the anti-American boycott. As a Hong Kong Chinese resident maintained, in boycotting American goods, "we are simply exercising our rights as members of the human race."[2]

The boycott movement reflected not merely such moral outrage but also practical social and economic concerns. It was directed against America's anti-Chinese movement, which threatened the interests and aspirations of all classes of Chinese around the Pacific basin. To ban the Chinese labor immigrants meant to deprive the Chinese lower classes of an opportunity to earn a living abroad in America, Hawaii, and the Philippines. The Chinese would no longer be able to join their friends and relatives already abroad. Family members were separated. Large numbers of Chinese in the Philippines and other regions of Southeast Asia were Fukienese. Both Fukienese and Cantonese were disaffected by the U.S. immigration laws. Racial discrimination and violence against the "exempted" groups of students, teachers, ministers, journalists, and travelers meant that the Chinese intelligentsia's professional opportunities abroad were threatened. And so were Chinese mercantile interests.

Nationalism as reflected in the anti-American boycott was not purely political; it had broad social and economic dimensions, which accounted for the coalition of all classes in the movement under the leadership of members of the intelligentsia and merchant class. Nationalism had a powerful appeal to people when it was fused with their social and economic concerns.

In part, the boycott movement reflected the aspiration of the Chinese businessmen to promote their economic rights and independence from foreign capitalist domination and control. Many Chinese merchants and businessmen sought to take advantage of the boycott to promote their own commercial interests and manufacturing enterprises.

As Linda Pomerantz observes, "The wealthy Chinese merchants in the United States had a vested interest in the development of a large and prosperous community of Chinese workers throughout the western states. The anti-Chinese movement jeopardized this goal . . . and hampered the merchants in their conduct of international trade"; thus, "the emergence of nationalist ideas [among the Chinese merchants in America] flowed naturally out of specific interests."[3] Indeed, the interests of the Chinese communities in the commercial network of the Pacific basin were more or less adversely affected. Hence the nationalistic boycott movement was to spread among the Chinese communities all around the Pacific basin. Nationalism was fused with social and economic concerns to propel the boycott movement.

It is important to note, however, that the boycott hurt both the boycotted and the boycotters. Moreover, interests could be differently perceived; many people would stress immediate interests and others, long-term interests. From the perspective of long-term interests, a well-organized boycott would press the U.S. government to modify its immigration laws in favor of Chinese of all classes. This would in the long run enhance the prosperity of the Chinese communities in America and in other regions of the Pacific commercial network. From this long-term perspective, the nationalistic boycott movenment was in harmony with people's concern with their economic interests.

From the perspective of the boycott's short-term impact, however, the nationalistic boycott movement may have seemed to be in conflict with individuals' concern for their immediate material interests. The Chinese merchants engaged in the importing and exporting business with America, for instance, would be hurt by the boycott, if they considered only its immediate effect. The Chinese merchants in the Pacific basin had a broad, common goal, to promote their general interest and to compete with foreign capitalism for a greater share in the international trade, but the long-term interest was often remote and uncertain. Therefore, difference in emphasis on either the immediate or long-term interests caused a split in the Chinese mercantile community.

In fact, many people were often primarily concerned with the boycott's immediate effect on their interests. So, those who were immediately affected by the boycott tended to oppose the boycott; and those who were not immediately affected were more inclined to support it. In particular, the merchants trading with America (dealers, wholesalers, and detailers of American goods in Hong Kong) would suffer immediate economic losses, so they opposed the boycott. But those who were exporting goods to supply the Chinese communities in America would support the boycott. And those who were not directly trading with America had more latitude to choose either to support or oppose the boycott.

In addition, the manufacturers who sought to take advantage of the boycott to promote their own enterprises would of course support the boycott, but those manufacturers who continued to rely on America for the supply of machines, techniques, and raw materials would soon retreat from the boycott. As for the intelligentsia, Hatano Yoshihiro observes that teachers, students, and journalists who had received a "modern bourgeois education" were the "propelling force" of the boycott.[4] But, as Kikuchi Takaharu points out, members of the intelligentsia were also divided in their attitudes, reflecting the immediate interests of one or another segment of the merchant class.[5]

Despite its common goal to resist foreign imperialism the disunity of the Chinese mercantile community was in part due to the omnipresence of foreign capitalism, with which the different segments of the Chinese community had formed economic ties in varying degrees and on which they all depended in varying degrees. The boycott and the concurrent "rights recovery" movement reflected the merchants' and businessmen's common political and economic aspiration to free themselves from foreign capitalist domination and control, but their common aspiration was frustrated by the reality of their economic ties with and dependency on foreign capitalism in China. This helps to explain why the boycott began to fade away just a few months after it was launched. With these assumptions in mind, let us proceed to examine the boycott and to test these assumptions.

A Divided Community: Various Responses to the Call for a Boycott

When the 1894 American Exclusion Treaty with China came up for renewal in December 1904, Chinese public opinion pressed the government to demand a revision of that treaty. On May 11, 1905, the

Shanghai Chamber of Commerce sent telegrams to the chambers of commerce of twenty-two cities all over China, calling on all Chinese merchants to join in a boycott. In response, the Hong Kong Chinese Commercial Union telegraphed Shanghai to express its approval of the resolution. But the telegraph added that "the matter of boycott had not been discussed due to its incompatibility with the British laws."[6]

Thus, from the beginning the Chinese Commercial Union in Hong Kong showed its weakness. Constrained by the colony's laws, it was reluctant to assume the leadership of a boycott movement. Without elite leadership, no organized boycott was possible. Chinese merchants in Shanghai launched a boycott of American goods on July 20 and Canton merchants responded on August 1. But the Hong Kong Commercial Union still remained quiet. The young revolutionary journalist Cheng Kuan-kung grew impatient. He wrote a poem lamenting that the colony's merchants were "as quiet as the winter cicadas."[7]

Only the local Chinese newspapers were engaged in a boycott in words. They propagated the boycott and disseminated the news of nationalistic activities of the Chinese at home and abroad. They called upon the Chinese government to protect the Chinese overseas and to use the threat of a boycott as a means of treaty revision. The Hong Kong Chinese newspapers vied with one another in denouncing Govornor General Yüan Shih-k'ai for discouraging and suppressing nationalistic agitations in Chih-li.[8]

Throughout the boycott the press stood in the forefront of the movement not only in Hong Kong but also in south China. The newspapers published by both revolutionaries (e.g., *Chung-kuo jih-pao, Kwangtung jih-pao, Yu-so-wei*) and constitutionalists (e.g., *Shih-pao, Hsiang-chiang shang-pao,*) competed with one another in reporting the progress of the boycott. They published letters from their readers expressing their views on the boycott, they revealed to the public the names of merchants dealing with American goods, and they urged people to join the boycott movement. Hong Kong became a major center of newspaper propaganda throughout the movement.[9] Even the conservative paper *Hua-tzu jih-pao* refused to accept advertisements of American goods.[10]

The leading article of the *Hua-tzu jih-pao* on July 26, entitled "Solidarity but No Rash Violence," blamed the incompetent Manchu government for the loss of China's sovereign rights and for the enslavement of her people by other countries. The article credited the merchants for arousing national consciousness and solidarity in the boycott and in the railroad redemption movements. But it warned against rash violence toward Americans in China, which occurred during the riot in Amoy on July 19, where people allegedly threw dirt into the American consulate, destroyed its flagpole, forced the Chinese employees to quit work, and threatened to set fire to the consulate. Such lawless action of the "ignorant people," said the *Hua-tzu jih-pao*, could cause an international incident and bring calamity to the nation. In short, it warned against "antiforeignism by barbarous means" (*yeh-man p'ai-wai*).[11] This was typical of the merchants' attitude towards the boycott. Even the revolutionary boycott activist and journalist Cheng Kuan-kung warned against mob violence of the "ignorant laborers."[12]

In the increasingly complex and heterogeneous society, which had begun to develop since the mid-1880s, the Tung Wah Hospital's role as an elite institution had gradually declined. By the 1900s it no longer played its earlier preeminent position of community leadership. The Canton merchants trading with foreign goods in Shanghai telegraphed to inform the Tung Wah Hospital that they had decided to stop ordering American goods. But, unwilling to get itself involved, the hospital transferred the telegram to the Hong Kong Chinese Commercial Union on August 6.[13] The hospital's abdication of social responsibility angered a large section of the colony's Chinese community as well as the overseas Chinese.[14] Later on, when the hospital again received a letter in January 1907 from the Oakland Chinese community soliciting support for an anti-American boycott, the hospital directorate replied that it would not intervene in any extramedical matters.[15] The Hong Kong Chinese Commercial Union was supposed to have taken over the responsibilities for such matters.

But the commercial union found itself in a difficult situation. It felt constrained by the colony's laws forbidding an organized boycott while it also felt the pressure of the Chinese compatriots at home and abroad urging an organized boycott. On August 8, 1905, some leading merchants of the commercial union (Fung Wah Chuen, Ho Tung, Lau Chu Pak, and Ho Kam Tong) consulted the barrister Mr. Pullok, who counseled against collective actions and public meetings.[16] But telegrams urging boycott continued to pour in.

On account of telegrams received from the Shanghai Boycott Committee and from the San Fransisco Chinese mercantile community, the Hong Kong Chinese Commercial Union advertised a public meeting in the press on August 11 to discuss the boycott, which was to take place on the following day in the premises of the union.[17] Even on such short notice the premises were fully crowded long before the appointed hours. Nearly four hundred persons assembled, representing all classes of the Chinese community, and another four hundred persons gathered outdoors. To the surprise and dismay of the public, however, the commercial union chairman Fung Wah Chuen opened the proceedings by reading a letter from the colonial authorities stating that "the meeting . . . cannot be held without the Governor's permit."[18] An uproar immediately interrupted Fung Wah Chuen's words. It was impossible to restore order, for the whole crowd vied with each other in shouting torrents of angry speech denouncing the uselessness of the commercial union and its management. A voice was raised in vain against the colonial government's ban on public meetings. The frustrated crowd lingered in or around the commercial union premises for nearly an hour before dispersing.[19]

Subsequently, the Committee of the Chinese Commercial Union met on August 14, attended by over thirty members. The debate on the boycott revealed the divided opinions of the colony's leading merchants. Ho Kam Tong (comprador to Jardine, Matheson & Co.) suggested a petition to the colonial authorities for permission to hold a merchants' meeting to discuss the boycott issue, saying that if the colony's merchants did not do something about the boycott, they would be censured by their fellow merchants in Shanghai and by the "400 million Chinese compatriots."[20]

The same concern was expressed by Fung Sau Tin (importer and exporter to California):

> In a boycott against American goods, I and my fellow exporters for San Fransisco would be the first to be adversely affected. But the boycott grows out of public indignation. So, if Hong Kong does not join the boycott, we will be blamed by the Chinese in other ports. [However], if the [Hong Kong] Government does not permit [an organized boycott], each firm should follow its own way—no one may force others [to join the boycott].

This statement by a merchant trading with America is particularly interesting because it revealed his conflicting feelings. He worried about the boycott's effect on his immediate commercial interest, but was also concerned about the "public indignation" of "the Chinese in other ports." Torn between a nationalist cause and a concern with his immediate material interest, Fung Sau Tin vacillated and then leaned towards his commercial interest.

Chan Keng Yu (Ch'en Keng Yu, son of a merchant in Hawaii named Chan Fong, and comprador to the Douglas Lapraik Shipping Co.) was more unequivocal. While believing that the Chinese were justified in staging a boycott to express their national indignation, he was opposed to an organized boycott in Hong Kong. He observed that ever since the coolie strike of 1884 the laws enacted to keep social order would not allow violation. Concerned that the boycott would disrupt the colony's trade, he insisted that each individual should decide for himself what to do and no one should urge others to join the boycott. But boycott sentiment was so strong that the Committee of the Chinese Commercial Union voted to petition the colonial government for permission to hold community meetings to discuss the matter.[21]

Meanwhile, Governor Matthew Nathan (1904–1907) had discussed the situation with the Chinese members of the legislative council, Ho Kai and Wei Yuk, who, the governor said, were "strongly opposed to the proposed meetings being allowed and were of the opinion that the 'boycott' was not wanted by any respectable merchant here, and that the proposal to enforce it was due entirely to the difficulty of resisting pressure from Shanghai unless the Government put its face against the movement." The Governor decided to reject the Chinese merchants' petition, stating that the boycott "can only be regarded as an attack on the commerce of a friendly power and . . . would react unfavourably on the trade of this free trade port."[22]

In opposing the boycott the Chinese elite represented by Ho Kai and Wei Yuk spoke only for some segments of the mercantile community. They were alienated from other segments of the Chinese community they purported to represent, which reflected the complex and heterogeneous nature of the Chinese community in Hong Kong in the 1900s. It was no longer possible to attain a societal consensus on important issues.

The commercial union chairman, Fung Wah Chuen, found himself in a difficult situation. In expressing sympathy with Chinese nationalist sentiment against the U.S. exclusion laws and in attempting to call Chinese public meetings to discuss the boycott, Fung Wah Chuen incurred the wrath of the colony's Western community. Yet, in readily submitting to the colonial government's order to call off the public meeting, he enraged the Chinese public. Anonymous placards were found everywhere, attacking Fung Wah Chuen and other prominent merchants of the commercial union for their inability to lead a boycott. Fung Wah Chuen also received anonymous threatening letters.[23] He decided to resign his position as chairman of the commercial union.[24] The Committee of the Chinese Commercial Union met on September 19 to elect a new chairman. Recommended by 146 firms, Yip Hoi Shan (a Fukienese) was elected chairman, and Chan Keng Yu, vice-chairman.

Thus, the disunity of the merchant elite in the Chinese Commercial Union and the government's ban on public meetings frustrated the boycotters and hampered the development of an organized boycott movement in Hong Kong. The anti-American boycott was left to the unorganized individuals and general public. Journalists, teachers, and students attempted to activate the boycott, and they were supported by some merchants and businessmen who sought to take advantage of the boycott to promote native enterprises against foreign capitalist economic domination over the Chinese. Businessmen's sectional self-assertion merged with patriotism in the boycott movement.

Disorganized Boycott Activities in the Colony

Even before the Chinese Commercial Union petitioned the colonial government on August 14, some importing and exporting of American goods had already been stopped. To avoid violation of the colony's laws, notices such as the following were posted in some stores: "We regret that owing to no stock of XX we are temporarily unable to supply customers with the stuff."[25] Placards and circulars were posted around the walls in the streets warning people against buying or using American products.

Kerosene oil, piece goods, and flour were the three major imports from America. American flour was especially valued for its superior quality. Yet a number of bakeries advertised in newspapers that they had "voluntarily substituted the highest rate Chinese and English flour" for American flour.[26] The boycott provided an opportunity for trade in Australian flour, and prominent among the firms to benefit were Messrs. Barretto and Co.[27] Tang Lap Ting, a California trade merchant, sold his imported American flour at a reduced price, and resolved not to place new orders until the abolition of the exclusion laws. Yeung Wan Po, a broker of flour and sundries for American firms, advertised that "to fulfill a citizen's duty" he was "willing to sacrifice personal interest" and quit his work until the exclusion treaty was revised.[28] Thus, Tang Lap Ting and Yeung Wan Po chose to sacrifice their immediate interests for the nationalist cause. As a Chinese resident wrote to the *South China Morning Post,* "The boycott, then, is the outcome of provocation; it is not a profit-making scheme. In supporting it we have actually to lose our money and risk our lives, but, notwithstanding that, we do so with pleasure."[29]

But it was easier for consumers to boycott American goods than for merchants who had to sustain economic losses. Not every merchant was like Tang Lap Ting and Yeung Wan Po, willing to sacrifice immediate interests for long-term interests that were remote and uncertain. Some shopkeepers sought to conceal from the public the true identity of American flour by changing its trademarks. In March 1906 six people were prosecuted for doing so. A similar case occurred as late as August 1, 1906, involving a comprador and some shopkeepers.[30]

On August 16, 1905, the Rice Merchants' Guild in the colony resolved to join the boycott. In supporting the nationalist cause the rice merchants sustained little economic loses, for rice was imported from Southeast Asia, not from America. The export of rice to the United States was little affected by the boycott. In other trades Chan Chen Cheong and Leung Chak Chau, who had relied on American material to operate a match-making company in Hong Kong, decided to close down their business until the exclusion treaty was revised.[31] The proprietor of the I-Ching Weaving Company advertised in August 1905 that to fulfill a citizen's duty he used only native material and not the American import.[32] *Yu-so-wei,* a newspaper run by the revolutionaries, refused to publish any commercial advertisement for American goods.[33] Feng Hui-ch'en (a clansman of the boycott martyr Feng Hsia-wei, and a merchant in Hong Kong for over ten years) resigned his position as an agent for the New York Life Insurance Company, "sacrificing personal interest for the preservation of public good."[34]

By September 19 the local press had reported "a serious diminution in local sales of American goods."[35] The British-American Tobacco Company was boycotted.[36] Many British and European firms in Hong Kong felt obliged to run advertisements in Chinese newspapers to remind the public that their goods (flour, cigarettes, yarns, cloth, shoes, beer, kerosene, and other imports) were manufactured in Europe and not in America. The British insurance companies did similar advertisements.[37] An American liner flying a British flag leaving Manila for Hong Kong was also subjected to boycott: one hundred and twenty out of one hundred and fifty Chinese passengers canceled their ticket reservations.[38] And a Chinese dentist confided to a foreign missionary that the public had threatened to boycott him because he had received his education in America.[39]

Since large numbers of Chinese in the United States came from the district of Hsin-ning in Kwangtung the Hsin-ning Cantonese bacame very active in the boycott movement. Here was an instance of how localism helped to enhance a nationalist cause. The Hong Kong merchants from Hsin-ning organized a commercial office, which collected subscriptions and sent several men back to their native district to propagate the cause. The boycott activist Siu King Chung's speech at the Kwang-hai academy was especially well-received by merchants and students. The activists used plain language, advertisements, and songs to propagate the boycott among the ordinary men, women, and children.[40] The *Shih-shih hua-pao*, a Canton pictorial, contributed a great deal to popularize the nationalist boycott cause.

Secondary school students in Hong Kong also became politically activated. During an examination in June 1905 at the Queen's College an English composition topic was: "To boycott American goods would be like cutting one's nose to spite one's face. Discuss the assertion."[41] The American Schlitz Beer Company donated a number of dictionaries to the Queen's College students. On their way home, on September 9, they tore up numerous such dictionaries to protest the United States exclusion laws.[42] When the *South China Morning Post* editorial called this "wonton mischief," Wai Ting Iu wrote on behalf of the students to remonstrate against such a remark.[43] The Canton pictorial *Shih-shih hua-pao* quickly picked up the story, publishing pictures of "patriotic students" in Hong Kong tearing up American books.[44]

Boycott as a Reflection of Manufacturers' Economic and Political Aspirations

In part, the boycott reflected the aspirations of many Chinese merchants and businessmen to promote their economic interests against foreign capitalist domination and control. Since 1895, in the aftermath of China's defeat in the Sino-Japanese war, the foreign powers had extended their industrial investments in China in railroads, mines, textiles, and other light industries. This gave a strong impetus to the development of a native modern industry. For as soon as the Chinese saw the immense advantage of the modern methods of industry, they began to invest in manufacturing enterprises, and they did so "with great passion" and "in the name of resisting foreign goods."[45]

Since 1895 Chinese-owned manufacturing enterprises as well as foreign-owned had increased in number.[46] Closely connected with the "rights recovery" movement, this passion to set up manufacturing enterprises was invigorated during and after the anti-American boycott in 1905–6. The historian Chu Shih-chia contends that the boycott resulted from a clash of interest between the Chinese "national bourgeoisie" and foreign capitalists. The former sought to use the anti-American boycott as a means to exclude foreign capital and interest from China and to develop Chinese "national industry" and "national capitalism."[47]

Kikuchi Takaharu similarly argues that the boycott and the rights recovery movement reflected the emerging national consciousness of China's rising national capitalists, who desired to develop national capitalism and a native modern industry. Kikuchi makes a distinction between *commercial capital* (*shôgyô shihon*) and *industrial capital* (*sangyô shihon*), with the industrial capitalists more actively supporting the boycott of foreign manufactured goods. Kikuchi further subdivides the commercial capitalists into two groups—those who did not directly trade with America and supported the boycott, and those who had close commercial ties with America and were often opposed to the boycott. Kikuchi further points out that even among the industrial capitalists, those who continued to rely on America for the supply of machines, techniques, and raw materials maintained an ambiguous attitude towards the boycott.[48]

The works of Chu Shih-chia and Kikuchi Takaharu provide much insight into the anti-American boycott movemnent. But they made too sharp a distinction between national capitalists, comprador capitalists, and bureaucratic capitalists. The capitalists cannot be so neatly classified because of the interpenetration of their capital. Similarly, Kikuchi's categories of commercial capital and industrial capital were in fact often intertwined. Kikuchi concedes the interpenetration and intertwining of these categories, but he asserts that comprador capitalists were more directly and to a larger degree tied to foreign capitalists than national capitalists were. While making these distinctions, he warns against making sweeping generalizations and emphasizes the need to study individual cases.

Similarly, Wang Ching-yü observes: "Born under the circumstances of the invasion of foreign capitalism, national capital could not cut itself free from compradore capital. On the contrary, in the incipient stage of Chinese capitalism, large sums of compradore capital were transferred into national capital." He cautions that "the emergence of Chinese capitalism was a process full of contradictions and complexities."[49]

What is important for our purpose here is that in the anti-American boycott, as Marie-Claire Bergere contends, "the Chinese bourgeoisie had consciously asserted itself as a class and given voice to political aims."[50] But the boycott did not merely reflect the nascent bourgeoisie's political aspiration to resist imperialism and to recover China's sovereign rights but also its economic aspiration to compete with foreign capitalists for a greater share in international trade and even its aspiration to assert economic independence from foreign capitalist domination and control, however unrealistic this may seem under the circumstances of omnipresent foreign capitalism at the time.

This economic aspiration was shared by the Chinese merchants and businessmen not merely in China's treaty ports but also in the entire commercial network of the Pacific basin. As the Reverend Dr. William D. Noyes (a Presbyterian missionary in Canton) observed: "We see also in the [boycott] movement the power of the Chinese merchants—they are not only in China, but in Japan, Korea, the

Straits Settlements, Siam, and in all these places they control considerable trade."[51]

Many Chinese businessmen sought to take advantage of the boycott to promote their own manufacturing enterprises. For them nationalism became a vehicle for sectional self-assertion. Business interests were being equated with national interests. The merchants' aspiration found rationalization in the leading article of *Hua-tzu jih-pao* on October 4, 1905, which asserted that Western countries acquired wealth and power by developing their commerce and industry, and in contrast, China lagged far behind, importing cloth from America, "costing the nation more than ten million dollars" each year; that the boycott of American goods was a golden opportunity to promote China's manufacturing enterprise and restore the nation's "interest and rights" (*li-ch'üan*); as a part of this campaign, the Hua-yang Textile Manufacturing Company was founded in Hong Kong.[52] The company produced underwear in the name of patriotism.

The Kwangtung Nanyang Tobacco Company, founded by Kan Chiu Nam (Chien Chao-nan) and Kan Yuk Kai (Chien Yü-chieh) in 1905, advertised in newspapers that each year China's import of foreign cigarettes "cost the nation ten million dollars"; and that the company aimed to help restore China's "interest and rights," while producing for the enjoyment of our compatriots the finest cigarette that "dispelled phlegm" and "stimulated energy."[53] Similarly, the Chu Cheong Lan Cigarette Company (based in Macao with offices in Hong Kong, Canton, and Singapore) advertised that it had prospered due to the patronage of "our fellow compatriots."[54] The Hong Kong boycott activist and journalist Cheng Kuan-kung was among those invited to speak at the company's founding ceremony.

Still another company, the Kwangtung Cigarette Company, with its general office in Hong Kong, advertised that it had produced the "best quality" cigarette for Chinese compatriots. A special brand of cigarette named after "The Great Man Feng Hsia-wei," the boycott martyr, was on sale to help promote the patriotic boycott movement.[55] A Sovereign-Rights Restoration Cigarette Factory (Wan-li yen-ch'ang) was founded to serve the compatriots and to help restore China's sovereign rights.[56] Commercial advertisement was promoted under the name of patriotism.

Chinese merchants in Hong Kong also ventured into the manufacturing of cosmetics. A Hong Kong Double Dragon Company was founded by Mok Lai Chi, producing perfume "superior" in quality to the American product.[57] The famed Kwong Sang Hong (Kwang Sheng Hang) was founded in 1905 with a capital of one hundred thousand dollars, which by 1914 was increased to six hundred thousand dollars. Its business was expanded to manufacture perfumery, lotions, face creams, powders, and toilet articles of all kinds.[58] This success story was the dream of all entrepreneurs in 1905—to take advantage of the boycott to assert their economic rights and independence from foreign capitalist domination and control.

But the prosperous Kwong Sang Hong still had to rely on the foreign capitalists' supplies of machines, techniques, and material. Similarly, the Kwangtung Nanyang Tobacco Company had to rely on Japanese techniques and management and also on American tobacco supplies.[59] And the Hua-yang Manufacturing Company's manager, Wu Tung-ch'i (Ng Tung Kai), was an importer and exporter to California.[60] With continued commercial ties to America, their participation in the boycott of American goods could only be half-hearted and temporary.

In an essay on the 1905 boycott Margaret Field finds a general pattern: "The merchants were most prominent in the talking stage, with a marked decline of their participation occurring, except in Canton, once severe economic pressure had been felt."[61] Merchants were the first to talk about the patriotic boycott movement and also the first to retreat from it when their economic interest was hurt. The "national bourgeoisie's" economic ties to, and dependency on, the foreign capitalists, predisposed it to vacillate and retreat from the boycott movement that it had done so much to launch.

Workers' Participation in Boycott: Sporadic and Unorganized

Under the watchful eye of the colonial authorities, the anti-American boycott in Hong Kong remained generally unorganized. It was largely a movement of the Chinese students, teachers, journalists, revolutionary intelligentsia, and the consumer public, in addition to those merchants and manufacturers who aspired to promote their economic interests against American capitalist competition. The Hong Kong working people's participation in the boycott was limited, although they were part of the consumer public who refused to buy American goods.

The chair and ricksha coolies disliked their formidable competitors, the electric trams. Many coolies were arrested by the police for posting wall posters to discourage people from taking trams. One such poster was a caricature featuring trams carrying animal passengers—monkeys, turtles, horses, rats, snakes, and dogs—implying that only beasts took trams. A coolie was arrested and fined twenty-five dollars for posting a placard stating that the Chinese should not travel by the Electric Tramway as it was run by an American company.[62] Having some difficulty getting its employees to work,[63] the Hongkong Electric Tramway Company had to request the Chinese press to inform the public that all its stocks belonged to the British, none to Americans.[64]

Some chair coolies willfully refused to serve the visiting American secretary of war William H. Taft and his party. Placards posted around the street walls attacked the Chinese Commercial Union's chairman Fung Wah Chuen for calling off the boycott meeting on August 12. Sin Wa Fung (a piece goods merchant) attempted to soothe him, asking him to ignore the abuses of the anonymous placards posted by "the unreasonable people of the lower-class society" (*hsia-liu she-hui*).[65]

At the naval yard a Chinese was given a small tube of rubber mixture and set to repairing a diving suit. He refused to work, saying in pidgin English: "No can, be'long American." But the rubber tube was in fact of English manufacture. An English newspaper correspondent ridiculed this episode as the "blind faith of the illiterate Chinaman."[66]

The local Chinese press reported that a head coolie named Liu "secretly sought to unite his fellow coolies . . . to refuse to carry American goods. . . . Many joined him to discuss the boycott." Believing that he had achieved his purpose, Liu returned to Canton, where carrying coolies were subsequently organized to engage in a boycott against the Americans.[67] But no coolie strike actually took place in Hong Kong. The Chinese Chamber of Commerce in Nagasaki, Japan, sent a letter, dated July 1, to the Hong Kong Chinese Commercial Union, calling on Hong Kong merchants to organize a boycott, and workers to stage a strike against Americans in the colony.[68] But to rely on the merchants of the Commercial Union to help promote a workers' strike in Hong Kong was to hope for the impossible. The Chinese commercial elite in the colony desired law and order, which was essential for business interests.

The Conservatism of the Colony's Business Elite

The most active members of the Chinese Commercial Union at the time consisted of over a dozen wealthy merchants and compradors. They expressed sympathy with Chinese nationalist sentiment against American mistreatment of the Chinese overseas, but for most of them economic consideration often took priority over nationalist sentiment when the two seemed in conflict. With close economic ties to foreign capitalism the wealthy merchants could only be conditional nationalists. A leading article in *Hua-tzu jih-pao* stated their position frankly: If merchants were forced into boycott against their own interests, it would work only for a moment but not for long. The best way to boycott American goods was to improve China's techniques and manufactures so as to wage a successful "commercial war" against foreign countries. But this would take time, and for the present there was no better way than to consult with the merchants trading in American goods so that they would not be "left out in the cold" while awaiting the actions taken by the American president.[69]

There were at least two hundred Chinese firms (*Kam-shan-chung*) in the entrepôt of Hong Kong that traded with America in 1905. Many of them exported goods (such as Chinese food stuffs) to supply the Chinese communities in America—these firms disliked the American exclusion law (which banned Chinese labor immigrants) and hence were inclined to support the boycott. But many other firms were dealers and traders of imported American goods (such as flour, oil, cloth)—these firms were adversely affected by the boycott, so they were opposed to the boycott. But the situation was rendered more complex by the fact that many firms were engaged in both exporting goods to America and importing goods from America—these firms were also adversely affected by the boycott, and were hence inclined to oppose the boycott. Moreover, those firms not directly trading with America were concerned about a rampant boycott's disrupting of the entrepôt's general trade. Thus, with their immediate interest at stake many Hong Kong commercial firms constituted a powerful, conservative force in the way of boycott. The colonial government's ban on public meetings also made the boycott less pervasive than its supporters had wished.

By comparison, the Chinese community in Thailand, for instance, was more determined and better organized. On August 1 more than a thousand people attended the boycott meeting in the T'ien-hua Hospital in Bangkok.[70] They sent telegrams to Chinese merchants in Singapore and Hong Kong asking them to stop all shipment of American goods to Thailand.[71] Despite repeated warnings, a vessel from Hong Kong loaded with forty-five hundred bags of American flour, arrived in Bangkok on August 23 and another two thousand bags on August 27, which were refused and returned to Hong Kong. This prompted the Chinese merchant organization in Thailand to write an open letter to *Hua-tzu jih-pao* in Hong Kong expressing their indignation and determination to boycott American goods. They insisted that it was the patriotic duty of every Chinese to join the boycott; they reproved the Hong Kong Chinese merchants for not fulfilling that duty. They seemed to say: We, no less than you, live under the constraints of a foreign government; yet we can do it, why can't you?[72]

But, unlike Thailand, which was on the receiving end of the trade in American goods, the entrepôt of Hong Kong was a distributing center. The Hong Kong dealers and wholesalers of American goods had a large stock of flour that had to be disposed of. So they shipped several thousand bags of flour to a Chinese firm in Saigon. For accepting the shipment, the firm in Saigon was later said to have voluntarily paid a fine of twenty-eight hundred dollars to the Canton boycott society.[73]

With vested interest in the colony's entrepôt trade, the Chinese commercial elite took a conservative view of how far the boycott should proceed. Their talk with the American secretary of war William H. Taft during his visit to China illustrated this conservative stand. Accompanied by six U.S. senators, twenty-two congressmen and the president's daughter, Alice Roosevelt, Secretary Taft arrived in Hong Kong on September 1, 1905, from Manila. He met with some "representative Hong Kong Chinese" to hear their views on the exclusion laws in the United States. They included Ho Kai, Wei Yuk, Fung Wah Chuen, Lau Chu Pak, Ku Fai Shan (a California trade merchant), and Leung Pui Chi. Three of these gentlemen were compradors to foreign firms.

The meeting took place in the presence of Governor Nathan in his office on September 5. The striking thing about this conversation between the Chinese merchant elite and Secretary Taft was their basic agreement regarding the need to remove the abuses in the administration of the exclusion laws rather than to abolish those laws. Ho Kai and his colleagues did not question America's exclusion of the Chinese laboring class; rather, they seemed mostly concerned about the mistreatment of Chinese merchants, students, and overseas Chinese gentlemen of wealth and education.[74] As an American resident in Hong Kong observed, "the merchants certainly do not care whether the coolie is excluded from America or not, as [they have] nothing in common with the coolie and [have] no regard for his interests."[75] This seemed to be a valid description of the Chinese gentlemen who talked with Secretary Taft. They did not speak for large segments of the Chinese community they purported to represent. By the 1900s the community had become increasingly complex and heterogeneous, with different attitudes and responses to important issues such as the boycott of American goods.

"Civilized Resistance": Boycott by "Civilized Means"

The Chinese elite and merchants were always sensitive to social unrest generated from below. During the anti-American boycott, most of the boycott activists from a commercial and intelligentsia background advocated "civilized resistance" (wen-ming ti-chih) and "civilized antiforeignism" (wen-ming p'ai-wai), that is, peaceful boycott of American goods without riot or violence. They distrusted the "barbarous antiforeignism" (yeh-man p'ai-wai) of the "lower class society" (hsia-liu she-hui).[76]

In Canton, Governor General Ts'en Ch'un-hsüan repeatedly warned against civil disorder and public agitation. He admonished the boycott activists in Kwangtung that they could peacefully address the mercantile communities but not "the idle people of the marketplace" (shih-ching yu-min) who might cause disturbances.[77] Posting wall posters to insult the party of visiting Americans (Secretary Taft and Alice Roosevelt) was also regarded by the authorities as an "uncivilized act" of the "ignorant" and "lawless people," and was therefore prohibited. One cartoon poster portrayed Miss Alice Roosevelt being carried by four turtles, meaning to induce chair coolies to boycott the Americans.[78] When the Hong Kong newspaper Shih-chieh kung-i pao (Commonweal) reprinted the cartoon poster, the colonial government banished its three staff members from Hong Kong for five years. Ho Kai and Wei Yuk told Governor Nathan that the banishment was fully justified.[79] The conservative newspaper *Hua-tzu jih-pao* insisted on "civilized boycott," calling the posting of the cartoon poster a "nonsensical act."[80]

Though the colonial government banned public meetings, a memorial service banquet was held in a restaurant on October 28, 1905, in honor of Feng Hsia-wei, the boycott martyr. The banquet was sponsored by the Enlightenment Society (K'ai-chih she) and chaired by Cheng Kuan-kung, a young revolutionary and founder-editor of *Kuang-tung jih-pao* (Kwangtung daily news).[81] More than two hundred people attended the banquet, which featured five speakers who were mostly from commercial and educational circles. Altogether 134 eulogies were received from 119 persons (including at least 8 women), 3 newspapers (*Kuang-tung jih-pao*, *Ch'ün-pao*, and *Shang-pao*, which was published by Hsü Ch'in, a constitutional monarchist and follower of K'ang Yu-wei), 4 student bodies, 4 merchants' associations (belonging to the Sze Yap "four districts" of Kwangtung), and 4 civic organizations.[82]

Some eulogies were composed in a militant tone, such as the one written by a *Ya-chou pao* journalist Ch'en Ch'ing-ch'en: "Though living in a land under foreign rule, we shall use the traitors' and public enemies' skulls as wine vessels."[83] The boycott activists and agitators were to be found from among the eulogy writers, which included students, teachers, and especially journalists and the T'ung-meng Hui revolutionaries (Feng Tzu-yu, Cheng Kuan-kung, Wang Ya-fu, Huang Shih-chung, Wu Yao-t'ing, Ch'en Shu-jen, etc.).

The way in which the memorial service was held (namely, making speeches, attending a banquet, and composing eulogies) revealed the intelligentsia background of the boycott activists; it also illustrated that under the watchful eye of the colonial government they were unable to rally the colony's populace for support in a mass movement. This was a major weakness of the boycott movement in Hong Kong, which was unlike the situation in Canton where the radical activists organized mass boycott demonstrations involving all classes of people. The inability of the Hong Kong activists to organize the masses could be attributed not merely to the colonial authorities' determination to ban it but also to the social conservatism of the colony's leading Chinese merchants.

Toward the end of 1905 some wealthy merchants in Hong Kong founded a boycott society known as the Society to Oppose the U.S.

Exclusion Treaty Against Chinese Laborers. Promoted by two wealthy businessmen, Li Yü-t'ang and Yang Hsi-yen, the boycott society was a conservative organization that did not worry the colonial authorities. It enlisted two advisers.[84] One was Ch'en Shao-pai, a journalist and revolutionary leader of the Hsing-Chung-hui and then of the T'ung-meng-hui in 1905. Another adviser was none other than Ho Kai, who had opposed the boycott movement. His conservative stand had been revealed in a conversation with William H. Taft in September and now again in the negotiations between the Chinese and the American merchants in mid-November and December of 1905.

Negotiations Between Chinese and American Merchants

Neither diplomatic pressure nor the threat of American gunboats at Canton could end the boycott in Kwangtung. The frustrated American merchants in Hong Kong and Canton decided to negotiate directly with the boycotters. Ignoring the objection of the Canton American consul, the American merchants asked the Canton boycott society and the Hong Kong commercial guilds to specify their demands that had to be satisfied before they would call off the boycott.

The Canton boycott society, the commercial guilds of Canton and Hong Kong, and the American Association of South China sent delegates to the meetings on Sha-mien and in Canton on November 13–14. The American merchants suggested a joint petition to the U.S. government. They also requested the Chinese to make a list of demands for conveyance to the American government. The delighted Canton merchants applauded and treated the American merchants to refreshment.[85]

To prepare a list of demands, the Canton boycott society sent delegates to Hong Kong to consult Ho Kai (a barrister), Tso Seen Wan (a barrister), Li Yü-t'ang (a wealthy businessman), Ch'en Shao-pai (a journalist), and Wu Tung-ch'i (a businessman).[86] These Hong Kong gentlemen took a conservative stand on the boycott issue. Li Yü-t'ang had business investments in insurance, shipping, banking, manufacturing (flour mill in Canton), and in trading business with America.[87] Wu Tung-ch'i was also a California trade merchant, a proprietor of the Kwong Mow Loong.[88] With such close trading relations with America, neither Li Yü-t'ang nor Wu Tung-ch'i wished to see a prolonged boycott. Eager to end the boycott, they were willing to accept a compromise settlement—some revisions rather than an abrogation of the exclusion treaty.

Li Yü-t'ang was a promoter of the Society to Oppose the U.S. Exclusion Laws, which enlisted Ch'en Shao-pai and Ho Kai as advisers. Ho Kai was, from the very beginning, opposed to a boycott in the colony. Ch'en Shao-pai, as a leader of the newly founded T'ung-meng-hui revolutionary organization, was more interested in seeking to channel the boycott towards an anti-Manchu movement than in the boycott itself. All these gentlemen were closely associated with the T'ung-meng-hui revolutionary cause. Thus, as the promoters, advisers, and supporters of the Society to Oppose the U.S. Exclusion Laws, these men were waving a boycott flag to stop the boycott. It was with these men that the Canton delegates consulted on the boycott issue. On behalf of the delegates, Ho Kai drafted a list of demands containing fifteen provisions.

On December 5 over a hundred people, including delegates from various cities, attended the Canton boycott meeting chaired by Cheng Kuan-ying. The Hong Kong merchant Sin Wa Fung took a leading part in discussing the draft. Both the Hong Kong merchants from Hsin-ning and the Macao boycott society expressed dissatisfaction with the draft. Delegates were, therefore, sent to Hong Kong again on December 7 to consult with the barristers Ho Kai and Tso Seen-wan and with the Hong Kong and Macao merchants.[89]

This consultation produced a revised draft of twelve provisions, which did not substantially differ, in content, from Ho Kai's earlier conversation with Secretary William H. Taft. The draft conceded the exclusion of Chinese unskilled laborers from America, although it demanded that skilled laborers and all employees for commercial stores should not be excluded. It insisted on better treatment by American officials for the Chinese officials, merchants, tourists, and students, as if they were members of a most favored nation. Article 9 of the draft demanded that Chinese laborers must be allowed to enter Hawaii and the Philippines, "provided that the legislature or local authorities of such Islands are willing to admit such laborers" (the American merchants added this condition). The draft also asserted that Chinese residents in America had the right to bring their parents, spouses, and unmarried children to America.[90]

This draft was read aloud by Sin Wa Fung in a meeting held in Hong Kong on December 8 attended by over eighty merchants from

Hong Kong, Macao, and Canton. Different views were voiced concerning the timing of the reply to American merchants. *Hua-tzu jih-pao* reported that no consensus of opinion was reached.[91] But according to the *South China Morning Post* a poll was taken on article 9; forty-seven voted in favor of it, three against, and subsequently the three consented.[92]

Controversy Over the Reply to American Merchants

Then, it was suddenly revealed to the public that the draft had been handed over to the American merchants in Hong Kong on December 9 without being first submitted as originally planned to Chinese communities in other ports and in San Francisco for approval. To a great number of boycotters, this was both abrupt and unauthorized. A mass meeting of several hundred people was organized by Huang Po-yao and Ch'en Kung-tse in Macao on December 13 condemning the twelve-article draft. The Canton boycott society telegraphed its delegates in Hong Kong to repudiate their unauthorized action. The Chinese community in San Francisco cabled the Canton Kwang-chi Hospital and the Hong Kong Commercial Union to repudiate the draft. The Chinese commercial communities in Hupei, Chekiang, Fukien, Vietnam, India, Australia, and South Africa all expressed their disapproval of the draft.[93]

A special meeting of the Canton boycott society was held on December 24 attended by more than a thousand people. Practically all present favored the abolition of the exclusion treaty. It was resolved to so inform the American merchants and the Hong Kong barristers Ho Kai and Tso Seen-wan, and to invalidate the draft-reply arbitrarily given to the Americans.[94]

In Hong Kong, the Chinese newspapers and the general public joined the hue and cry. A Hong Kong resident who had personally collected subscriptions of over six thousand dollars for the Canton boycott society was furious. He sent a long telegraph to the boycott society denouncing the betrayers for conceding the exclusion of Chinese laborers from America. Some members of the Wah On Co. (the California trade Kam-shan-chung General Guild) also cabled the Canton boycott society condemning the "traitors" for betraying fellow compatriots and demanding the expulsion of the draft signatories from the boycott society.[95] The Kam-shan-chung merchants were split into moderate and radical factions, as the Canton boycotters were.

Governor General Ts'en Ch'un-hsüan in Canton supported the moderates. He telegraphed Liang Ch'eng, the Chinese minister in Washington, that if the United States accepted the twelve provisions, he (the governor general) would do his utmost to prohibit the boycott and close down the boycott society. The Hong Kong newspaper *Hua-tzu jih-pao* warned the governor general to take back his words or face the consequence of a popular revolt.[96]

The controversy split the boycotters and aggravated the differences between some members of the young revolutionary organization, the T'ung-meng-hui. For several years, since 1901, revolutionaries in Hong Kong had been split into two factions—one centering around Ch'en Shao-pai, a veteran Hsing-Chung-hui leader, and the other around Cheng Kuan-kung, a young journalist. Ch'en Shao-pai maintained a close relation with the top stratum of the Chinese elite in the colony (such as Ho Kai), while Cheng Kuan-kung had wider contact with merchants, traders, and education circles. In these years lack of cooperation among the revolutionaries themselves stood in the way of revolutionary organization, until the autumn of 1905 when Feng Tzu-yu and Li Tzu-chung arrived in Hong Kong from Japan to serve as liaisons between Ch'en Shao-pai and Cheng Kuan-kung, which led to the foundation in October 1905 of the T'ung-meng-hui.[97]

But in less than two months the controversy over the boycott and the twelve-article reply to the American merchants rekindled the difference between Ch'en Shao-pai and Cheng Kuan-kung. As Hong Kong representatives negotiating with American merchants, Ho Kai, Ch'en Shao-pai, Li Yü-t'ang, Tso Seen-wan, and Wu Tung-ch'i were responsible for the twelve-article reply to the Americans, a document that provoked criticism and condemnations from Chinese communities at home and abroad. The newspaper *Yu-so-wei*, published by Cheng Kuan-kung, joined with others to refute the validity of the unauthorized twelve-article draft. The Enlightenment Society (K'ai-chih she) founded by Cheng Kuan-kung sponsored a Hong Kong-Macao Rectification Society (Pu-chiu she) with an aim "to rectify the situation." The conflict ended up with mutual denunciation between two revolutionary newspapers, the *Yu-so-wei* and *Chung-kuo jih-pao*, until Sun Yat-sen intervened.[98]

By early 1906, however, the boycott movement quickly lost its momentum, as public attention was diverted to a bitter controversy between the Chinese authorities and the Canton gentry and merchants over the financing of the construction of the Canton-Hankow railroad. Cheng Kuan-kung died in a plague in Hong Kong in the summer of 1906, aged twenty-six, ending the career of an energetic journalist and revolutionary.[99]

Thus, the great commotion in 1905–6 vividly revealed how much more complex and heterogeneous the Hong Kong Chinese community had become—with heated arguments and conflicting views concerning the boycott. The Tung Wah Hospital had declined from its earlier preeminent social position of the 1870s and 1880s. In a crisis situation the elite in the commercial union could no longer pretend to represent the consensus of the Chinese community in the colony.

Under the watchful eye of the colonial government, the boycott activists from the intelligentsia were unable to rally the populace in a coordinated mass boycott movement. By early 1906 the anti-American boycott had quickly spent its force. But another boycott was in the making—the anti-Japanese boycott of 1908.

E
I
G
H
T

The Anti-Japanese Boycott and Riot
in 1908

The businessman who is engaged in this profession [of manufac-turing soap] seeks not merely to gain profit but to help recover the nation's rights and interests.
　　　　　—Commercial advertisement by Chung Ching-yu,
　　　　　　　　　　a soap manufacturer, November 7, 1908

Those who deal clandestinely in foreign [Japanese] articles not only deserved monetary punishment but even the punishment of death was inadequate to the crime.
　　　　　—Yuan Heung Po, a Canton merchant, August 25, 1908

China is like a broken bird's nest, and one would be very unlikely to find a good egg in such a nest.
　　　　　—Cheong To Sang, a sea product merchant, August 25, 1908

The 1908 anti-Japanese boycott was aroused not merely by political but also by socioeconomic forces. It is important to examine the political and socioeconomic forces promoting the boycott. So far there has been no detailed English-language study on this important boy-cott movement.

Chinese Manufacturing Industry, Rights-Recovery Movement, and Boycotts

The Sino-Japanese War (1894–95) was an important watershed for the development of China's modern industry. The treaty of Shimonoseki that concluded the war in 1895 granted foreigners the legal right to operate factories with power-driven machinery in the treaty ports. Foreign-owned manufacturing enterprises in China, which had already existed prior to 1895, now began to increase in number; Chinese-owned industrial enterprises did also.

According to an incomplete estimate, in the four years from 1895 to 1898 the Chinese entrepreneurs founded over eighty manufacturing enterprises, with a capital of Ch.$17,810,000, in such industries as cotton spinning, flour milling, silk reeling, and mining. From 1899 to 1901 thirty more enterprises were set up with a capital of Ch.$5,359,000. More were founded subsequently, so that during the ten years from 1895 to 1904, a total of 168 enterprises were founded with a capital of Ch.$33,971,000. The four years from 1905 to 1908 witnessed even more rapid development of Chinese-owned industry—138 new enterprises with a capital of Ch.$61,219,000, including thirty-one in mining, six in metal working, over twenty in public utilities (water and electricity), twenty-one in cotton spinning and weaving, and some in silk reeling, flour milling, and in the making of matches, soaps, and so forth.[1]

These four years (1905–08) of rapid development in Chinese manufacturing industry also witnessed the rights recovery movement and two major boycott movements—the anti-American boycott of 1905–6, and the anti-Japanese boycott of 1908. Rather than mere coincidence, the development of industry, the rights recovery movement, and the boycotts were all closely related to one another.

In the aftermath of China's defeat in the Sino-Japanese War the foreign powers had engaged in a scramble for railway and mine concessions in China. Accelerated intrusion of foreign capital and thereby foreign control of China's railways, mines, and manufacturing industry provoked patriotic reactions from the Chinese. The Russo-Japanese War (1904–5) further aroused Chinese nationalism. Russia's defeat by an Eastern country had destroyed the myth of the invincibility of Western powers. A movement to recover China's sovereign rights and to facilitate Chinese control over its railways, mines, and industry, spread throughout the empire.[2]

In Kwangtung, a patriotic movement errupted in 1905–6 seeking to recover the construction rights over the Canton-Hankow Railway from American and Belgium companies. Led by gentry and merchant leaders in Canton this rights recovery movement appealed to the common people to subscribe capital in order to build and operate their own railways without foreign or state interference.[3] Nationalism was fused with economic interest to motivate large numbers of Chinese to join in the rights recovery movement.

Chinese entrepreneurs sought to obtain the economic right to control China's industry. They supported the anti-American boycott, seeking to take advantage of the boycott to promote their own manufacturing enterprises. Nationalistic boycott activities became a vehicle for sectional self-assertion; sectional interest was being equated with national interest. Commercial advertisements abounded with appeals to patriotism. For the Chinese entrepreneur, the founding of an enterprise in pursuit of his own interest was identical with the recovery of the nation's rights and interests. A Hong Kong soap manufacturer declared: "The businessman who is engaged in this profession [of manufacturing soap] seeks not merely to gain profit, but to help recover the nation's rights and interests."[4] He operated a soap company in the name of patriotism.

By 1908 the Chinese entrepreneurs' power and influence had grown in proportion to the rapid growth of their number and capital investments. The boycott of Japanese goods in 1908, occasioned by the *Tatsu Maru* incident, became even more strongly than the boycott of 1905 a reflection of Chinese merchants' aspiration to assert their interest against foreign capitalist competition and domination in China. Merchants and businessmen assumed leadership in the boycott movement, calling on the nation to resist foreign political and economic intrusions. Large numbers of the Chinese population responded to the call of patriotism, not merely because of moral outrage against the *Tatsu Maru* incident but also because they had suffered from Japanese capitalist inroads. Concern with economic interest helped to promote popular nationalism in the anti-Japanese boycott of 1908.

Japanese Capitalist Inroads: Competition between Chinese and Japanese

Prior to the Sino-Japanese War, in 1883, Japanese trade with China accounted for only 6.37 percent of China's direct foreign trade. At the conclusion of the war, in 1895, it increased to 9.90 percent, and thereafter continued to increase steadily. With her victory in the Russo-Japanese War in 1905, Japan emerged as a dominant power in East Asia. Japanese goods became popular in China and Japanese trade for the year 1906 jumped to 14.19 percent of China's external trade.[5]

The Chinese tea export trade faced competition from the Japanese. In the season of 1874–75 the United States imported more green tea from Japan (22.3 million pounds) than from China (20 million pounds).[6] With Japan's acquisition of Formosa, in 1895, tea from Formosa entered into competition with the oolong tea from China. The poor quality of Chinese teas made it very difficult for them to compete on the international market with the teas produced in India, Ceylon, or Japan.[7] Formosa also produced sugar. The Chinese sugar produced in Hui-chou and Ch'ao-chou in Kwangtung, subjected to high taxes, could not compete with Japanese-made sugar from Formosa on the market in China, thus depriving many Cantonese of much profit.[8] Due to the crude and primitive methods of extraction and hence its low quality, Chinese sugar was not popular on the international market.[9]

Similarly, machine-processed raw silk from Japan often beat Chinese silk in the expanding market in America. During the season of 1877–78 the raw silk exported from central China amounted to 52 percent of the export of raw silk from the East on the international market, but during the season of 1884–85 it decreased to 26 percent. This decrease of the export of Chinese silk was due to the great growth in the export of raw silk from Japan.[10] "The most notable aspect of the world silk trade was Japan's stunning success in capturing the expanding world market from China," Lillian M. Li has demonstrated. "Starting from a much smaller base, by 1907 Japan had over-taken China as the world's largest silk exporter."[11] In 1913 Japan provided 44.3 percent of the silk supply on the international market, and China 31.1 percent.[12] The Cantonese merchants took a strong aversion to Japanese competition, which adversely affected silk trade in Kwangtung.[13]

The basic strategy of Japanese capitalism was to use the capital earned by silk exports to finance the import of heavy industrial products (such as steel, machinery, and military equipments), and to develop the cotton textile industry to produce yarn and fabrics for export to the vast market of China.[14] The machine-made cotton yarn was more regular, stronger, better, and often cheaper than the native yarn. "The new and rapidly growing cotton industry in Japan [in 1882–91] was creating a demand for Chinese raw cotton, sending up the price and making it no longer possible for the yarn spun from it by primitive methods to compete with the foreign import." The import of Japanese yarn made successful competitive inroads in the 1890s and was firmly established in the China market by about 1900.[15] China provided a market for 90.3 percent of Japan's total cotton yarn exports in 1903, and 87 percent in 1905; then 84.3 percent in 1907, and 91.2 percent in 1909.[16]

In addition to tea, sugar, silk, and cotton yarn, Japanese porcelain also competed much more favorably with Chinese porcelain on the market, both in China and abroad. The Japanese were the most formidable competitors for the Chinese manufacturers because both were engaged in light industries, producing similar goods. As a result of Japan's economic competition on the market in China and abroad, large numbers of Chinese were adversely affected. Ten million people in Kwangtung and Fukien were more or less involved in sugar production; large numbers of them became idle as a result of the inroads of Japanese sugar.[17]

In the manufacture of cotton cloth, weavers in Kwangtung were also affected, as the following report testified:

> One of the principal industries in Fat Shan [Foshan] is the manufac-
> ture of cotton cloth. This has been a flourishing industry in that
> City for several decades and gave employment to thousands of
> men and women. It is carried on in hand-looms and many of the
> weavers work in their own houses. Over a million dollars of this
> textile are annually manufactured and sold in the interior or other
> provinces. The cloth is chiefly manufactured from imported foreign
> cotton yarn. It is reported that the demand for the native cloth this
> year [1908] has diminished considerably. Recently almost half the

number of shops dealing in this article have closed down, reasons given being dullness of trade, bad harvests, and keen competition of foreign piece goods.[18]

In Kwangtung this provided the socioeconomic forces promoting popular nationalism against the Japanese. It is not surprising that when an anti-Japanese boycott was touched off by the *Tatsu Maru* incident, which also occurred in Kwangtung, the Cantonese became the most active participants in the movement.

Depression in Hong Kong

Hong Kong occupied a position as a trading (rather than consuming) center, a port for landing, storing, and distributing goods intended for South China, Formosa, the Philippines, and other consuming areas in Southeast Asia. But for two or three years, since 1905, there had been decreased activity in trade—a depression. The Chinese yarn, piece goods, and flour merchants bitterly complained of a lack of demand from consuming areas. According to a report made in early spring of 1908 by the Hong Kong branch of the British China Association, the Japanese had taken the Newchwang trade, which used to be in Hong Kong hands, and had also taken the trade between Japan and Singapore and the Dutch Indies, with a detrimental effect on the Hong Kong sugar trade with Java. Rice now went directly from Siam to Peru instead of through Hong Kong. Kerosene oil was imported to the treaty ports in bulk instead of being distributed from Hong Kong. Flour, which used to be imported to Hong Kong and distributed far north and south, was shipped directly to Shanghai, Chefoo, Tientsin, and Vladivostok.[19]

Hitherto most yarn intended for South China had been purchased by Hong Kong dealers and resold to Haiphong, Canton, Swatow, and other ports. But the Japanese had started selling directly to these places, and as their steamers were able to go directly to these ports, Hong Kong also lost the transshipping business. Similarly, piece goods dealers in Hong Kong complained that much of their business had been taken away by direct importations. The Japanese were the most prominent in this direction, their competition being keenest in Swatow and Amoy. Japanese goods cut into the trade of similar British and Indian productions.

In short, with the Japanese and German firms pushing the direct business, Hong Kong felt the effects of losing its transshipping and its former position as the distributing center for South China, Formosa, and Southeast Asia.[20] In fact, with the rapid expansion of Japan's share in China's foreign trade, Japanese shipping also showed a remarkable expansion. The percentage of Japanese shipping entered from and cleared to foreign countries at the ports of China increased dramatically from 4.39 percent in 1896 to 20.83 percent in 1908, and 21.35 percent in 1909, the year after the boycott.[21]

It was at this time of economic competition with Japan and depression in Hong Kong that the *Tatsu Maru* incident occurred, touching off the anti-Japanese boycott. The Chinese merchants in Canton quickly seized the opportunity to assume leadership in the boycott, which became widespread in Kwangtung and Hong Kong.

The Tatsu Maru Incident

On February 5, 1908, a Japanese freighter, the *Tatsu Maru II*, was seized by Chinese gunboats in disputed waters off Macao because it was engaged in smuggling contraband arms and munitions into Kwangtung. The freighter was taken to Whampoa, where it was placed under guard, the Japanese flag being lowered and replaced by a Chinese flag. The Japanese government immediately denounced the seizure of the freighter as illegal, charging that it took place in Portuguese waters and that the captain of a Chinese gunboat had insulted Japan by striking her flag. The incident incensed public opinion in Canton. The Kwangtung Seventy-two Commercial Guilds' Association, headed by Ch'en Hui-p'u (Chan Wai Po), cabled to urge the Chinese foreign ministry to stand firm and protect China's sovereignty. Altogether 189 members of the gentry, headed by Teng Hua-hsi and Liang Ch'eng, sent a joint letter to Governor General Chang Jen-chün refuting the Japanese account of the *Tatsu Maru* incident and urging referral of the dispute to international arbitration. The governor general approvingly forwarded the gentry's letter to the foreign ministry in Peking for consideration. The Kwangtung and Kwangsi Fellow-Provincials' Association in Shanghai also wired the foreign ministry, requesting it never to compromise China's sovereign rights.[22]

Utterly refusing to compromise and threatening to dispatch warships to China, the Japanese repeatedly rejected Chinese proposals for joint investigation of the incident or arbitration by a third country. The Japanese ultimatum of March 13 demanded from the Chinese government a public apology, an indemnity, the release of the freighter, the punishment of officials responsible for the incident, and the purchase of the cargo of arms and ammunitions.[23] Under coercion, the Chinese government decided on March 15 to make a formal apology, to punish the responsible officials, to pay Japan ￥21,400 as an indemnity and remuneration for the arms (ninety-four cases of guns and forty cases of munitions) and an additional ten thousand taels of silver for demurrage.[24]

The overbearing manner of Japan in dealing with the incident and the Chinese government's humiliating capitulation to her exorbitant demands angered the Chinese people and aroused them to action. The Canton Merchants' Self-Government Society called a mass meeting on March 18 attended by about twenty-thousand people. The protesters presented a petition to Governor General Chang Jen-chün denouncing Peking's capitulation to the Japanese demands. On March 20, the day following the release of the *Tatsu Maru*, another mass meeting held in Canton resolved to launch a boycott of Japanese goods. Supported by merchants, gentry, students, women, and the general public of Kwangtung, the boycott soon spread to Hong Kong, Singapore, Manila, Honolulu, Sidney, and other cities where Cantonese merchants were engaged in business.[25]

The Canton Merchants' Self-Government Society

The Canton Merchants' Self-Government Society (Yüeh-shang tzu-chih hui or Kwangtung tzu-chih hui) was first founded in 1907 in response to the Manchu court's promise of constitutional reform and also in opposition to the British naval patrol of the pirate-infested West River. The British acting consul general in Canton, Harry H. Fox, described the Self-Government Society as a "notorious body which, under the cloak of the movement towards constitutional reform and the enlightenment of the Chinese people, carries on active propaganda against foreign interests and enterprise in China." The society "exercises a powerful influence over the Cantonese both in China and in all British colonies where Cantonese are to be found."[26]

According to the Canton Japanese consul Ueno, the Self-Government Society initially consisted of mainly middle and small merchants who advocated the national rights recovery against foreign powers. Its members came to include wealthy and reputable merchants of the Kwangtung Chamber of Commerce and politicians who "played with arguments."[27] Chiang K'ung-yin (Kong Hong Yin) was such a politician. He was a member of the upper gentry, being a *chin-shih* degree holder. But he was also a member of the new intelligentsia who had studied at Hôsei University in Japan and was closely associated with K'ang Yu-wei.[28] To enhance his political influence among the populace, the flamboyant Chiang K'ung-yin joined the Merchants' Self-Government Society. But the society's membership consisted mostly of merchants and some modern professional men (such as Lau Tze Kai, an American-educated dentist, and Tse Yam Luk, a pastor affiliated with the London Mission in Canton).[29]

The Self-Government Society's political activities were frowned upon by most members of the upper gentry in Canton, who set up an exclusive organization called Tzu-chih yen-chiu she (Self-government investigation association), which maintained closer relations with Canton officialdom. Tensions between the upper gentry and the merchants were revealed when the former filed a complaint with the Canton authorities, stating that Ch'en Hui-p'u (Chan Wai Po) and other merchants of the Self-Government Society schemed to use the boycott as a means to advance their private interests.[30] In fact, the merchants of the Self-Government Society came to exert more influence (than the upper gentry) over the general public.

The Merchants' Self-Government Society advocated constitutional reforms and also sought to promote merchants' interests. It was eager to assume leadership in such antiimperialist struggles as the boycott and rights recovery movements. The promotion of merchants' interests, the development of China's commerce and industry, and the antiimperialist struggles were all linked together. Leadership in the antiimperialist movements served to enhance the merchants' political power and influence; it also afforded them opportunities for economic development.[31] As we shall see, they launched a number of commercial and industrial enterprises while engaged in the antiimperialist struggles. The Self-Government Society became the leading organization in the anti-Japanese boycott, sending agents to various places in Kwangtung and Kwangsi to propagate the boycott.[32]

Boycott in Hong Kong

The *Tatsu Maru* incident aroused very bitter feelngs among the Chinese community of Hong Kong.[33] As public meetings were forbidden by the colonial authorities, the Chinese Commercial Union did not even attempt to call for meetings. The Chinese merchants could only engage in private communications, which, nevertheless, proved quite effective in enforcing the boycott. Most of the major trade guilds endorsed the boycott. On April 5, 1908, Chinese shippers in the colony resolved to boycott Japanese vessels leaving for Australia and America and to impose a fine of sixty dollars on any violators. As early as April 7 the Japanese insurance business was seriously affected by the boycott.[34] On April 6 the powerful Nam Pak Hong commercial guild resolved to boycott Japanese goods and to cable Chinese merchants in Nagasaki, Kôbe, and Yokohama to stop all shipment of Japanese goods to any firms belonging to the Nam Pak Hong association.[35]

Representatives of the silk goods firms met on April 8 and decided to stop ordering Japanese products.[36] The guilds of rice merchants, porcelain firms, Chinese dispensaries, and clock and watch dealers all endorsed the boycott.[37] The Hong Kong Cotton Piece Goods Guild also resolved to boycott Japanese goods, shipping, insurance, and money exchange and to expose and report boycott violators to the Canton Merchants' Self-Government Society, which had vowed to impose economic sanctions against violators.[38] By mid-April leading Japanese firms in Hong Kong had sustained heavy losses, with two insurance companies each losing twenty-thousand dollars a month.[39]

The Hua-an kung-so (Wah On Co.), a powerful guild of the Kam Shan Chung merchants in Hong Kong trading with America, Australia, and the Strait settlements, also joined the boycott, dealing a direct blow to Japanese shipping companies like Nippon Yûsen Kaisha, Osaka Shôsen, and Tôyô Kisen. This also served to spread anti-Japanese feelings among overseas Chinese communities in the United States, Canada, Australia, and throughout Southeast Asia.[40]

Many piece goods and sundry stores in Hong Kong put up posters saying that they sold no Japanese goods.[41] A Chinese firm destroyed a quantity of Japanese cigarettes, creating an emotional scene in Queen's Road.[42] A Hakka woman was said to have thrown away her Japanese-made clothes, porcelain, and lacquered ware.[43] Chinese cooks who served in various business firms decided in a meeting to cook no Japanese food.[44] To commemorate the "national disgrace" local merchants designed a kind of jewelry to urge Chinese women to support the boycott.[45] Envelopes bearing the words "national humiliation" were on sale. Some post carriers in Hong Kong reportedly refused to carry letters not contained in these envelopes. The Japanese consul in Canton pressed the Chinese authorities to prohibit the sale of the "national humiliation envelopes."[46]

In some ways the boycott was more widespread in Hong Kong than in Canton. Fines were imposed on merchants who violated the boycott resolutions; shipments of Japanese goods were refused and returned to Japan; and a Dare to Die Society threatened punishment for boycott breakers.[47] On April 23 the Japanese Chamber of Commerce in Nagasaki reported to Tokyo that the marine product export trade to Kwangtung had completely ceased, with sea products in storehouses; if this was allowed to continue, the livelihood of the Japanese fishermen would become difficult and businessmen would go bankrupt.[48]

Belatedly, the Japanese sought to mitigate the boycott by making a "goodwill" gesture toward the Chinese. To assist the flood victims in Kwangtung the Japanese government shipped to the Canton viceroy a large amount of relief articles, including seventy-one hundred rolls of cotton piece goods, seven thousand catties of flour, ten thousand tins of preserved cabbage, and twenty-five thousand bottles of medicine.[49] At the Chinese bazaar in Hong Kong Japanese merchants contributed liberally in aid of the flood relief fund. But Chinese feeling about the *Tatsu Maru* incident ran so high that no one would buy the goods contributed by the Japanese. Ultimately they were reportedly purchased for one hundred dollars by two Chinese gentlemen who then dumped the Japanese gifts into the sea, in a mock funeral ceremony attended by some invited friends.[50] The boycott was not merely a political movement; it also involved a conflict of economic interests that was not easily mitigated by the belated Japanese gesture of "goodwill."

The Boycott as a Reflection of Merchants' Economic Aspirations

The four years from 1905 to 1908 witnessed the rapid growth of Chinese-owned enterprises in China. It was also during these years that the concurrent nationalist movements broke out—to recover "national rights," to promote "national products," and to boycott foreign goods. The anti-Japanese boycott reflected an upsurge of Chinese nationalism against foreign imperialism. It also reflected the aspiration of the Chinese merchants to advance their interests against Japanese capitalist competition and domination in China.

Many merchants in Kwangtung founded new enterprises—in match-making, silk reeling, cotton spinning and weaving, sock-making, and tobacco manufacturing. The Kwang-hua-hsing Textile Company and the Yu-i Mortar and Bricks Company were founded at Hua-ti in 1908, with a capital of one hundred thousand dollars and three hundred thousand dollars respectively. The Seventy-two Commercial Guilds of Canton had an ambitious plan to raise a capital of ten million dollars to engage in shipping, manufacturing, and insurance business.[51] The Canton Merchants' Self-Government Society, the leading boycott organization, had sponsored a Liang-Kuang Shipping Corporation (Liang-Kuang yu-ch'uan hui-she), and was prepared to set up "large enterprises in banking, mining, agriculture, dairy farming, and industry."[52] In Kwangtung at least eight spinning and weaving companies[53] and eight large match factories were started in 1908.[54] Their products dealt a great blow to Japanese goods. The *South China Morning Post* reported that "the boycott was strongly directed against Japanese matches."[55]

The founding of the Yuen Hing Shat Yip Company in Ch'ing-yüan, Kwangtung, served to illustrate the Chinese entrepreneur's aspiration. Set up by Chu Kwan Yu, it was a piece goods and dyeing factory "on a very large scale . . . with foreign machines of the latest type." It commenced operations in July 1908 in the midst of the anti-Japanese boycott. It was reported to have turned out very fine specimens of woolen and cotton cloth. Many dealers said that "the weaving and the colour of the dyeing are both far superior to those manufactured in Japan." The new factory had received such a large number of orders from dealers that "more machinery has to be ordered at once as the output is not equal to the demand."[56] The Chinese manufacturers' aspiration to compete with the Japanese was given encouragement by some of "the most anti-foreign officials" in Canton. On the advice of Taotai Wen Tsung-yao, Viceroy Chang Jen-chün instructed civil and military officials of Kwangtung "to use only native cloth for the uniforms of soldiers and scholars and to strictly prohibit the use of foreign cloth."[57]

But the Canton merchants' resort to patriotic political activities as a means to promote native industry and to advance their sectional interests incurred the disapproval and jealousy of Canton's upper gentry members, who filed this complaint against a prominent leader of the Self-Government Society:

> This merchant [Chan Wai Po], who willfully owes money to the bank, has floated the [Liang-Kuang] Shipping Corporation. As he himself estimates that he is totally without reputation, he is using the *Tatsu Maru* incident as a cloak for self-advancement, sending telegrams to Chinese in other ports and overseas to vilify the government. People who were unaware of the truth thought that he was enthusiastic about public welfare; they have, therefore, flocked to buy shares in his business.[58]

The upper gentry members frowned upon the prominent merchants who used patriotism as a vehicle to advance their claim to wider civic recognition and to assert their sectional interests.

Chinese merchants in Hong Kong also frequently appealed to patriotism while conducting their business. The Japanese vice-consul in Hong Kong reported that a group of Chinese businessmen, including Ma Ying Piu (Ma Ying-piao) of the famed Sincere Company (a modern department store), set up a boycott organization called Shang-wu yen-chiu-she (Commerce investigation society) that regularly called business meetings. Speakers in such meetings often advocated the promotion of native industry and "the use of Chinese products by the Chinese," thus secretly adding fuel to the anti-Japanese boycott. They seized the opportunity presented by the boycott to plan a joint-stock company to manufacture fabrics, clothes, and towels.[59] This resulted in the founding of the Li Men Hing Kwok (Li-min hsing-kuo) Knitting Factory Company, in June 1908.

The company's founding statement proclaimed that China was weak and her people poor due to the underdevelopment of her industry; the company was set up in order to help enrich the Chinese compatriots and to "recover the nation's interests and rights and restore the country's prosperity (hsing-kuo)"; hence the name of the company, Li-min hsing-kuo, meaning "to benefit the people and restore the country's prosperity." The company was founded both as an act of patriotism and "an act of charity"—to give employment to poor women. The company also offered to sell its shares to the public at one dollar each. Eventually it hoped to collect a capital of a million dollars; the largest shareholders (those holding ten thousand shares or more) would run and manage the company.[60] Merchants resorted to nationalist language and activities to advance their claim to civic recognition. Patriotism became a vehicle for sectional self-assertion.

The company's founding members consisted of 108 men, mostly merchants, compradors, journalists, and insurance company managers. They included at least four active promoters of the anti-Japanese boycott in Hong Kong: Kwok Yik Chi (Kuo i-chih, comprador of Arnhold Kerberg & Co.), Leung Sui Hing (Liang Jui-heng, of Fu-an Insurance Co.), Pun Lan Sz (P'an Lan-shih, *Shih-pao* editor), and Chiu Shiu Pok (Chao Shao-p'u, of the Kung-ho firm). In addition, some other founders of the company were known to be strong boycott supporters, such as Wong Choi Chiu (Huang Tsai-ch'ao, of Sun Kon & Co., a department store)[61] and Yip Wai Pak (Yeh Hui-po, of Hua-i Co., a financial interest of the Pao-huang-hui).[62] But not all of the company's founders supported the boycott, for they included two merchants connected with the Japan trade: Yu Pun San (Yu Pin-ch'en, of Yung Fung Lung, dealer in medicine) and Chan Ket Chi (Ch'en Chi-chih, of Yung Ch'eng Co., dealer in Japanese sea products).[63] These two men secretly continued to conduct business with the Japanese in violation of the Nam Pak Hong boycott resolution.[64]

Although the Li Men Hing Kwok Knitting Factory Company founders hoped to raise one million dollars, its capital remained at one hundred thousand dollars in 1917. By 1915 there were at least seven major clothes knitting companies in Hong Kong that were financed exclusively with Chinese capital.[65] They competed with Japanese and other foreign imports, although they continued to rely on machines imported from America and England and raw silk materials from America, England, India, and Japan.[66]

As a result of the boycott, the export of Japanese goods to Hong Kong dropped from an amount worth ¥24,384,762 in 1907 to ¥18,538,739 in 1908, a decrease of ¥5,846,023, or 23.9 percent.[67]

Pao-huang-hui Constitutional Monarchists vs. T'ung-meng-hui Revolutionaries

The boycott provided the Pao-huang-hui constitutional reformers with an opportunity to expand their influence among the Chinese at home and overseas. Addressing boycott meetings of the Chinese communities in Kôbe, Liang Ch'i-ch'ao bitterly denounced Japanese imperialism. Many members of the Pao-huang-hui intelligentsia became boycott activists. They maintained close relations with the Canton Merchants' Self-Government Society. Ch'en I-k'an, a journalist and leader of the Pao-huang-hui in Hawaii, returned to Canton to take charge of the official publication of the Merchants' Self-Government Society, the *Kuo-shih-pao* (National affairs news) that had done so much to propagate the boycott.[68] Chiang K'ung-yin, a close associate of K'ang Yu-wei and Liang Ch'i-ch'ao, was also a boycott activist in Canton.[69] Based in Hong Kong were two leading Pao-huang-hui boycott activists, Hsü Ch'in and Wu Hsien-tzu, editors of *Shangpao* (*Sheung Po*).[70] Three more boycott activists in Hong Kong (Chiu Shiu Pok, Chan Lo Chun, and Kwok Yik Chi) may also be related to the Pao-huang-hui, for they took an active part in the commemoration of Confucius' Ascension Day on November 4, 1908.[71]

In contrast, many T'ung-meng-hui republican revolutionaries were opposed to the boycott. Attempting to counter the Pao-huang-hui influence and to break up the boycott, the Japanese authorities enlisted the service of Uchida Ryôhei, who was on close terms with revolutionaries like Sun Yat-sen. Corresponding with Uchida Ryôhei, Sun Yat-sen cabled from Singapore on April 27, saying that his party "had broken up the anti-Japanese groups in Singapore, Siam and Saigon"; Sun added, however, that he needed three hundred thousand yen to deal with K'ang Yu-wei's followers Hsu Ch'in and Chiang K'ung-yin, whose anti-Japanese activities were supported by the Canton officials.[72]

Induced by Uchida Ryôhei, a meeting of 132 Chinese students was held in Tokyo on April 22 that passed resolutions calling for an end to the boycott because it was said to have hurt the Chinese communities in Japan. Such resolutions were cabled to the foreign ministry and various other government offices and the press in China. But the Canton newspapers and the Self-Government Society rejected these as false documents originating from some students who were manipulated by two or three merchant traitors in Japan.[73]

Again, prearranged by Uchida Ryôhei, an enlarged meeting of the Chinese students in Japan was held in Tokyo on May 10. Of the more than one thousand Chinese students attending the meeting, 60 percent belonged to the antiboycott faction, 30 percent to the Pao-huang-hui boycott faction, with the remaining 10 percent neutral. The revolutionaries insisted that if there was to be a boycott, it should be directed against the Manchu government. Fistfighting between the two hostile factions resulted in the injury of more than thirty persons and the expulsion of the Pao-huang-hui boycott group from the meeting.[74]

Subsequently, the Pao-huang-hui boycott activists in Japan began to feel constrained and coerced by the Japanese authorities to restrain their anti-Japanese activities. Moreover, many Chinese merchants in Japan were opposed to the boycott because of its adverse effects on their commercial interests. Under these circumstances, some Pao-huang-hui members in Japan began to disassociate themselves from the boycott movement. Mai Shao-p'eng, for instance, eagerly sought to convince the Japanese authorities that he no longer supported the movement. This was in part due to the loses he had sustained in commercial investment as a result of the boycott.[75] However, the Pao-huang-hui activists in Hong Kong and Canton continued to assume leadership in the anti-Japanese boycott movement.

In contrast, the revolutionaries' newspapers in Hong Kong sought to deprecate the boycott, asserting that the boycott could only do harm to both Chinese merchants trading with Japan and Chinese students studying in Japan. They argued that the best ways to enrich and strengthen China against foreign powers were the pursuit of knowledge, the development of industry, and the promotion of democracy and nationalism.[76]

There were two major reasons why many T'ung-meng-hui revolutionaries were opposed to the boycott. First, they saw the Pao-huang-hui promotion of boycott as an expansion of the constitutional movement and hence an obstacle to the revolution in China. Second, the revolutionaries had great interest in the Japanese vessels' smuggling of weapons into China. Only a few months earlier, in 1907, the Hong Kong revolutionaries (Feng Tzu-yu, Hu Han-min, and Hsu Hsüeh-ch'iu) had conspired to employ a Japanese vessel named *Kôun Maru* to smuggle arms to Kwangtung for armed uprisings, although the conspiracy proved abortive in the end. In 1908 the *Tatsu Maru* was employed by a Macao Chinese merchant to smuggle weapons that he intended to sell for profit. Coveting these weapons, the Hong Kong revolutionaries (Feng Tzu-yu, Wen Tzu-ts'un, and Lin Kua-wu) conspired this time to raid the vessel, but before they could lay their hands on it, the *Tatsu Maru* incident occurred. At any rate, the boycott of Japanese goods could mean the discontinuation of the smuggling of firearms destined for the revolutionaries, who therefore were opposed to the boycott.[77]

But, in opposing the boycott the T'ung-meng-hui revolutionaries actually ran against the major current of the day. Chinese nationalism and anti-Japanese feelings were so intense, especially in Kwangtung, that the boycott went on unabated.

Boycott Politics in Hong Kong Mercantile Circles

The Hong Kong Chinese merchants dealing in Japanese goods and their Chinese partners in Japan both suffered severe losses as a result of the boycott. They sought to renew their business. But the boycott activists were on the alert. For importing Japanese ginseng, the firms of Weng Kat On had to pay three hundred dollars and Kwong On Wo two thousand dollars in fines. When investigated by the Hong Kong authorities these firms denied that they had ever been fined. They feared more the economic sanctions of their fellow merchants than government prosecution.[78] What sanctions could the Nam Pak Hong commercial association impose on a boycott breaker? First, the boycotters would ask the Chinese banks to stop dealing with him in financial matters. Next, they would ask other merchants to stop doing business with him. Then, fines would be imposed on him. Finally, threat of physical punishment and violence could follow.[79] Merchants feared violence and economic sanctions.

Japanese sea product merchants and ginseng merchants and their Chinese business partners in Yokohama were troubled by the lack of orders from Hong Kong. Repeatedly, they shipped in secret thousands of cutties of ginseng and dried fish to the Chinese dealers in Hong Kong, who, however, dared not accept them and had them returned to Yokohama.[80] Many marine product merchants in Japan were on the verge of bankruptcy. In desperation, Japanese and Chinese merchants in Yokohama, Kôbe, and Nagasaki now decided to bet on a forceful joint venture: they willfully shipped to Chinese dealers in Hong Kong two hundred tons of dried sea products on the *Kumano Maru*, which was due to arrive in Hong Kong on October 27. The Yokohama Sea Products Guild then petitioned the Japanese government in Tokyo requesting it to put pressure on the Chinese authori-

ties to forcefully suppress the Canton boycott organizations. Thereupon, Tokyo cabled Vice-Consul Funatsu Shinichirō in Hong Kong,
instructing him to see to it that the *Kumano Maru* shipment was
smoothly landed and transacted.[81]

While anxiously waiting for the arrival of the *Kumano Maru*, the
Chinese dealers in Hong Kong got together to discuss their strategy
to break the boycott. Within the Nam Pak Hong commercial guild
there were seven major firms engaged in the import and distribution
of Japanese goods (mostly sea products). They had suffered great
losses from the boycott. For several months they had almost closed
their doors for lack of business. They constituted the core of an
antiboycott faction in the Nam Pak Hong guild. But the majority of
the Nam Pak Hong firms had no trade relations with Japan, and the
majority decision to continue the boycott still prevailed. Nevertheless, the seven firms in desperation were determined to fight an open
battle against the boycott. They reasoned that the leading boycott
organization (the Canton Merchants' Self-Government Society) had
the power to effectively deal with one or two boycott breakers, but
confronting the joint actions of the seven major firms in Hong Kong,
the Self-Government Society's usual high-handed policy would hardly
work—so they hoped. They also calculated that their joint actions
would render the economic sanctions of the Nam Pak Hong guild
ineffective. The Nam Pak Hong in Hong Kong had served as a
barometer of the commercial climate in South China. If its stand on
the boycott was shaken merchant organizations in various parts of
China would change their attitudes too.[82]

So, the seven major Chinese importers of Japanese goods in Hong
Kong began to openly sell their commodities. They collectively re-
fused to pay the fines imposed on them by the boycott organizations.
By promising monetary benefit, they sought to induce merchants in
Hong Kong and Kwangtung to buy Japanese sea products from
them. Meanwhile, they approached the Japanese vice-consul in Hong
Kong with a grand strategy as follows: to bribe the merchants in
Hong Kong and Kwangtung into purchasing Japanese sea products,
a sum of thirty thousand dollars would be needed. Telegrams would
be sent to merchant communities in various places to inform them
that the boycott had been called off. The *Chung-kuo jih-pao* and the
Shih-chieh kung-i-pao (the two T'ung-meng-hui revolutionaries' newspapers, which had been opposed to the boycott) would be requested

to report the "dissolution of boycott by the Nam Pak Hong commercial association." Finally, the Japanese merchants would run an advertisement in the local Chinese press to express their appreciation to the Nam Pak Hong for the "satisfactory conclusion of the boycott."[83]

Delighted by this proposal, Vice-Consul Funatsu thought that now was the golden opportunity to deal a blow to the boycott organization. The vice consul called a meeting of Japanese businessmen on October 23 to discuss the grand strategy. Those present included the heads of ten major Japanese business concerns in Hong Kong—Seikin Bank, Nippon Yûsen Kaisha, Mitsubishi Company, Mitsui Bussan Company, Tôyô Kisen, Osaka Shôsen, Bank of Taiwan, Miyazaki Company, Antaku Company, and Ozawa Company. It was generally agreed that an opportunity to end the boycott had arrived. Yet grave concerns were also expressed that such a strategy of open battle and direct confrontation with the boycott organization at a time when the boycott had rather subsided might provoke and anger the boycotters and rekindle the fire of the whole boycott movement. But the market season for Japanese sea delicacies had started in late October and would reach its peak around the Chinese New Year's Day, when there would be a big demand for them. With great anxiety, the seven major Chinese importers were eager to resume trade and determined to break up the boycott.[84]

The boycott activists were provoked to actions. The newspaper published by the Canton Seventy-two Commercial Guilds' Association denounced the "cold-blooded beasts" who spread the false rumor about the end of the boycott. The newspaper alleged that the Japanese sea products contained poison. The Pao-huang-hui newspaper in Hong Kong, *Shang-Pao*, joined in to propagate the continuance of the boycott.[85] Lo Chor San (Lo Tso-ch'en, a Chinese merchant dealing in Japanese goods) reported to the Hong Kong Japanese consulate that on October 23 a Chinese who called for an end to the boycott was beaten up by the "ruffians" of the Dare to Die Society; and that a feeling of fear had been generated. Lo Chor San urged that more policemen and detectives be sent to the area where stores dealing in Japanese goods were located.

Rather than being a separate organization the Dare to Die Society was just a name under which leaders of the boycott movement threatened to impose coercive sanctions against boycott traitors.[86] On

October 21 and 26 the Japanese Consulate received letters from a Chinese merchant requesting police protection, for the loading of Japanese potatoes and onions for export to Haiphong and Saigon had been interfered with by the boycotters. Meanwhile, the *Kumano Maru* arrived in Hong Kong on October 27 with two hundred tons of dried sea products, part of which had been claimed by the Chinese merchants, although the rest remained unclaimed. This prompted the boycott agitators to take further actions.[87]

A shop assistant named Chiu Hong who worked for the Japanese sea product firm of Cheong Sing Hong was beaten up and had his ear cut by five or six "ruffians" sent by the Dare to Die Society. The Dare to Die Society also put up posters and wrote anonymous letters threatening to kill and cut off the ears of all boycott betrayers who coveted private profit. Many shopkeepers trading in Japanese goods had received anonymous notes warning: "We hear that you are a traitor. Take warning!"[88] In fear of their lives, the Chinese dealers of Japanese goods in Hong Kong completely stopped their transactions on October 29. Their grand strategy to break up the boycott fell to pieces.[89]

The importation of a large amount of Japanese sea products surely had aroused great aversion to it. Again, this was largely due to economic competition and conflict of interests. Nationalism was fused with economic interest to prompt the boycotters to action. While promoting the boycott, the Canton Merchants' Self-Government Society had floated in September 1908 a company called the Seventy-two Guilds Fishing Industry Company, with a capital of eight hundred thousand dollars, to promote the fishing industry in the South China Sea. The business of the company included fishing, fish curing, the manufacture of fish glue, and allied industries. It was also in September that the Canton Sea Delicacies Guild joined with the Piece Goods Guild and other guilds to call for more stringent measures in the enforcement of boycott. In one of their meetings, held at the Merchants' Self-Government Society's hall, copies of a circular were distributed to the public, stating that the Japanese sea products contained poison.[90] With economic interest in conflict, the end justified the means for the merchant boycotters.

Passions ran high among the Cantonese merchants, whose investment in the native fishing industry was threatened by the large importation of Japanese sea food products. Yuan Heung Po, a Canton sea delicacies merchant, had this to say: "Those who deal clandestinely in foreign [Japanese] articles not only deserved monetary punishment but even the punishment of death was inadequate to the crime." Cheong To Sang, another Canton sea products merchant, added:

> China is like a broken bird's nest, and one would be very unlikely to find a good egg in such a nest. If we do not hold firm from beginning to end we shall receive insults much more disgraceful from other (foreign) countries. If we do not devise means to save the situation of the present generation we ought to take steps to protect our sons and grandsons from receiving such treatment from the hands of foreigners.[91]

Concern with economic interest was fused with patriotism to propel the boycott movement. The merchant boycotters asserted their sectional interests in the name of patriotism. They threatened to cut more ears from anyone guilty of "unpatriotic behavior."

On November 2, the *Shih-pao* (*Shut Po*, edited by Pun Lan Sz, a boycott activist), published a Cantonese ballad entitled "The Story of the Ear Cutting: A Satire on a Merchant Who Had His Ear Cut Off in Hong Kong":

> Hello, My man! How many ears have you got?
> You had better be careful of your ear in the future.
> You had two and you let one be cut off.
> It makes you look out of shape.
> Who would be so unkind
> As to make you such a laughing stock?
> It is far worse than thieves in Canton
> Who are paraded in the street "with a notion stuck down the
>   back of their neck" [i.e., ears].
> It is indeed dangerous to have an ear that is so unpopular.
> Although it was not cut right off . . .
> It will make you frightened for some time to come.
> After this it will be harder for
> You to save your ears than it will be to save your life.
> If any company is willing to insure it
> You had better hurry up and come to terms.
> You have only so far lost one ear.
> You still have one left.
> Take care that you do not lose both.

There is a saying "I must draw an ear on the wall to listen to you"
    [i.e., when a man is lying].
If you lose the other you will be
Like a urinal pot without a handle (ear).
People will then object to your occupying a space.
Baskets without handles (ears) are no use.
It is very hard to put cording on them.
Every man has ears.
How is it that you alone cannot remember!
Aye. You had better wake up.
Let all your senses be awakened.
I am twisting your ear,
And will twist it till you are black in the face. [92]

As in the previous anti-American boycott of 1905, the Canton pictorial *Shih-shih hua-pao* rose to the occasion by printing pictures dramatizing the Dare to Die Chinese patriots cutting "nearly ten" traitors' ears in Hong Kong.[93]

Meanwhile, some Chinese merchants in Japan cabled merchants in Canton stating that the Japanese merchants had received orders for marine products in such bulk that they rejoiced exceedingly and organized a procession to celebrate the death of the boycott movement. Included in the procession were lanterns on which were painted fish, tigers, and other animals, all without tails—signifying that the Chinese could start a thing very well but could not put a tail to it and finish it.[94] Such lanterns were alleged to have been hung also before Japanese shops in Amoy. This was reported to have so annoyed and enraged a great number of the Chinese that riots were organized in Hong Kong.[95]

Riots in Hong Kong, November 1–2

News of the arrival of some thousands of packages of Japanese goods in the West Point warehouses aroused the anger of the boycotters. They selected Sunday, November 1 as the day for an organized attack on the shopkeepers dealing in Japanese articles. At 9:30 a.m. "an apparently organized gang of coolies" broke into a warehouse in Ko Shing Street and carried away many cases of Japanese marine products.[96] The police arrested twenty-two men and recovered most of the property. At 2:00 p.m. three more warehouses were broken into. Some Japanese marine products were taken and dumped into the sea. The police arrested nine men and recovered part of the property.[97] When the Japanese vice-consul Funatsu arrived on the scene, around 3:30 p.m., all seemed quiet, although two or three Chinese shouting at him: "Ti-chih! Ti-chih!" (resistance! resistance!).[98]

Around 7:30 at night, a number of men started wrecking the "ring and marble saloons" in the Western District. These saloons (imitations of Japanese pachinko-ya) were shops where games with rings and marbles were played and cheap articles (such as towels and soaps) were given away as prizes. Extra police were sent from the Central District but the "mob" had smashed the contents of a dozen of these "saloons." Meanwhile, around 8:00 p.m., a shop on Kwai Wah Lane in the Central District was attacked; more Japanese sea products were removed by the boycotters. The police arrived too late to stop them.[99]

The rioters numbered considerably over two hundred and fifty, and the Central District and the area toward West Point (where the Chinese merchants who dealt in Japanese goods had their shops and warehouses) became the scene of great disturbance, the uproar being at its height soon after 9:00 p.m. About twenty or thirty shops and warehouses were attacked during the first day of riots. Over two hundred policemen were mobilized to suppress the riots. Order was not restored until midnight.[100]

At 9:00 a.m. the next morning, November 2, a "ring and marble saloon" in Queen's Road was invaded and the goods thrown into the street. The police made eight arrests. When the Japanese vice consul arrived on the scene after 9:30 a.m., two or three Chinese again shouted boycott slogans at him.[101] "Business was at a standstill in the western district, and as the mob grew more riotous many shops were closed."[102] Around 11:00 a.m. "large mobs" congregated in several principal streets of the Central District. "A large crowd made an attack on a shop in Wing Kat Street but the Police charged them and drove them into Des Voeux Road."[103] The Japanese vice consul observed that the rioters' movements were so quick that it looked as if the police were chasing clouds of flies, quite unable to catch them. On the request of the Japanese consulate, a strong guard was placed over the Mitsui Bussan Kaisha's warehouse. Three or four Chinese dealers of Japanese marine products requested protection from the Japanese consulate, seeking to send their goods to the Mitsui Bussan Kaisha's warehouse for temporary safekeeping.[104]

With few exceptions, the crowds confined their actions to attacking Chinese shops suspected of selling Japanese goods. "No shops kept by Japanese were attacked nor were the keepers of any shops personally molested." The raids were well-organized.[105] But some Chinese joined the raid on stores in order to loot. A man who looted a blanket was beaten by the boycotters, who preferred to destroy the goods. A woman who attempted to carry away some towels was similarly treated. And some Chinese who endeavored to carry off umbrellas that had been thrown into the street were roughly handled.[106] So, while a number of raiders were disciplined and well-organized, a number of others were not—and the raid gave them a chance to loot. When the police interfered and arrested some of the crowd, riots broke out. Riots gave vent to the anticolonial sentiment of the Hong Kong populace, a sentiment nourished by a series of previous hostile confrontations with the authorities. The boycott issue and age-old anticolonialism were combined.

Around 1:30 p.m. a riot started near the International Hotel; the police drove the crowd toward the Land We Live In Hotel in Queen's Road West. Here the rioters were strengthened by "mobs" that poured in from the East Street (Taipingshan). The riotous crowd now numbered between five hundred and one thousand men. They hurled bricks, stones, bamboos, flower pots, and other things at the police. Some among the crowd were armed with bill hooks and boat hooks. Revolvers were discharged from the crowd firing at the police. Two men were dressed differently from the rest, each carrying a revolver in his right hand and a placard in his left. They cried "Ta, ta, ta-he" (strike, strike, strike).[107] About a score of policemen received wounds in their struggle with the rioting crowds. The police fired into the crowd. A bullet hit a coolie named Chu Loi through the buttocks. Bleeding profusely, he was conveyed to the Civil Hospital, where he died early the next morning. Another Chinese was shot in the thigh when he grappled with a Sikh policeman in an attempt to wrest the carbine away. Reports were current that six other Chinese were shot, although the police received no information regarding this.[108] According to the Japanese vice-consul Funatsu, there were "four or five [Chinese] killed or wounded" by gun shots.[109]

An excited Chinese gentleman called at the office of the *South*

China Morning Post protesting that the policemen's shooting of the Chinese coolie was a most unjustifiable outrage and that his countrymen were deeply incensed. It was a vain protest. In a subsequent court inquiry into the Chinese coolie's death, the jury (which consisted of Europeans) considered the shooting justified. Whenever social disturbances occurred the colonial government would confer with the Chinese elite. The registrar general called a meeting of the Chinese justices of the peace and the District Watch Committee. The riots caught them off guard and were beyond their control. They promised the government every assistance and "advised the adoption of stern measures to quell the disorder," [110] again revealing the coopted Chinese elite's alienation from the populace in the 1900s and their readiness to use coercion for social control.

Around 3:00 p.m. British troops numbering one hundred and fifty strong arrived at the junction of Bonham Strand and Queen's Road West. There they were met by Registrar General E. A. Irving and Ho Kam Tong, a prominent Chinese comprador, who continually advised the great crowd to disperse. The crowd took no heed of his words. The police scattered the crowd in all directions and soldiers paraded every street in the vicinity. Many Chinese business places closed their shops after dark, and those who stayed open had placards posted stating that they did not sell Japanese goods. In Wanchai, a number of warehouses contained Japanese goods. They were carefully guarded by the police and troops throughout the night. The riot had practically ended by midnight. [111]

The following day, November 3, happened to be the birthday anniversary of the Meiji emperor of Japan and the seventy-fourth birthday of the empress dowager of China. The latter event seemed to have passed in Hong Kong practically unheeded. In contrast, the subjects of the Japanese emperor observed the anniversary in Hong Kong with customary éclat. A large number of the leading residents and officials in the colony were invited to the Japanese vice consul's residence, which was decorated with flags and lanterns, the Anglo-Japanese alliance being symbolized by crossed flags at the entrance and fireworks. [112]

On this same day the Hong Kong police court was "crowded with unwashed [Chinese] coolies" in custody. In all, 119 arrests were made in the riots of the previous two days. Those arrested included a "gentleman" and a "businessman," but most of them were coolies.

One of the riot ringleaders was an aid employed in a fishmonger's stall at the Central Market. He was alleged to have urged the crowd to attack a shop when he was arrested. The magistrate at the police court discharged several juvenile offenders, but punishments were imposed on those convicted ranging from small fines to six months inprisonment and hard labor.[113]

Riot Instigators

According to Hong Kong police intelligence the National Disgrace Society in Canton sent twenty-five men to the colony. Enlisted into the service of these men were about a hundred Chinese in Hong Kong, comprised of vegetable hawkers and coolies who usually were employed to carry ammunition for the military authorities to the rifle ranges. At a given signal from one of the twenty-five men they attacked the stores of the Chinese merchants who dealt in Japanese goods and then walked away, leaving the goods to be picked up by "the rabble" as loot.[114]

The National Disgrace Society (Kuo-ch'ih-hui) originated with members of the Canton Merchants' Self-Government Society.[115] The Chinese authorities' capitulation to the Japanese demands leading to the release of the *Tatsu Maru* on March 19 was regarded as a national disgrace; hence the name of the society. Its members went to various places to propagate the boycott and incite anti-Japanese feelings.[116] Thus, it may be regarded as an offshoot of the Canton Merchants' Self-Government Society. Despatching emissaries to organize riots in the British colony, it was more radical than the leadership of the Self-Government Society, which had insisted on "civilized" resistance (i.e., peaceful boycott) against Japan. Under British protestation, Viceroy Chang Jen-chun defended the Self-Government Society as a responsible and reputable organization, and denied the existence of a National Disgrace Society in Canton.[117]

The leadership of the Self-Government Society published a circular notice on November 6 deprecating the "turbulent ruffians" responsible for the rioting in Hong Kong and exhorting the people in Canton to abstain from similar "uncivilized" acts and to keep the peace.[118] Nevertheless, since various members of the Self-Government Society had been so closely connected with the boycott that led to riots, both the British and Japanese officials blamed the Self-Government Society for the riots.[119]

Cracking Down the Boycott Activists

With the outbreak of the riots the Hong Kong government seized the opportunity to punish a number of boycott activists, whether or not they had any direct connections with them. Banishment orders were issued against four leading members of the Canton Merchants' Self-Government Society—Li Kai Hi (Li Chieh-ch'i), Lo Kuan She (Lo Kuan-shih), Lau Tze Kai, and Tse Yam Luk (who were in Hong Kong collecting money for the Canton Floods Relief Fund).[120] On November 20 three boycott activists in Hong Kong were ordered to leave the colony within a week—Chiu Shiu Pok (Chao Shao-p'u, proprietor of the Kung-ho firm and a founding member of the Li Men Hing Kwok Knitting Factory Co., who, according to Vice-Consul Funatsu, was most prominent in organizing the boycott and inciting the Dare to Die Society to action), Chan Lo Chun (Ch'en Lu-ch'üan, comprador of the Butterfield and Swire Co.), and Pun Lan Sz (P'an Lan-shih, a founding member of the Li Men Hing Kwok Knitting Factory Co. and editor of *Shih-pao*, which published the ballad about the ear-cutting of a boycott betrayer, thus violating the colonial government's order forbidding the local Chinese press to print news about the boycott). Also ordered to be banished was Kwok Yik Chi (Kuo I-chih, a founding member of the Li Men Hing Kwok Knitting Factory Co. and comprador of Arnhold Kerberg & Co.), but, thanks to the German firm's petition on his behalf, the banishment order against him was revoked.[121]

On November 24 banishment warrants were issued against six other prominent Chinese in the colony: Ho Tso Wan (Ho Tsao-yün, head of a boycott organization known as the Commerce Investigation Society), Leung Sui Hing (Liang Jui-heng, manager of the Fu-an Insurance Co. and a founding member of the Li Men Hing Kwok Knitting Factory Co.), Chan Hang Kiu (Ch'en Hsing-ch'iao, manager of the Kwong Man Tseung firm), Tsang Yan Po (Tseng En-p'u, Chinese medicine dealer and a native piece goods shipper for Tientsin), Nip Koon Man (Ni Kuan-wen, manager of the Kwong Yuen Tai firm), and Wu Hsien-tzu (Ng Hin Tsz, editor of *Shang-pao*).[122]

The Pao-huang-hui newspaper *Shang-pao* played a major role in instigating the boycott. For some time before the riots occurred, it had been "in the habit of indulging in veiled threats against such Chinese merchants as did not participate in the boycott," Governor Lugard complained.[123] The two editors of the newspaper, Wu Hsien-tzu and Hsü Ch'in, were ordered to be expelled from the colony. Thereupon Hsü Ch'in and several other Chinese connected with the riots fled to Bangkok, where they continued to agitate for boycott.[124] But Wu Hsien-tzu boldly chose to remain in Hong Kong to continue his struggle against the colonial authorities. He filed a petition on November 27 through solicitor Otto Kong King for revocation of the banishment order. Meanwhile, he distributed copies of a long farewell letter addressed to the colony's Chinese compatriots, propagating the nationalist cause of anti-Japanese boycott and denouncing the British authorities' "uncivilized" actions against the boycotters. What is more, Wu Hsien-tzu incited a number of merchants to sign a joint petition to the colonial authorities for the revocation of banishment warrants, intimating that if this demand was not met the boycott would turn against the British.[125]

Unwilling to publish a statement to repudiate his connection with the boycott and refusing to leave the colony, Wu Hsien-tzu was arrested by the police on December 1. His defiance to colonial authorities and his decision to test the validity of the legal proceedings against him aroused great interest and concern among the Chinese community in Hong Kong. On the day of his trial, December 4, several hundred Chinese thronged the court, only to be notified that the proceedings against him had been dropped and the suspect had been set free the previous day.[126] A remarkable young Pao-huang-hui journalist at twenty-eight years of age, Wu Hsien-tzu reflected the feeling of resentment among many Chinese in Hong Kong against the colonial authorities' high-handed measures.

The Colonial Government Softens Its Stand

A combination of circumstances forced the colonial government to relax the enforcement of banishment orders. First, the banishment of prominent merchants and newspaper editors for alleged complicity in the riots had caused a deep feeling of unrest among the Chinese in the colony. The Chinese felt that punishment had been inflicted without sufficient reason and in some cases unjustly. It was feared that any one might yet suddenly receive a notice of banishment. "None of the leading Chinese merchants felt themselves safe," Governor Lugard admitted.[127] This fear paralyzed trade. The Piece Goods Guild and the Metal Guild decided to suspend business for two weeks in protest against the government's action of deporting men without trial. The Hua-i Company, a Pao-huang-hui financial group, withdrew some thirty thousand dollars of its deposit from the Hong Kong and Shanghai Banking Corporation, setting an example for other Chinese merchants to follow. Rumors were spread that Chinese merchants would accept only hard cash but not the paper currency issued by the Hong Kong bank.[128]

Second, the dislocation of trade caused a panic in foreign business circles. The Hong Kong and Shanghai Banking Corporation, the Hong Kong Branch of the (British) China Association, and the Hong Kong (European) Chamber of Commerce all pointed out to the colonial authorities the need to restore confidence among the Chinese in the colony. They suggested that the government issue a proclamation stating that no further steps would be taken against anyone so long as the law was obeyed and disturbances did not take place. A proclamation to that effect was subsequently published.[129]

Finally, by December 1908, an anti-British movement was brought about by the *Fatshan* incident. A Chinese passenger was kicked to death by a Portuguese ticket collector on the British steamer *Fatshan* of the Butterfield and Swire Company on November 29. This incident had aroused bitter feelings of resentment against the British. The Canton Merchants' Self-Government Society started an agitation against the British shipping and British authorities. Apprehensive of a boycott against the British interests, the colonial government softened its stand on the banishment issue, set Wu Hsien-tzu free, and let the banishment orders against others lapse.[130] On January 9, 1909, the Hong Kong government officially withdrew banishment orders against the four leading members of the Canton Merchants' Self-Government Society.[131]

The Boycott Comes to An End

The anti-Japanese boycott was a prolonged movement that lasted about nine months, from March to December 1908. By January 1909, however, the boycott had nearly come to an end and trade with Japan was generally resumed in Hong Kong and Canton. This was due to several factors. First, the colonial government's banishment orders against prominent merchants and boycott activists had an important effect in halting the boycott, even though the government eventually softened its stand and relaxed the enforcement of such orders. Not all boycott activists were as bold as Wu Hsien-tzu, who dared to challenge the colonial authorities' banishment order. His colleague Hsü Ch'in had to flee to Bangkok. Other activists, such as Chiu Shiu Pok, Ho Tso Wan, and Leung Sui Hing, also had to flee the colony for some time until the banishment orders were relaxed.[132]

The banishment orders' deterrent effect on the boycott movement was best illustrated by the case of Chan Hang Kiu (Ch'en Hsin-ch'iao), who was thrown into panic on receiving an exile warrant. In a flurry, he went to see the registrar general to plea his innocence and agreed to publish a statement dissociating himself from the boycott.[133] He also requested Ho Kai to petition the government for cancellation of the exile warrant. In the meantime, he asked the comprador of the Japanese Seikin Bank to help him obtain an interview with Vice-Consul Funatsu, to whom he promised to help in the suppression of the boycott. The exile warrant against him was thereupon revoked by the colonial government.[134] Merchants feared the banishment order because it threatened to deprive them of their base of business operation and thus lead to bankruptcy. Merchants disliked bankcruptcy.

A second factor contributing to the resumption of trade with Japan was the conciliatory step taken by the Japanese vice-consul Funatsu, who proposed to hold *kondankai*, or "friendly meetings," between Chinese merchants and Japanese businessmen in Hong Kong. The vice-consul invited some twenty leading Chinese merchants and an equal number of Japanese businessmen to dinner at his official residence on December 27, 1908. One of the honored guests, Sin Tak Fan (chairman of the Tung Wah directorate), spoke about the need to promote the mutual understanding and mutual interests of China and Japan. To reciprocate the Japanese goodwill, Sin Tak Fan and the Chinese merchants invited the Japanese to another "friendly meeting" on January 2, 1909, at a Chinese merchants' club in Hong Kong.[135] Another important factor contributing to the end of the boycott was, ironically, the boycott riots of November 1–2, 1908, organized by the radical boycott activists from Canton. Because the riots had caused some death and injuries, had disrupted law and order, and had caused many stores and shops to close their doors for business, a number of merchants and shopkeepers had begun to take a dislike to the boycott.[136]

By January 1909 the anti-Japanese boycott had largely subsided, although it was briefly revitalized in April in opposition to the Japanese claim to the Pratas shoal (Tung-sha tao), and again in September and October of 1909, in protest against Japan's extension of the Mukden-Antung railway in southern Manchuria.[137] Japanese economic competition and the adverse effect of Japanese capitalist inroads continued to generate anti-Japanese feelings among the Chinese, serving as a motivating force for a long series of anti-Japanese boycott movements in subsequent years. In 1908 the T'ung-meng-hui failed to exploit the anti-Japanese current of the day for the cause of revolution. The problem of how to win the sympathy of the Chinese populace challenged the T'ung-meng-hui revolutionaries.

N

I

N

E

Hong Kong in the Chinese Revolution, 1911–12

Of every hundred Chinese in Hong Kong ninety-nine are in sympathy with the rebels, and perhaps seventy-five percent wildly and recklessly so. —China Mail, *November 7, 1911*

The animosity against foreigners which, always existent in the Chinese mind, has been inflamed by the recent revolution. . . . [This reveals] the real feelings of the mass of population towards Englishmen in this Colony. —Governor F. Henry May's *secret dispatch to London*

At various stages of the Chinese republican revolution Hong Kong played a critically important role. For example, the revolutions staged in Waichow (Hui-chou), both in 1900 and 1911, were headquartered in Hong Kong; so was the Canton uprising of the spring of 1911. In fact, during the years between 1895 and 1911 at least eight revolutionary attempts were organized in Hong Kong.[1] These, however, are not my major concern in this chapter. My purpose here is to examine how the Chinese revolution affected the Chinese community in Hong Kong in 1911–12. This chapter, as all earlier chapters, is concerned with three main themes—Chinese community structure, social unrest, and nationalism in the British colony of Hong Kong.

The Chinese revolution of 1911 gave an important stimulus to Chinese nationalism in Hong Kong. A large proportion of people from all classes in the colony were aroused to a new awareness of and concern with China's politics and problems. The laborers became politically activated, which found expression in their participation in popular jubilation over the fall of the Manchus in China as well as in labor strikes. These strikes were directed against empolyers, unlike most coolie strikes in the nineteenth century, which were usually directed against the colonial government regulations that threatened coolies' lives and work.

In the years around 1911–12 labor strikes against employers were sporadic and on a small scale. They generally posed no serious threat to social order in Hong Kong. It was not until the early 1920s that labor disputes turned into large-scale workers' strikes. But the trend towards organized labor began at the end of the nineteenth century, when various employees' guilds were activated and assumed some characteristics of Western-style trade unions. As we have seen in chapter 3, the consciousness of different interests of capital and labor was beginning to emerge in the 1880s and 1890s, and labor strikes for better wages and working conditions sporadically took place among employees in various trades. By the 1900s some republican revolutionaries had learned that to win labor support for their cause they had to stoop to working with laborers. They succeeded in organizing some workers to support the revolution.

T'ung-meng-hui Activities Among the Working People

Among the laborers in Hong Kong, the skilled and semiskilled workers such as seamen and mechanics were more literate than nonskilled coolies and were generally more responsive to the T'ung-meng-hui revolutionary ideas. The Cantonese seamen were among the earliest supporters of Sun Yat-sen's program. Their leaders, for example, Su Chao-cheng and Yang Yin, both natives of Sun Yat-sen's home county of Hsiang-shan, had joined the T'ung-meng-hui before 1911. Su Chao-cheng was a member of the Lien Yi and Chuang Yi societies set up by the revolutionaries in Hong Kong.[2]

The T'ung-meng-hui revolutionaries also began to establish close ties to the Chinese mechanics. Subjected to racial discrimination and frequently involved in labor disputes with their foreign employers, the mechanics in the colony became politically conscious and felt the need to combine their forces to defend their interest, looking to the revolutionaries for help. The T'ung-meng-hui activists came to the assistance of a Taikoo Dockyard mechanic named Wong Kwei Hung, who was unjustly fired by his foreign employer in November 1908, and another mechanic who was beaten up by his foreign supervisor. To avoid the colonial government's suspicion the T'ung-meng-hui activists set up offices under such names as Ch'ün-lo Country Villa, Tse-wen Literary Society, Ch'ün-i Study Society, and Ch'ün-ai Public Discussion Society. In these societies the revolutionaries held secret meetings with the mechanics, seeking to advance labor interests and to recruit them for the revolutionary cause.[3]

Ma Ch'ao-chün, a labor leader, played an important role in bringing together the mechanics and the revolutionaries. After a mechanic's apprenticeship for two years in Hong Kong, Ma Ch'ao-chün went to the United States in 1902 to work at a shipyard in San Francisco, where he joined the Triad Chih-kung-t'ang and met Sun Yat-sen in 1905. Following Sun Yat-sen to Japan, he joined the Tung-meng-hui, and was sent back to Hong Kong in the spring of 1906 to recruit laborers, especially his mechanic colleagues, for the revolution.[4] Close ties were being established between mechanics and revolutionaries.

The activists handed out printed bills to mechanics in late 1908, urging them to get organized to protect their own interests. Within three weeks over three thousand mechanics responded expressing interest in the organized movement. On March 24, 1909, the Hong Kong Chinese Mechanics' Association (Hsiang-kang Hua-jen chi-ch'i hui) was formally founded. On April 19, some five hundred or six hundred members gathered in a meeting to discuss how to organize themselves. The colonial government arrested three mechanic activists who made speeches in the meeting, although they were soon released to prevent a threatened mechanics' strike. Henceforth, to avert the colonial government's suspicion the mechanics held secret meetings on holidays under the disguise of recreation parties such as the Spring Time Picnic Party and Swimming Party. And small labor groups were formed with the cooperation of the T'ung-meng-hui revolutionaries.[5]

Meanwhile, the Chinese Institute for the Study of Mechanics (Chung-kuo yen-chi shu-shu) was founded on July 24, 1909, to provide education for the mechanics and their children. The teachers included T'ung-meng-hui revolutionaries (e.g., Chu Po-yüan), "enlightened" foremen, and masters of the mechanical workshops. Over two thousand people participated in the founding ceremony of this institute. Renamed The Chinese General Association for Engineering

Studies (Chung-kuo chi-ch'i yen-chiu tsung-hui) in 1910, it was registered with the Hong Kong government as "mainly an association of the employers." In fact, however, it was nothing less than an association dedicated to labor education and revolutionary activities. It set up several night schools for the mechanic laborers, raised money for the revolution, and recruited laborers to fight in the uprisings. In 1910 it helped to found a sister association in Canton named the Kwangtung General Association for Engineering Studies,[6] laying the basis for the future Cantonese mechanics' union.

To recruit labor forces for the revolution the T'ung-meng-hui intelligentsia "stooped" to establish connections with coolies and the *hui-t'ang* secret societies. For instance, they persuaded over thirty hotel workers in Hong Kong to join the T'ung-meng-hui.[7] The revolutionary Kot Him, before being executed in 1908, confessed to the Canton authorities:

> Our party comprises men of education and rank, but we all stoop when necessary to find adherents. We even join military bodies and take up employments as cooks, coolies, etc. . . . The Ko Lo Association are uncivilized; they still kidnap, rob people and have no education nor experience. They make no distinction between the Manchus and the Hans. We are now enlightening them with a view to their joining forces with us in order to successfully accomplish our great object.[8]

To organize armed uprisings in Kwangtung, the republican revolutionaries had, since 1895, sought to ally with the hui-t'ang secret society leaders who shared a common hostility towards the Manchus. The revolutionaries based in Hong Kong (such as Cheng Shih-liang, Yu Lieh, Tse Tsan Tai, Sun Yat-sen, and Ch'en Shao-pai) had joined the Triad society, hoping to turn it into an instrument for revolution. The Triads, however, were not easily converted into dedicated republican nationalists, which frustrated revolutionary intelligentsia like Kot Him. When the Triads joined the revolutionary uprisings against the Manchus they were often motivated, not by abstract patriotism, but by the lure of monetary gains (as mercenaries) and by a desire to protect their material interests against the government tax collectors (as in the case of the Triad salt smugglers in Waichow).[9] The revolutionaries hired mercenary detachments from among the *hui-t'ang* in Kwangtung to fight in the Canton uprising of

1895. By 1900 revolutionaries had closer and more extensive ties with the *hui-t'ang*. The detachments under the *hui-t'ang* leaders joined the military operation in the 1900 Waichow uprising.[10] And a hundred T'ung-meng-hui revolutionaries from Hong Kong joined in the Waichow revolution of 1911. They included "more than thirty waiters and porters presumably recruited through Triad channels from the big hotels in Hong Kong."[11]

The traditional bonds of provincialism and localism served the cause of nationalist revolution. Sun Yat-sen and other Cantonese revolutionaries often appealed to provincial and local ties to recruit their fellow Cantonese into the revolutionary camp. The Sze Yap Association in Hong Kong illustrated how localism served to enhance the nationalist cause. Originally it was composed of returned Californian and Australian coolie and artisan emigrants from Sze Yap (Four Districts), Kwangtung. As they had personally experienced persecution and discrimination in foreign countries, they became more politically aware than others that the individuals' well-being ultimately depended on the existence of a strong nation to protect them. The association came into prominence as a result of reorganization in Hong Kong around 1910 and was "excellent material ready to the hand of the conspirators against the Manchu dynasty."[12] In fact, as early as 1894 and especially since 1905 the revolutionaries from Sze Yap had been actively propagating revolution among the Sze Yap people both in Kwangtung and in the United States.[13]

Many republican conspirators from commercial backgrounds in Hong Kong came from Sze Yap. They included, among others, such leading activists as Ch'en Shao-pai, Li Chi-t'ang, Li Yü-t'ang, and Teng Chung-tse. Appealing to local ties, they had recruited into revolutionary forces the Sze Yap working people in the colony. The Sze Yap Association came to consist of merchants and traders as well as artisans and coolies, many of whom became members of the T'ung-meng-hui. Through the Sze Yap Association, money and men were procured from Hong Kong for the revolution at Canton.[14] The association became the most important and energetic agency of what the colonial authorities called the Young China Party in Hong Kong.[15] It provided much of the power and leadership for the patriotic movements in the colony to support the revolution in Canton—the jubilant celebration of the successful revolution, the fund-raising campaigns for the Canton revolutionary government, and the boycott of the Hong Kong Tramway.

Politicized Chinese Populace in the British Colony

The revolution of 1911 had a great impact on the British colony. A great proportion of people from all classes were aroused to a new awareness of and concern with China's politics and problems.

Since the Wu-ch'ang uprising of October 10, 1911, the feeling in Hong Kong was largely in favor of the revolution. This was reflected in the social unrest during the anniversary celebration of Confucius' birthday in the colony on October 18. In contrast to previous years when the imperial dragon flag was a prominent part of decorations put up by Chinese shopkeepers in the colony, the dragon flag this time was rarely displayed.[16] A crowd of about four hundred Chinese attacked the offices of the royalist Pao-huang-hui newspaper *Shang-pao* and of the Bank of China, forcing them to remove the dragon flags.[17]

Equally significant was the agitation for the removal of the queue, a symbol of submission to the Manchus. Within a few days after the October 10th Wu-ch'ang uprising thousands of men in Hong Kong had removed their queue. A barber's shop in Des Voeux Road offered to cut the queues free of charge for three days. On October 29, more than two hundred workers in a chair-making factory took collective action in cutting off their pigtails.[18]

The revolution in China greatly politicized the Chinese population of Hong Kong. As noted in the press, "they avail themselves of the newspapers to keep themselves acquainted with the latest happenings. . . . [M]ost of the lower class Chinese in the Colony are sympathetic towards the revolutionaries."[19] The comings and goings through Hong Kong of the revolutionaries added to the excitement in the British colony; many came from south China and Southeast Asia.[20] The revolutionaries also recruited Chinese in Hong Kong into their forces, reportedly offering each person eight taels of silver as monthly salary. And Huang Hsing was said to have purchased in Hong Kong tens of thousands of shirts and shoes for the rebels.[21] On October 24 the Manchu general Feng Shan passed through Hong Kong, where scores of hostile coolies at the dockyard jeered at the

two men for going on board to see the general. Over ten revolutionaries conspired to assassinate Feng Shan. They followed him on
board to Canton where, on the morning of October 25, he was killed
by a bomb.[22]

Meanwhile, a great number of refugees began to arrive at the
colony from Canton, Shanghai, and other ports in the north. Thousands of them came by steamboat and railway, creating an acute
housing problem in Hong Kong. Among the refugees from Canton
were about two thousand Manchus, some of whom were abused by
the Chinese in Hong Kong. Turbulence and insecurity in Canton
forced even high-ranking officials to send their families to take refuge
in Hong Kong on October 31.[23] The colony's population rapidly
increased. In 1911, over thirty thousand Chinese refugees took up
residence in Hong Kong. By 1914 the total population went over the
half-million mark.[24]

Spontaneous Popular Jubilation Over the Alleged Fall of Peking, November 6–7

The revolution made a great impact on the colony's Chinese population. It inspired high hopes and dreams of a better future and brought
together all classes of Chinese in support of the republican cause. On
November 6 news (which later proved untrue) was received by the
Chinese press in Hong Kong that Peking had fallen to the revolutionaries and the Manchus had fled. This provided "the occasion of the
most amazing outburst which has ever been seen and heard in the
history of this Colony," Governor Frederick Lugard reported to the
Colonial Office in London. "The entire Chinese population appeared
to become temporarily demented with joy. The din of crackers . . .
was deafening and accompanied by perpetual cheering and flag-
waving—a method of madness most unusual to the Chinese."[25]

The wide-spread excitement led a local English paper to affirm
that "of every hundred Chinese in Hongkong ninety-nine are in
sympathy with the rebels, and perhaps seventy-five per cent wildly
and recklessly so."

> [T]he rebel flag . . . appeared as if by magic, and floated from many
> an upper window and verandah, or was carried through the streets
> by excited mobs with an enthusiasm that could be called nothing

else than wild. For hours the trams [were] at the mercy of the Revolutionists. They were crowded by literally hundreds of excited youths who were waving white flags, and cheering each other till they grew hoarse. . . . [O]n many of the trams appeared scrolls bearing the four characters which might be rendered:'Long Live the Han [Chinese].'[26]

Several thousand people ran into the streets, some waving pictures of Sun Yat-sen and Li Yüan-hung.[27]

Some Chinese merchants complained of the conduct of queueless youths who came up to them in the street and called upon them to take their queues away. As G. R. Sayer recollected, "whereas in the spring of 1911 a Chinese discarded his queue at the risk of losing his head, in the spring of 1912 he risked his head who kept his queue."[28] Crowds surrounded shops and stores and insisted upon the inmates setting off firecrackers on pain of having their signboards destroyed.[29] A crowd of several hundred people gathered around the building of the royalist newspaper *Shang-pao*. Some broke into the office, smashing its windows and furniture. An editorial staff was brought into the street and compelled to set off firecrackers and wave a revolutionary flag. The stocks of paper and furniture were taken out to be burned on the street. A force of Indian constables and British officers arrived on the scene, and a fire brigade turned out to extinguish the fire. The resentful crowd threw stones at the police, who used the firehose to disperse the crowd.[30]

Popular jubilation continued on November 7. Setting off firecrackers and queue-cutting went on in various parts of the colony. Several barber shops, named *Wei-hsin* (renovation), *Wen-ming* (civilization), and *Hsin-Han* (new China), offered to cut queues free of charge for five days. The streets were thronged with people striking gongs and waving republican flags with the written characters "Long Live the Chinese Republic." The crowd demanded a holiday for schools. Several boat owners and workers also demanded a holiday to celebrate the alleged fall of Peking to the revolutionaries.[31] The Hong Kong Tramway Company complained that the Chinese crowds did not bother to pay tramfare for the ride.[32] The jubilant crowds consisted of revolutionary activists, republicans, shopkeepers, merchants, traders, boat owners, barbers, hawkers, and coolie workers. All rejoiced at the alleged fall of the Manchu government in Peking.

Turbulent Situation in Canton

Meanwhile, the situation in Canton only eighty miles away was extremely tense and turbulent. On October 18, 1911, Governor General Chang Ming-ch'i had received a communication from Hong Kong purporting to come from the revolutionary leader Huang Hsing, which threatened a general uprising in Kwangtung unless the governor general joined the revolution within five days. The loyalty of provincial troops to the governor general was already questionable. A scare in Canton was occasioned by the assassination of the Manchu general Feng-shan on October 25. Rumor went around on October 30 that the famous robber chief Lu Lan-ch'ing was marching on Canton to attack the city. Shops were shut and all gates closed. A large exodus from Canton to Hong Kong took place. Admiral Li Tsun sent his family to take refuge in Hong Kong on November 3. Fighting broke out at Waichow (Hui-chou) between the Ch'ing provincial troops and the revolutionaries. A white flag was hoisted in the Delta. Revolutionaries were gathering at Fatshan (Fo-shan). The city of Canton was full of troops, estimated at twenty-thousand under the command of the royalist Lung Chi-kwang. On November 6 a meeting of the Seventy-two Guilds, the Nine Charitable Institutions, and the chamber of commerce was held in Canton to consider a letter received from the revolutionaries in Hong Kong. Great efforts were made by the merchants in Canton to effect a peaceful change of government. They were anxious that Governor General Chang Ming-ch'i would retain control of the government of an independent Kwangtung province as its president.[33]

In the meantime, the revolutionaries in Hong Kong made a deal with the robber chief Lu Lan-ch'ing, promising him a large financial reward if he would support them in overthrowing the Ch'ing government. Consul General J. W. Jamieson had arranged for naval reinforcement from Hong Kong, to protect the British concession in Canton. The new model troops in Ch'ien-shan had hoisted a flag of independence from the Ch'ing government. Even the representatives of the Manchu banner forces in Canton told Governor General Chang Ming-ch'i on November 8 that they wished to go over to the revolutionaries' side, provided that their safety and that of their families were guaranteed. The tearful governor general promised to do everything he could to prevent fighting in the city. At 3 p.m. he proclaimed, in view of the unanimity of the people's demand for independence, that he would consider an early date for making a formal declaration.[34]

The British consul general J. W. Jamieson called on the governor general at 11 p.m., November 8. The governor general confided that the naval forces (under Admiral Li Tsun) could no longer be trusted, and that he could depend on only 10 percent of the provincial army, including General Lung Chi-kwang. Prostrate with grief and mental anxieties, Governor General Chang Ming-ch'i wept as he confessed that at last he had "decided to be traitor to his Emperor and avoid bloodshed." Jamieson endeavored to soothe him:

> Speaking not as His Majesty's Consul General to the Ruler of the two Kwan Provinces, but as one man to another, I think you have done the right thing: you have put your duty to God Almighty above everything else; if you find it impossible to stay here, my house on Shamien is at your disposal whenever you wish to use it.[35]

His excellency expressed great gratitude. Jamieson then bade farewell; he left with the impression that within the next twenty-four hours the governor general would probably "seek a solution of his difficulties in suicide." In fact, however, the governor general was quick to take advantage of Jamieson's kind offer. As soon as Jamieson left, the governor general quickly started packing. Jamieson was back on Shamien at 12:45 a.m., November 9, and within less than two hours, at 2:30 a.m., was awakened by one of the governor general's secretaries, saying that his excellency was there seeking protection. As he was in such a feeble state, Jamieson at once helped him to bed. Awakened at 8 a.m., the governor general was put on board a British destroyer, which left at once for Hong Kong. At noon, November 9, "the flag of independence, blue with white sun in the centre, was hoisted amidst great jubilation all over the city" of Canton.[36]

The independence of Canton was declared by the provincial assembly, which had, on the previous day, nominated Governor General Chang Ming-ch'i as president of the new Canton government, not knowing that he would flee.[37] Admiral Li Tsun had, by then, turned to the revolutionaries' side after secret negotiations in Hong Kong (with the Honorable Mr. Wei Yuk serving as a mediator). The provincial assembly met again on November 9 to nominate the revolutionary leader Hu Han-min as the military governor (Tu-tu) of Kwangtung. Accompanied by a number of prominent republican conspirators from Hong Kong, Hu Han-min arrived at Canton early on the morning of November 10 to become head of the new Canton revolutionary government.[38]

The ex-governor general, Chang Ming-ch'i, upon arrival in Hong Kong, took up residence in a house provided by the manager of the Hongkong and Shanghai Bank. The following day, November 10, he lunched at the Hong Kong Government House. Governor Lugard assured him of safty and hospitality while in Hong Kong. Chang Ming-ch'i left for Shanghai on November 17.[39]

Hong Kong Celebrates the Declaration of the Republic in Canton

The two Chinese legislative councillors, Ho Kai and Wei Yuk, reported to Governor Lugard that the Chinese decided to keep a holiday on November 13, with a demonstration to celebrate the declaration of the republic in Canton. The governor deprecated a demonstration, but Ho Kai and Wei Yuk explained that "the proposed demonstration was one of relief on learning that Canton had changed its allegiance without bloodshed, and was a very natural one, apart altogether from politics, as so many Hong Kong people had relatives in Canton." Governor Lugard reluctantly consented and directed the Chinese press to notify the residents that setting off firecrackers would be permitted only from 12 to 2 p.m., on the understanding that this was to signify joy at the absence of bloodshed in Canton.[40] In short, the British authorities pretended to understand that it was not politics but only the absence of bloodshed in Canton that the Chinese in the colony were to celebrate. But in reality the colonial authorities knew only too well that the Chinese community was jubilant for political reasons. Extremely sensitive about the involvement of the colony's Chinese in China's politics, the Hong Kong authorities sought to discourage this involvement wherever they could.

Prearranged by the republican revolutionaries and their supporters, November 13 was observed as a public holiday by the Chinese in the colony to celebrate the birth of the republican government in

Kwangtung.[41] In spite of a drizzling rain throughout the day, a flag flew from almost every house. Although the people in the streets were fairly orderly, an "unruly spirit" was displayed by groups of enthusiasts when they thought any of their countrymen were not sufficiently enthusiastic about the occasion. The crowds ordered residents to give proof of their loyalty by setting off firecrackers.[42] But, as a local English paper observed, little pressure was required, as the great majority of the Chinese population in the colony were revolutionists at heart and were only too willing to celebrate the downfall of Manchu rule in Canton. For at least an hour from noon, every Chinese street was given over to firecrackers, creating black smoke and deafening noise.[43]

The twin cities of Hong Kong and Canton were closely connected with each other in several important ways. Ethnically, most Hong Kong residents had relatives (and property) in Canton and its surrounding towns. Economically, the two cities formed inseparable ties, with Hong Kong serving as an entrepôt—importing goods for Canton merchants to distribute to the mainland and exporting goods that Canton had collected from inland. Such ethnic and commercial ties constituted the socioeconomic forces for patriotism among the Chinese in Hong Kong. They were deeply concerned about the political revolution in China. With the weak and corrupt Manchus overthrown and a new republican government set up in Canton, they wished the new government well, hoping that it would bring about better governance for their relatives in Canton and more trade and prosperity for themselves in Hong Kong. Politically, the republican conspirators who had used Hong Kong as a revolutionary base now became leaders of the new Canton government. They included a number of Hong Kong residents, particularly some prominent members of the Sze Yap Association. As we shall see, the successful republican revolution in China inspired many Chinese in Hong Kong to dream about a better political status for themselves, challenging the British colonial authorities.

Subscriptions for the Chinese Revolution

With the founding of the republican government in Canton on November 9, 1911, subscription campaigns were launched in Hong Kong to aid the cause of the revolution. As the new Canton government desperately needed money, it sought financial relief from the Chinese communities of Hong Kong, Canton, and overseas. A sum of about six hundred thousand dollars was obtained in a very short time in Hong Kong alone. A quarter of a million dollars more had been raised by November 14, the contributors to this loan being promised the return of double the amount subscribed at the end of twelve months.[44] The Canton government set up a subscription bureau in Hong Kong, which consisted of thirty businessmen and was headed by Yang Hsi-yen (from Sze Yap). It sought to raise a loan of five million dollars from the Chinese communities overseas (including one million from Hong Kong). The Sze Yap Association worked closely with the bureau in raising funds.[45]

In addition, various civic groups in Hong Kong volunteered to collect money for the Canton government. A citizens' subscription office was set up in December 1911 by two merchants, Li Chi-p'ei and Ch'en Keng-yü (Chan Keng Yu, who had opposed the revolution before 1911). Within a few days, they collected $3,227. Though a small sum, it reflected popular participation in subscription, with hundreds of people contributing small amounts of one or two dollars to the fund.[46] For a time, activists seemed to be everywhere soliciting contributions—on board the passenger vessels running between Canton, Hong Kong, and Macao, in restaurants and bars, in stores, and in the streets. In one meeting, the old clothes guild raised more than four thousand dollars. The seamen pledged portions of their salaries to the revolutionary government. [47] The mechanics association also helped in raising fund.[48] The students of the Yüeh-chih Girls' School raised money by selling their handiwork in an exhibition.[49] Hundreds of people in Hong Kong responded to the call to subscribe to provide medicine for the People's Army (*min-chün*) in Canton.[50]

At a time of revolutionary war the Chinese communities in Hong Kong and Canton showed concerns not only for the Cantonese but also for their countrymen in other parts of China. On October 26, 1911, an East Kwangtung Red Cross Society was founded by a group of Cantonese civic leaders, including Hong Kong businessmen such as Li Yü-t'ang (revolutionary veteran), Ma Ying-piao (of the Sincere Co.), Ch'en Ch'un-ch'uan (a Teochiu merchant of the Yuen Fat Hong), and Yin Wen-k'ai (doctor). They called upon their compatriots to contribute money to procure medicine and medical personnel for the wounded in Wuhan.[51]

In December 1911 the Hong Kong Chinese General Commercial Union joined with the Tung Wah Hospital and other charitable organizations in the colony to sponsor subscriptions for procuring food, clothes, and medicine for hundreds of thousands of war refugees in Hupei and flood refugees in Anhui.[52] Men and women went from door to door soliciting subscriptions. The amount of individual contributions ranged from ten or twenty cents or a dollar to a hundred dollars or more, the great majority being very small contributions. Tens of thousands of Chinese from all classes in the colony subscribed. In about a month, by January 18, 1912, a sum of eighty-two thousand dollars had been collected, in addition to a case of medicine, seven thousand clothes and one hundred and ten thousand pounds of cakes. All these were conveyed to the Chinese and Foreign Relief Society (Hua-yang i-chen hui) in Shanghai for distribution to the refugees.[53]

Merchants and students in Hong Kong also helped to promote the military expedition against the royalist forces in the north. Thirty-four Hong Kong merchants sponsored a fund drive to organize a Determined-to-Die Northern Expedition Troop in Canton under Chu Shao-t'ing's command.[54] Several thousand dollars were collected in a few days—a result of small contributions by many hundreds of Chinese residents in Hong Kong, again indicating the politicization of the populace in the British colony. The Hongkong Hotel employees pledged ten percent of their monthly income until the formal establishment of a republican government for a unified China. A group of theatrical troupes contributed over a thousand dollars. And men and woman fund-raisers frequented restaurants, brothels, and theaters soliciting contributions.[55] Over a hundred overseas Chinese from Southeast Asia had assembled in Hong Kong and were organized into an Overseas Chinese Bomb Troop.[56] A Women's Northern Expedition Troop was also created, which consisted of thirty or forty women, mostly teachers and students from Hong Kong and Macao.[57]

Eventually, the Kwangtung Northern Expedition Army consisted of about eight thousand well-armed troops, recruited mainly from the New Army, Chinese youths from overseas, T'ung-meng-hui members, and Triads. Under the general command of Yao Yü-p'ing, the expedition forces first sailed to Shanghai and then proceeded to Nanking. By defeating the Ch'ing forces at Shu-chow and Hsu-chow in Anhui, they contributed a great deal to secure Nanking for the republican revolutionary forces.[58] With Nanking secured, Sun Yat-sen and other revolutionaries entered into lengthy negotiations with the Ch'ing royalist Yüan Shih-k'ai. It was not until February 12, 1912, that the Manchus abdicated and Yüan Shih-k'ai pledged his support of the republic. On the following day, Sun Yat-sen stepped down as the provisional president of the republic in favor of Yüan Shih-k'ai. Tensions continued unabated, however, between the Kuomintang revolutionaries and Yüan Shih-k'ai's Peiyang forces in the north.

Rights Recovery Movement and Native Goods Promotion Movement

With the rapid growth of Chinese-owned industrial enterprises since 1905, Chinese nationalism was reflected in the concurrent movements to boycott foreign goods, to recover national rights, and to promote "national products." Chinese merchants and entrepreneurs used patriotism as a vehicle to assert their interests; as usual, sectional interests were being equated with national interests. Commercial advertisements in the Hong Kong native press abounded with appeals to patriotism in time of revolution as in time of boycott.

Restaurants sold cakes on which were imprinted the Hupei governor's seal and the republican flag. The national flags were used as trademarks for liquor. The Hua-lo-yüan Restaurant advertised that it would donate one day's earnings to the fund for the People's Army in Canton. A medicine labelled "manufactured blood" was advertised as a panacea for a "hundred diseases" and for "strengthening our race and state." The Oriental Printing Company printed large and small republican flags for sale to the Chinese compatriots. The Connaught Aerated Water Factory advertised to help "restore [China's] sovereign rights" by producing high quality aerated water for the compatriots.[59]

The Chinese Association for the Promotion of National Products was set up in Shanghai by Wu T'ing-fang and others. The Hong Kong Chinese Commercial Union supported its effort to recover China's sovereign rights by promoting native goods.[60] The China Felt Cap Factory produced "fashionable and beautiful straw hats" for sale to "our fellow compatriots," to help restore "our interests and sovereign rights."[61] The Yung-hsin Li-min Machine Weaving Company in Chiu-chiang, founded by five Hong Kong businessmen, aimed to help promote China's industry and thereby enrich the country and benefit the people.[62] The Kwang-hsin Weaving Company (with twin locations in Canton and Hong Kong, and agencies in Shanghai, Foochow, Chiang-men, Singapore and Penang) produced socks, shirts, and underwear to promote native goods and to help restore the nation's interests and sovereign rights.[63] For the Chinese entrepreneur, the promotion of an enterprise in pursuit of self-interest was identical with the recovery of the nation's interest and sovereign rights.

The inauguration of the Bank of Canton in Hong Kong on Western lines is another illustration of merchants' patriotism. It was closely related to the Canton Bank of San Francisco. With a registered capital of two million dollars provided by Chinese shareholders in the United States, Hong Kong, and Australia, the Bank of Canton aimed to "strive for the national polity, recover the nation's interests and rights, and promote commerce and facilitate communication."[64]

The Mongolia Issue

Chinese patriotism was also revealed in the Mongolia issue. The republican revolution had precipitated a declaration of Outer Mogolian independence from China on December 28, 1911. Russia steadily increased its influence and power over Outer Mongolia by arming and training the Mongol army. In November 1912 a Russian-Mongolian convention recognized Outer Mongolia's autonomy and Russia's economic privileges in Mongolia. In November 1913 China, Russia, and Outer Mongolia agreed on the formula of Chinese suzerainty and Outer Mongolian autonomy, which actually meant Russian domination over Mongolia.[65]

Russian advances in Outer Mongolia aroused a general anti-Russian feeling among the Chinese. Chinese newspapers in Peking published "inflammatory" articles and telegrams from the provinces showing that "the people throughout the country are greatly excited on the subject."[66] By November 1912 some twelve thousand Chinese troops had proceeded from northern military depots into Inner Mongolia to counter the Russian advance. Even as far west as Szechwan people volunteered for war with Russia, and as far south as Canton arrangements were made for dispatching troops to Mongolia.[67]

In late November 1912 when a "war fever" hit Canton, an appeal to the Dare to Dies was posted about the colony of Hong Kong to this effect: "Fight! Fight! To your horses and onward to St. Petersburg to blow up the Emperor of Russia." These notices were promptly torn down by the colony's police.[68] A Peking newspaper reported that a telegram was received from the Tu-tu (military governor) of Canton stating the the Chinese in Hong Kong had been very earnest regarding the Russo-Urga affair and had raised a large sum of money to be forwarded to Peking as soon as the Mongolian expedition was decided upon.[69] The Tu-tu had also received $3,620 from Chinese communities in Thailand.[70]

The Chinese in Hong Kong became so hostile to Russia that they boycotted a Russian aviator's flying exhibition in Shatin on Saturday and Sunday, December 14–15, 1912. Not a single Chinese was on board the special trains provided by the railway authorities going out to Shatin. It was the "most complete" boycott that had so far been witnessed in the colony. Later, in January 1913 the Chinese of Hanoi also boycotted the Russian aviator, and bills announcing his flights were torn down.[71] On April 12, 1913, a Chinese was charged with causing an obstruction in Water Street in Hong Kong, where he was addressing a crowd of some two hundred people and distributing pamphlets related to the Russian aggression in Mongolia. The defendant described himself as an engineering student at Kowloon Docks. On previous occasions he had managed to slip away on the approach of the police. But this time he was arrested and fined five dollars or seven days in prison.[72]

Political revolution was an agency of national awareness. The 1911 revolution stimulated national consciousness among the Chinese in many parts of the country. In Hong Kong, Chinese nationalism manifested itself in many ways—in the spontaneous popular jubilation over the fall of Manchus and the founding of the republic; in the subscription campaigns for the Chinese revolution; in the rights recovery movement and the national products promotion movement; in the Mongolian issue; and also in a movement to revive Confucianism.

Revival of Confucianism

During the years of republican revolution of 1911–1912, when the Chinese were supposed to be making a distinct departure from the beliefs and traditions of the past, there was paradoxically a movement to revive Confucianism in Hong Kong. In previous years the anniversary of Confucius' birthday (the 27th day of the eighth lunar month) did not attract much attention. But now it was celebrated with much enthusiasm. To make arrangements for the celebration a large committee was set up in late September 1911, which consisted of about three hundred and fifty prominent merchants and commercial firms in the colony.[73]

On October 18, 1911, most of the Chinese business stores were closed for the occasion, and the streets were decorated with colorful lanterns, flags, and Confucius' portraits. Joyous music was played.[74] At the Tai Ping Theatre, the president of the local Confucian Society, Lau Chu Pak (comprador to Messrs. A.S. Watson & Co.), addressed an audience of more than four thousand: "It was due to Confucius that the principle and virtue governing human relationships still existed in China; that the mind of the Chinese still has vitality; and that China is still conscious of what is justice."[75] Lau Chu Pak reported that the Hong Kong Confucian Society had set up eleven schools in Hong Kong and Kwangtung, with a total of over one thousand students being taught gratis. He praised Governor Sir Frederick Lugard for being concerned with the education of the Chinese youths in the colony, saying that this was in accordance with Confucius' teaching. Lau Chu Pak also reported that the Confucian Society had engaged three preachers to preach Confucius' doctrines on board the river steamers and elsewhere, and that such doctrines were also preached to appreciative audiences at the society's hall every Monday, Wednesday, and Friday evening. Lau Chu Pak concluded his long speech with the assertion that the moral principles and "uplifting power of Confucianism" would confer "a blessing on China as a nation."[76] The anniversary of Confucius' birthday during the first year of the republic on October 7, 1912, was again celebrated with extraordinary enthusiasm in Hongkong and Canton.[77]

But why the paradoxical revival of Confucianism during the years of republican revolution against the old political faiths? Confucianism provided a focus for the Chinese people in their search for identity as a nation. Indeed, the Hong Kong Confucian Society pointedly asserted that it aimed to develop "Confucian and Mencian nationalism" (K'ung Meng min-tsu chu-i).[78] At the same time, however, the colonial authorities encouraged the cult of Confucianism because the Confucian ideology promoted by the Chinese elite was conservative in nature, placing great emphasis on "instruction in moral principle" as "the life and soul of a nation," and on the inculcation in young people of the duties of loyalty, fraternity, and filial piety.

The British colonists heartily approved of this interpretation of Confucianism.[79] In the revival of Confucianism the main objective of both the Chinese elite and the colonial authorities coincided—to revive a conservative ideology for better social control. To both, the propagation of Confucianism was most opportune, indeed, for the years of the republican revolution saw rampant civil disobedience and popular unrest, which took the forms of "rowdysm," "hooliganism," and labor strikes in Hong Kong. It seemed that the merchants attempted to restore Confucianism as the hegemonic ideology that had held the Chinese community together under the elite's leadership in the good old days of the 1870s and 1880s. But in the new milieu of a complex, heterogeneous society in the twentieth century it proved only a vain, quixotic attempt.

"Rowdyism" and "Hooliganism"

The Chinese revolution politicized the masses of Hong Kong to an extent never previously attained. This was further reflected in popular civil disobedience, which took the form of rampant "hooliganism" and "rowdyism" in the streets. On November 18, 1911, Police Constable Clark was stoned by a crowd while attempting to make an arrest at Cross Street, Wanchai. On the following day, as Acting Sergeant Atwell arrested a Chinese for tearing an earring from a woman's ear in Hollywood Road, a large crowd gathered and attempted to drag the prisoner from the sergeant, who had to fire his revolver in the air to disperse the crowd. Another crowd made a demonstration outside the Yaumati Police Station on November 20, where the police were loudly hooted and jeered. The cause of this was the arrest of a man for the attempted snatching of a woman's wristlet.[80]

Purse snatching was nothing other than a petty crime, but the crowd's hostility to the colony's policemen bent on arresting the offender showed popular animosity towards British colonial rule. The most daring assault on the police occurred on November 20. As Sergeant Willis arrested a man for snatching a hat from a country-man, a large crowd of about one thousand assembled and demanded the release of the prisoner. Sergeant Willis, who spoke excellent Chinese, attempted to explain why the man was arrested, but the crowd was determined to rescue the offender. Shouting *ta fankwei* (strike the foreign devil), they threw bricks and stones at the police-man, who took shelter in the Fun Fong Bird Shop. The crowd furiously attacked and wrecked the shop.[81] Such cases of the colony's policemen being mobbed by the crowd were of frequent occurrence. Incidents involving stone-throwing at police continued to occur for several months, not only in Victoria City and Kowloon but also in villages.[82]

To deal with "rowdyism" and "hooliganism" an amendment of the Peace Preservation Ordinance of 1886 was rushed through the Legislative Council on November 30, reintroducing the flogging of prisoners.[83] During the three months from December 1911 to February 1912, fifty-one prisoners were flogged with the cat-o'-nine-tails for such offences as theft, assaults on the police, and resisting arrest. At the same time, two battalions of infantry and a battery of artillery were sent from India to reinforce the Hong Kong garrison.[84]

In ordinary times the snatching of jewelry from ladies was a form of crime so detested by the Chinese that they always gave the most eager assistance to the police. The fact that now in such criminal cases the crowd should have resented the arrest of the offender by the police was significant.[85] The Hong Kong populace, politicized by the Chinese revolution, expressed displeasure with colonialism in willful civil disobedience. On December 9, 1911, it was reported to Governor Lugard that "an antiforeign gang" loudly declared that Hong Kong should be returned to China, and that it was their intention to poison the whole of the troops on Christmas Day. This report might have originated among the European residents themselves, but it was circulated among the Chinese. The animus of the crowds was shown by their shouts to "strike" or "kill" the foreigners.[86]

In a confidential report to London Governor Lugard stated that the feeling of hostility towards the colonial authorities was "confined

to certain of the lower classes, some of whom riff-raff from Canton."
He commented that "their heads have become swollen by the con-
templation at a safe distance of the exploits of others in 'the emancipation of China from the foreign (Manchu) yoke', and their heads
deprived of the queue have become unbalanced."[87] Thus, the governor conceded that the Hong Kong Chinese populace, much inspired
by the emancipation of China from the Manchu foreign yoke, dreamed
about its own emancipation from British colonial rule. This showed
the close linkage between anti-Manchu and anti-imperialist sentiments. The fate of the Manchu dynasty and the position of foreign
powers in China were linked, as the theory of Sino-foreign synarchy
suggests. A "Sino-British synarchy" was created in China by the
unequal treaty system after 1860, a synarchy in which the Chinese
sovereignty was "overlaid or supplanted by that of the treaty powers."[88] The overthrow of the Manchus let loose a flood of anti-
imperialist sentiment and activities in the British colony. The Chinese
crowds seemed to feel that now the Manchus were gone the privileged foreigners had to go too. The Chinese revolution aggravated
their resentment against being treated as a subject people.

Mr. Murray Stewart, a prominent member of the legislative council, was "elbowed off the pavement in Queen's Road and into the
gutter by a half-naked Chinese coolie."[89] In some cases, European
ladies were attacked in the streets. The general manager of the Hongkong Tramway Company, J. J. Stodard Kennedy, urged the government to act with sufficient firmness against forces of disorder. As his
work involved "fairly close observation of large numbers of lower-
class Chinese," he "saw frequently a truculently insolent attitude of
the people travelling on cars and elsewhere towards Europeans." He
reported "the rush of Europeans to buy firearms."[90]

Governor Lugard observed that the feeling of hostility was not
shared by "respectable Chinese" in the colony.[91] Living in security
and prosperity under the British flag and maintaining close economic
ties to foreign capitalism, the "respectable Chinese" were eager to
cooperate with the colonial authorities to maintain peace and order.
They did not approve of popular outbursts of "rowdyism" and "hooliganism" as valid expressions of patriotism. In the legislative council
meeting, November 30, Ho Kai and Wei Yuk applauded Governor
Lugard's speech regarding the need to suppress street disturbances.
They voted for the amendment of the Peace Preservation Ordinance,

which authorized corporal punishment of "rowdies" in prison.[92] The wealthy Chinese merchants who served on the District Watchmen's Committee took energetic measures to help prevent further popular unrest by engaging lecturers to persuade the people to observe government regulations and keep the peace.[93]

Yet social unrest continued unabated. The colonial government became deeply concerned that the "peculiar and distorted views of 'independence' ["freedom" or *tzu-yu*] bred by the Revolution and interpreted to his own liking by every coolie, will have a permanent effect on the traditional submission to regulation which has hitherto simplified the duties of officials."[94] Unlike earlier cases of popular unrest such as those that occurred in 1884, 1888, 1894, 1895, and 1908 when strikers and rioters had some specific grievances and demands, the populace in 1911–12 held a general sense of discontent about British colonial rule. Confronted with "considerable disorder of a novel kind,"[95] the Chinese merchant elite were powerless to exert influence over their countrymen. In fact, some "respectable Chinese gentlemen" themselves were subjected to harassment of the "rowdies." On November 22, 1911, a gentleman was roughly elbowed off the pavement by a Chinese in Des Voeux Road Central. And on November 24 Mr. Kotewell's brother (a Eurasian) and two friends had their queues seized and pulled by "roughs." They hurried to a restaurant, from the verandah of which they saw several Chinese gentlemen similarly treated.[96]

Anticolonial civil disobedience was committed not merely by coolies but also by some shopkeepers who were among the disorderly crowds. On February 27, 1912, a shopkeeper named Chan Sing and several others assaulted the Indian Police Constable Roor Singh.[97] On January 2, 1912, a shopkeeper was arrested by a European constable for obstruction and for calling upon his folk to strike the officers.[98] And on November 24, 1911, a Chinese, "well-dressed and apparently of the better class, seized a public chair in which Mr. Bullock was riding, and in an insulting manner thrust his face with a cigar in his mouth into Mr. Bullock's face—he went away laughing."[99] Republican revolutionaries were also among the crowds involved in enforced queue-cutting and other cases.[100] A sense of revolution so permeated the colony that even school children became politicized. Two Chinese schoolboys, after leaving school on December 25, 1911, had an argument concerning the revolution. The tiff led to a quarrel and one boy took a pocket knife out of his pocket and slashed the other on the throat. The wounded boy was taken to the hospital.[101]

Compositors' Strike, October 20–December 12, 1911

The Chinese revolution contributed to the general feeling of unrest in Hong Kong. Popular unrest also took the form of labor strikes. Workers demanded legitimate rights to higher wages and better treatment from their European and Chinese employers. On October 20, 1911, a Chinese employee was assaulted by a European in the office of the *South China Morning Post*. Infuriated, all Chinese printers and compositors of the *Morning Post* went on strike. By mid-November, the strike was extended to the office of the *Hongkong Telegraph*, which came to the assistance of the *Morning Post*. The police arrested three leaders of the compositors' guild on the night of November 17, one of whom was banished to Macao. Immediately, on the following morning, a general strike of the compositors and printing machine hands was declared, involving about six hundred people. All the printing business in Hong Kong was affected.[102]

The Chinese Compositors' Guild was a modern trade union organization formed by the employees "as a weapon for enforcing their terms on [their] opponents." It maintained connections with the guild of the same trade in Canton.[103] As skilled workers could not be easily replaced, the sabotage of work in Hong Kong went on for several weeks. The strike was ordered by the guild with the idea that by paralyzing the whole printing and publishing business of the colony, the government would be forced to cancel the order of banishment issued against the guild leaders. When it became known that wholesale prosecutions were contemplated by the Chinese master printers, a large number of the men departed on the night of November 21 for Canton, the fares being paid out of the guild funds. The strikers threatened death to anyone who went back to their employment without the guild's sanction.[104]

The colonial authorities were convinced that "the strike was engineered by agitators who put their own curious interpretation on the revolutionary doctrine of 'independence' and wished to show the power of their guild," and that they seized on the opportunity offered by the "small trouble" of an assault by a European on a Chinese to order a strike.[105] The compositors employed in the Chinese newspaper offices had decided to resume work on December 3, but learning later on that day that the European papers did not intend to reengage the whole of their men, they revoked their decision.[106] It was not until December 12 that the compositors returned to work, in a few cases on rather better terms but generally on the same conditions as before, while a few of the more "troublesome" men lost their appointments altogether.[107] Beginning as a protest against the European employer's assault on a Chinese employee, it became clearly a case of labor dispute, with the organized workers of the guild turning against their European and Chinese employers in the printing business. This again reflected certain degree of community disintegration in Hong Kong in the years around 1911.

Canton Government's Attitude Towards Hong Kong Civil Disorder

What was the attitude of the Canton republican government toward the social unrest in the British colony? Ironically, it disapproved of the labor strike and anticolonial popular movements that were inspired by the revolution in Canton. Governor Lugard attributed the "very great increase of rowdyism" in Hong Kong to an influx of "bad characters" from the mainland. He requested the tutu (military governor) of Kwangtung, Hu Han-min, to help prevent the departure for Hong Kong of "bad characters" and to promote the "friendly feelings" between Canton and Hong Kong.[108] Eager to win British approval and support, the new revolutionary government in Canton responded favorably. In fact, the tutu had written to the Chinese Press Association in Hong Kong, deprecating "rowdyism" and labor strikes, which, the tutu said, did not help the revolutionary cause.[109] Yet Governor Lugard was apprehensive of the tutu's political power and influence over the Chinese in the colony. He asserted that it was not "advisable" for the tutu to directly cause the Hong Kong press to print the Canton official notice.

The Canton revolutionary government's attitude towards the British colonial government was no less paradoxical. The revolutionaries resented the colonial government for its hostility to the revolution.

But once in power, the Canton revolutionaries, although still resentful, sought to cultivate the goodwill and friendship of the colonial authorities.

The revolutionaries in Canton had a number of grievances against the Hong Kong authorities. During the course of revolution the British colonial authorities had not remained "neutral." Rather, they had placed numerous obstacles in the way of the revolution. On April 27, 1911, at the request of the Ch'ing government, Governor Lugard stopped all steamers and railway traffic from Hong Kong to Canton, to prevent the revolutionaries from sending reinforcements to the embattled Chinese city.[110] The colonial authorities had attempted to ban all revolutionary activities in the colony. A number of revolutionaries were banished from Hong Kong. Sun Yat-sen had been expelled and banned from the colony for fifteen years—since 1896. As late as November 19, 1911, when Sun applied for permission to visit Hong Kong, the colonial authorities reluctantly permitted him to pass through Hong Kong on the condition that he would not reside in the colony and use it as a base for political operations in China.[111] Apprehensive of the Chinese revolutionaries' political influence over the Chinese in Hong Kong, Governor Lugard added another condition—Sun should not be received with a great ovation.[112]

In fact, the British colonial government sought to discourage the Chinese revolution in every way, even after Canton had passed into the revolutionaries' hands. Keeping the docile Manchu government in power in Peking seemed preferable to having a nationalist revolutionary government that posed as a potential threat to foreign imperialism in China. At the end of November 1911 the Canton revolutionary government approached a British broker named Ray to charter ships for the transport of troops to North China presumably for an attack on Peking, but the Hong Kong government forbade such shipments. Failing this, the Canton revolutionaries decided that the troops would be conveyed in vessels of the China Merchants Steamship Company, a Chinese company. But Governor Lugard would not allow the vessels either to enter the Hong Kong harbor or to pass through the Hong Kong waters. Again, to discourage the revolution the traffic on the Kowloon-Canton Railway was suspended on November 6 and was not resumed until December 4, 1911.[113]

For these reasons, the Canton government held a strong anti-

British feeling, as the consul general, J. W. Jamieson, reported.[114]
The precarious new Canton government, however, did not wish to
alienate the omnipresent British imperialists. In fact, it sought to
cultivate the goodwill and friendship of the British colonial authorities in Hong Kong, because it looked to the banking institutions and
Chinese mercantile community in Hong Kong for assistance in financial matters. When the Hong Kong colonial secretary, Mr. C. Clement, visited Canton on December 9, 1911, he found the Chinese
officials "more than friendly"—they were inclined "to accept Hong
Kong as a model" rather than resent the British presence there.[115]

The Canton government's attempt to court British colonial authorities' goodwill eventually led to its alienation from the colony's Chinese
populace. To win British approval and support, the Canton government found itself in a position of deprecating popular unrest in Hong
Kong. It was an irony that the Canton revolutionary government
should have disapproved of the anticolonial popular movements in
Hong Kong, which were inspired by the revolution in Canton. The
tutu of Canton discouraged the Hong Kong compositors' strike in
1911. The year 1912 witnessed several labor strikes for higher wages
and better working conditions in the British colony.

Labor Strikes in 1912

The paucity of sources allows only brief discussion of these labor
strikes against employers, which in the years around 1912 still did
not pose a serious threat to social order in the colony. It was not until
the early 1920s that labor disputes turned into large-scale workers'
strikes. The strikes in 1912 were sporadic and on a small scale.

In May 1912 the washerman employees in Victoria went on strike
for better wages. The odd-job workers, paid on a daily scale, demanded an increase of wages from sixty to seventy cents a day, and
the regular workmen on monthly salary demanded a raise of two
dollars a month. To divide the employees, the masters acceded to
the demand of the regular workmen but not the odd-job workers.
Thereupon, all the employees including regular workmen staged a
strike. But after three days a settlement was reached.[116]

The Washermen's Guild possessed some characteristics of a modern trade union. The Mat-bag Packers' Guild and Painters' Guild did
as well. In August, some seventy mat bag packers employed at the

Sugar Refinery at Quarry Bay went on strike for several days. But it came to an end by August 13, when additional men were brought to work.[117] Unskilled workers had little bargaining power, because there were plenty of laborers around. There was also a strike of the employees of the Painters' Guild in August. The men demanded a raise of five cents a day. When this was granted, they further demanded a fixed minimum wage for all members of the guild. But the real cause was a wish to force masters to engage apprentices at full wages. The strike was shortly given up.[118] In September a strike occurred among the junkmen engaged in carrying stones for the new Harbor of Refuge at Mongkok. Their demand for higher wages was refused, but some small concessions by the contractors resulted in a resumption of work by all the junkmen except the two ringleaders, who lost their jobs.[119] In November there was still another strike of casual laborers employed in pounding rice. Some two hundred and fifty rice-pounders demanded a raise of wages from twenty-two cents to thirty cents a day. But their masters could easily replace such unskilled workers. The masters made small concessions, and the strikers returned to work at the end of a week.[120]

Finally, there were the chair and ricksha coolies, whose legal fares, set by the government, were so low as to cause constant complaint. The government made various regulations to control these traffic coolies. In protest against the increased amount of fines and penalties imposed on the offenders, 2,200 ricksha pullers and 1,340 chair bearers went on strike on October 29, 1912. The owners of the vehicles urged the government to suppress the strike. On the afternoon of October 30 the coolies agreed to resume work on the understanding that the punitive regulations be investigated.[121]

The Canton revolutionary government's attitude towards the labor movement underwent some changes. Before 1911 the T'ung-meng-hui revolutionaries had been active among workers in Hong Kong, especially skilled and semiskilled workers such as mechanics and seamen, seeking to assist them and to recruit them for the revolutionary forces. But once the revolutionaries came to power in Canton, they felt constrained by circumstances to turn their back on the labor movement. The precarious new government in Canton did not wish to alienate the British by encouraging "rowdyism" and labor unrest in Hong Kong. Looking to the banks and the Chinese merchants in Hong Kong for financial assistance, the new Canton government was eager to cultivate the goodwill of the British colonial authorities. In quest of British approval and support, the Canton government turned its back on the labor movement and ended up alienating the Chinese working people, which eventually helped to pave the way for its eclipse in August 1913.

The young Chinese republican government had not been liberal in its labor policy. Although the Provisional Constitution of the Chinese Republic, adopted in March 1912, provided for freedom of association, it made no special mention of workers. The freedom of association supposedly guaranteed by the constitution was much restricted by Article 224 of the Provisional Penal Code, whereby strikes were prohibited and severe penalties of fines and imprisonment were prescribed for the strikers and their leaders. The Kuomintang's espousal of the worker's cause would come only in 1919, after the May Fourth incident.[122]

In Hong Kong the labor movement enjoyed no legal protection. The Trades Union Acts of 1871, 1876, and 1906, instituted in Great Britain, did not apply to the colony of Hong Kong. Consequently, every association formed by workers for the purpose of promoting better wages was illegal, its action being "in restraint of trade"; each of its members was liable to be prosecuted and imprisoned for conspiracy and also accountable for damages for inducing employees to leave their employment.[123] In short, collective actions by the colony's workers in labor disputes enjoyed no legal protection. Frustrations in life and in work nurtured among the lower-class Chinese a strong feeling of animosity towards the colonial authorities, which was frequently expressed in extralegal means, such as assaults on the colony's police and British officials.

Assaults on Governor Sir F. Henry May

Sir Frederick Lugard's tenure as governor of Hong Kong expired in early 1912. Ho Kai and Wei Yuk joined with other unofficial members of the legislative council to petition London for an extension of his term. The petitioners praised Governor Lugard's administration, saying that it "has commanded the respect and admiration not only of the British, but also to a very marked degree of the Chinese community." The petitioners suggested that if Lugard's term as governor could not be extended, then Sir F. Henry May should be appointed as the new governor.[124] The veteran former official of Hong Kong enjoyed such a strong reputation for being a disciplinarian that London now decided to appoint him as the new governor. Lugard left Hong Kong on March 16, 1912, to take up the government of Nigeria. The colonial secretary, Claud Severn, administered the Hong Kong government until the arrival of Sir F. Henry May on July 4.[125] But the comings and goings of the governors made no difference to the working people in Hong Kong and brought no change to their daily struggle for a living.

Governor May was an old China hand. He had been with the Hong Kong colonial service for twenty-eight years, from 1881 to January 1911, when he had been transfered to Fiji as governor and high commissioner for the South Pacific. With a command of both Cantonese and Mandarin Chinese, he had held various positions in Hong Kong. Yet he was best known by the Chinese as the former head of the police and jail. As the police chief for nearly a decade, he had distinguished himself in suppressing both the coolie strike in 1895 and the popular resistance to British occupation of the New Territories in 1899. He did not commend himself to the coolies; he often had trouble finding chair and ricksha coolies willing to work for him. He was the author of several publications, including a *Guide to Cantonese* and manuals for use in the police force.[126] After an absence from the colony for one and a half years, the fifty-two-year-old Sir F. Henry May, a man of "a fearless impetuosity," returned to Hong Kong as its new governor on July 4, 1912.[127]

In a secret dispatch to the Colonial Office in London, Sir Henry revealed with remarkable frankness "the real feelings of the mass of the population towards Englishmen in this Colony." He was gravely concerned about "the animosity against foreigners which, always existent in the Chinese mind, has been inflamed by the recent [Chinese] revolution." He pointed out that from the time of his arrival in Hong Kong, on July 4, 1912, up to the end of the boycott of the tramway in February 1913 assaults on the police were of weekly occurrence. These took the form of, at times, the attempted rescue of prisoners and, on other occasions, throwing missiles from verandahs at the police. The governor himself was subjected to physical attacks. A stone was thrown into his motor car as he sat in it with his wife. On another occasion a bundle of lighted firecrackers was thrown at a vehicle while Sir Henry and his wife were in it; it struck the footboard. On still other occasions sticks, orange peels, and other missiles were thrown at the car, also while the governor was riding in it.[128] The ex-police chief was greatly annoyed.

The gravest assault on Sir Henry May took place the very day of his arrival to take up the reins of the government—July 4, 1912. Having inspected the guards of honor at Blake Pier, Governor and Lady May and their daughters got into sedan chairs, which were accompanied with the procession to City Hall to receive an address of welcome from the community. Sir Henry's chair was on the right and Lady May's chair on the left. There were four Indian constables on each side. Behind them were other police, and the streets were lined with troops. The sedan chairs had proceeded about fifty yards when suddenly a Chinese carrying a revolver ran out between the troops and between the second and third Indian constables, put his hand and elbow on the chair occupied by Sir Henry, and pointed the revolver point blank at Sir Henry's head. The Indian constable Kala Singh promptly threw up the assailant's arm, while Sergeant Garrod ran forward to seize his wrist. The pistol discharged, but the bullet missed Sir Henry and lodged in the canopy of Lady May's chair. The assailant struggled with Sergeant Garrod and attempted in vain to fire a second shot but was overpowered by the sergeant.[129] As he was led away, the local English press reporters heard (apparently from among the Englishmen in the crowd of spectators) cries of "Lynch him," "Kill him," and "Let us have him."[130]

The prisoner, named Li Hon Hung, was a Cantonese, twenty-four years of age, and the son of a former Hong Kong constable from a lower-class background. After his arrest, he declared that he was determined to assassinate Sir Henry May, owing to his detestation of the British. Li Hon Hung named several grievances against the British colonial authorities: first, the ill-treatment of Chinese in Hong Kong and in South Africa, including the compulsory repatriation of Chinese coolies employed in the mines in the latter place. Second, the prohibition of the circulation in Hong Kong of Chinese copper coins issued in Canton, which, he claimed, was an interference with the Canton republican government. And third, Li Hon Hung's father had been dismissed from the Hong Kong police force by then police chief Henry May, because, while holding the position of a detective in the Hong Kong service, Li's father was also found to be in the pay of Canton officials.[131] Thus, personal grievances and patriotic feelings converged to impell Li Hong Hung to action. Li Hon Hung was subsequently tried on July 17 in a large courtroom filled with some five hundred persons, in addition to the Chinese crowds who gathered round the entrance to the law court to catch a glimpse of the defendant. His lordship sentenced Li Hon Hung to life imprisonment with hard labor.[132]

On July 6 a deputation representing various Chinese elite associations waited upon his excellency the governor at Government House with reference to the assassination incident. Sir Kai Ho Kai, acting as the spokesman, expressed "the horror and consternation of the Chinese at the dastardly outrage, and expressed their profound sympathy." The local English press described the audience with the governor as follows:

> The deputation assured the Governor of the loyalty of the Chinese to the British Crown and of the esteem and affectionate attachment that they had for Sir Henry May as His Majesty's representative, as a personal friend and a Chinese well-wisher. . . . The Governor, in reply, thanked the deputation and said he knew at the time the crime was committed that it would be abhorrent to none more than to the Chinese community, and had at once attributed it either to some person having spite or to some members of the secret societies to whom the policy of the British Government in maintaining law and order was distasteful. The Governor felt sure that law-abiding Chinese would render assistance in maintaining good government in the Colony. The deputation then withdrew.[133]

"The loyalty of the Chinese to the British Crown" and "the esteem and affectionate attachment . . . for Sir Henry May,"—perhaps these words truly expressed the feelings of some prosperous elite Chinese in the colony but not of the lower-class masses, the overwhelming majority of the Chinese population.

The attempt on Governor Sir Henry May's life had not been connected with any political plot. In Sir Henry's view, it was "the act of a man who if not mad must be of weak intellect."[134] Whatever his personal view of the assailant's intellect, Sir Henry frankly conceded in a secret despatch to London that "the real feelings of the mass of the population towards Englishmen in this Colony" could be described in one word—"animosity." The governor pointed to the following incident for illustration: when the police searched the assailant's lodging, they found a letter written by a Chinese woman of the peasant class in whose miserably poor dwelling the assailant had lodged. The letter was intended to be sent to her relative in Canton. The police opened the letter to see if it gave any clue to a plot. It dealt with many domestic details such as the recent sale of a pig and concluded with these words: incidently, "yesterday my lodger fired a pistol at the Governor of Hong Kong and *most unfortunately* missed him." The governor himself commented that the woman "merely regretted that I had not been killed, as one might regret that one's terrier had missed a rat in the ditch."[135]

The Chinese revolution therefore served as a vehicle for accentuating the anticolonial discontentment of the people as well as fostering nationalistic sentiment, which found expression again in the organized tramway boycott in 1912–13.

T
E
N

The Boycott of the Hong Kong Tramway, 1912–13

All of us . . . should refuse to travel by the company's trams. . . . Indeed all our fellow-countrymen should speedily awake.
—*An-ya Pao*, Canton,
November 28, 1912

The boycott of the Hong Kong Electric Tramway was precipitated by the tramway company's refusal to accept Chinese coins (minted in Canton) in payment of fare. It aroused strong feelings of hostility among the Chinese in Hong Kong against the European-operated tramway company. The boycott lasted more than two months, from late November 1912 to early February 1913. Why were the Chinese feelings so strong and the boycott so persistent? Who promoted the boycott? What motivated the populace to engage in boycott? What did the boycott reveal about social relations in the British colony and about the Chinese revolutionary government in Canton? The answers to these questions must begin with the politics of Canton and Hong Kong.

Prelude to Boycott: Canton and Hong Kong Politics

The Kwangtung revolutionary government had led a precarious existence since its founding on November 9, 1911. It exercised little authority beyond the city of Canton and its suburbs. At the head of the Canton government was Hu Han-min, the tutu of Kwangtung. Under him, Ch'en Chiung-ming ranked first as military official, commanding some twenty thousand to thirty thousand well-armed men. Another commander, Lung Chi-kwang, had an army of Kwangsi and Yün-nan men whose numbers had dwindled from twelve thousand to three thousand by July 1912. There were other groups of soldiers (such as that of Li Tang, an ex-robber, in Ho-nan, Kwangtung), but the connection between them and the Kwangtung provincial government seemed very vague.[1]

The Kwangtung provincial treasury had been managed very badly. Lacking efficient machinery for collecting taxes, the government expenditure exceeded its income. The monthly receipts of the Canton government were one million two hundred and fifty thousand dollars and the expenditures two million. The financial supplies from Chinese abroad (to which the Chinese community of Hong Kong had contributed between two and three million dollars) had all been spent or embezzled. The government then issued notes worth twenty-two million dollars without any reserve to secure them, resulting in the notes being at a discount of between 30 and 40 percent. In July 1912 the Canton government approached the Hongkong and Shanghai Banking Corporation for a loan against the security of the government Cement Works at Canton. Failing to obtain this, it again looked to Chinese abroad for loans. The financial situation seemed desperate.[2]

The founding of the republican government in Canton had inspired high hopes and dreams among the Chinese in Hong Kong and Canton. They had responded with much enthusiasm to the monetary subscriptions for the new government. Within two or three months, however, that enthusiasm quickly began to wane, as the new government proved incapable of maintaining financial and political stability in the province. In fact, "moneyed men in Hongkong and Canton and abroad are getting tired of pouring their money into a sieve, and they require some kind of security before subscribing much more."[3]

With close commercial ties to Canton, the Chinese merchants in Hong Kong were seriously concerned about the problems in Canton. As early as November 23, 1911, they calculated that they had lost "over five million dollars already by the stoppage of trade."[4] As the situation had become worse by the summer of 1912, Ho Kai and Wei Yuk came up with a collaborationist idea. In a confidential conversation on July 12 they proposed to Governor Henry May that if financial aid could be given to the Canton government, it would accept British supervision of its expenditure and British advice in matters of administration. This coincided with Governor May's imperialist scheme to "reorganize" the administration of Kwangtung "under tactful and unostentatious British supervision and advice, backed if necessary by financial assistance." Governor May's only fear was the "demonstrations by a mob which might resent even the semblance of the loss of independence." In response to the governor's suggestion, the London colonial authorities remarked that "it would be an excellent thing . . . to get the Province straight." But they decided not to do so for fear of provoking protests from other powers, who might start protectorates over other provinces in China.[5]

While Ho Kai, Wei Yuk, and Governor Henry May were contemplating a collaborationist-imperialist scheme, the Canton government tried every possible device to improve its financial situation. It attempted to induce the Chinese merchants of Kwangtung and Hong Kong to form a Canton and Hong Kong Co-operative Financial Company with a capital of five million dollars. This company would purchase Canton banknotes from the market at market price and deposit them with the Provincial Treasury Bank, hoping thereby to improve the notes' market value.[6] But very few people had taken up the company's shares. In Hong Kong, "on account of various obstacles and difficulties" merchants were unable to give their strenuous assistance.[7] The greatest difficulty was, according to Governor May, the conviction of many Chinese merchants that the Canton government under Hu Han-min was in grave danger of collapse. Abhorring the Canton government's exertion of influence over the colony's Chinese population, and convinced that Canton government would soon collapse, Governor May threw a number of obstacles in its way, as if intending to hasten its fall. He warned the promoters of the Canton and Hong Kong Co-operative Financial Company that the levy of subscriptions was viewed with disfavor by the colony's government.[8] Thus discouraged by the colonial authorities, the promotion of the financial company was formally abandoned on September 3, 1912.[9]

Yet, the dire financial straits gave the Canton government little option. The superintendent of the Canton Government Money Department, Chau Lo, came to Hong Kong to contact the Money Changers' Guild to push the circulation in the colony of the Canton banknotes. "The Society of Chinese Abroad for the Promotion of Patriotic Subscriptions" called upon the various Chinese guilds in the colony to send delegates to a meeting on October 5 at the Sze Yap Association in order to promote the Canton notes. It was resolved at the meeting that "the Canton notes should be taken as the standard and accepted in accordance with their face value," and that "the various Guilds should themselves draw up a scale of fines to be imposed for any breach of this requirement and appoint special officers to deal with the matter." The colonial authorities sought to ban such promotion activities in the colony, declaring it illegal to circulate foreign banknotes and instructing police to stop the "mischief."[10]

The Canton government made further attempts to obtain patriotic subscriptions from overseas Chinese. Leaflets were distributed in Hong Kong calling upon patriotic Chinese in the colony to make monetary contributions to the republic—to avoid raising foreign loans and to protect "the rights and privileges of our nation." Again, the colonial authorities banned such subscriptions. The Canton government then proposed to issue lottery loan bonds to the value of ten million dollars in small shares of ten dollars, with the periodic drawings of many prizes.[11] But the colonial government also banned the bonds.[12]

In sum, colonial authorities threw a number of obstacles in the way of the Canton government, which sought desperately to alleviate its financial situation. They prohibited the circulation of Canton banknotes in Hong Kong, banned the Canton and Hong Kong Cooperative Financial Company, and forbade the Canton lottery loan bonds. Such a series of unfriendly acts antagonized what the colonial authorities called the Young China Party in Hong Kong.[13] The most important and energetic agency of this party was the Sze Yap Association, which played a major role in the boycott of the Hong Kong Tramway. A description of the boycott and analysis of the boycott promoters and their motivations follows.

Boycott of Tramway

The boycott was touched off by the Hongkong Tramway Company's refusal to accept Chinese coins in payment of fare. On November 22, 1912, handwritten bills and caricatures advocating a boycott of the trams were posted all over the colony from Shaukiwan to West Point. As mentioned previously, one caricature depicted the passengers of a tramcar as pigs, kangaroos, and other beasts. On November 24 a demonstration against the tramways took place at Shaukiwan. A crowd of about one thousand people gathered at the tramway terminus and threatened the tramcars, calling "boycott." When Police Sergeant Ogg arrested a man, the crowd shouted out to strike the Sergeant and began to throw stones. A second man, who struggled violently with the police, was arrested. Inspector Gourlay had to threaten the crowd with his revolver before the arrested men could be removed to the police station.[14]

More notices urging a boycott were posted around the colony. Very few people used the trams on November 26. A disturbance took place in the Central District between Central and Western Markets. About one thousand people gathered in Des Voeux Central. The crowd mobbed and intimidated the tram passengers. A large force of police proceeded to the scene from the Central Station. The crowd threw stones and other missiles at the police. The police made four arrests, after which police pickets patrolled the tram route night and day. On November 28 fifty soldiers were sworn in as special constables to ride in the trams and as night pickets.[15]

The determination of the Chinese people to boycott the trams surprised the European community in the colony. Prior to the boycott the tramcars were daily crowded with Chinese commuters, because the alternative was the jinricksha, a slower and more expensive means of locomotion. As the local English press reported, "in a Colony like Hongkong, where some thousands of Chinese are employed in factories and workshops, where time-sheets are kept, time means money. So that if the boycott means a heavy loss to the Tramway Company, it involves at the same time a considerable sacrifice on the part of the boycotters." Despite several successive days of rain in early December, which added to the inconvenience of not taking the tram, the boycott continued unabated.[16]

The boycott involved some cases of violence. At Wanchai, West Point, and other places, a number of passengers who alighted from the tramcar were said to be stabbed in the buttocks with sacking needles. But only one case of assault came to the notice of the police: a Chinese domestic servant employed by an European employee of the tramway company was attacked by several Chinese in the Central

Market after alighting from a tramcar.[17] Very few Chinese were using the trams, but of the few that were doing so, a large proportion were women, which seemed to indicate that apprehension of violence or intimidation was not sufficient cause for refusal to ride in the tramcars.[18]

Government Measures

Eager to end the boycott, the colonial authorities enacted a Boycott Prevention Ordinance on December 15, and threatened to proclaim certain areas of the city as "boycott areas," hence to levy a special tax on their inhabitants to compensate the tramway company for its losses. Deeply concerned that the governor might arbitrarily proclaim "boycott areas," Ho Kai gained assurance from him that "leading inhabitants" of a particular district would be consulted before the proclamation was issued.[19]

On December 18, 1912, Governor May convened a meeting of about one hundred and fifty leading members of the Chinese commercial community. Addressing them on the subject of boycott, the governor said that the Hong Kong Tramway Company had in the past incurred a great loss in accepting Canton coins, which were lighter and cheaper than Hong Kong coins; that the company's current decision to refuse Canton coins was purely a business transaction and not meant to be an insult to China; and that the boycott was "unreasonable and foolish and . . . unjust," for the boycotters were trying to destroy a commercial concern of much benefit to the community and in which considerable Chinese capital was invested. The governor then urged the leading Chinese to show that the boycott was a misunderstanding by traveling themselves and bidding their employees to travel by tramway. After the governor's speech, Sir Kai Ho Kai, the Honorable Mr. Wei Yuk, and others spoke about the need to end the boycott. Many of these "leading Chinese" then proceeded to ride in the tram cars, hoping to set an example for others.[20]

Subsequently, on December 20, a meeting was held at the Chinese Commercial Union at which both Ho Kai and Wei Yuk made speeches justifying the actions of the tramway company and the Hong Kong government. The meeting was, however, poorly attended.[21] Ho Kai reminded the audience that if the malcontents brought about the destruction of Hong Kong prosperity, they would bring misery not only to thousands in the colony but also to "millions in China," since the Chinese British subjects would no longer be as ready as in the past to help their poorer brothren in Kwangtung with money.[22] In other words, the "collaborationist patriot" Ho Kai reminded the Chinese in the colony that the "millions in China" would be better served, not by boycott but by cooperation with the colonial government to maintain prosperity in Hong Kong. Patriotism was subject to different interpretations; it took different forms.

Hoping to induce the Chinese to use tramcars, the tramway company carried passengers free of charge for three days, from December 21 to 23. On the first day of free rides the tramcars were practically monopolized by Indian soldiers and Chinese children, who crowded the cars for fun all day, and there was little room for others with ordinary traveling purposes. On the second day the tramcars were occupied by a fair proportion of Chinese adults. And on the third and last day of free rides the cars were almost completely monopolized by the former Chinese patrons of the cars with their customary baggage. After the three-day free rides were over, however, the tramcars were again deserted by the Chinese and the boycott remained in full force.[23]

Once again it had been demonstrated that fear of intimidation was not a sufficient reason to explain the boycott movement. As we shall see, several reasons combined to sustain the anticolonial boycott movement.

Threatening Letters to Collaborators

Some "leading" Chinese who eagerly collaborated with the colonial authorities in an attempt to end the boycott received threatening letters. Mr. Lau Chu Pak received one from the Dare to Die Society. The Honorable Mr. Wei Yuk (Wei Po-shan) received more than one. Here is a threatening letter addressed jointly to Wei Yuk and Chan Kang Yu (Ch'en Keng-yü):

> This is for your information, Po Shan. I cannot see that you have during your past life distinguished yourself in any other way than in flattering others, especially foreigners. . . . [T]o our surprise you alleged that the tramway boycott was promoted by the upper classes, and societies had been formed for the purpose. . . . Let me ask

you who are the originators of these societies, where are these societies and what proof have you of their existence. On receipt of this letter you must publish in the papers for my information the people you have procured, otherwise I will show you no mercy. You are the only man who brings ruin upon us Chinese. The longer you remain in Hong Kong, the longer we Chinese residents cannot enjoy peace. . . . The tramway boycott is but an undertaking of individuals, yet that offensive [Governor] May caused an ordinance to be enacted by the Government. . . . [I]nstead of putting forth any argument against the enactment of the Ordinance, you on the other hand act with hostility towards us Chinese residents; and in fact you have conferred no single benefit on your fellow-countrymen. Why do you despise your fellow-countrymen so much? Have you not been informed that the wife of your younger brother carried on the business of a sly prostitute every night? Indeed your history is too dirty for my pen to describe. In fact you deserve to die for the various actions you have done. Now in conjunction with our fellow countrymen, I have determined to see whether you or we have to die first and to know how long you can enjoy the happiness of being a cuckold.

Chan Hon Tat. 23 December, 1912[24]

Thus, the letter had two major complaints: first, "that offensive May's" enactment of the Boycott Prevention Ordinance, which threatened to impose a special tax on Chinese residents. Second, Wei Yuk's habit of flattering foreigners, despising his fellow countrymen, and collaborating with colonial authorities, informing them that the boycott was promoted by upper-class Chinese.

Boycott Promoters and Their Motivations

The tramway company's refusal to accept Chinese coins threatened the interests of several social groups that joined together to sustain the boycott. They included the small bankers, money changers, and other middlemen who made profits by the manipulation of exchange between Hong Kong currency and Chinese coins. The Nam Pak Hong and Kam Shan Chung Chinese merchants who traded with California were also involved in money exchange. They were closely associated with the Sze Yap Association, which in turn was closely connected with the Canton revolutionary government and with political agitators in Hong Kong who saw the tramway's refusal of Chinese coins as a slur on Chinese dignity and "an affront to the newly-awakened spirit of nationalism."[25] In other words, several overlapping social groups, prompted either by economic interest or by a sense of nationalistic pride, or by both, became active promoters of the boycott of trams.

The money changers played an important role in instigating the boycott.[26] Their number had risen from 104 in 1905 to 420 in 1912. They were associated with the compradors, shroffs, and other middlemen who acted as intermediaries between employer and employee in the payment of wages. Especially important were merchants and bankers who received remittances from Chinese overseas and transmitted them to relatives in China. Since their profits came from money exchange, they felt threatened by the prohibition of Chinese coins in the colony; they welcomed the boycott of trams as a means of expressing their resentment.

According to the government estimate, the Nam Pak Hong–Kam Shan Chung merchants received from Chinese residents abroad remittances in gold in the amount of about fifty-six million dollars per annum for payment to Chinese in Hong Kong, Canton, and its vicinity. These merchants charged no commission but made the payments in subsidiary coin and pocketed the whole of the discount. Their profit amounted to some two million dollars a year. Naturally, they were opposed to the rehabilitation of Hong Kong subsidiary coins, and to the prohibition of the circulation in the colony of Chinese and other foreign coins and the consequent removal of some media of manipulation of exchange. The Hong Kong government was convinced that it was the money changers and the Nam Pak Hong and Kam Shan Chung merchants who actually organized the boycott.[27]

Many of these merchants were members of the powerful Sze Yap Association, the patriotic Young China Party in Hong Kong.[28] The moving spirit of the Sze Yap Association was Li Yü-t'ang, the T'ung-meng-hui veteran who had served as the new Canton government treasurer. Li was the owner of the Chin-li-yüan Chinese medicine firm, which handled the remittance of one hundred and ninety thousand dollars from overseas for the T'ung-meng-hui in 1912.[29] Li was also the principal promoter of the Canton and Hong Kong Financial Co-operative Company, which aimed to help the Canton government financially but had to be abandoned on September 3, 1912, due to the opposition of the colonial authorities.

For these overlapping groups of money changers, bankers, middlemen, Nam Pak Hong and Kam Shan Chung merchants, and the Sze Yap Association patriots the tramway company's refusal of Chinese coins both hurt their interest and put a slur on Chinese dignity. Motivated by both patriotism and economic interest, they promoted the boycott of tramway. Invoking political sentiment of the Chinese populace against British colonialism, they won popular support.

The Canton Government Attitude Towards the Boycott

What was the attitude of the Canton government toward the boycott of trams in Hong Kong? Carefully watched by the British, some Canton officials sought to disassociate the Canton government from the boycott movement. In an interview with the colony's registrar general on December 20, 1912, the visiting Canton police chief Chan King-wah (Ch'en Chin-hua) affirmed that his government "in no way sympathized with the boycott which . . . was the outcome of spontaneous action on the part of the lower and more ignorant classes." He added that his government would do all in its power to assist the Hong Kong authorities in suppressing the boycott.[30]

But Governor May was not satisfied with this affirmation. He was doubtful regarding how far the opinion of the Canton police chief was endorsed by the Canton government, because "objectionable" articles fostering the boycott were repeatedly published in the Canton press, including the official newspaper *Chung-kuo jih-pao.*[31] A notice from "the whole commercial community of Canton and Hong Kong," published in *An-ya Pao,* Canton, November 28, 1912, read in part as follows:

> The recent centralization of the Republican Government and the union of the five races under our Republic enjoy the universal support of all friendly civilized nations. . . . Recently, however, the Electric Traction Company . . . has issued a notice discriminating against Chinese Silver Coins and refusing to accept them, a step evidently designed to cast a slur on our Republic and to repudiate friendship with our people. . . . therefore all of us should not allow ourselves to be boycotted but should refuse to travel by the company's trams. Anybody who permits himself to be boycotted and travels by the tramway is no better than a brute beast. Indeed all our fellow-countrymen should speedily awake.[32]

This notice revealed the Chinese humor by asserting that since the Hong Kong Tramway Company was boycotting the Chinese republic, the Chinese "should refuse to travel by the company's trams."

Similarly, the Canton official newspaper *Chung-kuo jih-pao* published letters from its correspondents in Hong Kong, asserting that the tramway company's rejection of all Chinese coins showed its "deliberate hostility against the Chinese," and that boycott was "the only means available of marking their displeasure."[33] Such articles were reprinted in Hong Kong Chinese newspapers.

Despite the colonial authorities' protestation, the Canton official newspaper continued to publish "mischievous" articles calculated to incite the inhabitants of Hong Kong to persist in the boycott.[34] One article related that two Chinese ladies, on alighting from a tramcar, were subjected to abuse by bystanders: something was thrown into their mouths, their dresses were soiled, and the ladies were told that they had no patriotic pride. Articles like this were printed for the purpose of keeping the boycott alive.[35] Many of these articles were attributed to the Sze Yap Association patriots.[36] It was not until January 3, 1913 that the tutu of Canton, Hu Han-min, took action to stop such publications.[37] The Canton government seemed too weak or too divided to exercise an effective control over the press.[38]

In sum, the boycott seemed to be tacitly endorsed by some Canton authorities connected with the Sze Yap Association who had grudges against the Hong Kong government for putting too many obstacles in the way of the Chinese revolution, and who regarded the rejection of Chinese coins in the colony as an insult to the Chinese republic.

Working People in Boycott

But the major actors in the boycott remained the Hong Kong crowds— the general population who refused to take trams, the lower-class people who mobbed the tramcars, who posted notices and caricatures on the street, and who intimidated and assaulted the few boycott violators. Without popular sympathy and support, no boycott could be launched. Governor May deplored the loss of influence by the "leading Chinese" over the colony's population. Sir Kai Ho Kai concurred, admitting that the "respectable Chinese community and the merchants who had the largest stake in the Colony were terrorised by the lower orders." He urged "strong measures to deal with the unruly and rowdy lower classes and to re-establish the lost influence of their whilom leaders."[39] The crisis situation once again revealed the extent of community disaggregation in the colony during the 1910s.

What were the motives of the "lower classes" participating in the boycott? How did they become activated? An appeal to patriotism alone could hardly mobilize the masses to a sustained and persistent boycott lasting more than two months. Patriotism had to be combined with an appeal to mundane interest in order to mobilize the populace in a prolonged social movement. The crowds in Hong Kong were activated by both economic reasons and the politics of anticolonialism. Among the working population, the most active supporters of the boycott of trams were chair coolies, ricksha coolies, the mechanics' union (which was closely connected with the patriotic Sze Yap Association and T'ung-meng-hui), and other artisans interested in the launch traffic and ricksha traffic that were reaping a golden harvest in the tram boycott.[40]

Besides, large numbers of laborers supported the boycott because they felt the threat of economic losses as a consequence of the tramway's refusal of Chinese coins. Many Chinese shops and business houses were in the habit of supplying their workers and employees with Chinese coins to travel by trams and ricksha.[41] The coal coolies and other workmen were often forced by their foremen or employers to accept payment of wages in Chinese coins, which were lighter and cheaper than the Hong Kong coins.[42] These workmen were angered by the tramway company's refusal to accept Chinese coins in payment of fare. And the general population had suffered indignities by being turned away from the tramcars for failure to produce Hong Kong coins.[43] When the colonial government came to support the tramway company it aggravated popular indignation against the government.

Chinese Patriotism and Anticolonialism

Workers' concern with economic losses converged with the politics of anticolonialism to propel the boycott movement. As the governor conceded, a boycott could not be started without working on and winning the political sympathies of the people, who had but scant respect for the colonial government.[44] The anticolonial political sentiment of the populace was deeply rooted in history. Of all social classes in Hong Kong, the coolie laborers were the most inclined to dislike colonial rule, as they were the most exploited and abused. The colonial setting made them susceptible to the influence of patriotic forces from various sources, such as the mandarins and Triads during the Sino-French War in 1884, the Pao-huang-hui in 1908, and the T'ung-meng-hui in 1911–13. Sir Henry May, the much-hated governor of Hong Kong, admitted that from the first day of his arrival on July 4, 1912, he had "noticed signs of aggressiveness and antipathy to Europeans on the part of the Chinese population."[45] This was an understatement, considering the attempt on his life that day and subsequent similar threats.

The Chinese revolution of 1911 had politicized the people in Hong Kong to an extent never previously attained. It had inspired high hopes and dreams among the Chinese in the colony for a better status and a better future for themselves. This was further reflected in a number of incidents. A Chinese constable was walking along the road in Hung-hom when a Chinese, who was in company with a number of others, called after him: "This constable is slave enough to serve a foreign power during the boycott." The man was arrested and sentenced to a fine of fifty dollars or two months' hard labor.[46] Popular animosity to British colonial rule was a theme of notices posted in the streets:

> Attention! Attention! Attention!
> Why was a meeting of the various merchants convened by the Governor of Hong Kong? It was on behalf of the Tramway. After the tea and refreshments at the conclusion of the meeting, he made them return home by the tram. Some of those present, being far sighted, slunk away beforehand, but some of them who were fond of flattering others, travelled by the Tramway. Indeed we people must not behave like shifting sands, but we pray that all our Chinese will unite in mind that offensive May be driven back to his home.[47]

In his confidential dispatch to London, Governor May reported that he had received warnings that further attempts might be made upon his life.[48]

Another notice was posted in the street on December 20, 1912, by "Ip of the Branch Society for Secret Assassination," who denounced

the leading merchants riding in the trams as "cold-blooded animals
. . . fond of flattering others":

> They are indeed no better than oxen and horses, willingly obeying
> the directions of foreigners. We presume that they would even vie
> with one another to be the first in yielding their wives and concu-
> bines to foreigners, and would consider such an undertaking as
> glorious. . . . We hope that after the issue of this notification, the
> merchants of the various Guilds will exhort their fellow-country-
> men far and wide to persist in the boycott. . . . Give strict obser-
> vance without fail.[49]

Still another street poster proclaimed:

> The Electric Tramway Company has adopted a new law refusing to
> accept dragon coins. A boycott must be put up. The five races must
> combine together. Those who take no notice of my word will be
> exploded to death. All brethren must look out, avoiding the bomb.[50]

This notice contained a nationalist aspiration derived from the
newly founded Chinese republic—namely, to combine China's "five
major nationalities" of Han Chinese, Manchus, Mongolians, Hui,
and Tibetans in a grand unity against foreign imperialism.

The ideology of popular protest was an amalgamation of the common people's inherent beliefs and the more structured ideology derived from the T'ung-meng-hui activists: people's inherent hatred of
the *fankwei* merged with the Republican revolutionaries' derived idea
of national unity of all Chinese against foreign imperialism. As George
Rude has observed, "the 'derived' ideology . . . can only be effectively absorbed [by the populace] if the ground has already been well
prepared."[51] The long series of strikes, riots, and boycotts that had
taken place since 1842 against British colonialism, together with the
T'ung-meng-hui revolutionaries' activities among the people, had
prepared a popular ground for the absorption of nationalism and
republicanism, which found expression in the mass jubilation over
the founding of the republic and in the boycott of the tramway in
1912–13.

Tensions between Chinese and foreign residents gave rise to a
rumor that there was talking among the Chinese of a "general rising"
against foreigners in connection with the boycott.[52] The Europeans
observed with uneasiness the display of China's republican flag from

many residences and places of business on the New Year's Day, 1913. As the local English press reported,

> The universal display of the five-striped banner in Chinatown suggests a spirit of defiance which was not discernible in the old days. The hundreds of flags seen flying all belonged to the same pattern, and the poles were likewise of a standard pattern, facts which suggest organization.[53]

The English press complained that the hoisting of China's national flag was likely to encourage the "wrong impression . . . as to the ownership of the island." When children in the Hong Kong vernacular schools were asked: "To which country does Hong Kong belong?," ninety-eight percent of them said Hong Kong was Chinese territory.[54]

To End the Boycott

It is significant that the boycott of the tramway caused only some inconvenience of traffic; it caused neither major street riots nor the disruption of work or trade, which would have alienated large numbers of Chinese traders and merchants who generally disliked social disorder. The tramway company's rejection of Chinese coins, supported by the colonial government, split the merchants in Hong Kong. Those who were engaged in the money exchange business and overseas remittance were adversely affected by the colony's rejection of Chinese coins. So they helped to promote the boycott of trams—and they did so in the name of patriotism. But those who were not directly engaged in money exchange were more inclined to collaborate with the colonial authorities in ending the boycott. With economic ties to foreign capitalism, the prosperous merchants especially had vested interest in desiring law and order in the colony. In fact, considerable Chinese capital was invested in the tramway company. Mr. Lau Chu Pak was known to be an important shareholder and a director of the tramway company.[55] He had sought to collaborate with the colonial authorities to help suppress the boycott, for which he had received a threatening letter from boycotters.

Yet shopkeepers, store owners, and traders were adversely affected by the rejection of Chinese coins, as large numbers of them used to supply their workers and employees with the cheaper Chinese coins to travel by trams. They were inclined to support the boycott. The boycott of trams lasted for more than two months (from late November 1912 to early February 1913), partly because it caused neither major social disturbances nor commercial disruption. If the shopkeepers, merchants, and businessmen faced the prospect of a financial loss, they would exert their influence to help end the boycott.

Such a prospect came from the colonial government's threat, in January 1913, to carry into practice the Boycott Prevention Ordinance. A government notice threatened to proclaim ten districts as "boycott areas," whose inhabitants would be subjected to a special tax to compensate the tramway company for losses incurred by the boycott. The governor in executive council, however, would give audience to representatives from each area to hear their views as to why any area should be exempted from the levy.[56]

This high-handed measure created more animosity among the Chinese residents against the Hong Kong government. In fact, the London Colonial Office belatedly disapproved of the governor's measure. But it proved to be effective in ending the boycott. Merchants hated financial losses. Facing the prospect of a personal financial loss, many Chinese merchants began to take steps with an aim to stop the boycott. A meeting took place in the Tung Wah Hospital on the night of January 8, 1913, attended by about fifty merchants and shopowners representing all districts of Hong Kong. Addressing the meeting, Mr. Lau Chu Pak (a wealthy businessman, shareholder, and director of the tramway company) explained the "reasonableness" of the tramway company's action in collecting only Hong Kong coins on the trams. He said that the enforcement of the boycott ordinance would make not only the landlords but also the tenants suffer:

> Some of you say it is only the lower class who are boycotting . . . [but] don't attribute everything to the lower classes. Many of the lower classes are your servants or your workmen. . . . Those who are masters of shops, employers of labour or managers of big firms, can prove to the Government that they have no interest in the boycott by disallowing the conveyance allowance, and giving their men tram tickets instead.[57]

Finally, the meeting resolved to call on all the guilds and associations in the colony to cooperate in breaking down the boycott.

Meanwhile, representatives of the "boycott areas" appeared before the executive council to request an extension of time before the special levy was imposed so that they could endeavor to use their influence to help end the boycott. The local Chinese press, too, began to publish articles explaining that the tramway company's action originated purely from financial loss and did not mean "contemptuous rejection of Chinese coins," and that the boycott had arisen from "misunderstanding."[58] The Chinese press expressed its "sincere hope that the storm of boycott will abate without delay [so] that no special rate may be levied to the injury of us Chinese."[59] Appealing to the working people to end the boycott, the Chinese press also publicized the colony's law that every workman might demand payments of his wages to be made in Hong Kong coins, and that any foreman who compelled any workman to accept Chinese coins would be liable to prosecution in court on charge of fraud.[60]

In the meantime, a considerable number of employers had undertaken to purchase monthly tram tickets for their employees.[61] At the request of the "leading Chinese," one hundred thousand tickets at half price were sold in books to Chinese shops and business houses that were in the habit of supplying their employees with Chinese coins to travel by the tramway and, during the boycott, to travel by ricksha. This was a compromising and face-saving device to compensate the Chinese employers, who were confronted with the financial loss by the tramway company's refusal of Chinese coins.[62]

As a result of all these measures, large numbers of the working population were induced to take trams, so that by February 4, 1913, the governor was able to telegraph London that the boycott had ceased and the ordinance had been suspended.[63]

Implications

The Boycott Prevention Ordinance incurred more animosity among the Chinese inhabitants against the colonial authorities. It also created tensions within the colony's Chinese community. As Ho Kai had observed, by boycotting the tramway company, the Chinese themselves would be the losers, because monetary compensation for the company would be collected by the colonial government in the form of increased taxation "so that the people whom the Chinese boycotters were injuring were their own compatriots and not the

British at all." "By that means, bitterness would be aroused, and all brotherly feeling, sympathy, good will and readiness to help in time of need, on the part of the leading Chinese, would be alienated."[64]

The London Colonial Office considered the Hong Kong Boycott Prevention Ordinance as "a most extraordinary piece of legislation," because the special tax provision was "certain to inflict a great deal of hardship or injustice" on the Chinese residents. "It is quite indefensible and a very serious step to have taken without the previous consent [of the Colonial Office]. Sir H. May must have quite lost his balance," commented Colonial Office authorities. London, therefore, ordered Governor May to have the ordinance repealed and to immediately terminate any steps that might have been taken in enforcing the special tax provision.[65] In fact, the governor's threat to enforce the tax provision forced the Chinese residents to bow grudgingly to the will of the colonial authorities.

Thus, by February 4, 1913, the boycott had been halted, but the governor's high-handed measures had further incurred Chinese animosity against British colonialism. The boycott of the Hong Kong tramway shed much light not merely on the complex sociopolitical relations and structure in the colony but also on the relations between the Canton government and the British colonial authorities in Hong Kong. The latter's ban on Chinese coins was widely perceived to be a slur on Chinese dignity. The British had put up a number of obstacles in the way of the Chinese revolution, despite the eagerness of the Canton revolutionary government to court British goodwill. Ironically, in its vain attempts to win British approval and support, the Canton revolutionary government turned its back on the labor movement in Hong Kong and ended up alienating the Chinese populace in the colony. In fact, the earlier enthusiasm of the Chinese public for the Canton government quickly waned when the government proved incapable of maintaining financial and political stability in Kwangtung province. This contributed to the eclipse of the Canton revolutionary government in August 1913, as the Chinese communities in Canton and Hong Kong abandoned the Canton government and pledged their allegiance to President Yüan Shih-k'ai in Peking.

Conclusion

This study explores three main themes concerning the history of Hong Kong—the changing urban community structure and social relations, the changing nature and patterns of social unrest, and the growth of nationalism among Chinese merchants, populace, and intelligentsia in Hong Kong under British colonial rule. These themes are examined in the context of Chinese history during the seven decades from 1842 to 1913. This conclusion recapitulates these themes.

Under British colonial rule, Hong Kong had its own path of historical development. Peculiar sociopolitical experience made it different from China in some ways, although its society remained distinctly Chinese. The British acquired Hong Kong primarily for the promotion of trade, not for territorial conquest. Therefore, they were initially willing to leave the Chinese to their own devices so long as public order was maintained and trade enhanced.

In 1842 Hong Kong was a new frontier settlement with little preexisting local power structure. The town grew rapidly as the Chinese from the neighboring districts congregated there seeking employment opportunities. In the unsettled conditions of the colony during the 1840s and the early 1850s, Chinese pioneers and adventurers from very humble origins like Loo Aqui and Tam Achoy had risked their lives to serve the British during the Opium War in return for land and privileges with which to acquire wealth. They used their wealth to serve the Chinese community and thereby emerged as its leaders. They built temples that served as community centers. The British colonial policy of segregation allowed them to manage Chinese public affairs. They arbitrated civil and commercial disputes among the Chinese to help maintain public order. But they were not allowed to possess private armed power, unlike the Chinese strongmen commanding armed followers in other frontier settlements like Taiwan or Kweichow. As Esherick and Rankin justly affirm in their volume of essays on local elites and patterns of dominance, "different environments and resources available to elites in different areas of China . . . produce different types of elite."[1] The relations between Chinese and Europeans in Hong Kong were marked by both cooperation and tensions, harmony and conflict. When order and security were at stake, the British colonial authorities were quick to resort to coercive force. The power of the Chinese elite was severely constrained by the modern colonial state.

The composition of the Chinese elite in Hong Kong began to change in the 1850s and 1860s with the influx of Chinese families and capital during the Taiping uprising in China. New elements of wealthy, respectable merchants joined the elite group. Aspiring Chinese used all the resources available to promote their power and influence. In Hong Kong connections with the British served as an important vehicle for social advancement. Chinese contractors, merchants, and compradors formed business connections with the British colonists. Resources for the aspiring Chinese also included native place–dialect ties as well as the transregional associations. These two were not perceived as mutually exclusive. With the formation of such associations as the District Watch Committee in 1866 and the Nam Pak Hong Guild in 1868, a sense of Chinese community dominated by a merchant elite in Hong Kong was greatly enhanced. And it was further strenghtened by the founding of the famed Tung Wah Hospital in 1872.

During the 1870s and 1880s the elite exerted an unchallenged cultural hegemony over the populace. They shared some common cultural values and traditions, such as beliefs in *feng-shui*, *pa-tzu*, omens, religious worship, family loyalty, and Confucian ideology. It was these shared values that bound the Chinese community together and distinguished it from the Europeans in the colony. Like the gentry elite in China, the gentrified merchant elite in Hong Kong sought to foster social consensus based on Confucian ideals of social harmony and elite paternalism. Consensus was maintained through compromise and elite mediation in conflict situations. The Tung Wah elite arbitrated civil disputes. Through community service and philanthropy, the elite affirmed its claim to social superiority. It used all available social and economic resources to cultivate loyalties based on vertical ties of occupation, kinship, and ethnicity. Such loyalties reinforced Confucian ideals of social order, harmony, and a sense of hierarchy. The elite propagated Confucianism as the hegemonic ideology.

The colony's socioeconomic structure provided a fertile ground for the hegemonic Confucian ideology. Chinese merchants often hired their trusted kinsmen and fellow provincials as assistants, office clerks and workers, and domestic servants. Vertical, paternalistic relationship was usually maintained among them. Urban Hong Kong was in large part a city of small shopkeepers who perceived themselves as upholders of tradional Chinese way of life and sustainers of Confucian culture. The elite used all resources available to induce popular deference and subordination; and in return it had to fulfill its moral obligations to the populace by providing public service and representing the community in its dealings with the colonial government. But the elite management of public affairs was carefully watched by the government. Unlike elites in late imperial China who possessed power in tax collections and military force, the Hong Kong elite exercised no such power. The local arena of Hong Kong as a British colony limited the power of its Chinese elite.

Up to the mid-1880s the colonial government's segregationist policy allowed the Chinese community to function under its elite leadership. The elite's periodic display of cultural symbols of wealth, power, and authority rivaled those at the official *yamen* compounds in imperial China. Yet, high trees attract the wind. Such constant display of power incurred European suspicion. The colonial situation brought the local elite into a complex, interlocking web of ambivalent relationships with the British and the Canton authorities. The colonial government needed Chinese community leaders' cooperation in maintaining law and order in the colony, but it also looked upon them with a watchful, suspicious eye, particularly when the elite became closely connected with the Canton officials. Both Canton and Hong Kong authorities claimed allegiance from the colony's Chinese residents; the local elite therefore served two lords, seeking to manipulate the situation to its own advantage. Colonial experience made the local elite different from Chinese elites on the mainland.

The popular insurrection of 1884 marked an important turning point in the colony's history. It made a lasting impression on the colonial government, which henceforth sought to impose direct rule over the Chinese community. To accelerate political integration, the government assumed more control over the elite organizations and created new channels for social advancement for the aspiring Chinese individuals who were coopted into the government power structure. Henceforth government connections became the most important avenue to the top elite status. The elite's cooperation with the government was reinforced by its economic ties to foreign capitalism in the colony. The elite-sponsored Tung Wah Hospital and Po Leung Kuk were intended both to promote popular welfare and to facilitate social control. During the 1890s tensions surfaced between the lower-class Chinese and the elite who collaborated with the government to keep them in line. The mob attack on the Tung Wah chairman in 1894 symbolized the decline of the old elite's power and prestige in the new social milieu.

From the mid-1880s to the 1900s society became more heterogeneous as a result of population growth and economic expansion. It became more difficult to attain community consensus. The developing capitalist enterprise employing large number of workers was conducive to the growing consciousness of different interests of capital and labor. A younger generation of merchants, businessmen, professionals, and new intelligentsia emerged. It was a generation more Western-oriented than the old elite and more inclined to innovations and new commitments. Although still bound to many traditional ideas, values, and customs, some members of the new intelligentsia became iconoclastic, ready to challenge some parts of Chinese culture and tradition. They denounced as superstitions some old cultural values and practices (such as the aforementioned *feng-shui*, *pa-tzu*, omens, religious worship, and herbal medicine) that had bound together the old elite and community in earlier times.

The dividing of the elite into factions reflected the tendency toward community disintegration during the period from the mid-1880s to the 1900s. In China, the scope of local elite management of public affairs rapidly increased after the Taiping rebellion and continued to expand in subsequent years until 1911, when it collided with the state power and resulted in the overthrow of the Ch'ing government.[2] By contrast, in the British colony of Hong Kong, elite management developed in just the opposite direction: the assertion of state power and political integration after the mid-1880s meant the progressive decline in the scope of their management of public affairs. Again, the colonial experience made Hong Kong different from China.

The new generation of Chinese merchants and intelligentsia in the colony became increasingly politicized by the main currents of events in China, from the Sino-French War in 1884–85 to the revolution of 1911. During these years both elite and populace became more politically activated.

Hong Kong's historical development was not, as the standard works maintain, a story of continuous growth and stability with a politically apathetic Chinese population. Rather, the development was punctuated by a long series of social crises in which both coolies and merchants expressed their dissatisfaction with British rule.

Regarding the historiography of colonialism, Peter Worsley aptly observes that whereas the history of colonialism written by imperialists is "the story of what the White man did," "nationalist historiography has developed a contrary myth: a legend of 'national' resistance which omits the uncomfortable fact of collaboration."[3] The history of Hong Kong reveals patterns of social relations much more complex and subtle than either imperialist or nationalist myth. The relationship between the colonizers and the colonized was full of ambiguities and paradoxes. As stated in the beginning of this book, George Balandier's definition of the "colonial situation" is useful but needs modification. Whereas Balandier stresses "the fundamentally antagonistic character of the relationship" between colonizers and colonized,[4] this study of Hong Kong shows an ambivalent relationship, characterized by both collaboration and hostility, harmony and conflict, partnership and antagonism simultaneously. Antagonism was often caused by unequal partnership, racial tensions in a colonial situation, and the colonial policy of social and political control.

There was a long tradition of Chinese resistance to British colonial rule in Hong Kong. Some anticolonial social protests (e.g., the 1884 popular insurrection, the 1895 controversy over the Light and Pass Ordinance, the series of incidents involving willful civil disobedience in 1911–12, and the boycott of the tramway in 1912–13) were linked to Chinese nationalism; but others were not, depending on historical circumstances. In the coolie strikes of 1888 and 1895, for instance, coolies were thinking primarily in terms of how their livelihood was affected by the colonial government regulations, not in terms of Chinese nationalism. During the period under study anticolonialism was often conservative in character. On many occasions it was directed against the specific colonial government measures affecting the lives and work of the Chinese subjects. Such conservative anticolonialism did not aim to terminate British colonial rule.

Forced by economic hardship and sociopolitical unrest on the mainland to seek work and opportunities in Hong Kong, the colony's Chinese residents were essentially pragmatic and realistic in attitude. While merchants cooperated with their foreign business partners, coolies worked for their foreign employers to make a living. At the bottom of the social hierarchy, coolies were often preoccupied with their daily subsistence and were parochial in outlook. They were divided by dialect and native district differences into rival and hostile groups competing with each other for job opportunities.

Yet, in a colonial situation such coolie parochialism was not too formidable to overcome. When their livelihood was threatened by the colonial government measures, coolies of different dialect groups often joined in strike. A series of coolie disturbances (in 1861, 1863, 1872, 1883, 1884, 1888, 1894, and 1895) disrupted trade and hurt the interests of the Chinese merchants, who naturally sought to cooperate with the British to help maintain law and order. As community leaders, the merchant elite also had moral obligations to mediate and resolve conflict situations. Under certain historical circumstances, like those that came together in 1884 (when the laborers' livelihood was threatened by the French war act and by the colonial government's repressive measures, and when popular sentiment was inflamed by the nationalistic Canton officials), the laborers' anticolonialism came to acquire a nationalistic overtone. But incipient popular nationalism aroused in 1884 proved ephemeral. Local issues affecting the laborers' livelihood remained of primary importance to them. National issues, if not aligned with local issues, had little appeal to coolies.

National consciousness did not easily develop among the colony's coolies, because it involved a certain degree of abstract conceptualization often unrelated to the problems of their everyday lives. In ordinary times coolies' living conditions were hardly conducive to the nurturing of the concept of "loyalty and selfless devotion to China as my nation-state." The street hawkers, for instance, were preoccupied with their daily worries and problems: their sleeping rooms were filthy and overcrowded; their congee, fruits, vegetables, or other commodities quickly got stale or rotten, especially in the hot and humid summer months; they complained about their fussy customers; they quarreled with shopkeepers who would not allow them to place their stalls in front of shops; they also quarreled among themselves for better stands for their stalls; and they had to watch out for police who imposed fines and dragged them to the magistrate's court. And so on and so forth.[5] Coolies preoccupied with these practical matters could not easily turn into dedicated patriots possessing a sense of collective identity with and loyalty to China as a sovereign nation-state.

This observation does not mean to deprecate workers as incapable of "high" passions of nationalism. To pay close attention to coolies' preoccupation with mundane matters is not to slight the coolie workers. Quite the contrary, it is to affirm the legitimacy of such preoccupation. Living a bare subsistence existence, coolies had to attend to their immediate material needs for food, clothing, and shelter. In their daily struggle to earn a living these mundane needs were not "trivial" matters. To dismiss these as "trivial" would be "a slander on the moral status of fundamental material needs," to use James C. Scott's words.[6] A nationalist cause that addressed the issues of laborers' needs and concerns would be more likely to attract their interest and support.

Nationalism was a complex phenomenon with cultural, political, and socioeconomic dimensions. Nationalism was Janus-faced. It took many different forms. So far as there were different views concerning what was in the best interest of the nation, there would be different forms of nationalism. They ranged from elitist nationalism to populist nationalism, from militant, exclusive nationalism to conservative collaborationist nationalism (i.e., collaboration with imperialism at the sacrifice of some sovereign rights in the hope of eventually building a strong nation to fight imperialism). With close economic ties to foreign capitalism, many Chinese merchants in Hong Kong favored peaceful reforms along Western capitalist lines to strengthen China under British tutelage. They did not regard popular outbursts of strikes and riots as "valid" expressions of patriotism.

Elitist and collaborationist nationalism, on the other hand, had little appeal to coolies because it was built on a sectional foundation that identified merchants' interests with national interests. The immediate economic interest and social concerns were of primary importance to the laborers in their daily struggle to earn a living. But the elitist nationalists from among the merchants and intelligentsia often failed to address the local issues relating to the workers' pressing social needs and economic problems. This helps to explain why the elitist nationalists did not win much support from laborers for the nationalist causes from 1887 to 1900.

The boycott movements of 1905 and 1908 represented an upsurge of political and economic nationalism among the Chinese against foreign imperialism. In part, the boycotts also reflected the aspiration of the Chinese businessmen to assert their interests against foreign capitalist competition and domination in China. Nationalism became a vehicle for sectional self-assertion. Leadership in the anti-imperialist movements served to enhance the merchants' political power and influence; it also afforded them opportunities for economic development. Appealing to Chinese patriotism against foreign political and economic imperialism, boycott activists from among the merchants and intelligentsia were able to rally some degree of popular support. The crowd's attacks on Hong Kong Chinese stores selling Japanese goods and the street riots of 1908 gave vent to the popular anti-Japanese and anticolonial sentiments. Yet, the extent of workers' participation in the boycotts compared unfavorably with the 1884 coolie strike organized by the coolies themselves. Coolies would respond to a nationalist cause, if it was fused with an appeal to their social needs and economic interests. Subsequently the T'ung-meng-hui revolutionaries did seek to politicize the laborers by "stooping" to work with them, and thus helped to win popular support in Canton and Hong Kong for the Chinese revolution in 1911.

The revolution of 1911 greatly politicized Chinese of all classes in Hong Kong. Chinese nationalism in the British colony found lively expression in various ways: spontaneous popular jubilation over the fall of the old government; monetary subscriptions for the Canton revolutionary government; the compositors' strike; civil disobedience; an assassination attempt on the Hong Kong governor; the boycott of the Hong Kong tramway. Ironically, eager to cultivate the British colonial authorities' goodwill, the newly founded Canton revolutionary government deprecated labor strikes and popular unrest in Hong Kong, which were inspired by the revolution itself. The Canton revolutionaries thus became identified as the new ruling elite that again was primarily interested in maintaining social order, securing government revenue, suppressing workers' demands, and thus helped to alienate itself from the populace in 1913.

The Chinese revolution helped to create a general sense of social unrest in the British colony. It gave an important stimulus to popular nationalism, as the populace was aroused to a new awareness of and concern with China's politics and problems. Popular national consciousness was reflected in the labor strikes, the mob attacks on colonial officials and other acts of civil disobedience, and the tramway boycott. Many members of the Chinese elite, however, refused to accept such popular outburts as "legitimate" expressions of patriotism. To help restore order and discipline, elite members like Lau Chu Pak sought to revive Confucianism as a hegemonic ideology and means of social control. They advocated Confucian and Mencian nationalism (*K'ung-Meng min-tsu chu-i*), seeking to use the conservative Confucian cultural tradition as a focus for the Chinese people in their search for identity as a nation. Again, nationalism took many different forms; it was both a mobilizing and a divisive force in history.

Notes

Introduction

1. Eitel, *Europe in China*, pp. ii, iv, 290, 294, 318, 568, 569.
2. Wood, *A Brief History of Hongkong*.
3. Endacott, *A History of Hong Kong; Fragrant Harbor, A Short History of Hong Kong* (Hong Kong: Oxford, 1962); *Government and People in Hong Kong; Hong Kong Eclipse*, edited by Alan Birch.
4. These are Paul Cohen's words in his analysis of American historical writing on China. See Cohen, *Discovering History in China*, p. 4.
5. Milner, "Colonial Records History; British Malaya," pp. 774, 779, 783.
6. Lethbridge, *Hong Kong: Stability and Change*, p. 65.
7. Wesley-Smith, *Unequal Treaty, 1898–1997*; Miners, *Hong Kong Under Imperial Rule, 1912–1941*; Edwin Ride, *BAAG, British Army Aid Group, Hong Kong Resistance, 1942–45* (Hong Kong: Oxford, 1981); Crisswell, *The Taipans*; Lo Hsiang-lin, *Hong Kong and Western Cultures*; Ng Alice Lun Ngai-ha, *Interactions of East and West*; H. A. Turner, *The Last Colony: But Whose? A Study of the Labour Movement, Labour Market, and Labour Relations in Hong Kong* (Cambridge: Cambridge University Press, 1980); Joe England and John Rear, *Industrial Relations and Law in Hong Kong* (Oxford: Oxford University Press, 1981); Paul Gillingham, *At the Peak: Hong Kong Between the Wars* (Hong Kong: Macmillan, 1983); Jaschok, *Concubines and Bondservants*; Kevin P. Lane, *Sovereignty and the Status Quo: The Historical Roots of China's Hong Kong Policy* (Boulder: Westview Press, 1990); Tsang, *Democracy Shelved*; Chan Lau Kit-ching, *China, Britain, and Hong Kong, 1895–1945*, which is largely a diplomatic history.
8. Cameron's *Hong Kong: The Cultured Pearl* and *An Illustrated History of Hong Kong* are anecdotal histories for general readers.

9. Two books deal with social and political crises: John Cooper, *Colony in Conflict: The Hong Kong Disturbances, May 1967–January 1968* (Hong Kong: Swindon, 1970) and Gregor Benton, *The Hongkong Crisis* (London: Pluto Press, 1983), the latter on the recent Sino-British negotiations over Hong Kong's future.

10. Balandier, "The Colonial Situations," pp. 34–61.

11. Moore, *Social Origins of Dictatorship and Democracy*, pp. 522–523.

12. Cohen, "The New Coastal Reformers," in Paul A. Cohen and John E. Schreker, eds., *Reform in Nineteenth-Century China* (Harvard University East Asian Research Center, 1976), pp. 256–257.

13. Rowe, *Hankow: Conflict and Community*, pp. 347–349. For some discussion of "cultural hegemony," see E. P. Thompson, "Patrician Society, Plebeian Culture," pp. 382–405; T. J. Jackson Lears, "The Concept of Cultural Hegemony: Problems and Possibilities," pp. 567–593; Ellen Kay Trimberger, "E. P. Thompson: Understanding the Process of History," pp. 211–243; Suzanne Desan, "Crowds, Community, and Ritual in the Work of E. P. Thompson and Natalie Davis," pp. 47–71.

14. Rankin, *Elite Activism*, pp. 6–17.

15. Kuhn, *Rebellion and Its Enemies*, pp. 213–216.

16. David Strand, *Rickshaw Beijing: City People and Politics in the 1920s* (Berkeley and Los Angeles: University of California Press, 1989), pp. 143, 256.

17. Honig, *Sisters and Strangers*, pp. 249. Shaffer, *Mao and the Workers*, also shows that traditional workers formed the core of the labor movement in Hunan precisely because of their preindustrial ties.

18. Thompson, *The Making of the English Working Class*, pp. 9, 11, 13.

19. Hershatter, *The Workers of Tianjin*, pp. 239–240.

20. Honig, *Sisters and Strangers*, pp. 5–6, 76, 78.

1. Historical Setting: The Making of An Entrepôt

1. See Wang Gungwu, *China and the Chinese Overseas* and *Community and Nation*.

2. For the creation of an Amoy trading system see Chin-keong Ng, *Trade and Society: The Amoy Network on the China Coast, 1683–1735* (Singapore: Singapore University Press, 1983).

3. Chiu, *The Port of Hong Kong*, pp. 16–17.

4. Smith, "The Chinese Settlement of British Hong Kong," pp. 26–27.

5. Smith, "The Chinese Settlement of British Hong Kong," p. 26; Eitel, *Europe in China*, pp. 169–171, 181–183, 186.

6. Endacott, *A History of Hong Kong*, p. 65.

7. Ping-ti Ho, *Studies on the Population of China*, pp. xi, 183–189.

8. Yen Chung-p'ing et al., *Chung-kuo chin-tai ching-chi shih*, pp. 362–367. Wakeman, *Strangers at the Gate*, pp. 179–180.

9. Mei, "Socioeconomic Origins of Emigration," p. 468.

10. Wakeman, *Strangers at the Gate*, p. 15.

11. Mei, "Socioeconomic Origins of Emigration," pp. 470–471.

12. Wakeman, *Strangers at the Gate*, p. 187.

13. Ming Kou Chan, "Labor and Empire," p. 15.

14. Albert Feuerwerker, *The Chinese Economy*, p. 17, states that while the Chinese "handicraft industry as a whole was not seriously undermined between 1870 and 1911, . . . significant structural changes in the handicraft industrial sector took place in these four decades . . . and the strain and dislocation occasioned by these developments adversely affected substantial parts of population."

15. The Cohong system in Canton did not in fact maintain a rigid monopoly over China's foreign trade. A "semi-free trade" was carried out by British private traders, American opium merchants, Chinese "shopmen," compradors, and Junks beyond the limits of Canton. British traders, nevertheless, sought to promote a complete free trade with China, thereby precipitating the Opium War. See Yen-ping Hao, *The Commercial Revolution*, pp. 14–33.

16. Jones, "The Ningpo Pang," p. 74.

17. Wakeman, *Strangers at the Gate*, pp. 98–101.

18. Ming Kou Chan, "Labor and Empire," p. 16.

19. Hsü Hsin-wu, *Ya-p'ien chan-cheng ch'ien*, p. 63.

20. Mei, "Socioeconomic Origins of Emigration," pp. 473–474.

21. Smith, "Emergence of a Chinese Elite in Hong Kong," pp. 82–84.

22. Smith, "The Chinese Settlement of British Hong Kong," pp. 82–84.

23. Legge, "The Colony of Hong Kong," p. 184.

24. The Chinese population in Hong Kong increased from 54,072 in 1854, to 70,651 in 1855, to 85,280 in 1859, and to 92,441 in 1860, the year when Kowloon was added to the colony. See *Historical and Statistical Abstract*.

25. Smith, "Emergence of a Chinese Elite in Hong Kong," pp. 89–91.

26. Chiu, *The Port of Hong Kong*, pp. ix, 1, 3, 16–17.

27. Endacott, *An Eastern Entrepot*, pp. ix, xi, xii.

28. Hobsbawm, *The Age of Revolution*, p. 136; David B. Davis, *Slavery and Human Progress* (New York and Oxford: Oxford University Press, 1984).

29. P'eng Chia-li, "Shih-chiu shih-chi Hsi-fang ch'in-lüeh-che, pp. 235–239, 255.

30. Mei, "Socioeconomic Origins of Emigration," pp. 493–494, 485.

31. *The China Mail*, March 30, 1854.

32. Ch'en Tse-hsien, "Shih-chiu shih-chi sheng-hsing ti ch'i-kung chih," pp. 169–171; P'eng Chia-li, "Shih-chiu shih-chi Hsi-fang ch'in-lueh-che," pp. 238, 254.

33. Kani Hiroaki, *Kindai Chūgoku no kuri to choka* (Coolies and "slave girls" of modern China) (Tokyo: Iwanami Shobō, 1979), p. 31; P'eng Chia-li, "Shih-chiu shih-chi Hsi-fang ch'in-lueh-che," pp. 250–251.

34. Kani Hiroaki, *Kindai Chūgoku*, pp. 31–33.

35. Coolidge, *The Chinese Immigration*, p. 428.

36. Kani Hiroaki, *Kindai Chūgoku*, p. 24.

37. Eitel, *Europe in China*, p. 259. But Kani Hiroaki, *Kindai Chūgoku*, p. 31, gives a figure of 20,026 Chinese emigrants landed in San Francisco in 1852.

38. Denby, *China and Her People*, 2:110.

39. P'eng Chia-li, "Shih-chiu shih-chi Hsi-fang ch'in-lueh-che," pp. 251–252, 257, 258–259.

40. Mei,"Socioeconomic Origins of Emigration," p. 490.

41. Endacott, *A History of Hong Kong*, p. 132.

42. Noda Jitsunosuke, *Honkon jijō*, pp. 284–285, 288; Wright and Cartwright, *Twentieth-Century Impressions*, pp. 244–245.

43. Yen Chung-p'ing, *Chung-kuo chin-tai ching-chi shih*, pp. 239–241; Endacott, *An Eastern Entrepot*, pp. xiv-xv, 146; Wright and Cartwirght, *Twentieth-Century Impressions*, pp. 116–120, 200–210. Noda Jitsunosuke, *Honkon jijō*, pp. 160–164.

44. Denby, *China and Her People*, 2:93.

45. Endacott, *A History of Hong Kong*, pp. 126–127.

46. Pomerantz, "The Chinese Bourgeoisie," pp. 3–5.

47. Hyde, *Far Eastern Trade*, pp. 86–87, 115.

48. Hyde, *Far Eastern Trade*, pp. 85, 106.

49. Choa Chee Bee's *Wills*, dated May 8, 1890 and June 28, 1900.

50. Choa Leep Chee's *Will*, June 17, 1909; Wright and Cartwright, *Twentieth-Century Impressions*, p. 176.

51. Feldwick, *Present Day Impression*, p. 595.

52. Ng Li Hing's *Will*, October 25, 1913.

53. By 1917 the Chinese population in Siam numbered 900,000. John K. Fairbank, E. O. Reischauer, and A. M. Craig, *East Asia: The Modern Transformation* (Boston: Houghton Mifflin, 1965), pp. 430, 459.

54. Lü-Kang Ch'ao-chou shang-hui ch'ang-wu li-shih-hui, *Lü-Kang Ch'ao-chou shang-hui*, p. 6.

55. Smith, "Emergence of a Chinese Elite in Hong Kong," p. 93.

56. Feldwick, *Present Day Impression*, p. 586; Wright and Cartwright, *Twentieth-Century Impressions*, p. 229.

57. Fairbank, Reischauer, and Craig, *East Asia*, p. 733.

58. Lee Poh Ping, *Chinese Society in Nineteenth-Century Singapore* (Kuala Lumpur: Oxford University Press, 1978), p. 87, gives as the Chinese population of Singapore:

	1881	1891	1901
Hokkien	24,981	45,856	59,117
Cantonese	14,853	23,397	30,729
Hakka	6,170	7,402	8,514
Teochiu	22,644	23,737	27,564
Hainanese	8,319	8,711	9,451
Straits-born	9,527	12,805	15,498
Total:	86,766	121,908	164,041

59. Feldwick, *Present Day Impression*, pp. 590–591.

60. Feldwick, *Present Day Impression*, p. 588.

61. Wright and Cartwright, *Twentieth-Century Impressions*, p. 248; Cheng Tzu-ts'an, *Chih-nan-lu*, p. 491. Feldwick, *Present Day Impression*, p. 558.

62. CO129.391.26748, Governor May to Lewis Harcourt, July 23, 1912, p. 138.

63. Remer, *The Foreign Trade of China*, p. 44.

64. Cheng Tzu-ts'an, *Chih-nan-lu*, pp. 1–78, 100–104.

65. Cheng Tzu-ts'an, *Chih-nan-lu*, pp. 78–99, 105–106.

66. Cheng Tzu-ts'an, *Chih-nan-lu*, pp. 240–252; 280–287.

67. Yen Chung-p'ing, *Chung-kuo chin-tai ching-chi shih*, pp. 65–66.

68. Remer, *The Foreign Trade of China*, p. 160.

69. In writing this paragraph I am indebted to the readers for Columbia University Press for their inspiring and erudite comments on my manuscript. See also Yuen Sang Leung, "Regional Rivalry in Mid-Nineteenth Century Shanghai."

70. Cohen, *Between Tradition and Modernity*, pp. 256–257.

71. Wright and Cartwright, *Twentieth-Century Impressions*, p. 194.

2. A Frontier Settlement: The Chinese Community Under Alien Rule, 1840s–1860s

1. Lau Siu-kai, *Society and Politics*, p. 7.

2. Headley J. Stephen, "Hong Kong is the Lifeboat, Notes on Political Culture and Socialization," *Journal of Oriental Studies* (September 1970), 8:210.

3. Pomerantz Shin, "China in Transition," p. 30, aptly characterizes early Hong Kong as "a frontier outpost."

4. Fieldhouse, *The Colonial Empires*, pp. 242, 243, 293.

5. Norton-Kyshe, *The History of the Laws and Courts*, 1:4–6.

6. Smith, "The Chinese Settlement of British Hong Kong," pp. 26–28.

7. Endacott, *An Eastern Entrepot*, pp. 96–98.

8. Norton-Kyshe, *The History of the Laws and Courts*, 1:29.

9. Endacott, *Government and People in Hong Kong*, p. 37.

10. *The Friend of China*, Nov. 2, 1844, pp. 561, 563, 565; Shuang Ai, *Hsiang-chiang chiu-shih*, pp. 105–107.

11. *The Friend of China*, Nov. 2, 1844, p. 561.

12. Eitel, *Europe in China*, pp. 224, 226.

13. *The Friend of China*, Nov. 2, 1844, p. 561.

14. For these popular outbursts against Europeans in the Canton delta and in Macao and Hong Kong, see Eitel, *Europe in China*, pp. 158, 214–216, 218–219, 255, 269.

15. Shuang Ai, *Hsiang-chiang chiu-shih*, pp. 75–78; Norton-Kyshe, *The History of the Laws and Courts*, 1:228–230, 296–299.

16. A recent study by Dian H. Murray, *Pirates of the South China Coast, 1790–1810* (Stanford: Stanford University Press, 1987), argues that pirates in earlier times were "entrepreneurs," who preyed on shipping, engaged in the salt trade, and operated protection rackets; that some pirate chiefs were easily induced into defections by the Ch'ing government offers of monetary

rewards and military ranks; and that the pirates were nonideological, collaborating with the government as much as fighting against it.

17. Hobsbawm, *Bandits*, p. 143.

18. For a critique of Hobsbawm's "social bandits" see Cheah Boon Kheng, "Hobsbawm's Social Banditry," pp. 34–51.

19. Fox, *British Admirals*, p. 107.

20. Norton-Kyshe, *The History of the Laws and Courts*, 1:228–230, 296–299; Shuang Ai, *Hsiang-chiang chiu-shih*, pp. 75–78.

21. Norton-Kyshe, *The History of the Laws and Courts*, 1:228–230, 296–299; Shuang Ai, *Hsiang-chiang chiu-shih*, pp. 75–78.

22. See Smith's articles, "The Chinese Settlement of Hong Kong," pp. 26, 28; and "Emergence of a Chinese Elite in Hong Kong," pp. 80–82.

23. "The Districts of Hong Kong and the Name Kwan-Tai-Lo," p. 333.

24. Smith, "The Chinese Settlement of British Hong Kong," p. 29, and "Emergence of a Chinese Elite in Hong Kong," pp. 87–88.

25. Eitel, *Europe in China*, pp. 168–169.

26. *The Hongkong Daily Press*, April 23, 1880.

27. Elizabeth Sinn, "A Preliminary Study," pp. 3–4.

28. Ibid., pp. 4–5. In Chinese cities on the mainland, traditional Chinese traders and sojourners in an alien setting tended to cluster into groups and created associations based on common native place and occupation; see Jones, "The Ningpo Pang," pp. 73–96.

29. Armentrout-Ma, "Urban Chinese at the Sinitic Frontier," pp. 107–135.

30. Lu Yen et al., *Hsiang-kang chang-ku*, 11:1–4.

31. Pryor, "Housing Conditions in Hong Kong," pp. 92.

32. Kani Hiroaki, *General Survey of the Boat People*, p. 73. But fishermen of all dialect groups shared these common beliefs and customs regarding the shipwreck portents.

33. Douglas W. Sparks, "The Teochiu: Ethnicity in Urban Hong Kong," *JHKBRAS* (1976), 16:26, shows that "differences between ethnic groups in Hong Kong in rituals, beliefs, and family structure, etc. are minimal . . . particularly in the urban areas."

34. Hayes, "Secular Non-Gentry Leadership," p. 114.

35. Ibid., pp. 121–124. The management of temples and shrines and the organization of festivals were generally in the hands of the *kaifong* land-dwellers, for the Tanka boat people were traditionally just worshippers and "lookers-on." The boat people were "parasites on the temple ashore founded by a land-dweller"; see Kani Hiroaki, *A General Survey of the Boat People*, pp. 80–81. Loo Aqui was an exception. He was an ex-boatman who had acquired wealth that enabled him to earn the preeminent position of an elite.

36. Hayes, "Secular Non-Gentry Leadership," pp. 125–126.

37. *Hsiang-kang wen-wu-miao shih-lüeh.*

38. Sinn, *Power and Charity*, pp. 16, 217.

39. Lethbridge, "The Tung Wah," p. 151. For *kaifong* in contemporary Hong Kong, see Wong, *The Kaifong Associations*, and her article, "Chinese

Voluntary Associations in Southeast Asian Cities and the Kaifongs in Hong Kong," *JHKBRAS* (1971), 11:62–73.

40. Hayes, "Secular Non-Gentry Leadership," p. 126; Sinn, *Power and Charity*, p. 17.

41. Rankin, *Elite Activism*, p. 18; and Linda Pomerantz Shin, "China in Transition," pp. 38–41. More on gentry managers in chapter 3.

42. *Report . . . Tung Wah*, pp. xvii–xviii.

43. See also Sinn, *Power and Charity*, p. 18.

44. Eitel, *Europe in China*, pp. 302–304.

45. Smith, *Chinese Christians*, pp. 75–86.

46. Eitel, *Europe in China*, pp. 306–309; Lu Yen et al., *Hsiang-kang chang-ku*, 2:155–161.

47. *The China Mail*, Nov. 27, 1856.

48. Eitel, *Europe in China*, pp. 310–311.

49. Norton-Kyshe, *The History of the Laws and Courts*, 1:417.

50. Ibid., 1:418–421; Shuang Ai, *Hsiang-chiang chiu-shih*, pp. 79–91; Lu Yen et al., *Hsiang-kang chang-ku*, 2:162–164.

51. Endacott, *A History of Hong Kong*, p. 94.

52. Shuang Ai, *Hsiang-chiang chiu-shih*, pp. 90–91.

53. Lu Yen et al., *Hsiang-kang chang-ku*, 2:162–164.

54. Eitel, *Europe in China*, pp. 315–317; Wakeman, *Strangers at the Gate*, pp. 159–173; Steven A. Leibo, "Not So Calm an Administration: The Anglo-French Occupation of Canton, 1858–1861," *JHKBRAS* (1988), 28:16–33.

55. Norton-Kyshe, *The History of the Laws and Courts*, 1:;495. In 1858 the total Chinese population of Hong Kong was 74,041.

56. Eitel, *Europe in China*, pp. 319–320.

57. Yüan Pang-chien, "Hsiang-kang kung-jen yün-tung li-shih ti chi-ko t' eh-tien" (Some characteristics in the history of labor movement in Hong Kong), *Chin-tai-shih yen-chiu* (1989), 1:178.

58. Eitel, *Europe in China*, p. 132.

59. *The China Mail*, July 23, 1891; Smith, "Emergence of the Chinese Elite in Hong Kong," pp. 90–91.

60. Eitel, *Europe in China*, p. 316.

61. Eitel, *Europe in China*, p. 395.

62. Norton-Kyshe, *The History of the Laws and Courts*, 2:1–4.

63. Eitel, *Europe in China*, p. 368.

64. Norton-Kyshe, *The History of the Laws and Courts*, 1:328, 495.

65. *The China Mail*, January 3 and 17, 1861.

66. *The China Mail*, October 8 and 29, 1863.

67. Hayes, *The Hong Kong Region*, p. 15; see also Hayes, "The Nature of Village Life," pp. 55–72, and James Hayes, "Rural Leadership in the Hong Kong Region: Village Autonomy in A Traditional Setting," in Goran Aijmer, ed., *Leadership on the China Coast* (London and Malmo: Curzon Press, 1984), pp. 32–52.

68. Tilly, "Rural Collective Action in Modern Europe," p. 26.

69. Esherick and Rankin, *Chinese Local Elites*, p. 11.

70. Johanna Menzel Meskill, *A Chinese Pioneer Family: The Lins of Wu-feng, Taiwan, 1729–1895* (Princeton: Princeton University Press, 1979), p. 255, observes that "the frontier spawned local leaders with private power, including private armed power, who interposed themselves between the populace and the apparatus of a remote Chinese government. It was a custom which they would retain even after Taiwan was incorporated into the Chinese state."

71. Edward A. McCord, "Local Military Power and Elite Formation: The Liu Family of Xingyi County, Guizhou," in Esherick and Rankin, *Chinese Local Elites*, p. 188, states: "In the mid-nineteenth century, militia leadership served as the agency for the Liu family's remarkable rise to a position of local dominance, but the condition of widespread rebellion and social disorder ultimately made this rise possible. Likewise only the special conditions of the 1911 Revolution in Guizhou gave Liu Xianshi the chance to parlay his family's local military power into provincial military domination."

72. Lu Yen et al., *Hsiang-kang chang-ku*, 11:3–7; Norton-Kyshe, *The History of the Laws and Courts*, 1:633–641.

73. Gerth and Mills, *From Max Weber*, p. 78, assert, "A state is a human community that (successfully) claims the monopoly of the legitimate use of physical force within a given territory." See also Tilly, *From Mobilization to Revolution*, p. 52.

74. Loo Aqui was declared bankrupt in 1855 because he stood security for the mismanaged estate of a Punti Cantonese merchant. He no longer appeared as a public figure after his bankruptcy, although his two sons (who had inherited most of his wealth before 1855) were to be of elite status in the 1870s. Tam Achoy remained prosperous as a contractor until his death in 1871, although he did not participate actively in public affairs in his later years because his health was affected by his habitual opium-smoking. Kwok Acheong, owner of a fleet of steamships, also remained prosperous until his death in 1880. See Smith, "Emergence of a Chinese Elite in Hong Kong," pp. 82, 88, 97–98.

75. Smith, "Emergence of a Chinese Elite in Hong Kong," pp. 89–90.

76. Lethbridge, "The District Watch Committee," p. 127.

77. "The Nam Pak Hong Commercial Association of Hong Kong," *JHKBRAS* (1979), 19::222.

78. Lin Hsi, "Ch'ung Hsiang-kang ti Yuan-fa-hang t'an-ch'i" (On the Yuan-fa-hang of Hong Kong), *Ta Ch'eng*, August 1, 1983, 117:51, gives a glimpse of close personal relations between Ko Man Wah (from Teochiu), Wong Shing (from Hsiang-shan), and Leung On (from Shun-te).

79. Lethbridge, "The District Watch Committee," pp. 117–119.

80. Ibid.

81. Nam Pak Hong kung-so, *Hsin hsia luo-ch'eng*, p. 23; English translation is cited from "The Nam Pak Hong Commercial Association of Hong Kong," p. 217. See also Nam-pak-hong kung-so, comp., *Nan-pei-hang kung-so ch'eng-li i-pai-chou-nien chi-nien t'e-kan* (Centenary publication of the Nam Pak Hong) (Hong Kong; 1968), pp. 17–19.

82. Nam-pak-hong kung-so, comp., *Hsin hsia luo-ch'eng*, pp. 23–24; "The Nam Pak Hong Commercial Association of Hong Kong," pp. 218, 221–222.

83. Eitel, *Europe in China*, p. 282.

84. Smith, "Emergence of a Chinese Elite in Hong Kong," pp. 81, 88, 98; Yen-p'ing Hao, *The Comprador in Nineteenth-Century China*, p. 195.

85. Esherick and Rankin, *Chinese Local Elites*, p. 308.

86. "The Nam Pak Hong Commercial Association of Hong Kong," p. 222.

87. Thompson, "Patrician Society, Plebeian Culture," p. 389.

3. The Chinese Community in a Colonial Situation, 1870s–1900s

1. *Report . . . Tung Wah*, pp. vii, xix, xxix, xxx, xliv; *The Hongkong Daily Press*, April 26, 29, 1869.

2. Tung-shih-chü (Board of directors), comp., *Hsiang-kang tung-hua san yüan pai-nien shih-lüeh* (One hundred years of the Tung Wah group of hospitals, 1870–1970) (Hong Kong: 1970), 1:15–16 (English), 90–92 (Chinese); *The China Mail*, February 14, 1872; *Report . . . Tung Wah*, pp. xliii–xlv.

3. *Report . . . Tung Wah*, pp. xlv–xlvii.

4. For details of the Tung Wah management and organization, see Sinn's excellent study, *Power and Charity*, pp. 54–60, 273–274.

5. To give a few examples, Ko Man Wah from Teochiu, one of the Tung Wah founders, served as a director in its initial preparatory stage from 1869 to 1871. Later on other Teochiu men who served on the directorate included O Chun Chit (1874), Chan Wun Wing (1877), Ko Soon Kam (1892), Chan Tin San (1907), Wong Siu Ham (1915), and Chan Tsz Tan (1920). Some wealthy Hokkienese, too, served on the directorate, such as Yip Oi Shan (1880), Choa Chee Bee (1900), Ng Li Hing (1902, 1905), Ng Sau Sang (1907), O Ting Sam (1909), and To Sze Tun (1919); see Tung-shih-chü, *Hsiang-kang tung-hua san yüan*, 1:61–63, 65, 67–70.

6. They included a former boatman Kwok Acheong, Eurasians such as Robert Ho Tung, and Christians such as Wong Shing and Chan Tai Kwong, who remained deeply committed to many traditional Chinese customs, ideas, and values. Smith, "Emergence of the Chinese Elite in Hong Kong," pp. 97–98, 107, 109, 112.

7. Po Leung Kuk, *Hsiang-kang Pao-liang-chü pai-nien shih* includes a history of the institution on pp. 135–153 and a long table of chronological events and a list of directors on pp. 211–274.

8. Lethbridge, "Evolution of a Voluntary Association," pp. 41, 47. For a detailed account of the Po Leung Kuk charitable work, see Kani Hiroaki, *Kindai Chūgoku*, pp. 38–57, 351–374.

9. Sinn, *Power and Charity*, pp. 64–67, 69–74; 98–113.

10. Sinn, *Power and Charity*, pp. 59–60, 89, 96.

11. Sinn, *Power and Charity*, pp. 96–98.

12. Wang Tao, "Hsiang-hai chi-tsung" (My Sojourn in Hong Kong: Excerpts), *Renditions: A Chinese-English Translation Magazine* (Spring and Autumn 1988), nos. 29–30, p. 39.

13. *Hong Kong Government Gazette*, July 13, 1878, p. 352.

14. Bird, *The Golden Chersonese*, pp. 87, 91–92.

15. Rankin, *Elite Activism*, pp. 6–17.

16. Kuhn, *Rebellion and Its Enemies*, pp. 213–216.

17. Rankin, *Elite Activism*, pp. 7, 9, 18.

18. Indeed, throughout the late Ch'ing period the Chinese government desperately needed funds to pay for the expenses and/or indemnities incurred by such national disasters as the Sino-French War (1884–85), the Sino-Japanese War (1894–95), and the Boxer uprising in 1900. The sale of honors greatly expanded so that "brevet titles and ranks flooded the overseas market." In addition to financial need, the sale of titles was also intended as a means of securing overseas Chinese allegiance and as a political weapon to counterrevolutionary influence in the overseas Chinese communities. See Yen Ching-huang, "Ch'ing's Sale of Honours, pp. 20–32.

19. Esherick and Rankin, *Chinese Local Elites* p. 11.

20. This section on the Ko family is reconstructed mainly from a series of articles written by Ko Man Wah's grandson (Ko Soon Kam's son), Kao Chen-pai, "Hsiang-kang Tung-hua i-yüan" pp. 2–5; Lin Hsi (Kao Chen-pai), "Ch'ung Hsiang-kang ti yüan-fa-hang t'ang ch'i" (Yuen Fat Hong of Hong Kong), *Ta-ch'eng* (August 1983), 117:47–52; (Sept. 1983), 118:45–51; (Oct. 1983), 119:34–39; (Nov. 1983) 120:46–54.

21. Lethbridge, "A Chinese Association in Hong Kong," p. 154.

22. *China Mail*, July 26, 27, 29, 1872.

23. *China Mail*, July 30, 1872.

24. "Report on Chair and Ricksha Coolies," pp. 57–61.

25. "Report on Chair and Ricksha Coolies," p. 2.

26. *British Parliamentary Papers*, vol. 26, p. 128.

27. "Correspondence Relative to the Magistrate's Court," 11:219–224.

28. "Correspondence Relative to the Magistrate's Court," 11:208–216.

29. *China Mail*, May 31, 1899. See an interesting article by Nacken, "Chinese Street-Cries," p. 129.

30. Nacken, "Chinese Street-Cries," pp. 128–129.

31. *China Mail*, May 31, 1899.

32. *Daily Press*, May 23, 24, 1883.

33. *China Mail*, May 22, 1883; *Daily Press*, May 23, 1883.

34. English translation of the *Hua-tzu jih-pao* article in *China Mail*, May 26, 1883. The earliest issue of *Hua-tzu jih-pao* now available dated only from 1895.

35. *Daily Press*, May 24, 1883.

36. CO129/222/20878, Bowen to F. Stanley, Oct. 21, 1885, p. 413.

37. *Daily Press*, May 24, 1883.

38. Sinn, *Power and Charity*, pp. 5–6, also makes this observation.

39. *China Mail*, October 8, 1884.

40. Hu Ch'uan-chao, *Tun-mo liu-fen*, chuan 2:14b, 21b; 3:7a.

41. CO129/217/19555, Marsh to Derby, #340, Oct. 6, 1884, p. 422.

42. CO129/225/7651, Marsh to Granville, March 24, 1886, pp. 328–331; Sinn, *Power and Charity*, pp. 141–146.

43. CO129/225/7651, sub-enclosure 1, pp. 337–338.

44. CO129/225/7651, pp. 332–341; CO129/230/9720, Foreign Office to Undersecretary of State, Colonial Office, June 3, 1886, pp. 179–185.

45. Sinn, *Power and Charity*, pp. 88–89, 132, 151.

46. On Wu T'ing-fang's and Wong Shing's appointments, see Endacott, *Government and People in Hong Kong*, pp. 97, 101–102.

47. Cheng, "Chinese Unofficial Members," pp. 12–20.

48. *Hong Kong Directory (1884)*, pp. 348–349; (1893), pp. 612–613.

49. Lethbridge, "The District Watch Committee, pp. 118–122.

50. Sinn, *Power and Charity*, pp. 152–153, 207.

51. *China Mail*, Sept. 12, 1889; Feb. 1, 1894. Ho Kai once spoke on racial discrimination and social inequality when he was serving on the Sanitary Board in 1887. But such occasions were rare. The board more frequently discussed things like the "begging nuisance" in the street and "the alleged nuisance arising from the practice of drying shark fins' refuge upon the roofs of houses," and so forth. Since 1935 the Sanitary Board has been superseded by the Urban Council, which is today "contemptuously tagged as the 'Garbage Council' by many Hong Kong residents"; Lau Siu-kai, *Society and Politics*, p. 115.

52. Endacott, *Government and People in Hong Kong*, pp. 95, 109–110.

53. This relationship between the government and the capitalist elite has remained essentially unchanged today. For a theoretical discussion of this in contemporary Hong Kong, see Lau Siu-kai, *Society and Politics*, pp. 123–130; Lau, however, neglects the tensions in the government-elite relationship, over-stating "an atmosphere of harmony between the government and the Chinese elite" (p. 129).

54. Eitel, *Europe in China*, pp. 569–570.

55. A Hong Kong Chinese commercial directory of 1915 listed eleven foreign banks employing 185 Chinese staff, including compradors, cashiers, clerks, shroffs, and accountants. Also listed were eighty-one "comprador departments of European firms," employing some seven hundred Chinese staff. A few companies were operated under a joint Chinese and foreign partnership. See Cheng Tzu-ts'an, *Chih-nan-lu*, pp. 107–114, 140–146, 150, 157, 162; and *Hong Kong Directory* (1893), p. 633.

56. *British Parliamentary Papers*, 26:330.

57. *China Mail*, January 3, 1891, March 23, 1897.

58. *Hong Kong Directory* (1884), p. 362; (1893), p. 632.

59. Carl Smith, "English-Educated Chinese Elites," p. 83.

60. Cheng Tzu-ts'an, *Chih-nan-lu*, pp. 177, 180, 187–189; Feldwick, *Present Day Impression*, p. 580; and Wright and Cartwright, *Twentieth-Century Impressions*, p. 229.

61. Bergere, "The Role of the Bourgeoisie," pp. 249–250, states: "one way or another, whether from the aspect of finance, supply, equipment, or distribution, all Chinese business of any size operated within a context of foreign domination. . . . It can be said that in all relations established with foreigners, the Chinese bourgeoisie was in a position of total economic dependence."

62. Wright and Cartwright, *Twentieth-Century Impressions*, pp. 245–246.

63. Wang Ching-yü, "Shih-chiu shih-chi wai-kuo ch'in-Hua, pp. 70–72.

64. Wang Ching-yü, "Birth of the Chinese Bourgeoisie," p. 29.

65. Legge, "The Colony of Hong Kong," p. 180.

66. Bergere, "The Role of the Bourgeoisie," pp. 250–253.

67. Yen-ping Hao, *The Comprador in Nineteenth-Century China*, p. 217; Bergere, "The Role of the Bourgeoisie," p. 238.

68. CO129/198/3979, Hennessy to Colonial Office, telegrams, 2–3, March, 1882, p. 43.

69. Kani Hiroaki, *Kindai Chūgoku*, p. 114.

70. Thompson, "Eighteenth-Century English Society," p. 150.

71. Kani Hiroaki, *Kindai Chūgoku*, pp. 360–362, 369–370.

72. *China Mail*, December 5, 1890.

73. *China Mail*, December 6, 1890.

74. *China Mail*, January 14, 1893.

75. *Report . . . Tung Wah*, pp. 35, 38.

76. *British Parliamentary Papers*, 26:412.

77. *The Hong Kong Weekly Press*, May 24, 1894, p. 420. CO129/263/10936, Robinson to Ripon, pp. 194–200, enclosure.

78. *Daily Press*, May 25, 1894, suspected: "The coolie class are blindly led by busybodies among their countrymen occupying higher stations in life. It is men in good positions with anti-foreign proclivities who disseminated wild stories to bring the Government and its officers into detestation."

79. *British Parliamentary Papers*, 26:412.

80. *The Hong Kong Weekly Press*, May 24, 1894, p. 402.

81. *The Hong Kong Weekly Press*, May 24, 1894, p. 403.

82. The Commission's long *Report . . . Tung Wah* provides much information about the hospital's history, operation, and organization.

83. Sinn, *Power and Charity*, pp. 206–207.

84. *Historical and Statistical Abstract of the Colony of Hong Kong, 1841–1930*.

85. Remer, *The Foreign Trade of China*, p. 160.

86. Lu Yen et al., *Hsiang-kang chang-ku*, 8:47–65.

87. Wood, *Report on the Chinese Guilds*, pp. 7, 19–20. This is a brief report of twenty-six pages. Material on employees' guilds is difficult to obtain, and so far as I am aware, very little research has been done on labor problems in Hong Kong during the period under study.

88. Wood, *Report on the Chinese Guilds*, pp. 7, 19–20.

89. Feldwick, *Present Day Impression*, p. 575.

90. Wright and Cartwright, *Twentieth-Century Impression*, pp. 245–246.

91. Chan, "The Organizational Structure of the Traditional Chinese Firm," pp. 229–232.

92. Feldwick, *Present Day Impression*, pp. 579–580; Smith, "English-Educated Chinese Elites," pp. 82–84.

93. Tse Tsan Tai, *The Chinese Republic*, pp. 7–8.

94. Huang Chia-jen, "Hsieh Tsuan-t'ai," p. 14.

95. *Daily Press*, May 30, 1894.

96. *China Mail*, January 20, 1896.

97. *China Mail*, March 12, 1896.

98. *China Mail,* January 21, 1896.
99. *Hsiang-kang Chung-hua tsung shang-hui,* pp. 7, 17.
100. *China Mail,* June 16, 1900.
101. *Hua-tzu jih-pao,* December 9, 16, 1895.
102. *China Mail,* December 23, 1895.
103. *Correspondence Relative to the Magistrate's Court,* 13:202, 205.
104. *China Mail,* Dec. 23, 1895; *Hua-tzu jih-pao,* Dec. 24, 1895.
105. *China Mail,* Dec. 23, 1895; *Hua-tzu jih-pao,* Dec. 24, 1895.
106. *The China Mail,* December 24, 1895.
107. *Hua-tzu jih-pao,* December 27, 1895.
108. Norton-Kyshe, *The History of the Laws and Courts,* 2:473.

4. Coolies in the British Colony

1. CO129/193/13140, Gov. Hennessy to Earl of Kimberley, June 15, 1881, pp. 204, 206.
2. CO129/193/13140, pp. 204, 206.
3. CO129/250/19830, Major-General Digby Barker to Lord Knutsford, Aug. 31, 1891, enclosure 2, pp. 788–789.
4. "Correspondence Relative to the Magistrate's Court," 11:219–224.
5. CO129/193/13140, p. 206.
6. *The China Mail,* May 23, 1883.
7. "Report on Chair and Ricksha Coolies", p. 3.
8. CO129/193/13140, pp. 201, 203.
9. Wood, *A Brief History of Hongkong,* p. 228.
10. Smith, "The Chinese Settlement of British Hong Kong," p. 27.
11. *The Friend of China and Hongkong Gazette,* Nov. 2, 1844, p. 561.
12. *China Mail,* July 29, August 1, 3, 1872.
13. *The Hong Kong Guide 1893,* p. 137.
14. *China Mail,* April 2, 1895.
15. "Report on Chair and Jinricksha Coolies," pp. 65, 31.
16. *Blue Book: Colony of Hong Kong, 1901* (Hong Kong: Noranha, 1902), p. T2.
17. *China Mail,* January 4, 1902.
18. *Blue Book: Colony of Hong Kong 1901,* p. I24, I26.
19. "Report . . . on Chair and Jinricksha Coolies," pp. 11–12, 87.
20. Wood, *A Brief History of Hong Kong,* pp. 215–216.
21. "Report on Chair and Jinricksha Coolies", pp. 31, 74, 82–83, 89.
22. "Report on Chair and Ricksha Coolies", pp. 20, 38, 61, 69, 129, 144. *The Hongkong Daily Press,* October 10, 1906.
23. "Report on Chair and Ricksha Coolies," pp. 115–116.
24. "Report on the Chair and Ricksha Coolies," pp. 122–123.
25. Henry Norman, *The Peoples and Politics of the Far East,* p. 20.
26. "Report on Chair and Ricksha Coolies," pp. 7, 90.
27. *British Parliamentary Papers,* 26:99; "Report on the Chair and Ricksha Coolies," pp. 2, 61; Li Tsin-wei, *Hsiang-kang pai-nien shih,* pp. 131–132.

28. "Report on Chair and Ricksha Coolies," p. 56.

29. *British Parliamentary Papers*, 26:128.

30. "Report on Chair and Ricksha Coolies," pp. 10, 80–81.

31. Mortimer Menpes and Henry A. Blake, *China* (London: Adam and Charles Black, 1909), p. 48.

32. This description of the coolie house is put together from *China Mail*, July 27, 29, 30, August 3, 1872; March 13, 19, 1894; March 29, 30, April 1, 4, 1895; *Daily Press*, March 13, 1894; *British Parliamentary Papers*, 26:128; and Teng Chung-hsia, *Chung-kuo chih-kung yün-tung chien-shih*, pp. 2–3, 50.

33. Butters, *Labour*, p. 111.

34. "Report on Chair and Ricksha Coolies," pp. 82, 105–108.

35. "Report on Chair and Ricksha Coolies," pp. 5, 57, 58, 79, 107.

36. "Report on Chair and Ricksha Coolies," pp. 8, 31, 38, 44, 57.

37. Stanton, *The Triad Society*, pp. 26–28; *Daily Press*, November 12, 1884; CO129/227/13330, E. Marsh to Earl Granville, June 15, 1886, enclosure, p. 321.

38. CO129/227/13330, p. 321.

39. CO129/217/19557, Marsh to Derby, October 11, 1884, pp. 473–474; *Daily Press*, October 10, 1884; CO129/227/13330, enclosure 1, in Marsh to Granville, #204, June 15, 1886, pp. 306, 321–322, 349–351.

40. CO129/227/13330, p. 370, 334, 322.

41. CO129/262/7340, Governor Bowen to Ripon, March 22, 1894, p. 449; Stanton, *The Triad Society*, p. 28.

42. *Daily Press*, November 12, 1884.

43. Chesneaux, *Secret Societies*, pp. 34, 188; CO129/227/13330, p. 341.

44. Morgan, *Triad Societies in Hong Kong*, p. 65.

45. *Daily Press*, May 29, 1883.

46. *Daily Press*, May 30, 1883.

47. Eitel, *Europe in China*, pp. 337, 445, 458.

48. *Daily Press*, October 20, 1906.

49. *Daily Press*, October 19, 1906.

50. *China Mail*, May 19, June 2, 1905. The police courts were often "filled with [European] soldiers and sailors arrested for brutishly drunk in a brothel, kicking and beating chair-coolies, or trying to rape Chinese women"; Pope-Hennessy, *Verandah*, p. 238.

51. *China Mail*, June 1, 7, 1904; June 20, 1909.

52. *China Mail*, February 20, 1904.

53. *China Mail*, July 22, 1896; "Correspondence Relative to the Magistrate's Court," 13:29, 32.

54. "Correspondence Relative to the Magistrate's Court," 19:66; vol. 20.

55. "Correspondence Relative to the Magistrate's Court," 21.

56. CO882, 4(33):5–6.

57. CO882, 4(33):9, 10, 43, 44, 47.

58. CO882, 4(33):20–21.

59. CO882, 4(33):36–37.

60. CO882, 4(33):14, 23, 25, 26, 29, 31, 32. "Correspondence Relative to the Magistrate's Courts" 3 (January–April 1878), police court case No. 146.

61. Endacott, *A History of Hong Kong*, p. 172.

62. Eitel, *Europe in China*, pp. 541, 545.

63. Endacott, *A History of Hong Kong*, p. 173.

64. See the numerous cases in "Correspondence Relative to the Magistrate's Court," 6:257, 273, 277, 335, 357, 381, 511, 523–703.

65. *China Mail*, June 5, 1899; March 15, 1900.

66. "Correspondence Relative to the Magistrate's Court," vol. 2.

67. CO129/193/12802, Governor Hennessy to the Earl of Kimberly, May 26, 1881, enclosure: report by E. J. Eitel, p. 115.

68. Endacott, *A History of Hong Kong*, p. 187.

69. CO129/193/12802, Governor Hennessy to the Earl of Kimberly, no. 73, May 26, 1881, pp. 111–112, and enclosure: report by Dr. E. J. Eitel, pp. 116, 117.

70. Pope-Hennessy, *Verandah*, pp. 272–273.

71. *China Mail*, July 4, 1904.

72. *Daily Press*, February 12, 1912; *Hua-tzu jih-pao*, February 10, 1912.

73. *Daily Press*, May 27, 1913.

74. Quoted in Joseph Chailley-Bert, *The Colonisation of Indo-China*, trans. Arthur B. Brabant (Delhi: B. R. Publishing, 1892, repr. 1985), p. 69.

75. Chailley-Bert, *The Colonisation of Indo-China*, p. 69.

76. Turner, *Kwang Tung*, p. 111. For the amount of $10,000 spent by the Chinese, see *China Mail*, Jan. 20, 1896.

77. *Daily Press*, June 25, 1897.

78. *Hua-tzu jih-pao*, June 25, 1897; Cameron, *Hong Kong: The Cultured Pearl*, pp. 138–141; *Daily Press*, June 25, 1897.

79. Cameron, *Hong Kong: The Cultured Pearl*, p. 138.

80. Chang Chih-pen, *Hsiang-kang chang-ku*, p. 29.

81. *Hua-tzu jih-pao*, June 23, 24, 1902.

82. Cameron, *Hong Kong: The Cultured Pearl*, p. 111.

83. Chang Sheng, *Hsiang-kang hei she-hui fuo tung chen-hsiang*, p. 50.

84. Quoted from Roberta A. Dayer, "The Young Charles S. Addis: Poet or Banker?" in King, ed., *Eastern Banking*, p. 18.

85. Norman, *The Peoples and Politics of the Far East*, p. 18.

5. *Popular Insurrection in 1884 During the Sino-French War*

1. Shih Man-yu, "Ma-chiang feng-yün—I-pa-pa-ssu-nien Fuchou jen-min fan-k'ang Fa-kuo ch'in-lüeh ti tou-cheng." Lin Ch'i-ch'üan, "Shih-chiu shih-chi mo Taiwan t'ung-pao fan-tui Fa-kuo." Eastman, "The Kwangtung Anti-foreign Disturbances."

2. Eastman, *Throne and Mandarins*, chapters 2–4.

3. For ch'ing-i and ch'ing-liu see Eastman, *Throne and Mandarins*, pp. 16–29, and Rankin, " 'Public Opinion,' " pp. 453–477.

4. *The Hongkong Daily Press*, September 4, 9, 1884.

5. CO129.217.18738, Marsh to Derby, no. 336, September 25, 1884, pp. 382, 386–388. *Daily Press*, September 4, 15, 19, 1884.

6. *The China Mail*, September 26, 30, 1884.

7. *China Mail*, September 30, October 1, 1884; *Daily Press*, October 3, 1884.

8. *China Mail*, October 3, 1884; *Daily Press*, October 4, 6, 1884.

9. *Daily Press*, October 4, 6, 10, 1884.

10. *China Mail*, October 3, 1884; *Daily Press*, October 4, 1884.

11. *Daily Press*, October 4, 1884; *China Mail*, October 3, 1884.

12. *China Mail*, October 2, 1884.

13. *China Mail*, October 4, 1884; *Daily Press*, October 6, 1884.

14. *China Mail*, October 6, 1884; *Daily Press*, October 6–7, 1884.

15. *Daily Press*, October 7, 1884.

16. *China Mail*, October 14, 1884.

17. *Chang Wen-hsiang kung ch'üan-chi*, 119:11–13, 15–17. CO129.219.20728, Foreign Office to Colonial Office, December 3, 1884, pp. 338–340; CO129.219.20997, Foreign Office to Colonial Office, December 9, 1884, enclosure 2, pp. 356–357. *China Mail*, September 30, 1884. Eastman, "The Kwangtung Anti-foreign Disturbances," pp. 13, 14, 19, 20–21. Wang Liang, *Ch'ing-chi wai-chiao shih-liao*, 47:10, 18.

18. *Shu-pao*, January 19, March 2, 30, October 31, November 5, 1884; January 16, 23, 31, February 6, 8, 28, March 5, 13, 20, April 2, 1885.

19. *Shu-pao*, October 23, 24, November 9, 1884; February 8, 10, 1885. *Daily Press*, October 18, 1884.

20. *Daily Press*, September 16, October 23, 1884.

21. *Daily Press*, October 23, 1884; CO129.217.18738, Marsh to Derby, no. 336, September 25, 1884, pp. 379–382.

22. *Daily Press*, August 25, 1884.

23. CO129.217.19555, Marsh to Derby, no. 340, October 6, 1884, pp. 426–427.

24. CO129.217.19557, pp. 480–482.

25. CO129.217.19557, pp. 470, 476–477, 492–493.

26. *Chang Wen-hsiang kung ch'üan-chi*, 122:14; Wang Liang, *Ch'ing chi wai-chiao shih-liao*, 48:5.

27. *Chang wen-hsiang kung ch'üan-chi*, 122:12, 14; 73:8–9.

28. Hsü I-sheng, "Chia-wu Chung-Jih chan-cheng ch'ien, *Ching-chi yen-chiu* (Peking; 1956), 5:112–115; *Chang Wen-hsiang kung ch'üan-chi*, 73:16–17, 25–26; 12:27–29; 122:1, 19, 34.

29. *Chang Wen-hsiang kung ch'üan-chi*, 122:33.

30. *Chang Wen-hsiang kung ch'üan-chi*, 15:16–17.

31. *Chang Wen-hsiang kung ch'üan-chi*, 11:11.

32. *China Mail*, December 15, 1896.

33. Morgan, *Triad Societies in Hong Kong*, p. 65.

34. *China Mail*, October 15, 1884.

35. CO129.217.19555, p. 426.

36. CO129/217/19555, p. 422.

37. CO129.217.19555, pp. 434–435

38. CO129.217.19957, pp. 482–483.

39. CO129.217.19555, pp. 434–438.

40. CO129.217.19555, pp. 434–438.

41. CO129.217.19555, pp. 434–438; *China Mail*, October 6, 1884.

42. According to *Daily Press*, October 6, 1884, "some of the most intelligent and influential Chinese in the Colony have also strongly advocated . . . a return to public flogging."

43. Of the sixty unofficial justices of the peace in Hong Kong, only seven were Chinese, all of British nationality as a condition of their appointment. They included Chan Kwan I (large real estate owner and comprador to the Augustine Heard and Co. in the late 1850s), Wong See Tye (comprador to Belilios and Co.), Choa Chee Bee (Fukienese, comprador to the Wahee, Smith and Co., Sugar Refinery), Woo Lin Yuen (Fukienese, secretary of the Man On Insurance Co.), Luk Sau Theen (of the Yew Cheong Hong), Wei Yuk (educated in Britain, comprador to the Chartered Mercantile Bank of India, London, and China), and Ho Kai (anglicized young barrister with a medical degree from the University of Abadeen and a law degree from Lincoln's Inn). For some of these men see Smith, "English-Educated Chinese Elites," pp. 85–86; Tung-shih-chü, *Hsiang-kang Tung-hua san-yüan*, 1:61, 63, 64, 67; Po Leung Kuk, *Hsiang-kang Pao-liang-chü shih-lüeh*, pp. 125–126.

44. *China Mail*, October 6, 1884.

45. *Daily Press*, September 23, 1884.

46. *Hong Kong Directory* (1884), pp. 362–363; *Chronicle and Directory*, pp. 265, 268.

47. CO129.198.3979, Hennessy to Colonial Office, telegrams, March 2–3, 1882, p. 43. Another reason for the rejection was the project's connection with the Danish-Russian–backed Great Northern Telegraph Company, whose engineers were to be employed to supervise the construction of the cable. See Carl Smith, "How A-mei Pioneered."

48. *China Mail*, October 8, 1884.

49. Hu Ch'uan-chao, *Tun-mo liu-fen*, 2:14b, 21b; 3:7a. Thanks to Elizabeth Sinn for calling my attention to this work.

50. *Chang Wen-hsiang kung ch'üan-chi*, 73:7.

51. *Daily Press*, September 9, 10, 1884.

52. CO129.198.3979, p. 45.

53. CO129.220.5502, Bowen to Derby, no. 89, February 23, 1885, pp. 281–282.

54. *Daily Press*, August 26, 1884.

55. *Tien-shih-chai hua-pao*, pp. 3, 4, 51, 92.

56. Paul Linebarger, *Sun Yat-sen*, p. 177.

57. *Shu-pao*, November 5, 1884, March 21, 1885; *Daily Press*, November 1, 1884.

58. *Daily Press*, September 22, 23, 1884.

59. *Daily Press*, September 2, October 7, 1884.

60. CO129.217.19557, enclosure 2, pp. 480–482.

61. *China Mail*, October 7, 1884, quoted in Sinn, "The Strike and Riot of 1884," p. 69.

62. *Daily Press*, October 6, 11, 1884.

63. *Daily Press*, October 4, 6, 8, 9, 16, 1884; *China Mail*, October 4, 6, 1884.

64. *Chang Wen-hsiang kung ch'üan-chi* 73:6–7. Viceroy Chang Chih-tung was fairly well-informed about situations in Hong Kong, because he employed informers and spies of both Chinese and foreign nationalities. "A Frenchman in Hong Kong often gave us secret reports. About French activities there, we know seven or eight out of ten," he confided to the Tsungli Yamen; *Chang wen-hsiang Kung ch'üan-chi*, 16:17, 122:6.

65. CO129.217.19555, enclosure 3, p. 439.

66. Merlat, "En Marge de L'Expedition du Tonkin," pp. 228–229, states that the organized Hong Kong workers did not loot, not only because of the vigilance of British police and troops but also because workers were aware that such acts could only hurt their cause.

67. CO129.217.19555, p. 423.

68. *Daily Press*, October 4, 1884.

69. CO129.218.20342, War Office to Colonial Office, Marsh to Granville, no. 204, enclosure 1, June 15, 1885, p. 341; CO129.217.19557, p. 493.

70. CO129.218.20342, enclosure, p. 460.

71. *Daily Press*, October 25, November 1, 1884; CO129.218.20862, Marsh to Derby, no. 358, November 1, 1884.

72. *Daily Press*, November 1, 1884.

73. *Daily Press*, October 11, 16, 1884.

74. CO129.217.19557, pp. 480–483; *Daily Press*, October 8, 1884.

75. *Daily Press*, October 7, 1884.

76. *Shu-pao*, October 12, 1884.

77. For a discussion of "collaborationist patriotism" see Tsai, "Predicament of the Comprador Ideologists," pp. 191–225.

78. Referring to the dockworkers in the strike of 1884, Chesneaux, *Secret Societies*, p. 126, states: "It is worth noting that when—for the first time in its history—the Chinese industrial proletariat took the initiative and staged a truly political strike, which was successful, it was a secret society that gave the call to action." See also Bastid-Brugere, "Current of Social Change," 11:575.

79. Unlike Eric Hobsbawm's "social bandits" who "took care not to harm the local people." See *Bandits*, pp. 13, 143.

6. Coolie Unrest and Elitist Nationalism, 1887–1900

1. Among their many works are Kohn, *The Idea of Nationalism*; Carlton Hayes, *The Historical Evolution of Modern Nationalism* (New York, 1931); Deutsch, *Nationalism and Social Communication*; and Eric J. Hobsbawm, *Nations and Nationalism Since 1780: Programme, Myth, Reality* (Cambridge University Press, 1990).

2. Willson H. Coates and Hayden V. White, in *The Ordeal of Liberal Humanism: An Intellectual History of Western Europe, Since the French Revolution*, 2 vols. (New York: McGraw-Hill, 1970), 2:25–26, maintain: "Nationalism developed during the early nineteenth century in the service of the emerging liberal ideal. It had taken on the character of an instrument of liberal reform in France during the Revolution and assisted in the exportation of liberalism to France's neighbors in Continental Western Europe. . . . The connection between nationalism and liberalism was, however, not a necessary one. Just as an earlier, nascent national feeling had been exploited by divine-right monarchs like Louis XIV, so the more intense modern nationalism could be used to achieve conservative or autocratic purposes." See also Louis L. Snyder, *Varieties of Nationalism: A Comparative Study* (Hinsdale, Ill.: Dryden Press, 1976).

3. Eley, "Nationalism and Social History," pp. 90–91.

4. Eley, "Nationalism and Social History," p. 99.

5. Joseph R. Levenson, *Modern China and Its Confucian Past* (New York: Anchor Books, 1964), p. 61.

6. Benjamin Schwartz, *In Search of Wealth and Power: Yen Fu and the West* (Cambridge: Harvard University Press, 1964), p. 19.

7. Rankin, *Elite Activism*, pp. 26, 327.

8. Liu Kwang-ching, "The Confucian as Patriot and Pragmatist: Li Hung-chang's Formative Years, 1823–1866," *Harvard Journal of Asiatic Studies* (1970), 30:5–45; and Liu Kwang-ching, "Politics, Intellectual Outlook, and Reform: The T'ung-wen Kuan Controversy of 1867," in Paul A. Cohen and John E. Schrecker, eds., *Reform in Nineteenth-Century China* (Cambridge: East Asian Research Center, Harvard University, 1976), pp. 87–88.

9. David Pong, "Confucian Patriotism and the Destruction of the Woo-sung Railway, 1877," *Modern Asian Studies* (1973), 7(4):647–676.

10. Bays, *China Enters the Twentieth Century*, pp. 216–220.

11. John E. Schrecker, *Imperialism and Chinese Nationalism: Germany in Shantung* (Cambridge: Harvard University Press, 1971), pp. 250–254.

12. Young, *The Presidency of Yuan Shih-k'ai*: p. 106.

13. Gerald E. Bunker, *The Peace Conspiracy: Wang Ching-wei and the China War, 1937–1941* (Cambridge: Harvard University Press, 1972), p. 145.

14. Eley, "Nationalism and Social History," pp. 86, 99, 104.

15. *Shu-pao*, January 28, 1885.

16. See Onogawa Hidemi, *Shinmatsu seiji shisō kenkyū*, pp. 4–5, 41, 45, 47–50, 52–53; Hu Pin, *Chung-kuo chin-tai kai-liang chu-i ssu-hsiang* (Reformist thought in modern China) (Peking: Chunghua shuchu, 1964), pp. 67–68; Lloyd E. Eastman, "Political Reformism in China before the Sino-Japanese War," *JAS* (August 1968), 27(4):695–710.

17. Paul A. Cohen, "Wang T'ao and Incipient Chinese Nationalism," *JAS* (August 1967), 26(4):559–574, and *Between Tradition and Modernity*.

18. Tseng Chi-tse, "China: The Sleep and the Awakening," pp. 1–10; Mou An-shih, *Yang-wu yün-tung* (The foreign matter movement) (Shanghai: 1956), p. 128; Li En-han, *Tseng Chi-tse*, p. 276.

19. Ho Kai, "To the Editor." Ling-yeong Chiu, "The Debate on National Salvation: Ho Kai Versus Tseng Chi-tse," *JHKBRAS* (1971), vol. 11.

20. Ho Kai and Hu Li-yüan, "Tseng-lun shu-hou," *HINHSCC*, 3:10b, 23a, 24b, 25b–26a, 28b.

21. Hu Li-yüan, "Hsin-cheng lun-i hsu" (Preface to the Discourse on the New Government), *HINHSCC* 4:1–4.

22. *China Mail*, May 21, 1895.

23. Ho Kai and Hu Li-yüan "Hsin-cheng lun-i," 6:23b–24a, 32a.

24. Ho Kai and Hu Li-yüan, "Hsin-cheng pien-t'ung," 21.25a.

25. Hsü Chieh-lin, "Nihon to Chūgoku ni okeru shoki rikken-shisō no hikaku kenkyū" (A comparative study of early constitutional ideas in Japan and China), *Kokka Gakkai Zasshi* (December 1970), 83(9–10):716.

26. Hu Pin, *Chung-kuo chin-tai kai-liang chu-i ssu-hsiang*, p. 72.

27. Tsai, "Comprador Ideologists," pp. 65–69.

28. Jung-fang Tsai, "Syncretism," pp. 19–33.

29. See the two English letters he wrote in 1909 published in the Queen's College journal *The Yellow Dragon* (May 1909), 10(8):147–151.

30. Hu Li-yüan, *HINHSCC*, chuan 29, and 39.

31. Ho Kai and Hu Li-yüan, "Hsin-cheng lun-i," 4:18b, 6.20a–21a; "Ch'üan-hsüeh-p'ien shu-hou," 18.4.

32. Hu Pin, *Chung-kuo chin-tai kai-liang chu-i ssu-hsiang*, pp. 73–74; Yen-p'ing Hao, "Cheng Kuan-ying: The Comprador as Reformer," *JAS* 29(1):20–22.

33. Chang Chih-tung, *Ch'üan-hsüeh p'ien*, nie-p'ien, 22a.

34. See Tsai, "Reflections," pp. 99–118.

35. Ho Kai and Hu Li-yüan, "Ch'üan-hsüeh p'ien shu-hou," 18.12a.

36. Kohn, *The Idea of Nationalism*, p. 455.

37. Ho Kai and Hu Li-yüan, "Hsin-cheng an-hsing" (Administration of the new government), *HINHSCC*, 10.19b–21a, 23a. 11.8a; "Hsin-cheng pien-t'ung," 19.20b.

38. Tse Tsan Tai, *The Chinese Republic*, p. 15.

39. Watanabe Tetsuhiro, "Ka Kei," pp. 63–64.

40. The estimated number of attendants varied—over fifteen hundred people according to both the *Hongkong Daily Press* and the *China Mail;* some seven hundred and fifty according to the *Hongkong Telegraph* (January 23, 1899); over seventeen hundred according to Li Tsin-wei, ed., *Hsiang-kang pai-nien shih*, pp. 24–28.

41. Li Tsin-wei, *Hsiang-kang pai-nien shih*, pp. 24–28; *China Mail*, January 23, 1899; *Daily Press*, January 23, 1899; *Hongkong Telegraph*, January 23, 1899.

42. *China Mail*, January 23, 1899.

43. *China Mail*, January 23, 1899.

44. *China Mail*, January 24, 1899.

45. Ho Kai and Wei Yuk, "Letter to Rear-Admiral Lord Charles Beresford," pp. 221–222.

46. Ho Kai and Wei Yuk, "Letter to Rear-Admiral Lord Charles Beresford," pp. 221–222.

47. Orwell, *Burmese Days*, p. 40.

48. *Hongkong Hansard*, December 21, 1899, p. 40.

49. Wesley-Smith, *Unequal Treaty, 1898–1997*, p. 84; R. G. Groves, "Militia, Market, and Lineage," pp. 42, 62; Despatches and Other Papers Relating to the Extension of the Colony of Hong Kong (Hong Kong: Noronha, 1899), pp. 51–52.

50. Great Britain Colonial Office, *Hong Kong Correspondence (June 20, 1898 to August 20, 1900) Regarding the Extension of the Boundaries of the Colony* (November 1900), pp. 305–306.

51. Groves, "Militia, Market and Lineage," pp. 43–52; Wesley-Smith, *Unequal Treaty, 1898–1997*, pp. 82–87.

52. Colonial Office, *Hong Kong Correspondence*, pp. 307–317.

53. Tse Tsan Tai, *The Chinese Republic*, pp. 8–9; Feng Tzu-yu, *Ko-ming i-shih*, 1:9, 18; Schiffrin, *Sun Yat-sen*, pp. 71, 82; *China Mail*, March 12, 1895; Rhoads, *China's Republican Revolution*, p. 41.

54. CO129.285.25027, confidential despatch from Major-General Black to Joseph Chamberlain, October 8, 1898, pp. 395–396; Tse Tsan Tai, *The Chinese Republic*, p. 13.

55. Schiffrin, *Sun Yat-sen*, pp. 180–208; Tse Tsan Tai, *The Chinese Republic*, p. 19; Feng Tzu-yu, *Ko-min i-shih*, 1:113, 4:92.

56. Ho Kai, "Chih Hsiang-kang tsung-tu," 5:16–19; Thanks to Dr. Chun-tu Hsueh for providing me with the original English document.

57. Schiffrin, *Sun Yat-sen*, pp. 205–213.

58. Ho Kai, "An Open Letter on the Situation."

59. *China Mail*, August 1, 1900.

60. Wright and Cartwright, *Twentieth-Century Impressions*, pp. 353–354.

61. Peter Worsley, *The Three Worlds*, p. 292.

62. Linda Colley, "Whose Nation?" pp. 111, 116. Peter N. Stearns and Herrick Chapman, *European Society in Upheaval: Social History Since 1750* (New York: MacMillan, 1992, third edition), p. 245, observe: "Traditionally hostile to nationalism, aristocratic interest groups [in Europe], along with conservative parties, began converting to it in the 1880's because it let them retain political influence despite democracy. The nation's interest, spokespersons argued, demanded protection for agriculture, a strong military, and an expanding empire. Beneath all these resounding arguments were benefits to the aristocracy."

63. CO129.271.7908, Gov. Robinson to Joseph Chamberlain, March 11, 1896, pp. 439, 441.

64. *British Parliamentary Papers*, 26:325.

65. CO129.237.13476, Gov. Des Voeux to Lord Knutsford, May 31, 1888, pp. 527–532.

66. CO129.237.13476, pp. 531–536.

67. CO129.237.13476, pp. 536–539; *British Parliamentary Papers*, 26:326.

68. *China Mail*, March 1 and 2, 1894.

69. CO129.262.7340, Gov. Robinson to The Marquess of Ripon, March 22, 1894, enclosure, p. 449.

70. CO129.262.7340, enclosure, pp. 449–450; *Daily Press*, March 13, 1894.
71. CO129.262.7340, enclosure, pp. 454–456.
72. *China Mail*, March 13, 1894.
73. CO129.262.7340, enclosure, p. 456.
74. CO129.262.7340, enclosure, pp. 456–460; *Daily Press*, March 14, 15, 16, 1894.
75. CO129.263.11451, Gov. Robinson to the Marquess of Ripon, May 26, 1894, enclosure, pp. 203–206.
76. *China Mail*, March 30, 1895.
77. *British Parliamentary Papers*, 26:6–7.
78. *Legislative Council Sessional Papers 1896.*
79. *China Mail*, March 23–29, 1895; CO129.266.5241, Gov. Robinson's telegram to the Marquess of Ripon, March 25, 1895; CO129.266.7333, Robinson to the Marquess of Ripon, March 27, 1895.
80. *China Mail*, March 26, 1895.
81. *China Mail*, March 26, 1895.
82. *China Mail*, March 28, 29, 1895.
83. *China Mail*, March 29, 1895.
84. *China Mail*, March 29, 1895.
85. Orwell, *Burmese Days*, pp. 112, 72.
86. *China Mail*, March 29, 1895.
87. *China Mail*, March 29, 1895; CO129.267.7713, Gov. Robinson to Marquess of Ripon, April 2, 1895, enclosure E.
88. *China Mail*, March 30, 1895; CO129.267.7713.
89. *China Mail*, April 1, 1895.
90. *China Mail*, April 1, 1895.
91. CO129.267.7713.
92. CO129.267.7713, enclosure F.
93. *China Mail*, April 3–4, 1895.
94. *China Mail*, March 29, 1895.

7. The Anti-American Boycott, 1905–6

1. See Chang Ts'un-wu, *Kuang-hsü sa-i-nien*; Tsai, *Chinese Experience*, pp. 62–76; Tsai, *China and the Overseas Chinese*, pp. 60–108; McKee, *Chinese Exclusion*, and "The Chinese Boycott Reconsidered," pp. 165–191.
2. *South China Morning Post*, Nov. 7, 1905.
3. Pomerantz, "The Chinese Bourgeoisie," p. 27.
4. Hatano Yoshihiro, *Chūgoku kindai kōgyōshi*, pp. 269–270.
5. Kikuchi Takaharu, *Chūgoku minzoku undō*, pp. 43, 55.
6. *Hua-tzu jih-pao*, May 17, 1905.
7. A Ying, *Fan-Mei Hua-kung*, p. 7.
8. *Hua-tzu jih-pao*, May 17, 22, 25, 26, July 8, 1905; *Yu-so-wei*, July 13, 1905.
9. Kwong Tak Aaron Chan, "Local Chinese Elites in Hong Kong and the Problem of Divided Loyalties: The 1905 Anti-American Boycott and the 1908

Anti-Japanese Boycott," B.A. thesis, University of Hong Kong, 1987, pp. 73–75.

10. *Hua-tzu jih-pao,* August 19, 21, 1905.

11. *Hua-tzu jih-pao,* July 26, August 2, 1905.

12. *Yu-so-wei,* July 16, 1905.

13. *Hua-tzu jih-pao,* August 15, 1905.

14. *China Mail,* September 18, 1905.

15. Kwong Tak Aaron Chan, "Local Chinese Elites in Hong Kong," p. 77.

16. *Hua-tzu jih-pao,* August 15, 1905.

17. *Hua-tzu jih-pao,* August 11, 1905.

18. Which reads: "No Chinese shall hold or be present at any Chinese public meeting whatever, not being a meeting solely for religious worship, without a permit under the hand of the Governor, which may be issued to the occupier of the house in or near which the meeting is to take place or to the person convening the meeting." *China Mail,* August 14, 1905.

19. *China Mail,* August 14, 1905; *Hua-tzu jih-pao,* August 14, 1905.

20. *Hua-tzu jih-pao,* August 15, 1905.

21. CO129.329.35986, Gov. Nathan's confidential despatch to Alfred Lyttleton, September 8, 1905, enclosure 1; *China Mail,* August 14, 29, 1905; *Hua-tzu jih-pao,* August 15, 30, 1905.

22. CO129.329.35986; *China Mail,* August 29, 1905; *Hua-tzu jih-pao,* August 30, 1905; *Morning Post,* August 30, 1905.

23. *Morning Post,* August 15, 1905; Kwong Tak Aaron Chan, "Local Chinese Elites in Hong Kong," p. 66.

24. *Hua-tzu jih-pao,* August 30, 1905.

25. *China Mail,* August 14, 1905.

26. *Hua-tzu jih-pao,* August 15, 17, 21, 22, 30, September 1, 2, October 10, December 21, 1905.

27. Wright and Cartwright, *Twentieth-Century Impressions,* p. 218; *Hua-tzu jih-pao,* September 27, 18, October 10, 1905.

28. Ting Yu, "1905-nien Kuang-tung," pp. 23–24, 29; Ho Tso-chi, "I-chiu-ling-wu nien, p. 40.

29. *Morning Post,* November 7, 1905.

30. *Hua-tzu jih-pao,* March 21, August 1, 1906.

31. Ting Yu, "1905-nien Kuang-tung," p. 29; Ho Tso-chi, "I-chiu-ling-wu nien," p. 40.

32. *Yu-so-wei,* March 3, 1906.

33. *Yu-so-wei,* July 22, 1905.

34. *Hua-tzu jih-pao,* August 12, November 2, 1905. "The boycott contributed to the decision of the New York Life Insurance Company to withdraw its agents from central China altogether"; Remer, *A Study of Chinese Boycotts,* p. 37.

35. *Morning Post,* September 19, 1905.

36. CO129.332.32996, letter from the director of the British-American Tobacco Co. to the secretary of state for the colonies, September 13, 1905.

37. *Hua-tzu jih-pao,* July 22, 28, August 16, 21, 25, September 1, December 19, 1905.

38. *Hua-tzu jih-pao,* August 28, 1905; Ting Yu, "1905-nien Kuang-tung," pp. 31–32.

39. *Morning Post,* Nov. 23, 1905.

40. *Hua-tzu jih-pao,* Oct. 4, 1905; Ting Yu, "1905-nien Kuang-tung," pp. 26–27, 29; Ho Tso-chi, "I-chiu-ling-wu nien," pp. 33–34, 40; *Yu-so-wei,* July 25, 1905.

41. Gwenneth Stokes, *Queen's College 1862–1962* (Hong Kong: Standard Press, 1962), p. 73.

42. *Hua-tzu jih-pao,* October 11, 1905.

43. *Morning Post,* October 10, 11, 1905.

44. *Shih-shih hua-pao* (November 1905), no. 6.

45. Yen Chung-p'ing, *Chung-kuo mien-fang-chih,* p. 124.

46. Feuerwerker, *The Chinese Economy,* p. 36.

47. Chu Shih-chia, *Mei-kuo p'o-hai.*

48. Kikuchi Takaharu, *Chūgoku minzoku undō,* pp. 19, 22, 42, 55.

49. Wang Ching-yü, "Birth of the Chinese Bourgeoisie," p. 46.

50. Bergere, "The Role of the Bourgeoisie," p. 252.

51. *Morning Post,* November 23, 1905.

52. *Hua-tzu jih-pao,* October 4, 1905; *Yu-so-wei,* February 24, 1906.

53. *Hua-tzu jih-pao,* December 18, 1905. *Shao-nien-pao,* August 23, 1906.

54. *Yu-so-wei,* July 6, 1905, February 24, 1906.

55. *Hua-tzu jih-pao,* October 5, 7, 9, 13, 27, November 16, 1905.

56. *Yu-so-wei,* February 24, March 4, 1906; *Shao-nien pao,* September 27, 1906.

57. *Hua-tzu jih-pao,* September 1, 1905, March 19, 1906; *Yu-so-wei,* February 24, 1906.

58. Feldwick, *Present Day Impression,* pp. 593–594.

59. Tōa Dōbunkai, *Honkon Kantō,* 1:20–21.

60. Cheng Tzu-ts'an, *Chih-nan-lu,* pp. 156, 26. Kikuchi Takahara, *Chūgoku minzoku undō,* p. 41, speaks of the same predicament concerning the Ta-sheng Textile Company set up by Chang Chien who continued to rely on the machines and raw cotton imported from America.

61. Field, "The Chinese Boycott of 1905," p. 80.

62. *Hua-tzu jih-pao,* August 21, 23, 1905; *China Mail,* August 22, 1905.

63. *China Mail,* August 22, 1905.

64. *Hua-tzu jih-pao,* August 16, 21, 23, 1905.

65. *Hua-tzu jih-pao,* August 30, 23, 1905.

66. *Morning Post,* August 19, 1905.

67. *Hua-tzu jih-pao,* July 14, August 5, 1905; *Yu-so-wei,* July 14, 1905; Ting Yu, "1905-nien Kuang-tung," p. 18.

68. *Hua-tzu jih-pao,* August 15, 1905.

69. *Hua-tzu jih-pao,* December 21, 1905.

70. Ting Yu, "1905-nien Kuang-tung," p. 32.

71. Charge d'Affaires Schuyler's telegram to the U.S. Secretary of State,

August 10, 1905, in *Papers Relating to the Foreign Relations of the United States, 1905* (New York: Kraus Reprint, 1969), p. 844.

72. *Hua-tzu jih-pao,* August 22, September 18, 1905; Ting Yu, "1905-nien Kuang-tung," p. 33; Ho Tso-chi, "I-chiu-ling-wu nien," pp. 41–42.

73. *Hua-tzu jih-pao,* October 19, 1905.

74. CO129.329.35986, Gov. Nathan to Alfred Lyttleton, September 8, 1905, enclosure, "Memorandum of a Conversation." *China Mail,* September 12, 1905; *Hua-tzu jih-pao,* September 12, December 8, 1905.

75. *China Mail,* August 3, 1905.

76. *Hua-tzu jih-pao,* August 17, September 4, 1905.

77. *Hua-tzu jih-pao,* August 14, 21, 1905.

78. *Hua-tzu jih-pao,* September 4, 5, 13, 1905.

79. CO129.329.35986; *Hua-tzu jih-pao,* September 6, 1905.

80. *Hua-tzu jih-pao,* August 17, September 4, 1905.

81. *Hua-tzu jih-pao,* November 3, 1905; Feng Tzu-yu, *Hua-ch'iao ko-ming,* p. 14.

82. *Hua-tzu jih-pao,* October 30, 31, November 1–9, 1905.

83. *Hua-tzu jih-pao,* November 2, 1905.

84. Feng Tzu-yu, *Ko-ming i-shih,* 2:222–223, 1:277–278.

85. *Hua-tzu jih-pao,* November 15–16, 1905; *Morning Post,* November 16, 1905.

86. Feng Tzu-yu, *Ko-ming i-shih,* 3:230; *Hua-tzu jih-pao,* November 25, December 5, 12, 1905.

87. *HKHJMJSL,* pp. 7–8; Feng Tzu-yu, *Ko-ming i-shih,* 3:255.

88. Cheng Tzu-ts'an, *Chih-han-lu,* pp. 26, 156, 738, 739.

89. *Hua-tzu jih-pao,* December 7, 1905.

90. *Hua-tzu jih-pao,* December 11, 1905; *Morning Post,* December 11, 1905; Rhoads, "Nationalism and Xenophobia," p. 180.

91. *Hua-tzu jih-pao,* December 9, 1905.

92. *Morning Post,* December 11, 1905.

93. Hua-tzu jih-pao, December 9, 12, 14, 15, 16, 18, 20, 25, 29, 1905.

94. *Hua-tzu jih-pao,* December 26, 27, 1905.

95. *Hua-tzu jih-pao,* December 18, 1905.

96. *Hua-tzu jih-pao,* January 4, 1906.

97. Feng Tzu-yu, *Ko-ming i-shih,* 3:228–229.

98. Feng Tzu-yu, *Ko-ming i-shih,* 3:230, 1:104; *Hu-tzu jih-pao,* December 15, 16, 1905.

99. Feng Tzu-yu, *Ko-ming i-shih,* 1:127.

8. The Anti-Japanese Boycott and Riot in 1908

1. Li Shih-yüeh, "Lun i-chiu-ling-wu," pp. 67–69; Wang Ching-yü, *Chung-kuo chin-tai kung-yeh,* pp. 869–920.

2. Li Shih-yüeh, "Lun i-chiu-ling-wu," p. 72; Tōa Dōbunkai, *Shina no kōgyō,* p. 60.

3. See Chan, *Merchants, Mandarins,* pp. 10, 131–142.

4. *Hua-tzu jih-pao,* November 7, 1908.

5. T. Roger Banister, *External Trade of China,* pp. 155–156, 175.

6. Remer, *The Foreign Trade of China,* p. 48.

7. Banister, *External Trade of China,* p. 151.

8. Kikuchi Takaharu, *Chūgoku minzoku undō,* pp. 77–78.

9. Banister, *External Trade of China,* p. 130.

10. Remer, *The Foreign Trade of China,* p. 50.

11. Li, "Silks by Sea," p. 196.

12. Remer, *The Foreign Trade of China,* pp. 138–141.

13. Ch'iu Chieh, "Hsin-hai ko-ming shih-ch'i," p. 189.

14. Kikuchi Takaharu, *Chūgoku minzoku undō,* pp. 65–66, 78.

15. Banister, *External Trade of China,* pp. 148, 150.

16. Yen Chung-p'ing, *Chung-kuo mien-fang-chih,* p. 132.

17. Kikuchi Takaharu, *Chūgoku minzoku undō,* pp. 77–78.

18. *Daily Press,* July 22, 1908.

19. CO129.351.21665, confidential report of the China Association to British Foreign Office, May 20, 1908, enclosure 3: "Suggested reasons for the arrested prosperity of Hong Kong," p. 692.

20. CO129.351.21665, enclosure 3, p. 693.

21. Banister, *External Trade of China,* p. 174.

22. *Wai-wu-pu Ch'ing-tang,* vol. 2: Kwangtung Seventy-two Commercial Guilds' Association to Wai-wu-pu, Kwang-hsu 34.2.8; Canton Viceroy to Wai-wu-pu, KH 34.2.13; and the Liang-Kuang Fellow-Provincials' Association to Wai-wu-pu, KH 34.2.14.

23. The Tatsu Maru incident is narrated in Remer, *A Study of Chinese Boycotts,* pp. 40–45, and Rhoads, *China's Republican Revolution,* pp. 135–136.

24. Remer, *A Study of Chinese Boycotts,* pp. 40–41; *Wai-wu-pu Ch'ing-tang,* vol. 4: Viceroy Chang Jen-chün to Wai-wu-pu, KH 34.11.4, enclosure.

25. Kikuchi Takaharu, *Chūgoku minzoku undō,* pp. 69, 73; Remer, *A Study of Chinese Boycotts,* p. 41; *Wai-wu-pu Ch'ing-tang,* vol. 2:: Canton Viceroy to Wai-wu-pu, KH 34.2.17; vol. 3: Japanese Minister Hayashi to Wai-wu-pu, KH 34.3.8.

26. CO129.349.270508/09, Gov. Lugard to the Earl of Crewe, December 24, 1908, enclosure 7, p. 574.

27. Consul Ueno to Foreign Minister Hayashi, April 17, 1908, *Nihon gaikō bunsho,* 41:69–70.

28. Uchida Ryōhei to Ishii, April 29, 1908, *Nihon gaikō bunsho,* 41:73.

29. CO129.360.7004, p. 466.

30. *Wai-wu-pu Ch'ing-tang,* vol. 3: Wai-wu-pu to the Canton Viceroy, KH 34.3.15.

31. Ch'iu Chieh, "Hsin-hai ko-ming shih-ch'i," p. 189, 191, 192.

32. *Wai-wu-pu Ch'ing-tang,* vol. 2: Japanese Consulate to Shanghai taotai, KH 34.2.18; vol. 3: Japanese Minister Hayashi's letter to Wai-wu-pu, KH 34.3.2.

33. *China Mail,* November 2, 1908.

34. Ekiko's telegrams to Hayashi, April 7, 8, 9, 1908, *Nihon gaikō bunsho*, 41:66–67.

35. *Morning Post*, April 9, 1908; *China Mail*, April 8, 1908; *Hua-tzu jih-pao*, April 10, 1908.

36. *China Mail*, April 8, 1908.

37. *China Mail*, April 10, 11, 15, 1908; *Hua-tzu jih-pao*, April 1, 1908.

38. Kikuchi, *Chūgoku minzoku undō*, p. 72.

39. Rhoads, *China's Republican Revolution*, p. 138.

40. Kikuchi Takaharu, *Chūgoku minzoku undō*, pp. 71–73; *China Mail*, April 8, 1908.

41. Kikuchi Takaharu, *Chūgoku minzoku undō*, pp. 72–73; *Daily Press*, August 24, 1908; *China Mail*, April 15, 1908.

42. *China Mail*, April 7, 1908.

43. *Hua-tzu jih-pao*, April 8, 1908.

44. *China Mail*, June 20, 1908.

45. *Hua-tzu jih-pao*, April 10, 1908.

46. *Hua-tzu jih-pao*, April 14, May 5, 23, 1908.

47. Japanese Foreign Minister Komura to Vice-Consul Funatsu, September 12, 1908, *Nihon gaikō bunsho*, 41:90.

48. Nagasaki Chamber of Commerce to the Japanese Foreign Minister, April 23, 1908, *Nihon gaikō bunsho*, 41:71–72.

49. *Daily Press*, August 27, 1908.

50. *Morning Post*, November 3, 1908.

51. Kikuchi Takaharu, *Chūgoku minzoku undō*, pp. 77–79.

52. Ch'iu Chieh, "Hsin-hai ko-ming shih-ch'i," p. 189.

53. Kikuchi Takaharu, *Chūgoku minzoku undō*, p. 79.

54. Rhoads, *China's Republican Revolution*, p. 139.

55. *Morning Post*, November 4, 1908. Three years prior to the boycott, some Chinese match manufacturers had resorted to counterfeiting Japanese products; this was done by the I-ho Match Co., in July 1905; *Yu-so-wei*, July 13, 1905.

56. *Daily Press*, September 11, 1908.

57. *Daily Press*, September 4, 1908.

58. *Wai-wu-pu Ch'ing-tang*, vol. 3: Wai-wu-pu to Canton Viceroy, KH 34.3.15.

59. Kikuchi, *Chūgoku minzoku undō*, p. 79.

60. *Hua-tzu jih-pao*, July 1, 1908.

61. *Hua-tzu jih-pao*, July 1, 1908.

62. Funatsu to Komura, December 12, 1908, *Nihon gaikō bunsho*, 41:114.

63. *Hua-tzu jih-pao*, July 1, 1908.

64. Funatsu to Komura, October 24, 1908, *Nihon gaikō bunsho*, 41:96; Kikuchi Takaharu, *Chūgoku minzoku undō*, p. 81.

65. Cheng Tzu-ts'an, *Chih-nan-lu*, pp. 737–740.

66. Noda Jitsunosuke, *Honkon jijō*, pp. 294–295.

67. Noda, *Honkon jijō*, p. 228.

68. Kikuchi Takaharu, *Chūgoku minzoku undō*, p. 75.

69. Uchida Ryōhei to Ishii, April 29, 1908, *Nihon gaikō bunsho*, 41:73; *Wai-wu-pu Ch'ing-tang*, vol. 3: Japanese Minister Abe to Wai-wu-pu, KH 34.4.9.

70. Vice-Consul Funatsu to Foreign Minister Komura, December 12, 1908, *Nihon gaikō bunsho*, 41:114; CO129.349.270508/09, enclosure 3, p. 559; Hu Ying-han, *Wu Hsien-tzu*, p. 8.

71. *Hua-tzu jih-pao*, November 3, 1908.

72. Uchida to Ishii, April 29, 1908, *Nihon gaikō bunsho*, 41:73.

73. Consul Ueno to Foreign Minister Hayashi, April 30, 1908, *Nihon gaikō bunsho*, 41:74; Kikuchi Takaharu, *Chūgoku minzoku undō*, pp. 88–89; *Wai-wu-pu Ch'ing-tang*, vol. 3, telegram from "All Cantonese Students in Japan" to Wai-wu-pu, KH 34.3.23.

74. Kikuchi Takaharu, *Chūgoku minzoku undō*, pp. 88–89, 90.

75. Matsumoto Takehiko, "Tai-Nichi bōikotto," pp. 232, 235, 241–243. See also Sugano Tadashi, "Tatsu Maru jiken," pp. 17–32.

76. Kikuchi Takaharu, *Chūgoku minzoku undō*, pp. 91–92. Consul Ueno to Foreign Minister Hayashi, April 17; Consul Segawa to Foreign Minister Hayashi, June 12; Vice-Consul Funatsu to Foreign Minister Komura, October 24, 1908, *Nihon gaikō bunsho*, 41:70, 80–81, 98.

77. Feng Tzu-yu, *Ko-ming i-shih*, 3:238; 4:188–194. According to *Wai-wu-pu Ch'ing-tang*, vol. 2: Wai-wu-pu's telegram to Chinese Consul in Portugal, KH 34.2.19, the Tatsu Maru was commissioned by a Macao Chinese merchant named T'an Pi-li to smuggle firearms for sale to "bandits" in China.

78. Funatsu to Komura, October 6, 1908, *Nihon gaikō bunsho*, 41:92–93.

79. Funatsu to Komura, October 24, 1908, *Nihon gaikō bunsho*, 41:97.

80. Komura to Funatsu, October 12, 13, 1908, *Nihon gaikō bunsho*, 41:93–94.

81. Komura to Funatsu, October 24, 1908, *Nihon gaikō bunsho*, 41:95–96.

82. Funatsu to Komura, October 24, 1908, *Nihon gaikō bunsho*, 41:96–97.

83. Funatsu to Komura, October 24, 1908, *Nihon gaikō bunsho*, 41:97–98.

84. Funatsu to Komura, October 24, 1908, *Nihon gaikō bunsho*, 41:97–98.

85. Funatsu to Komura, October 30, 1908, *Nihon gaikō bunsho*, 41:99–100.

86. CO129.361.13949, Colonial Office to Foreign Office, March 25, 1909, enclosure 1, p. 2.

87. Funatsu to Komura, Oct. 27, 30, 1908, *Nihon gaikō bunsho*, 41:99, 100–101; *Daily Press*, October 28, 1908.

88. *Daily Press*, November 4, 1908.

89. Funatsu to Komura, October 30, 1908, *Nihon gaikō bunsho*, 41:101.

90. *Daily Press*, September 16, 1908.

91. *Daily Press*, August 25, 1908.

92. CO129.349.47462, Gov. Lugard to the Earl of Crewe, November 25, 1908, enclosure 4, pp. 258, 274–275.

93. *Shih-shih hua-pao*, November 1908, no. 25, p. 2.

94. *Morning Post*, November 3, 1908.

95. *Daily Press*, November 3, 1908; *China Mail*, November 2, 1908;

CO129.349.270508/09, subenclosure to enclosure 7, p. 578; *Wai-wu-pu Ch'ing-tang*, vol. 4: Viceroy Chang Jen-chün's telegram to Wai-wu-pu, KH 34.10.27.

96. *Daily Press*, November 3, 1908; *China Mail*, November 2, 1908; *Morning Post*, November 3, 1908; *The Hongkong Weekly Press*, November 9, 1908, p. 330.

97. CO129.349.47462, enclosure 1: Report on the Riots by Captain Superintendent of Police F. J. Badeley, dated November 7, 1908, p. 261; Vice-Consul Funatsu to Foreign Minister Komura, November 2, 1908, *Nihon gaikō bunsho*, 41:101–102.

98. Funatsu to Komura, November 2, 1908, *Nihon gaikō bunsho*, 41:102.

99. CO129.349.47462, enclosure 1, p. 261; *Daily Press*, November 3, 1908.

100. *Hua-tzu jih-pao*, November 3, 1908; *China Mail*, November 2, 1908.

101. Funatsu to Komura, November 2, 1908, *Nihon gaikō bunsho*, 41:102.

102. *Daily Press*, November 3, 1908.

103. CO129.349.47462, enclosure 1, p. 262.

104. Funatsu to Komura, November 2, 1908, *Nihon gaikō bunsho*, 41:102; *Daily Press*, November 3, 1908.

105. CO129.349.47462, enclosure 1, p. 263; *Daily Press*, November 3, 1908. According to the *Morning Post*, November 3, 1908, a Japanese toy shop in Peel Street was wrecked, but this was not confirmed by the Japanese Consulate records or other sources.

106. *Morning Post*, November 3, 1908.

107. *Morning Post*, November 13, 1908; CO129.349.47462, enclosure 3, p. 269.

108. *Daily Press*, November 3, 4, 1908; *China Mail*, November 2, 1908; *Morning Post*, November 3, 13, 1908; CO129.349.47462, enclosure 1, p. 262, enclosure 3, pp. 270–272; *Hua-tzu jih-pao*, November 3, 4, 1908.

109. Funatsu to Komura, November 2, 1908, *Nihon gaikō bunsho*, 41:102.

110. *Morning Post*, November 3, 4, 13, 1908.

111. *Hua-tzu jih-pao*, November 3, 4, 1908; *Daily Press*, November 3, 1908; *China Mail*, November 2, 3, 1908.

112. *Daily Press*, November 4, 1908; *Hua-tzu jih-pao*, November 4, 1908.

113. CO129.349.47462, enclosure 2, p. 264; *Morning Post*, November 3, 1908; *Daily Press*, November 5, 1908.

114. CO129.349.45592, Lugard to the Earl of Crewe, November 12, 1908, enclosure: Chief Detective Inspector's report, pp. 219–220; *Wai-wu-pu Ch'ing-tang*, vol. 4: British Minister to Wai-wu-pu, KH 34.11.2.

115. *Wai-wu-pu Ch'ing-tang*, vol. 3: Japanese Minister Hayashi to Wai-wu-pu, KH 34.3.8.

116. Canton Japanese Consul Ueno to Foreign Minister Hayashi, April 7, 17, 1908, *Nihon gaikō bunsho*, 41:65–66, 69–70.

117. *Wai-wu-pu Ch'ing-tang*, vol. 4: Viceroy Chang Jen-chun's telegram to Wai-wu-pu, KH 34.11.7.

118. CO129.349.270508/09, pp. 574–580.

119. Funatsu to Komura, November 20, 1908, *Nihon gaikō bunsho*, 41:107;

Wai-wu-pu Ch'ing-tang, vol. 4: telegram from Japanese Attache Abe to Wai-wu-pu, KH 34.10.24.

120. CO129.360.7004, p. 466.

121. CO129.349.270508/09, p. 551; CO129.349.43433, Lugard's telegram to the secretary of state for the Colonies in London, November 27, 1908, p. 295; Funatsu to Komura, November 22, *Nihon gaikō bunsho*, 41:108, 111.

122. Funatsu to Komura, November 27, 1908, *Nihon gaikō bunsho*, 41:111; CO129.349.270508/09, pp. 557–558.

123. CO129.349.47462, p. 259.

124. *Daily Press*, December 4, 12, 1908; Funatsu to Komura, December 12, 1908, *Nihon gaikō bunsho*, 41:115.

125. Funatsu to Komura, December 12, 1908, *Nihon gaikō bunsho*, 41:114; CO129.349.270508/09, pp. 550–551, 559–561.

126. *Hua-tzu jih-pao*, December 4, 5, 1908.

127. CO129.355.8247, p. 100; CO129.349.270508/09, p. 563.

128. Funatsu to Komura, December 4, 12, 1908, *Nihon gaikō bunsho*, 41:112, 114; *Daily Press*, December 4, 1908. The Hua-i Company, a Pao-huang-hui financial group, was founded in July 1905; see *Yu-so-wei*, July 16, 1905.

129. CO129.349.270508/09, enclosure 5, pp. 563–572; *Hua-tzu jih-pao*, December 7, 8, 1908; Funatsu to Komura, December 4, 12, *Nihon gaikō bunsho*, 41:112, 114.

130. Funatsu to Komura, December 12, 1908, *Nihon gaikō bunsho*, 41:114.

131. CO129.360.7004, pp. 462–463.

132. Funatsu to Komura, December 29, 1908, *Nihon gaikō bunsho*, 41:122.

133. CO129.349.270508/09, pp. 549, 555.

134. Funatsu to Komura, December 4, 12, 1908, *Nihon gaikō bunsho*, 41:112–114.

135. Funatsu to Komura, December 12, 29, 1908, *Nihon gaikō bunsho*, 41:116–117, 124.

136. Funatsu to Komura, December 12, 1908, *Nihon gaikō bunsho*, 41:116.

137. Rhoads, *China's Republican Revolution*, pp. 140–141; Orchard, "China's Use of the Boycott," p. 253.

9. Hong Kong in the Chinese Revolution, 1911–12

1. For Hong Kong's role in the Chinese republican revolution, see Chan, "Chinese Revolutionaries"; Hsieh, "Triads, Salt Smugglers"; Hsieh, "Peasant Insurrection"; Schiffrin, *Sun Yat-sen*; Rhoads, *China's Republican Revolution*. K. C. Fok, *Lectures on Hong Kong History*, pp. 53–65; Chan, *China, Britain and Hong Kong*, chapters 1–2.

2. Wales, *The Chinese Labor Movement*, p. 209; Chan, "Labor and Empire," p. 35.

3. Ch'en Ta, "Wo-kuo nan-pu ti lao-kung kai-k'uang," pp. 3–4.; Furuyama Takashi, "1920–22 nen Honkon rōdōsha no tatakai," pp. 48–49.

4. Chan, "Labor and Empire," pp. 33–34.

5. Ch'en Ta, "Wo-kuo nan-pu ti lao-kung kai-k'uang," p. 4; Furuyama Takashi, "1920–22 nen Honkon rōdōsha no tatakai," p. 49.

6. Furuyama Takashi, "1920–22 nen Honkon rōdōsha no tatakai," pp. 49–50; Ch'en Ta, "Wo-kuo nan-pu ti lao-kung kai-k'uang," pp. 4–7.

7. *Kwangtung hsin-hai ko-ming shih-liao*, p. 98.

8. *The Hongkong Daily Press*, December 17, 1908.

9. Hsieh, "Triads, Salt Smugglers," pp. 146–164.

10. Borokh, "Early Role of Secret Societies," pp. 135–144.

11. Hsieh, "Triads, Salt Smugglers," p. 148.

12. CO129.394.68512/13, Governor May to the Hon. Lewis Harcourt, December 16, 1912, p. 85.

13. Liu Yu-tsun and Ch'eng Lu-hsi, "Hsin-hai ko-ming yun-tung chung ti T'ai-shan," pp. 92–113.

14. CO129.399.7204, Gov. May to the Hon. Lewis V. Harcourt, January 22, 1913, p. 268.

15. CO129.394.40743, Governor May to the Hon. Lewis Harcourt, December 2, 1912, p. 6.

16. *Hua-tzu jih-pao*, October 20, 1911.

17. *Daily Press*, October 19, 20, 1911; *Hua-tzu jih-pao*, October 20, 1911.

18. *Daily Press*, October 24, 1911; *Hua-tzu jih-pao*, October 24, 31, 1911.

19. *Daily Press*, October 23, 1911.

20. *Daily Press*, October 24, 1911; *Hua-tzu jih-pao*, October 24, 1911.

21. *Hua-tzu jih-pao*, October 24, 1911.

22. *Hua-tzu jih-pao*, October 26, 28, 1911.

23. *Daily Press*, October 31, November 1, 8, 1911; *Hua-tzu jih-pao*, October 24, 26, 28, 30, November 1, 7, 1911.

24.

YEAR	NON-CHINESE	CHINESE	TOTAL
1910	20,806	415,180	435,986
1911	18,893	445,384	464,277
1912	21,163	446,614	467,777
1913	21,470	467,644	489,114
1914	20,710	480,594	501,304

Historical and Statistical Abstract of the Colony of Hong Kong, 1841–1930.

25. CO129.381.41103, Gov. Lugard to the Hon. Lewis Harcourt, November 23, 1911, confidential, pp. 196–197.

26. *China Mail*, November 7, 1911. See also *Hua-tzu jih-pao*, November 7, 1911.

27. *Hua-tzu jih-pao*, November 7, 8, 1911.

28. G. R. Sayer, *Hong Kong 1862–1919; Years of Discretion*, Hong Kong: Hong Kong University Press, 1975, p. 112.

29. *Daily Press*, November 8, 1911.

30. *Daily Press*, November 8, 1911; *Hua-tzu jih-pao*, November 8, 1911.

31. *Hua-tzu jih-pao*, November 8, 1911.

32. *Hua-tzu jih-pao,* November 11, 1911.

33. CO129.381.41103, pp. 197, 206, and enclosure 8, pp. 221–223.

34. CO129.381.41103, enclosure 8, pp. 223–224.

35. CO129.381.41103, p. 225.

36. CO129.381.41103, p. 225.

37. *Daily Press,* November 10, 1911.

38. Chiang Yung-ching, *Hu Han-min hsien-sheng nien-p'u,* p. 122.

39. CO129.381.41103, pp. 197, 205, 208.

40. CO129.381.41103, pp. 198, 210; *Hua-tzu jih-pao,* November 13, 1911.

41. *Daily Press,* November 13, 1911.

42. *Daily Press,* November 14, 15, 1911; Japanese Acting Consul General Funatsu Tatsuichirō to Foreign Minister Uchida, no. 371, November 14, 1911.

43. *Daily Press,* November 14, 15, 1911; Funatsu Tatsuichirō to Foreign Minister Uchida, no. 371, November 14, 1911.

44. *Daily Press,* November 14, 1911.

45. *Hua-tzu jih-pao,* November 17, 18, 1911; T'an Yung-nien, *Hsin-hai ko-ming hui-i-lu,* p. 378.

46. *Hua-tzu jih-pao,* December 9, 19, 1911.

47. *Hua-tzu jih-pao,* December 12, 15, 18, 1911.

48. Ch'en Ta, "Wo-kuo nan-pu lao-kung kai-k'wang," p. 6.

49. *Hua-tzu jih-pao,* December 15, 28, 1911.

50. *Hua-tzu jih-pao,* December 9, 21, 22, 1911.

51. *Hua-tzu jih-pao,* October 23, 30, November 2, 6, 1911.

52. *Hua-tzu jih-pao,* December 13, 18, 19, 30, 1911, January 8, 1912.

53. *Hua-tzu jih-pao,* December 29, 1911, January 8, 10, 13, 19, 20, 21, 26, 1912.

54. *Hua-tzu jih-pao,* December 8, 9, 12, 1911.

55. *Hua-tzu jih-pao,* December 8, 9, 12, 14, 18, 19, 22, 30, 1911, January 23, 1912.

56. *Hua-tzu jih-pao,* December 9, 11, 12, 1911; *Kwangtung hsin-hai ko-ming shih-liao,* p. 168.

57. *Kwangtung Hsin-hai ko-ming shih-liao,* p. 102.

58. *Kwangtung Hsin-hai ko-ming shih-liao,* pp. 79, 171–173, 177–178, 180.

59. *Hua-tzu jih-pao,* November 11, 15, 18, December 18, 28, 1911; January 26, March 22, 1912.

60. *Hua-tzu jih-pao,* January 12, 1912, February 21, 1913.

61. *Hua-tzu jih-pao,* April 11, 1913.

62. *Hua-tzu jih-pao,* March 15, 1912.

63. *Hua-tzu jih-pao,* January 20, 1912.

64. *Daily Press,* March 25, 1912. *Hua-tzu jih-pao,* December 26, 27, 1911, January 26, 1912.

65. Fairbank, Reischauer, and Craig, *East Asia,* pp. 647, 790; *Daily Press,* November 27, 1912.

66. *Daily Press,* November 26, 1912.

67. *Daily Press,* November 28, December 5, 1912, June 4, 1913.

68. *Daily Press,* December 2, 1912.

69. *Daily Press*, December 23, 1912.
70. *Hua-tzu jih-pao*, March 6, 1913.
71. *Daily Press*, December 16, 23, January 25, 1913.
72. *Daily Press*, April 13, 1913.
73. *Hua-tzu jih-pao*, September 28, 1911.
74. *Hua-tzu jih-pao*, October 18, 20, 1911.
75. *Daily Press*, October 25, 1911; *Hua-tzu jih-pao*, October 21, 1911.
76. *Daily Press*, October 25, 1911; *Hua-tzu jih-pao*, October 21, 1911.
77. *Daily Press*, October 8, 1912.
78. *Hua-tzu jih-pao*, December 27, 1911.
79. *Daily Press*, October 8, 1912.
80. *Daily Press*, November 22, 1911.
81. *Daily Press*, November 22, 1911; CO129.381.171411/12, Gov. Lugard to the Hon. Lewis Harcourt, December 11, 1911, pp. 351–352.
82. CO129.381.171411/12, pp. 352–357; *Daily Press*, November 25, 27, 28, 1911.
83. CO129.381.171411/12, p. 359; *Daily Press*, December 1, 9, 1911. CO129.388.3503, Gov. Lugard to Lewis Harcourt, January 5, 1912, enclosure 2, pp. 57–58, 59.
84. Norman Miners, *Hong Kong Under Imperial Rule, 1912–1914*, p. 4.
85. *Daily Press*, December 1, 1911.
86. CO129.381.171411/12, p. 346.
87. CO129.381.171411/12, p. 346.
88. Fairbank, *The Cambridge History of China*, vol. 10, part 1, pp. 259–263.
89. CO129.402.30413, Gov. May to Harcourt, July 28, 1913, p. 283.
90. CO129.388.5840, Gov. Lugard to Lewis Harcourt, February 2, 1912, enclosure 2, p. 223.
91. CO129.381.171411/12, pp. 346–347.
92. *Hong Kong Hansard:* Session 1911, November 30, 1911, p. 245.
93. *Administrative Reports for the Year 1911*, pp. c6, c18; *Administrative Reports for the Year 1912*, p. c7.
94. *Administrative Reports for the Year 1911*, p. c18.
95. CO129.381.171411/12, p. 345.
96. CO129.381.171411/12, pp. 355, 356.
97. CO129.389.11256, Gov. Lugard to Lewis Harcourt, March 13, 1912, pp. 114–115.
98. *Daily Press*, January 3, 1912.
99. CO129.381.171411/12, pp. 355–356.
100. CO129.388.3503, p. 56; *Daily Press*, December 22, 1911.
101. *Daily Press*, December 27, 1911.
102. *Administrative Reports for the Year 1911*, pp. c20–21; *Daily Press*, November 20, 1911.
103. A. E. Wood, *Report on the Chinese Guilds*, pp. 3, 9, 11.
104. *Daily Press*, November 23, 27, 1911.
105. *Administrative Reports for the Year 1911*, p. c21.
106. *Daily Press*, December 4, 1911.

107. *Administrative Reports for the Year 1911*, p. c21; *Daily Press*, December 4, 12, 1911.

108. CO129.388.3503, p. 60.

109. CO129.381.171411/12, p. 358.

110. CO129.383.19953, enclosure, p. 614.

111. CO129.385.37602, Foreign Office to Colonial Office, November 22, 1911, p. 196.

112. CO129.381.41103, p. 216.

113. CO129.388.3503, pp. 53–54.

114. CO129.381.171411/12, p. 347. Governor Lugard's contention that the Canton government's anti-British feeling was directed merely at Jamieson personally was not at all convincing, because Jamieson was not a private person but rather the British consul-general representing British interests in Canton.

115. CO129.381.171411/12, p. 347.

116. *Administrative Reports for the Year 1912*, p. c20; *Daily Press*, May 21, 1912.

117. *Daily Press*, August 8, 13, 1912.

118. *Administrative Reports for the Year 1912*, pp. c20–21.

119. *Administrative Reports for the Year 1912*, p. c21.

120. *Administrative Reports for the Year 1912*, p. c21.

121. *Daily Press*, October 30, 31, 1912.

122. Augusta Wagner, *Labor Legislation in China*, pp. 203–204. Yet there were some cases in which republicans and intellectuals, as individuals, were engaged in labor movement in various parts of China in the early years of the Republic prior to 1919; see Wales, *The Chinese Labor Movement*, p. 21, and Chesneaux, *The Chinese Labor Movement, 1919–1927*, pp. 131–137.

123. *Daily Press*, November 15, 1911.

124. CO129.381.1899, petition to the secretary of state for the colonies, December 29, 1911, p. 562.

125. *Hongkong Annual Report for 1912*, p. 31.

126. Wright and Cartwright, *Twentieth-Century Impressions*, pp. 106–107; Endacott, *Government and People in Hong Kong*, p. 137; *Hong Kong Annual Report for 1911*, p. 25.

127. Sayer, *Hong Kong, 1862–1919*, p. 112.

128. CO129.402.30413, Gov. Henry May to Lewis Harcourt, July 28, 1913, pp. 282–284.

129. *Daily Press*, July 19, 1912.

130. Miners, "The Attempt to Assassinate the Governor in 1912," p. 282.

131. CO129.397.20702, Reuter's telegram, July 4, 1912, pp. 248, 250; CO129.391.26076, Gov. May to Lewis Harcourt, July 24, 1912, p. 151; *Hong Kong Annual Report for 1912*, p. 31; *South China Morning Post*, July 3, 5, 9, 1912. The ill-treatment of the Chinese in South Africa was much publicized by Hong Kong Chinese newspapers. *Yu-so-wei* (March 5, 1906), for instance, related an incident where the British troops brutally suppressed a Chinese

coolie riot, murdering over four hundred coolies and cutting off the coolie leaders' hands and feet.

132. *Daily Press*, July 19, 1912; *Morning Post*, July 19, 1912.

133. The deputation consisted of the most prominent Chinese including Sir Kai Ho Kai, the Honorable Mr. Wei Yuk, Messrs. Ho Fook, Ho Kam Tong, Wong Kam Fuk, Fung Wah Chuen, Ng Hon Chi, Lau Chu Pak, Un Li Chun, and other representatives of the Tung Wah Hospital, the Po Leung Kuk, and the District Watchmen Committee. *Daily Press*, July 8, 1912.

134. CO129.391.26076, p. 151.

135. CO129.402.30413, pp. 282–283; London colonial officials' emphasis.

10. Boycott of the Hong Kong Tramway, 1912–13

1. CO129.391.26748, Gov. May to Lewis Harcourt, confidential, July 23, 1912, pp. 133–134.

2. CO129.391.26748, pp. 137, 147.

3. CO129.391.26748, p. 137.

4. CO129.381.41103, Gov. Lugard to Lewis Harcourt, November 23, 1911, p. 200.

5. CO129.391.26748, pp. 132, 138, 140–142.

6. CO129.391.26748, p. 147.

7. CO129.392.34364, Gov. May to Lewis Harcourt, confidential, October 4, 1912, p. 192.

8. CO129.391.29319, Gov. May to Lewis Harcourt, confidential, August 16, 1912, p. 319.

9. CO129.392.34364, p. 191.

10. CO129.392.37573, Gov. May to Lewis Harcourt, confidential, October 31, 1912, pp. 366, 370, 372, 376, 377, 379.

11. CO129.392.34364, pp. 189, 195–198.

12. CO129.393.40485, Gov. May to Lewis Harcourt, confidential, November 21, 1912, pp. 262–263, 266; CO129.394.68012/13, Gov. May to Harcourt, confidential, December 13, 1912, p. 56.

13. CO129.394.40743, Gov. May to Lewis Harcourt, confidential, December 2, 1912, p. 6.

14. *The Hongkong Daily Press*, November 25, 26, 1912; CO129.394.40743, p. 7.

15. CO129.394.40743, p. 7; *Daily Press*, November 27, 28, 1912.

16. *Daily Press*, December 6, 1912.

17. CO129.402.30413, Gov. May to Lewis Harcourt, secret, July 28, 1913, pp. 277, 291.

18. CO129.394.40743, p. 7.

19. *Hongkong Hansard, 1912*, pp. 108–109; *Daily Press*, December 16, 1912; CO129.394.68512/13, Gov. May to Lewis Harcourt, December 16, 1912, enclosure, pp. 86–90.

20. CO129.394.2222, Gov. May to Lewis Harcourt, confidential, December 30, 1912, pp. 187–190; *Daily Press*, December 19, 1912.

21. CO129.394.2222, p. 175.

22. *The Hongkong Telegraph,* December 23, 1912.

23. *Hongkong Telegraph,* December 23, 27, 1912; CO129.394.2222, p. 176; *Daily Press,* December 23, 24, 25, 27, 1912.

24. CO129.402.30413, enclosure p. 294.

25. *Hong Kong Annual Report* (1912), p. 31; G. R. Sayer, *Hong Kong 1862–1919, Years of Discretion,* Hong Kong: Hong Kong University Press, 1975, p. 113.

26. *Daily Press,* December 27, 1912.

27. CO129.394.2222, pp. 177–178.

28. CO129.394.40743, p. 6; CO129.394.68512/13, p. 85.

29. Feng Tzu-yu, *Ko-ming i-shih,* 3:255.

30. CO129.394.2222, pp. 176–177.

31. CO129.394.68512/13, p. 86; CO129.394.2222, p. 177.

32. CO129.402.30413, enclosure, p. 286.

33. CO129.402.30413, enclosure, pp. 287–288.

34. CO129.402.30413, pp. 289–291.

35. *Daily Press,* December 18, 1912.

36. CO129.394.68512/13, p. 86.

37. CO129.402.30413, p. 276.

38. CO129.394.2222, p. 177.

39. CO129.394.2222, p. 196.

40. CO129.394.2222, p. 195.

41. CO129.401.20488, Gov. May to Lewis Harcourt, confidential, May 26, 1913, p. 218.

42. CO129.399.4390, Gov. May to Lewis Harcourt, confidential, January 10, 1913, p. 45.

43. CO129.394.2222, p. 195.

44. CO129.394.2222, pp. 195–196; CO129.402.30413, pp. 281–282.

45. CO129.399.6640, Gov. May to Lewis Harcourt, confidential, January 31, 1913, p. 355.

46. *Daily Press,* December 25, 1912.

47. CO129.402.30413, p. 292.

48. CO129.402.30413, p. 277.

49. CO129.402.30413, p. 293.

50. *Daily Press,* November 29, 1912.

51. Rude, *Ideology and Popular Protest,* p. 29.

52. *Daily Press,* January 13, 1913.

53. *Daily Press,* January 7, 1913.

54. *Daily Press,* January 13, 1913.

55. Feldwick, *Present Day Impression,* p. 575.

56. *Daily Press,* January 6, 1913; CO129.399.4390, p. 43.

57. *Morning Post,* January 10, 1913.

58. *Kung Wo Po,* Hong Kong, January 8, 1913, enclosure 2 in CO129.399.4390, p. 45.

59. *Hua-tzu jih-pao,* January 8, 1913, enclosure 2 in CO129.399.4390, p. 46.

60. *Kung Wo Po, Chung Ngoi San Po,* and *Hua-tzu jih-pao,* January 8, 1913, in enclosure 2, CO129.399.4390, pp. 44–46.

61. CO129.399.4390, p. 41.

62. CO129.401.20488, Gov. May to Lewis Harcourt, confidential, May 26, 1913, p. 218; CO129.399.4396, Gov. May to Lewis Harcourt, confidential, p. 159.

63. CO129.399.4203, Gov. May to the Secretary of State for the Colonies, telegram, p. 370.

64. *Hongkong Telegraph,* December 23, 1912, in CO129.394.2222, enclosure, p. 191.

65. CO129.394.68512/13, pp. 83, 91; CO129.399.8860, p. 413.

Conclusion

1. Esherick and Rankin, *Chinese Local Elites,* p. 11.

2. See Rankin, *Elite Activism,* pp. 3, 27.

3. Worsley, *The Three Worlds,* p. 4.

4. Balandier, "The Colonial Situation," pp. 34–61.

5. *Correspondence Relative to the Magistrate's Court,* 10:571–573; 11:208–216, 219–224; 14:109; and *The Hongkong Daily Press,* May 5, 17, 19, 1883.

6. James C. Scott, *Weapons of the Weak: Everyday Forms of Peasant Resistance* (New Haven: Yale University Press, 1985), p. 296.

Character List

An-ya Pao (On Nga Po) 安雅報

Chan Chen Cheong (Ch'en Chin-hsiang) 陳進祥
Chan Chun-chuen (Ch'en Ch'un-ch'üan) 陳春泉
Chan Hang Kiu (Ch'en Hsing-ch'iao) 陳杏橋
Chan Keng Yu (Ch'en Keng-yü) 陳賡虞
Chan Ket Chi (Ch'en Chi-chih) 陳吉之
Chan King Wah (Ch'en Ching-hua) 陳景華
Chan Kwan Shan (Ch'en K'un-shan) 陳崑山
Chan Lo Chun (Ch'en Lu-ch'üan) 陳露泉
Chan Pek Chun 陳碧泉
Chan Quan-ee 陳關意
Chan Wai Po (Ch'en Hui-p'u) 陳惠普
Chang Chih-tung 張之洞
Chang Jen-chün 張人駿
Chang Ming-ch'i 張鳴岐
Chang P'ei-lun 張佩綸
Chang Tzu-mu 張自牧
Chau Siu Ki 周少岐

Ch'en Chih　陳熾
Ch'en Ch'ing-ch'en (Chan Hing Sum)　陳慶琛
Ch'en Chiung-ming　陳烱明
Ch'en I-k'an (Chan Yi Hon)　陳儀侃
Ch'en Kung-tse (Chan Kung Chak)　陳公澤
Ch'en Pao-ch'en　陳寶琛
Ch'en shao-pai　陳少白
Ch'en Shu-jen (Chan Shu Jen)　陳樹人
Cheng Kuan-kung　鄭貫公
Cheng Kuan-ying　鄭觀應
Cheng Shih-liang (Cheng Shi Leong)　鄭士良
Cheong Ah-lum　張亞霖
Cheong Sing Hong (Ch'ang Sheng Hang)　昌盛行
Cheung Kwong Yuen　張廣源
Chiang K'ung-yin (Kong Hong Yin)　江孔殷
chih-kung-t'ang　致公堂
ch'ing-i　清議
ch'ing-liu　清流
Chiu Hong　趙洪
Chiu Shiu Pok (Chao Shao-p'u)　趙少樸
Chiu Yue-tin　招雨田
Choa Chee Bee　蔡紫微
Choa Leep Chee　蔡立志
Choi Si-kit　蔡士傑
Chou Fu　周馥
Chu Cheong Lan (Chu Ch'ang Lan)　朱昌蘭
Chu Chih-hsin　朱執信
Chung-kuo chi-ch'i yen-chiu tsung-hui　中國機器研究總會
Chung-kuo jih-pao　中國日報
Chung-kuo yen-chi shu-shu　中國研機書塾
Chung Wan (Choong Wan)　中環

En-p'ing (Yan-ping)　恩平

fankwei　番鬼
Fatshan (Fo-shan)　佛山
Feng Hsia-wei　馮夏威
Feng Hui-ch'en　馮蕙晨
Feng Kuei-fen　馮桂芬
Feng-shan　鳳山
feng-shui　風水

Feng Tzu-yu　馮自由
Fu-jen wen-she　輔仁文社
Fuk Tak Kung　福德公
Funatsu Shinichirō　船津辰一郎
Fung Ming Shan　馮明珊
Fung Ping Shan　馮平山
Fung Sau Tin (Feng shou-t'ien)　馮壽田
Fung Wah Chuen　馮華川

Ghee Hin　義興
Goh Guan Hin　吳源興

Hakka　客家
Ho Amei　何亞美
Ho Asik　何阿錫
Ho Fook　何福
Ho Kai　何啓
Ho Kam Tong　何甘棠
Ho Tso Wan (Ho Tsao-yün)　何藻雲
Ho Tung　何東
Hokkien　福建
Hoklo　福佬
Ho-nan (Ho-nam)　河南
hsia-liu she-hui　下流社會
Hsiang-kang Hua-jen chi-ch'i hui　香港華人機器會
Hsiang-shan (Heung-shan)　香山
hsieh-tou　械鬥
Hsin-an (Hsin-ngan, Sun-on)　新安
Hsin-cheng chen-ch'üan　新政真詮
Hsin-Han　新漢
Hsin-hui (Sun-wai)　新會
Hsin-ning (Sun-ning)　新寧
Hsing-Chung-hui　興中會
Hsü Ch'in　徐勤
Hsü Hsüeh-ch'iu　許雪秋
Hsün-huan jih-pao　循環日報
Hu Han-min　胡漢民
Hu Li-yüan　胡禮垣
Hua-tzu jih-pao　華字日報
Hua-yang i-chen hui　華洋義賑會
Huang Hsing　黃興

Huang Po-yao 黃伯耀
Huang Shih-chung 黃世仲
Huang Yung-shang 黃詠商
hui-t'ang 會堂
Hung Hom 紅磡
Hung Jen-kan 洪仁玕
Hung-Mo-Miu 紅毛廟

K'ai-chih-she 開智社
kaifong 街坊
K'ai-p'ing (Hoi-ping) 開平
Kam Shan Chung 金山庄
Kan Chiu Nam (Chien Chao-nan) 簡照南
Kan Yuk Kai (Chien Yü-chieh) 簡玉階
K'ang Yu-wei 康有爲
Ko Man Wah 高滿華
Ko Sing Tze 高繩之
Ko Soon Kam 高舜琴
kondankai 懇談會
Kōun Maru 幸運丸
Ku Fai Shan 古輝山
Kuan Ti (Kwan Tai) 關帝
Kumano Maru 熊野丸
K'ung-Meng min-tsu chu-i 孔孟民族主義
kung-so 公所
Kuo-ch'ih hui 國恥會
Kuo-chih-pao 國事報
Kuo Sung-tao 郭嵩燾
Kwan Hoi Chun 關愷川
Kwan Sun Yin 關心焉
Kwok Acheong 郭亞祥
Kwok Chuen 郭泉
Kwok Lok 郭樂
Kwok Yik Chi (Kuo I-chih) 郭翼之
Kwong Fook I-ts'z 廣福義祠
Kwong Sang Hong 廣生行
Kwun Yum (Kuan Yin) 觀音

Lau Chu Pak 劉鑄伯
Lau Lo-tak 劉老澤
Lau Wai Chuen 劉渭川

Lee Shu Fan (Li Shu-fen) 李樹芬
Leung Chak Chau (Liang Tse-chou) 梁澤周
Leung On 梁安
Leung Pui Chi 梁培芝
Leung Sui Hing (Liang Jui-heng) 梁瑞珩
Li Cheng-kao 李正高
Li Chi-t'ang 李紀堂
li-ch'üan 利權
Li Hung-chang 李鴻章
Li Kai Hi (Li Chieh-ch'i) 李戒欺
Li Leong 李良
Li Men Hing Kwok (Li-min hsing-kuo) 利民興國
Li Sing 李昇
Li Tak Cheung 李德昌
Li Tsun 李準
Li Tzu-chung 李自重
Li Yü-t'ang (Li Yuk Tong) 李煜堂
Li Yüan-hung 黎元洪
Liang Ch'eng 梁誠
Liang Ch'i-ch'ao 梁啓超
Liang-Kuang yu-ch'uan hui-she 兩廣郵船會社
Lin Kua-wu (Lam Kua Ng) 林瓜五
Liu Hsüeh-hsün 劉學詢
Liu Kuang-han 劉光漢
Liu Yung-fu 劉永福
Lo Chi Tin 盧芝田
Lo Chor-san (Lo Tso-ch'en) 羅佐臣
Lo Hok Pang 羅鶴朋
Lo Koon Ting 盧冠廷
Lo Kuan She (Lo Kuan-shih) 羅關石
Loo Aqui 盧亞貴
Lu Hao-tung (Lok Hou Tong) 陸皓東
Lu Lan-ch'ing 陸蘭清
Lung Chi-kuang 龍濟光
Luk Sau-theen 陸壽田

Ma Ch'ao-chün 馬超俊
Ma Chien-chung 馬建忠
Ma Tsui Chiu (Ma Hsü-ch'ao) 馬敍朝
Ma Ying Piu (Ma Ying-piao) 馬應彪
mai-pan-hua 買辦化

Mai Shao-p'eng 麥少彭
Man Cheong (Wen-ch'ang) 文昌
Man Mo Temple 文武廟
min-chün 民軍
Mitsui Bussan 三井物産
Mok Lai Chi (Mo Li-chih) 莫禮智
mui-tsai 妹仔

Nam Pak Hong 南北行
Nan-hai (Nam-hoi) 南海
Nanyang 南洋
Ng Choy 伍才
Ng Li Hing 吳理卿
Nip Koon Man (Ni Kwan-wen) 聶冠文
Nippon Yūsen Kaisha 日本郵船會社

O Chun Chit 柯振捷
Osaka shōsen 大阪商船

pa-tzu 八字
P'an-yü (Pun-yu) 番禺
pang 幫
Pao-huang-hui 保皇會
P'eng Yü-lin 彭玉麟
Ping Tau Fa Yuen 兵頭花園
Po Leung Kuk 保良局
Pu-chiu-she 補救社
Pun Lan Sz (P'an Lan-shih) 潘蘭史
Pun Wan Nam (P'an Wan-nan) 潘晚南
punti 本地

Saiyingpun (Sei Ying Poon) 西營盤
Sam Yap 三邑
sangyō shihon 産業資本
Seikin Bank 正金銀行
Shang-pao 商報
Shang-wu yen-chiu-she 商務研究社
Shen Nung 神農
Shen Pao-chen 沈葆楨
shen-shang 紳商
shen-tung 紳董

Sheung Wan　上環
Shih-chieh kung-i-pao　世界公益報
shih-ching yu-min　市井游民
shih-k'o chi-chih　適可即止
Shih-pao　實報
Shih-shih hua-pao　時事畫報
shōgyō shihon　商業資本
Shu-pao　述報
Shun-te (Shun-tak)　順德
Si-tap-si　屎塔士
Sin (Sinn) Tak Fan　冼德芬
Sin Wa Fung (Shan Hua-feng)　單華豐
Siu King Chung (Hsiao Ching-chung)　蕭警鍾
Su Chao-cheng　蘇兆徵
Sun Yat-sen　孫逸仙
Swatow (Shan-t'ou)　汕頭
Sze Yap　四邑

ta-fankwei　打番鬼
Tai-Lai-Pai-Tong　大禮拜堂
Taipingshan　太平山
Tam Achoy　譚亞才
Tam Chi Kong　譚子剛
Tang Lap Ting (Teng Li-t'ing)　鄧立亭
tanka　蛋家
Tatsu Maru　辰丸
Teng Chung-tse (Tang Chung Chak)　鄧仲澤
Teng Hua-hsi (Tang Wah Hei)　鄧華熙
Teochiu (Ch'ao-chou, Chiu-chau)　潮洲
Tien-shih-chai hua-pao　點石齋畫報
Tin Hau (T'ien-hou)　天后
To Sze Tun　杜四端
Toishan (T'ai-shan)　台山
Tong Lai Chuen　唐麗泉
Tōyō Kisen　東洋汽船
Tsang Yan Po (Tseng En-p'u)　曾恩普
Tse Tsan Tai　謝纘泰
Ts'en Ch'un-hsüan　岑春煊
Tseng Chi-tse　曾紀澤
Tso Seen Wan　曹善允
tu-tu　都督

t'uan-chia　圍甲

t'ung-hsiang hui-kuan　同鄉會館

Tung Kun (Tung-kuan)　東莞

T'ung-meng-hui　同盟會

Tung Wah Hospital　東華醫院

Tzu-chih yen-chiu-she　自治研究社

Uchida Ryōhei　內田良平

U I-kai　胡爾楷

Waichow (Hui-chou)　惠州

Wanchai　灣仔

Wan-li yen-ch'ang　挽利煙廠

Wang Ching-wei　汪精衞

Wang Hsien-ch'ien　王先謙

Wang T'ao　王韜

Wang Ya-fu　王亞斧

Wei-hsin　維新

Wei Wah On　韋華安

Wei Yuk　韋玉

wen-ming p'ai-wai　文明排外

wen-ming ti-chih　文明抵制

Wen Tsung-yao　温宗堯

Wen Tzu-ts'un　温子純

Wing On　永安

Wong Choi Chiu (Huang Tsai-ch'ao)　黃在朝

Wong Kwei Hung (Huang Kuei-hung)　黃桂鴻

Wong See-tye　黃社帶

Wong Shing　黃勝

Woo Lin Yuen　胡連元

Wu Hsien-tzu (Ng Hing Tsz)　伍憲仔

Wu T'ing-fang　伍廷芳

Wu Tung-ch'i (Ng Tung Kai)　吳東啓

Wu Yao-t'ing (Ng Yiu Ting)　伍耀廷

Ya-chou-pao　亞洲報

Yang Ch'ü-yün (Yeung Ku-wan)　楊衢雲

Yang Hsi-yen (Yeung Sai Ngam)　楊西巖

Yang Shih-hsiang　楊士驤

Yang Yin　楊殷

Yao Yü-p'ing (Yiu Yue Ping)　姚雨平

Yaumati 油麻地
yeh-man p'ai-wai 野蠻排外
Yeh Ming-ch'en 葉名琛
Yeh Te-hui 葉德輝
Yen Fu 嚴復
Yeung Wan Po 楊雲坡
Yin Wen-k'ai 尹文楷
Yip Hoi Shan 葉藹山
Yip Wai Pak (Yeh Hui-po) 葉惠伯
Yu Lieh 尤列
Yu Pun San (Yü Pin-ch'en) 余斌臣
Yu-so-wei 有所謂
Yu Yuk Chi (Yü Yü-chih) 余育之
Yüan Shih-k'ai 袁世凱
Yüeh-shang tzu-chih-hui 粵商自治會
Yuen Fat Hong 元發行
Yung-hsin li-min 永新利民
Yung Wing (Jung Hung) 容閎

Selected Bibliography

Abbreviations

Chih-nan-lu: Cheng Tzu-ts'an, comp. *Hsiang-kang Chung-hua shang-yeh chiao-t'ung jen-ming chih-nan-lu* (The Anglo-Chinese commercial directory of Hong Kong). Hong Kong: 1915.

CO129: Great Britain. Colonial Office Records. Series CO129. Governor's Dispatches and Replies from the Secretary of State for the Colonies. 1841–1913.

CO882: Great Britain. Colonial Office Records. Series CO882. Confidential Prints, Eastern. 1860–1913.

HINHSCC: Hu Li-yüan, *Hu I-nan hsien-sheng ch'üan-chi* (Complete works of Hu Li-yüan). Hong Kong: 1917.

HKHJMJSL: Woo Sing Lim, comp. *Hsiang-kang Hua-jen ming-jen shih-lüeh* (Prominent Chinese in Hong Kong). Hong Kong: 1937.

JAS: Journal of Asian Studies

JHKBRAS: Journal of the Hong Kong Branch of the Royal Asiatic Society

"Report . . . on Chair and Jinricksha Coolies": "Report of the Commission Appointed by His Excellency the Governor to Enquire into and Report on the Question of the Existing Difficulty of Procuring and Retaining Reliable Chair and Jinricksha Coolies for Private Chair and Jinrickshas." Hong Kong: *Hong Kong Legislative Council Sessional Papers 1901*.

Report . . . Tung Wah: Report of the Commission Appointed by His Excellency Sir William Robinson, K.C.M.G., to Enquire into the Working and Organization of the Tung Wah Hospital, Together with the Evidence Taken Before the Commission, and Other Appendices. Hong Kong: Noronha, 1896.

A Ying, ed. *Fan-Mei Hua-kung chin-yüeh wen-hsüeh chi* (A collection of literature on the anti-American exclusion treaty). Shanghai: Chung-hua shu-
chü, 1962.

Armentrout-Ma, Eve. "Urban Chinese at the Sinitic Frontier: Social Organizations in the United States' Chinatowns, 1849–1898." *Modern Asian Studies* (1983), 17(1):107–135.

——*Revolutionaries, Monarchists, and Chinatowns: Chinese Politics in the Americas
and the 1911 Revolution*. Honolulu: University of Hawaii Press, 1990.

Balandier, George. "The Colonial Situation: A Theoretical Approach." In
Emmanuel Wallerstein, ed., *Social Change: The Colonial Situation*. New
York: Wiley, 1966.

Banister, T. Roger. *A History of the External Trade of China, 1834–81, Together
with a Synopsis of the External Trade of China, 1882–1931, Being an Introduction to the Customs Decennial Reports, 1922–1931*. Shanghai: 1931.

Bastid-Brugere, Marianne. "Current of Social Change." In J. K. Fairbank
and K. C. Liu, eds., *The Cambridge History of China*. Vol. 11, part 2, *Late
Ch'ing, 1800–1911*, pp. 536–602. Cambridge: Cambridge University Press,
1980.

Bays, Daniel H. *China Enters the Twentieth Century: Chang Chih-tung and the
Issues of a New Age, 1895–1909*. Ann Arbor: University of Michigan Press,
1978.

Benton, Gregor. *The Hongkong Crisis*. London: Pluto, 1983.

Beresford, Charles. *The Break-up of China*. New York: Harper and Row,
1899.

Bergere, Marie-Claire. "The Role of the Bourgeoisie." In Mary C. Wright,
ed., *China in Revolution: The First Phase, 1900–1913*, pp. 229–295. New
Haven: Yale University Press, 1968.

Bird, Isabella L. *The Golden Chersonese and the Way Thither*, London: John
Murray, 1883; Kuala Lumpur: Oxford University Press, 1967, reprint.

Borokh, Lilia. "Notes on the Early Role of Secret Societies in Sun Yat-sen's
Republican Movement." In Jean Chesneaux, ed., *Popular Movements and
Secret Societies in China 1840–1950*, pp. 135–144. Stanford: Stanford Univer-
sity Press, 1972.

British Parliamentary Papers: China. Vols. 25 and 26. Shannon: Irish University
Press, 1971.

Butters, H. R. *Labour and Labour Conditions in Hong Kong*. Hong Kong: 1939.

Cameron, Nigel. *Hong Kong the Cultured Pearl*. Hong Kong: Oxford University Press, 1978.

——*An Illustrated History of Hong Kong*. Hong Kong: Oxford University Press,
1991.

Chadwick, Osbert. "Report on the Sanitary Condition of Hong Kong." In
British Parliamentary Papers: China, 26:93–160. Shannon: Irish University
Press, 1971.

Chan, Lau Kit-ching. *China, Britain, and Hong Kong, 1895–1945*. HongKong:
Chinese University Press, 1990.

Chan, Mary Man-yue. "Chinese Revolutionaries in Hong Kong, 1895–1911." Master's thesis, University of Hong Kong, 1963.

Chan, Ming Kou. "Labor and Empire: The Chinese Labor Movement in the Canton Delta, 1895–1927." Ph.D. diss., Stanford University, 1975.

Chan, Wai Kwan. *The Making of Hong Kong Society: Three Studies of Class Formation in Early Hong Kong.* Oxford: Clarendon Press, 1991.

Chan, Wellington K. K. *Merchants, Mandarins, and Modern Enterprise in Late Ch'ing China.* Cambridge: Harvard University East Asian Research Center, 1977.

——"The Organizational Structure of the Traditional Chinese Firm and Its Modern Reform." *Business History Review* (Summer 1982), 56(2):218–235.

Chang Chih-pen, comp. *Hsiang-kang chang-ku* (Hong Kong historical records). Hong Kong: Feng Nien Ch'u-pan-she, 1959.

Chang Chih-tung. *Chang Wen-hsiang kung ch'üan-chi*, 228 chüan. (Complete works of Chang Chih-tung). Taipei: Wen-hai, 1963.

——*Ch'üan-hsüeh p'ien* (Exhortation to learning). Taipei: Wen-hai, n.d., reprint.

Chang Sheng. *Hsiang-kang hei she-hui fuo-tung chen-hsiang* (A truepicture of the underground society's activities in Hong Kong). Hong Kong: T'ien-ti, 1980.

Chang Ts'un-wu. *Kuang-hsü sa-i-nien Chung-Mei kung-yüeh feng-ch'ao* (The controversy over the Sino-American treaty in 1905). Taipei: Institute of Modern History, Academia Sinica, 1966.

Cheah Boon Kheng. "Hobsbawm's Social Banditry, Myth, and Historical Reality: A Case in the Malaysian State of Kedah, 1915–1920." *Bulletin of Concerned Asian Scholars* (October–December 1985), 17(4):34–51.

Ch'en Ta. "Wo kuo nan-pu ti lao-kung kai-k'uang" (General conditions of the laborers in the south of our country). *T'ung-chi yüeh-k'an* (December 1929), 1(10):1–42.

Ch'en Ta-t'ung, comp. *Pai-nien shang-yeh* (A century of commerce). Hong Kong: 1941.

Ch'en Tse-hsien. "Shih-chiu shih-chi sheng-hsing ti ch'i-kung chih" (The contract labor system prevalent during the nineteenth century). In Ch'en Han-sheng et al., eds., *Hua-kung ch'u kuo shih-liao*, 4 vols. (Historical sources on Chinese emigrant laborers), 4:144–173. Peking: Chung-hua shu-chü, 1981.

Cheng, T. C. "Chinese Unofficial Members of the Legislative and Executive Councils in Hong Kong up to 1941." *Journal of the Hong Kong Branch of the Royal Asiatic Society* (1969), 9:7–30.

Cheng Tzu-ts'an, comp. *Hsiang-kang Chung-hua shang-yeh chiao-t'ung jen-ming chih-nan-lu* (The Anglo-Chinese commercial directory of Hong Kong). Hong Kong: 1915.

Chere, Lewis M. "The Hong Kong Riots of 1884: Evidence for Chinese Nationalism." *Journal of the Hong Kong Branch of the Royal Asiatic Society* (1980), 20:54–65.

Chesneaux, Jean. *Secret Societies in China in the Nineteenth and Twentieth Centuries.* Hong Kong: Heinemann, 1971.

——*The Chinese Labor Movement 1919–1927.* Stanford: Stanford University Press, 1968.

Chesneaux, Jean., ed. *Popular Movements and Secret Societies in China, 1840–1950.* Stanford: Stanford University Press, 1972.

Chiang Yung-ching. *Hu Han-min hsien-sheng nien-p'u* (Chronological biography of Mr. Hu Han-min). Taipei: Tang-shih wei-yüan hui, 1978.

Chin, Ying-hsi. *Hsiang-kang shih-hua* (Anecdotal history of Hong Kong). Kuang-chou: Kuang-tung jen-min ch'u-pan-she, 1988.

China Mail, The. (A Hong Kong daily). 1853–1914

Chinn, Thomas W., H. Mark Lai, and P. P. Choy, eds. *A History of the Chinese in California: A Syllabus.* San Francisco: Chinese Historical Society of America, 1973.

Ch'iu Chieh. "Hsin-hai ko-ming shih-ch'i ti yüeh-shang tzu-chih hui" (The Canton Merchants' Self-Government Society during the period of the 1911 revolution). *Chin-tai shih yen-chiu* (1982), no. 3, pp. 183–200.

Chiu, Ling-yeong. "The Life and Thoughts of Sir Kai Ho Kai." Ph.D. diss., University of Sydney, 1968.

Chiu, T. N. *The Port of Hong Kong: A Survey of Its Development.* Hong Kong: Hong Kong University Press, 1973.

Chiu, Weng-kai Stephen. "Strikes in Hong Kong: A Sociological Study." Master's thesis, University of Hong Kong, 1987.

Choa, Gerald H. *The Life and Times of Sir Kai Ho Kai.* Hong Kong: Chinese University Press, 1981.

Choa Chee Bee. *Wills.* May 8, 1890 and June 28, 1900.

Choa Leep Chee. *Will.* June 17, 1909.

Chronicle and Directory for China, Japan, the Philippines, Borneo, Annam, Cochin China, Siam, Straits Settlements, Malay States, etc. Hong Kong: 1884.

Chu Shih-chia, ed. *Mei-kuo p'o-hai Hua-kung shih-liao* (Historical materials concerning the American persecution of Chinese laborers). Peking: Chung-hua shu-chü, 1958.

Cohen, Paul A. *Between Tradition and Modernity: Wang T'ao andReforms in Late Ch'ing China.* Cambridge: Harvard UniversityPress, 1974.

——*Discovering History in China: American Historical Writing on the Recent Chinese Past.* New York: Columbia University Press, 1984.

Cohen, Paul A. and John E. Schreker, eds. *Reform in Nineteenth-Century China.* Cambridge: Harvard University East Asian Research Center, 1976.

Colley, Linda. "Whose Nation? Class and National Consciousness in Britain 1750–1830." *Past and Present* (November 1986), no. 113, pp. 97–117.

Coolidge, Mary. *The Chinese Immigration.* New York: Henry Holt, 1909.

"Correspondence Relative to the Magistrate's Court, Police, and Prisons." 21 vols. Handwritten ms. Hong Kong: 1876–1908.

Crisswell, Colin N. *The Taipans Hong Kong's Merchant Princes.* Hong Kong: Oxford University Press, 1981.

Denby, Charles. *China and Her People: Being the Observations, Reminiscences, and Conclusions of an American Diplomat.* 2 vols. Boston: L. C. Page, 1906.

Desan, Suzanne. "Crowds, Community, and Ritual in the Work of E. P. Thompson and Natalie Davis," in Lynn Hunt, ed., *The New Cultural History*, pp. 47–71. Berkeley and Los Angeles: University of California Press, 1989.

Deutsch, Karl W. *Nationalism and Social Communication: An Enquiry into the Foundations of Nationality.* Cambridge: M.I.T. Press, 1953.

"The Districts of Hong Kong and the Name Kwan-Tai-Lo." *The ChinaReview* (1872–73), 1:333–334.

Eastman, Lloyd. "The Kwangtung Anti-foreign Disturbances during the Sino-French War." *Papers on China*, 13:1–31. Cambridge: Harvard University East Asian Research Center, 1959.

——*Throne and Mandarins: China's Search for A Policy During the Sino-French Controversy, 1880–1885.* Cambridge: Harvard University Press, 1967.

Eitel, E. J. *Europe in China: The History of Hongkong from the Beginning to the Year 1882.* Hong Kong: Kelly and Walsh, 1895. Taipei: Cheng-wen Publishing Company, 1968, reprint.

Eley, Geoff. "Nationalism and Social History." *Social History* (January 1981), 6(1):83–107.

Endacott, G. B. *A History of Hong Kong.* Rev. ed. Hong Kong: Oxford University Press, 1973.

——*Government and People in Hong Kong, 1841–1962: A Constitutional History.* Hong Kong: Hong Kong University Press, 1964.

——*Hong Kong Eclipse.* Ed. Alan Birch. Hong Kong: Oxford University Press, 1978.

Endacott, G. B., ed. *An Eastern Entrepot: A Collection of Documents Illustrating the History of Hong Kong.* London: Her Majesty's Stationary Office, 1964.

Esherick, Joseph W. "1911: A Review." *Modern China* (April 1976), 2(2):141–183.

——*Reform and Revolution in China: The 1911 Revolution in Hunan and Hubei.* Berkeley: University of California Press, 1976.

Esherick, Joseph W. and Mary B. Rankin, eds., *Chinese Local Elites and Patterns of Dominance.* Berkeley and Los Angeles: University of California Press, 1990.

Fairbank, John K. *Trade and Diplomacy on the China Coast: The Opening of the Treaty Ports, 1842–1854.* Cambridge: Harvard University Press, 1953. Rev. ed., 1969.

Fairbank, John K., ed. *The Cambridge History of China.* Vol. 10, part 1, *Late Ch'ing, 1800–1911.* Cambridge: Cambridge University Press, 1978.

——*The Cambridge History of Modern China.* Vol. 12, part 1, *Republican China, 1912–1949.* Cambridge: Cambridge University Press, 1983.

Fang Han-ch'i. "I-pa-pa-ssu nien Hsiang-kang jen-min fan-ti tou-cheng (The 1884 Hong Kong people's anti-imperialist struggle). *Chin-tai shih chih-liao* (1957), no. 6, pp. 20–30.

Faure, David. *The Structure of Chinese Rural Society: Lineage and Village in the*

Eastern New Territories, Hong Kong. Hong Kong: Oxford University Press, 1986.

Faure, David, J. Hayes, and A. Birch, eds. *From Village to City: Studies in the Traditional Roots of Hong Kong.* Hong Kong: University of Hong Kong Press, 1984.

Feldwick, W., ed. *Present Day Impression of the Far East and Prominent and Progressive Chinese at Home and Abroad: The History, People, Commerce, Industries, and Resources of China, Hong Kong, Indo China, Malaya, and Netherlands India.* London: Globe Encyclopedia, 1917.

Feng Tzu-yu. *Hua-ch'iao ko-ming k'ai-kuo shih* (A history of the overseas Chinese [activities] in the revolution and founding of the republic). Taipei: 1953.

——*Ko-ming i-shih* (Reminiscences of the revolution). 5 vols. Taipei: Shang-wu, 1965. Originally published in 1939.

Feuerwerker, Albert. *The Chinese Economy, ca. 1870–1911.* Ann Arbor: Michigan Papers in Chinese Studies, no. 5, 1969.

——*The Foreign Establishment in China in the Early Twentieth Century.* Ann Arbor: Michigan Papers in Chinese Studies, no. 29, 1976.

Field, Margaret. "The Chinese Boycott of 1905." *Papers on China,* 11:63–98. Cambridge: Harvard University East Asian Research Center, 1957.

Fieldhouse, D. K. *The Colonial Empires: A Comparative Survey from the Eighteenth Century.* New York: Dell, 1966.

Fok, K. C. *Lectures on Hong Kong History: Hong Kong's Role in Modern Chinese History.* Hong Kong: Commercial Press, 1990.

——"Wan-Ch'ing ch'i-chien Hsiang-kang tui nieh-ti ching-chi fa-tsan chih yin-hsiang" (Hong Kong's impact on the interior's economic development during the late Ch'ing period). *Hsüeh-shu yen-chiu* (Guangzhou) (1988), no. 2, pp. 70–74.

Fox, Grace. *British Admirals and Chinese Pirates, 1832–69.* London: Kegan Paul, Trench, Trubner, 1940.

The Friend of China and Hongkong Government Gazette. Hong Kong: 1844.

Furuyama Takashi. "1920–22 nen Honkon rōdōsha no tatakai" (The Hong Kong laborers' struggle in the years 1920–22). *Rekishi hyōron* (1977, no. 8), no. 328. pp. 43–60.

Gaikō shiryō-kan Archives (Reports of Japanese Foreign Ministry Archives in Tokyo).

Gerth, H. H. and C. Wright Mills, eds. *From Max Weber: Essays in Sociology.* New York: Oxford University Press, 1958.

Giddens, Anthony. *Capitalism and Modern Social Theory: An Analysis of the Writings of Marx, Durkheim, and Max Weber.* Cambridge University Press, 1971.

Great Britain. Colonial Office Records:
Series CO129. Governor's Dispatches and Replies from the Secretary of State for the Colonies.
Series CO132. Hong Kong Government Gazettes.
Series CO133. Annual Blue Book of Statistics.
Series CO882. Confidential Prints, Eastern.

Groves, R. G. "Militia, Market, and Lineage: Chinese Resistance to the Occupation of Hong Kong's New Territories in 1899." *Journal of the Hong Kong Branch of the Royal Asiatic Society* (1969), 9:31–64.

Guldin, Gregory E. "'Overseas' at Home: The Fujianese of Hong Kong." Ph.D. diss., University of Wisconsin, 1977.

Hao, Yen-p'ing. *The Comprador in Nineteenth Century China: Bridge Between East and West*. Cambridge: Harvard University Press, 1970.

——*The Commercial Revolution in Nineteenth-Century China: The Rise of Sino-Western Mercantile Capitalism*. Berkeley: University of California Press, 1986.

Hatano Yoshihiro. *Chūgoku kindai kōgyōshi no kenkyū* (Studies in the early industrialization in China). Kyoto: Tōyōshi Kenkyūkai, 1962.

Hayes, James. *The Hong Kong Region 1850–1911: Institutions and Leadership in Town and Countryside*. Hamden: Shoe String, 1977.

——"The Nature of Village Life." In David Faure, James Hayes, and Alan Birch, eds., *From Village to City: Studies in the Traditional Roots of Hong Kong Society*, pp. 55–72. Hong Kong: Centre of Asian Studies, University of Hong Kong, 1984.

——*The Rural Communities of Hong Kong: Studies and Themes*. Hong Kong: Oxford University Press, 1983.

——"Secular Non-Gentry Leadership of Temple and Shrine Organizations in Urban British Hong Kong." *JHKBRAS* (1983), 23:113–136.

Hershatter, Gail. *The Workers of Tianjin, 1900–1949*. Stanford: Stanford University Press, 1986.

Historical and Statistical Abstract of the Colony of Hong Kong, 1841–1930. 3d ed. Hong Kong: Noronha, 1932.

Ho Kai. "To the Editor." *The China Mail*. February 16, 1887.

——"An Open Letter on the Situation." *The China Mail*. August 22, 1900.

——"Chih Hsiang-kang tsung-tu li-shu Man-Ch'ing cheng-fu tsui-chuang ping ni-ting p'ing-chih chang-ch'eng ch'ing chuan-shang ke-kuo tsan-ch'eng shu" (Letter to the Governor of Hong Kong listing the crimes of the Manchu government and proposing the regulations for peaceful rule, requesting to be forwarded to all countries for their approval). In *Kuo-fu ch'üan-chi (Complete works of Sun Chung-shan)*, 5:17–19, Taipei: Wen-wu, 1957.

Ho Kai and Hu Li-yüan. "Tseng-lun shu-hou" (Review of Tseng Chi-tse's article). In *Hu I-nan hsien-sheng ch'üan-chi*, chüan 3 (The complete works of Hu Li-yüan). Hong Kong: 1917.

——"Hsin-cheng lun-i" (Discourse on the new government). In *Hu I-nan hsien-sheng ch'üan-chi*, chüan 6. Hong Kong: 1917.

——"Hsin-cheng pien-t'ung" (Flexibility of the new government). In *Hu I-nan hsien-sheng ch'üan-chi*, chüan 21. Hong Kong: 1917.

——"Ch'üan-hsüeh p'ien shu-hou" (Review of Chang Chih-tung's Exhortation to Learning). In *Hu I-nan hsien-sheng ch'üan-chi*, chüan 18. Hong Kong: 1917.

Ho Kai and Wei Yuk. "Letter to Rear-Admiral Lord Charles Beresford, C.B.,

M.P." In Charles Beresford, *The Break-up of China*. New York: Harper and Row, 1899.

Ho, Ping-ti. *Studies on the Population of China, 1368–1953*. Cambridge: Harvard University Press, 1959.

Ho Tso-chi. "I-chiu-ling-wu nien fan-Mei ai-kuo yün-tung" (The 1905 anti-American patriotic movement). *Chin-tai shih chih-liao* (1956), no. 1, pp. 1–90.

Hobsbawm, Eric J. *The Age of Revolution, 1789–1848*. New York: New American Library, 1962.

——*Bandits*. Rev. ed. New York: Pantheon, 1981.

——*Nations and Nationalism Since 1780: Programme, Myth, Reality*. Cambridge: Cambridge University Press, 1990.

Hobsbawm, Eric J. and Terence Ranger, eds. *The Invention of Tradition*. New York: Cambridge University Press, 1983.

Hoe, Susanna. *The Private Life of Old Hong Kong: Western Women in the British Colony, 1841–1941*. Hong Kong: Oxford UniversityPress, 1991.

The Hongkong Daily Press. 1870–1913.

The Hong Kong Directory and Hong List for the Far East. Hong Kong: 1884, 1893.

Hong Kong Government Publications:
Administrative Reports for the Year–.
Hong Kong Annual Report
Hong Kong Blue Book for the Year–.
Hong Kong Government Gazette.
Hong Kong Hansard: Reports of the Meetings of the Legislative Council.
Hong Kong Legislative Council Sessional Papers.

The Hong Kong Guide 1893. Hong Kong: Oxford University Press, 1982, reprint.

The Hongkong Telegraph. 1881–1913.

The Hongkong Weekly Press. 1895–1909.

Honig, Emily. *Sisters and Strangers: Women in the Shanghai Cotton Mills, 1919–1949*. Stanford: Stanford University Press, 1986.

Hsiang-kang Chung-hua tsung-shang-hui ch'eng-li ch'i-shih chou-nien chi nien t'e-k'an (The souvenir of the seventieth anniversary of the Chinese General Chamber of Commerce). Hong Kong: 1970.

Hsiang-kang Tung-hua san yüan pai-nien shih-lüeh, comp. Tung-shih-chü (One hundred years of the Tung Wah group of hospitals, 1870–1970, compiled by the board of directors). Hong Kong: 1970.

Hsiang-kang wen-wu-miao shih-lüeh (The story of the Hong Kong Man Mo Temple). Hong Kong: n.d.

Hsieh, Winston. "Triads, Salt Smugglers, and Local Uprisings: Observations on the Social and Economic Background of the Waichow Revolution of 1911." In Jean Chesneaux, ed., *Popular Movements and Secret Societies in China 1840–1950*, pp. 145–164. Stanford: Stanford University Press, 1972.

——"Peasant Insurrection and the Marketing Hierarchy in the Canton Delta, 1911." In Mark Elvin and G. William Skinner, eds., *The Chinese City Between Two Worlds*, pp. 119–141. Stanford: Stanford University Press, 1974,

Hsü Hsin-wu. *Ya-p'ien chan-cheng ch'ien Chung-kuo mien-fang-chih shuo-kung-yeh ti shang-p'in sheng-ch'an yü chih-pen chu-i meng-ya wen-t'i* (Commercial production of the Chinese handicraft cotton textile industry prior to the Opium War and the issue of the sprouting of capitalism). Chiang-shu: Jen-min Ch'u-pan-she, 1981.

Hsü I-sheng. "Chia-wu Chung-Jih chan-cheng ch'ien Ch'ing cheng-fu ti wai-tsai" (The foreign debt of the Ch'ing government prior to the 1894 Sino-Japanese War). *Ching-chi yen-chiu*, no. 5, pp. 105–127. Peking: 1956.

Hsueh, Chun-tu. "Sun Yat-sen, Yang Ch'ü-yün, and the Early Revolution-aries in China." In Chun-tu Hsueh, ed., *Revolutionary Leaders of Modern China*, pp. 102–122. New York and London: Oxford University Press, 1971.

Hu Ch'uan-chao. *Tun-mo liu-fen* (Notes on the [Sino-French] war). 1898. Taipei: 1973, reprint.

Hu Ying-han. *Wu Hsien-tzu hsien-sheng chuan-chi* (A biography of Mr. Wu Hsien-tzu). Hong Kong: Sze-ch'iang, 1953.

Hua-tzu jih-pao (Chinese daily, Hong Kong). 1895–1913.

Huang, Chia-jen. "Tsai Hsiang-kang kao ko-ming ti Hsieh Tsuan-t'ai" (The revolutionary in Hong Kong, Tse Tsan Tai). *Ta-hua* (September 1970), 1(3):13–15.

Huang I-feng. "Ti-kuo chu-i ch'ing-lüeh Chung-kuo ti i ko chung-yao chih-chu: mai-pan chieh-chi" (One important pillar of imperialism's incursion on China: the comprador class). *Li-shih yen-chiu* (1965), 91:55–70.

Hunt, Lynn, ed. *The New Cultural History*. Berkeley and Los Angeles: University of California Press, 1989.

Hyde, Francis E. *Far Eastern Trade, 1860–1914*. New York: Barnes and Noble, 1973.

Jaschok, Maria. *Concubines and Bondservants: The Social History of a Chinese Custom*, London: Zed Books, 1988.

Johnson, David, Andrew J. Nathan, and Evelyn S. Rawski. eds.*Popular Culture in Late Imperial China*. Berkeley and Los Angeles: University of California Press, 1985.

Jones, Susan Mann. "The Ningpo Pang and Financial Power at Shanghai." In Mark Elvin and G. W. Skinner, eds., *The Chinese City Between Two Worlds*, pp. 73–96. Stanford: Stanford University Press, 1974.

K'ang Yu-wei. "Pao-kuo hui san-yüeh erh-shih-ch'i jih ti-i tz'u yen-shuo" (Speech at the first meeting of the Society to Protect the Emperor on March 27, 1898). In Yu Pao-hsuan, ed., *Huang-ch'ao hsü-ai wen-p'ien* (A compilation of reformist essays in the Ch'ing dynasty), 5:19–22. Shanghai: 1902.

Kani Hiroaki. *Kindai Chûgoku no kuri to choka* (Coolies and "slave girls" of modern China). Tokyo: Iwanami Shoten, 1979.

——*A General Survey of the Boat People in Hong Kong*. Hong Kong: Chinese University of Hong Kong, 1967.

Kao Chen-pai. "Hsiang-kang Tung-hua i-yüan yü Kao Man-ho" (The Tung Wah Hospital of Hong Kong and Ko Man Wah). *Ta-hua* (October 1970), 1(4):2–6.

——"Hsin-hai Ch'ao Shan ko-ming yü Kao Shen-chih" (The 1911 revolution in Ch'ao-chou and Swatow and Ko Sing Tze). *Ta-hua* (May 1971), 1(11):2–5.

——(Lin Hsi). "Ch'ung Hsiang-kang ti Yüan-fa-hang t'ang ch'i" (On the Yuen Fat Hong of Hong Kong). *Ta-ch'eng* (August 1983), 117:47–52; (September 1983), 118:45–51; (October 1983), 119:34–39; (November 1983), 120:46–54.

Kikuchi Takaharu. *Chūgoku minzoku undō no kihon kōzō, taigai boikotto no kenkyū* (The basic structure of the Chinese nationalist movement: a study of anti-foreign boycotts). Enlarged ed. Tokyo: Kyuko Shoin, 1974.

King, Frank H. H. *The History of the Hong Kong and Shanghai Banking Corporation.* 3 vols. Cambridge: Cambridge University Press, 1988–90.

King, Frank H. H., ed. *Eastern Banking: Essays in the History of the Hong Kong and Shanghai Banking Corporation.* London: Athlone Press, 1983.

Kohn, Hans. *The Idea of Nationalism: A Study in its Origin and Background.* New York: 1944, 1967, reprint.

Kuhn, Philip A. *Rebellion and Its Enemies in Late Imperial China: Militarization and Social Structure, 1796–1864.* Cambridge: Harvard University Press, 1970.

Kwangtung hsin-hai ko-ming shih-liao (Historical sources of the 1911 revolution in Kwangtung). Kwangchou: Kwangtung Jen-min Ch'u-pan-she, 1981.

Lao She (Shu Ch'ing-ch'un). *Rickshaw: The Novel Lo-t'o Hsiang Tzu.* Trans. Jean M. James. Honolulu: University of Hawai Press, 1979.

Lau Siu-kai. *Society and Politics in Hong Kong.* Hong Kong: Chinese University Press, 1982.

Lears, T. J. Jackson. "The Concept of Cultural Hegemony: Problems and Possibilities," in *American Historical Review* (June 1985), pp. 567–593.

Lee Poh Ping. *Chinese Society in Nineteenth-Century Singapore.* Kuala Lumpur: Oxford University Press, 1978.

Legge, James. "The Colony of Hong Kong." *The China Review* (1874), vol. 3, reprinted in *Journal of the Hong Kong Branch of the Royal Asiatic Society* (1971), 11:172–193.

Lethbridge, H. J. "The District Watch Committee: 'The Chinese Executive Council of Hong Kong.'" *Journal of the Hong Kong Branch of the Royal Asiatic Society* (1971), 11:116–141.

——"A Chinese Association in Hong Kong: The Tung Wah." *Contributions to Asian Studies* (January 1971), 1:144–158.

——"The Evolution of a Chinese Voluntary Association in Hong Kong: The Po Leung Kuk." *Journal of Oriental Studies* (January 1972), 10(1):33–50.

——"Condition of the European Working Class in Nineteenth-Century Hong Kong." *Journal of the Hong Kong Branch of the Royal Asiatic Society* (1975), 15:88–112.

——*Hong Kong: Stability and Change.* Hong Kong: Oxford University Press, 1978.

Leung, Yuen Sang. "Regional Rivalry in Mid-Nineteenth Century Shanghai: Cantonese vs. Ningpo Men." *Ch'ing-shih Wen-t'i* (December 1982), 4(8):29–50.

Li, Lillian. "Silks by Sea: Trade, Technology, Enterprise in China and Japan." *Business History Review* (Summer 1982), 56(2):192–217.

Li En-han. *Tseng Chi-tse ti wai-chiao* (Tseng Chi-tse's diplomacy). Taipei: 1966.

Li Ming-jen. "I-pa-pa-ssu nien Hsiang-kang pa-kung yün-tung" (The 1884 Hong Kong strike movement). *Li-shih yen-chiu* (March 1958), no. 3, pp. 89–90.

Li Shih-yüeh. "Lun i-chiu-ling-wu i-chiu-ling-pa nien Chung-kuo min-tsu kung-yeh ti fa-chan" (On the development of China's industry, 1905–1908). *Jen-wen tsa-chih* (1959), no. 1, pp. 67–78.

Li Tsin-wei, ed. *Hsiang-kang pai-nien shih* (Centenary history of Hong Kong). Hong Kong: Nan-chung, 1948.

Liang Ch'i-ch'ao. *Wu-hsü cheng-pien chi* (A history of the coup d'état of 1898). Taipei: Chung-hua, 1959.

Lin Ch'i-ch'uan. "Shih-chiu shih-chi mo Taiwan t'ung-pao fan-tui Fa-kuo wu-chuang ch'in-lüeh ti tuo-cheng" (The struggle of the Taiwan compatriots against French military invasion in the late nineteenth century). *Hsia-men ta-hsüeh hsüeh-pao* (1978), no. 1.

Linebarger, Paul. *Sun Yat-sen and the Chinese Republic*. New York: Century, 1925.

Liu, Tse-sheng. *Hsiang-kang ku-chin* (Hong Kong's past and present). Kuang-chou wen-hua ch'u-pan-she, 1988.

——*Hsiang-chiang yeh-t'an* (Hong Kong evening talk). Hong Kong: Shan-lien shu-tien, 1990.

Liu Yü-tsun and Ch'eng Lu-hsi. "Hsin-hai ko-ming yün-tung chung ti T'ai-shan hsien yü Hua-ch'iao" (T'ai-shan county and the overseas Chinese during the 1911 revolution). In Hung Ssu-ssu, ed., *Hsin-hai ko-ming yü Hua-ch'iao*. Peking: Jen-min ch'u-pan-she, 1982.

Lo Hsiang-lin. *Hong Kong and Western Cultures*. Tokyo: 1963.

Lü-Kang Ch'ao-chou shang-hui san-shih chou-nien chi-nien t'e-k'an (Thirty years of the Ch'ao-chou Chamber of Commerce in Hong Kong: A special commemorative publication). Hong Kong: 1951.

Lu Yen et al., *Hsiang-kang chang-ku* (Hong Kong historical records). 12 vols. Hong Kong: Kwang-chiao-ching, 1977–1989.

Lust, John. "Secret Societies, Popular Movements, and the 1911 Revolution." In Jean Chesneaux, ed., *Popular Movements and Secret Societies in China*, pp. 165–200. Stanford: Stanford University Press, 1972.

Ma Hsü-ch'ao Archives (Private archives of a commercial firm).

McKee, Delber L. *Chinese Exclusion Versus the Open Door Policy, 1900–1906: Clashes over China Policy in the Roosevelt Era*. Detroit: 1977.

——"The Chinese Boycott of 1905–1906 Reconsidered: The Role of Chinese Americans." *Pacific Historical Review* (May 1986), 55(2):165–191.

Maeda Takarajirō, comp. *Honkon gaikan* (A general view of Hong Kong). 1919.

Mann, Susan. *Local Merchants and the Chinese Bureaucracy, 1750–1950*. Stanford: Stanford University Press, 1987.

Matsumoto Takehiko. "Tai-Nichi bōikkotto to zai-Nichi Kakyō—dai-ni Tatsu-maru jiken o megutte" (Anti-Japanese boycott and overseas Chinese in Japan: the Case of the *Tatsu Maru II."* In Shingai kakumei kenkyū-kai, ed., *Kikuchi Takaharu sensei tsuitō ronshō: Chūgoku kingendai-shi kenkyū* (Essays on the modern and contemporary Chinese history in memory of the late Professor Kikuchi Takaharu), pp. 221–250. Tokyo: Kyuko Shoin, 1985.

Mei, June. "Socioeconomic Origins of Emigration: Guangdong to California, 1850–1882." *Modern China* (October 1979), 5(4):463–501.

Menpes, Mortimer and Henry A. Blake. *China.* London: Adam and Charles Black, 1909.

Merlat, Odette. "En Marge de L'Expedition du Tonkin, Les Emeutes de Quen-Tcheou et de Hong-Kong." *Revue Historique* (October-December 1956), no. 216, pp. 219–229.

Mills, Lennox A. *British Rule in East Asia.* New York: Russell and Russell, 1942, 1972 reprint.

Milner, A. C. "Colonial Records History: British Malaya." *Modern Asian Studies* (1987), 21(4):773–792.

Miners, Norman. *Hong Kong Under Imperial Rule, 1912–1941.* Hong Kong: Oxford University Press, 1987.

——"The Attempt to Assassinate the Governor in 1912." *Journal of the Hong Kong Branch of the Royal Asiatic Society* (1982), 22:279–285.

Moore, Barrington, Jr. *Social Origins of Dictatorship and Democracy: Lord and Peasant in the Making of the Modern World.* Boston: Beacon, 1966.

Morgan, W. P. *Triad Societies in Hong Kong.* Hong Kong: Government Press, 1960.

Murray, Dian H. *Pirates of the South China Coast, 1790–1810.* Stanford University Press, 1987.

Nacken, J. "Chinese Street-Cries in Hong Kong." *China Review* (1873), vol. 11. Reprinted in *Journal of the Hong Kong Branch of the Royal Asiatic Society* (1968), 8:128–134.

Nam Pak Hong kung-so, comp. *Hsin-hsia luo-ch'eng chi ch'eng-li pa-shih-liu chou-nien chi-nien t'e-k'an* (A special publication in commemoration of the completion of the new hall and the eighty-sixth anniversary). Hong Kong, 1954.

"The Nam Pak Hong Commercial Association of Hong Kong." *Journal of the Hong Kong Branch of the Royal Asiatic Society* (1979), 19:216–226.

Ng, Alice Lun Ngai Ha. *Interactions of East and West: Development of Public Education in Early Hong Kong.* Hong Kong: Chinese University Press, 1984.

Ng Li Hing. *Will,* October 25, 1913.

Nihon gaikō bunsho (Documents in Japan's foreign relations). Comp. Gaimu-shō (Japanese Foreign Ministry). Tokyo: Nihon Kokusai Rengō Kyōkai, 1958.

Noda Jitsunosuke. *Honkon jijō* (The state of affairs in Hong Kong). Tokyo: Gaimushō Tsūshōkyoku, 1917.

Norman, Henry. *The Peoples and Politics of the Far East: Travels and Studies in the British, French, Spanish and Portuguese Colonies, Siberia, China, Japan, Korea, Siam, and Malaya.* New York: Scribners's, 1895.

Norton-Kyshe, James W. *The History of the Laws and Courts of Hong Kong from the Earliest Period to 1898.* 2 vols. Hong Kong: Vetch and Lee, 1898, 1971 reprint.

Onogawa Hidemi. *Shinmatsu seiji shisō kenkyū* (Studies in late Ch'ing political thought). Enlarged ed. Tokyo: Misuzu Shobō, 1969.

Orchard, Dorothy J. "China's Use of the Boycott as a Political Weapon." *The Annals of the American Academy of Political and Social Science* (November 1930), 152:252–261.

Orwell, George. *Burmese Days.* New York: Harcourt Brace Jovanovich, 1934.

Papers Relating to the Flogging of Prisoners in Hong Kong: 1879. CO882: Colonial Office Confidential Prints (Eastern), vol. 4, no. 33.

Peng Chia-li. "Shih-chiu shih-chi Hsi-fang ch'in-lüeh-che tui Chung-kuo lao-kung ti luo-lüeh" (The Western invaders' pillage of Chinese laborers during the nineteenth century). *Ching-chi yen-chiu-shuo chi-k'an.* Peking: Chung-kuo she-hui k'e-hsüeh ch'u-pan-she (1979), vol. 1.

Po Leung Kuk (board of directors), comp. *Hsiang-kang Pao-liang-chü pai-nien shih* (Centenary history of the Po Leung Kuk in Hong Kong). Hong Kong: 1978.

——*Hsiang-kang pao-liang-chü shih-lüeh* (History of the Po Leung Kuk, Hong Kong, 1878–1968). Hong Kong: 1969.

Pomerantz, Linda. "The Chinese Bourgeoisie and the Anti-Chinese Movement in the United States, 1850–1905." *Amerasia Journal* (Spring-Summer 1984), 11(1):1–33.

Pope-Hennessy, James. *Verandah: Some Episodes in the Crown Colonies, 1867–1889.* New York: Knopf, 1964.

Pryor, E. G. "A Historical Review of Housing Conditions in Hong Kong." *JHKBRAS* (1972), 12:89–116.

——"The Great Plague of Hong Kong." *JHKBRAS* (1975), 15:61–70.

Rankin, Mary B. *Elite Activism and Political Transformation in China: Zhejiang Province, 1865–1911.* Stanford: Stanford University Press, 1986.

——"'Public Opinion' and Political Power: Qingyi in Late Nineteenth-Century China." *Journal of Asian Studies* (May 1982), 41(3):453–477.

Remer, C. F. *A Study of Chinese Boycotts.* Baltimore: Johns Hopkins University Press, 1933; Taipei: Ch'eng-wen, 1966, reprint.

——*The Foreign Trade of China.* Shanghai: 1926; Taipei: Ch'eng-wen, 1972, reprint.

Report of the Committee Appointed by His Excellency Sir William Robinson to Enquire into the Working and Organization of the Tung Wah Hospital, Together with the Evidence Taken Before the Commission, and Other Appendices. Hong Kong: Noronha, 1896.

"Report of the Committee Appointed by His Excellency the Governor to Enquire into and Report on the Question of the Existing Difficulty of Procuring and Retaining Reliable Chair and Jinricksha Coolies for Private Chair and Jinrickshas." Hong Kong: *Hong Kong Legislative Council Sessional Papers 1901.*

"Report on the Census of the Colony for 1901." Hong Kong: *Hong Kong Legislative Council Sessional Papers 1901.*

Rhoads, Edward J. M. *China's Republican Revolution: The Case of Kwangtung.* Cambridge: Harvard University Press, 1975.

——"Merchant Association in Canton, 1895–1911." In Mark Elvin and G. W. Skinner, eds. *The Chinese City Between Two Worlds,* pp. 97–118. Stanford: Stanford University Press, 1974.

——"Nationalism and Xenophobia in Kwangtung (1905–1906): The Canton Anti-American Boycott and the Lienchow Anti-Missionary Uprising." *Papers on China,* 16:154–197. Cambridge: Harvard University East Asian Research Center, December 1962.

Rowe, William T. *Hankow: Commerce and Society in a Chinese City,1796–1889.* Stanford: Stanford University Press, 1984.

——*Hankow: Conflict and Community in a Chinese City, 1796–1895.* Stanford: Stanford University Press, 1989.

Rude, George. *Ideology and Popular Protest.* New York: Pantheon, 1980.

Schiffrin, Harold Z. *Sun Yat-sen and the Origins of the Chinese Revolution.* Berkeley and Los Angeles: University of California Press, 1968.

Scott, James C. *Weapons of the Weak: Everyday Forms of Peasant Resistance.* New Haven: Yale University Press, 1985.

Selden, Mark. "The Proletariat, Revolutionary Change, and the State in China and Japan, 1850–1950." In Immanuel Wallerstein, ed., *Labor in the World Social Structure,* pp. 58–120. Beverly Hills: Sage, 1983.

Shaffer, Lynda. *Mao and the Workers: The Hunan Labor Movement,1920–23.* Armonk, N.Y.: M. E. Sharp, 1982.

——"The Chinese Working Class: Comments on Two Articles." *Modern China* (October 1983), 9(4):455–464.

Shao-nien-pao (Hong Kong). 1905–06.

Shih Man-yu. "Ma-chiang feng-yün—I-pa-pa-ssu nien Fuchou jen-min fan-k'ang Fa-kuo ch'in-lüeh ti tou-cheng" (Ma-chiang events— the 1884 Fuchou people's struggle against the French invaders). *Fu-chien shih-ta hsüeh-pao,* no. 3, 1978.

Shih-shih hua-pao (Canton). 1905–1913.

Shin, Linda Pomerantz. "China in Transition: The Role of Wu T'ing-fang (1842–1922)." Ph. D. diss., University of California at Los Angeles, 1970.

Shu-pao (Canton). 1884–85.

Shuang Ai. *Hsiang-chiang chiu-shih* (Hong Kong old events). Hong Kong: Yi Ch'un ch'u-pan-she, 1974.

Silin, Robert H. "Marketing and Credit in a Hong Kong Wholesale Market." In W. E. Willmott, ed., *Economic Organization in Chinese Society,* pp. 327–352. Stanford: Stanford University Press, 1972.

Sinn, Elizabeth. "Materials for Historical Research: Source Materials on the Tung Wah Hospital, 1870–1941: The Case of A Historical Institution," pp. 1–41. The Hong Kong Studies Seminar Program, the University of Hong Kong, October 15, 16, 23, 1982.

——"The Strike and Riot of 1884—A Hong Kong Perspective." *Journal of the Hong Kong Branch of the Royal Asiatic Society* (1982), 22:65–98.

——*Power and Charity: The Early History of the Tung Wah Hospital, Hong Kong.* Hong Kong: Oxford University Press, 1989.

——"A Preliminary Study of the Development of District Associations in Pre-War Hong Kong." Paper presented at the University of Hong Kong, December 1986.

Skinner, G. William. "Regional Urbanization in Nineteenth-Century China." In G. W. Skinner, ed., *The City in LateImperial China,* pp. 211–249. Stanford: Stanford University Press, 1977.

Skocpol, Theda, ed. *Vision and Method in Historical Sociology.* Cambridge: Cambridge University Press, 1984.

——*State and Social Revolution: A Comparative Analysis of France, Russia, and China.* Cambridge: Cambridge University Press, 1979.

Smith, Carl. "The Chinese Settlement of British Hong Kong." *Chung Chi Journal* (May 1970), no. 48, pp. 26–32.

——"The Emergence of a Chinese Elite in Hong Kong." *Journal of the Hong Kong Branch of the Royal Asiatic Society* (1971), 11:74–115.

——"English-Educated Chinese Elites in Nineteenth-Century Hong Kong." In *Hong Kong, the Interactions of Traditions and Life in the Towns,* pp. 65–96. Hong Kong: Hong Kong Branch of the Royal Asiatic Society, 1975.

——"How A-mei Pioneered a Modern Canton." *South China Morning Post,* April 12, 1978.

——*Chinese Christians: Elites, Middlemen, and the Church in Hong Kong.* Hong Kong: Oxford University Press, 1985.

South China Morning Post. 1904–1913.

Stanton, William. *The Triad Society or Heaven and Earth Association.* Hong Kong: Kelly and Walsh, 1900.

Stearns, Peter N. and Herrick Chapman. *European Society in Upheaval: Social History Since 1750.* 3d ed. New York: Macmillan, 1992.

Strand, David. *Rickshaw Beijing: City People and Politics in the 1920s.* Berkeley and Los Angeles: University of California Press, 1989.

Sugano Tadashi. "Tatsu Maru jiken to zai-Nichi Chūgokujin no dōkō" (The *Tatsu Maru* incident and the tendency of the Chinese residents in Japan). *Nara daigaku kiyō* (December 1982), 11:17–32.

Taiwan Ginkō, comp. *Honkon jijō gaiyō* (General affairs of HongKong). Taihoku: 1915.

T'an Yung-nien. *Hsin-hai ko-ming hui-i-lu* (Memoirs of the 1911 revolution). Taipei: Wen-hai, 1957.

Teng Chung-hsia. *Chung-kuo chih-kung yün-tung chien-shih* (A brief history of laborers in China). Peking: Jen-min ch'u-pan-she, 1957.

Thompson, E. P. "Eighteenth-Century English Society: Class Struggle Without Class?" *Social History* (May 1978), 3(2):133–165.

——"Patrician Society, Plebeian Culture." *Journal of Social History* (Summer 1974), 7(4):382–405.

——"The Moral Economy of the English Crowd in Eighteenth Century." *Past and Present* (1971), 50:76–136.

——*The Making of the English Working Class*. New York: Vintage, 1966.

Tien-shih-chai hua-pao (Shanghai), 1884.

Tilly, Charles. "Rural Collective Action in Modern Europe." In Joseph Spielberg and Scott Whiteford, eds., *Forging Nations: A Comparative View of Rural Ferment and Revolt*, pp. 9–40. East Lansing: Michigan State University Press, 1976.

——*From Mobilization to Revolution*. Reading, Mass.: Addison-Wesley, 1978.

Ting Yu. "1905-nien Kuang-tung fan-Mei yün-tung" (The 1905 anti-American movenment in Kwangtung). *Chin-tai shih tzu-liao* (1958), no. 5, pp. 8–55.

Tōa Dōbunkai, comp. *Honkon Kantō chūzaihan chōsa hōkokusho* (Investigation report by the teams stationed in Hong Kong and Canton). Hand-written manuscript, 1908.

——*Shina no kōgyō* (China's industry). Tokyo: 1916.

Trimberger, Ellen Kay. "E. P. Thompson: Understanding the Process of History," in Theda Skocpol, ed., *Vision and Method in Historical Sociology*, pp. 211–243. Cambridge: Cambridge University Press, 1984.

Tsai, Jung-fang. "Comprador Ideologists in Modern China: Ho Kai (Ho Ch'i 1859–1914) and Hu Li-yüan (1847–1916)." Ph.D. diss., University of California at Los Angeles, 1975.

——"Syncretism in the Reformist Thought of Ho Kai (Ho Ch'i, 1859–1914) and Hu Li-yüan (1847–1916)." *Asian Profile* (February 1978), 6(1):19–33.

——"The Predicament of the Comprador Ideologists: He Qi (Ho Kai, 1859–1914) and Hu Li-yüan (1847–1916)." *Modern China* (April 1981), 7(2):191–225.

——"Reflections on Some Chinese Reformers' and Conservatives' Views of Freedom (Tzu-yu) in Late Ch'ing Times." *Proceedings of the Fifth International Symposium on Asian Studies 1983*, pp. 99–118. Hong Kong: Asian Research Service, 1983.

——"The 1884 Hong Kong Insurrection: Anti-Imperialist Popular Protest During the Sino-French War." *Bulletin of Concerned Asian Scholars* (January-March 1984), 16(1):2–14.

Tsai, Shih-shan Henry. *China and the Overseas Chinese in the United States, 1868–1911*. Fayetteville: University of Arkansas Press, 1983.

——*The Chinese Experience in America*. Bloomington: Indiana University Press, 1987.

Tsang, Steve Y. S. *Democracy Shelved: Great Britain, China, and Attempts at Constitutional Reform in Hong Kong, 1945–1952.* Hong Kong: Oxford University Press, 1988.

Tse Tsan Tai. *The Chinese Republic: Secret History of the Revolution*. Hong Kong: South China Morning Post, 1924.

Tseng Chi-tse. "China: The Sleep and the Awaking." *Asiatic Quaterly Review* (January 1887), 3:1–10.

Turner, John A. *Kwang Tung, or Five Years in South China*. London: S. W. Partridge, 1894.

U. S. Congress, House of Representatives. *Papers Relating to the Foreign Relations of the United States*. 1905 and 1906. New York: Kraus Reprint, 1969.

Wagner, Augusta. *Labor Legislation in China*. Peking: Yenching University , 1938.

Wai-wu-pu: Wai-chiao tang-an (Chinese Foreign Ministry Archives, Kwang-tung): *Yao-hsiang mei-ch'ang an* (The case of Yao-hsiang Coal Co.), KH32.1.2–1.23.

Wai-wu-pu Ch'ing-tang (Chinese Foreign Ministry Ch'ing Archives): *Erh-ch'en-wan (Tatsu Maru)*.

Wakeman, Frederic, Jr. *Strangers at the Gate: Social Disorder in South China, 1839–1861*. Berkeley and Los Angeles: University of California Press, 1966.

Wakeman, Frederic, Jr., and Carolyn Grant. eds. *Conflict and Control in Late Imperial China*. Berkeley and Los Angeles: University of California Press, 1975.

Wales, Nym. *The Chinese Labor Movement*. New York: John Day, 1945.

Wang Ching-yü. "Shih-chiu shih-chi wai-kuo ch'in-Hua shih-yeh chung ti Hua-shang fu-ku huo-tung" (The investment by Chinese merchants in foreign enterprises that invaded China in the nineteenth century). *Li-shih yen-chiu* (1965), 4:39–74.

——"Birth of the Chinese Bourgeoisie: A Tentative Discussion." *Chinese Studies in History* (Summer 1984), 17(4):27–48.

Wang Ching-yü, comp. *Chung-kuo chin-tai kung-yeh tzu-liao, ti-erh-chi, 1895–1914 nien* (Source materials on the history of modern industry in China, second collection, 1895–1914). Peking: 1960.

Wang Gungwu. *Community and Nation: Essays on Southeast Asia and the Chinese.* Singapore: Heinemann, 1981.

——*China and the Chinese Overseas*. Singapore: Times Academic, 1991.

Wang Liang, comp. *Ch'ing-chi wai-chiao shih-liao* (Sources in diplomatic history of the Ch'ing dynasty). Taipei: Wen-hai, 1964, reprint.

Watanabe Tetsuhiro. "Ka Kei, Ko Reien no shinseiron" (Ho Kai and Hu Li Yüan's theory of the new government). *Ritsumeikan bungaku* (1961), no. 197, pp. 59–75.

Wesley-Smith, Peter. *Unequal Treaty, 1898–1997: China, Great Britain, and Hong Kong's New Territories*. Hong Kong: Oxford University Press, 1980.

Wong, Aline K. *The Kaifong Associations and the Society of Hong Kong*. Taipei: Oriental Cultural Service, 1972.

Woo Sing Lim (Wu Hsing-lien). *Hsiang-kang Hua-jen ming-jen shih-lüeh* (The prominent Chinese in Hong Kong). Hong Kong: Five Continents, 1937.

Wood, A. E. *Report on the Chinese Guilds of Hongkong, Compiled from Material Collected by the Registrar General*. Hong Kong: Noronha, 1912.

Wood, Winifred A. *A Brief History of Hongkong*. Hong Kong: South China Morning Post, 1940.

Worsley, Peter. *The Three Worlds: Culture and World Development.* Chicago: University of Chicago Press, 1984.

Wright, Arnold and H. A. Cartwright, eds. *Twentieth-Century Impressions of Hongkong, Shanghai, and Other Treaty Ports of China: Their History, People, Commerce, Industries, and Resources.* London: Lloyd's Greater Britain Publishing, 1908.

Wright, Mary C., ed. *China in Revolution: The First Phase, 1900–1913.* New Haven: Yale University Press, 1968.

Wu Tsai-ch'iao, comp. *Hsiang-kang Min-ch'iao shang-hao jen-ming-lu* (Directory of Hokkienese commercial firms in Hong Kong). Hong Kong: 1947.

Yen Ching-huang. "Ch'ing's Sale of Honours and the Chinese Leadership in Singapore and Malaya, 1877–1912." *Journal of Southeast Asian Studies* (September 1970), 1(2):20–32.

——*Coolies and Mandarins: China's Protection of the Overseas Chinese During the Late Ch'ing Period (1851–1911).* Singapore: Singapore University Press, 1985.

Yen Chung-p'ing. *Chung-kuo mien-fang-chih shih kao 1829–1937* (A draft history of cotton spinning and weaving in China, 1829–1937). Peking: K'o-hsüeh ch'u-pan-she, 1963.

Yen Chung-p'ing et al., comps. *Chung-kuo chin-tai ching-chi shih t'ung-chi tzu-liao hsüan-chi* (Selected statistics on China's modern economic history). Peking: K'o-hsüeh ch'u-pan-she, 1955.

Yeung, Peter. "Publications on Hong Kong from China." *Hong Kong Library Association Journal* (1982), no. 6, pp. 9–19.

Yip Oi Shan. *Will.* June 17, 1907.

Young, Ernest P. *The Presidency of Yuan Shih-k'ai: Liberalism and Dictatorship in Early Republican China.* Ann Arbor: University of Michigan Press, 1977.

Yu-so-wei. Hong Kong: 1905–6.

Index

A Ying, 318*n*7
Addis, Charles S., 123
Amaral, Gov. J. M. F., 41
America, 2, 25, 27, 30, 31, 182–83, 190.
  See also United States
Amoy, 28, 212
Anglo-Japanese Alliance, 231
Anhui, 251
Annam, 32, 125
Antaku Company, 225
Anti-American boycott in 1905–1906,
  11, 182–206, 208, 209, 295; business
  elite's attitude toward, 198–200; by
  "civilized means," 200–2; contro-
  versy over, 204–6; in Hong Kong,
  190–93; local newspapers in, 186–87;
  manufacturers' aspirations in, 193–
  96; negotiations between Chinese
  and American merchants in, 202–
  204; origins and nature of, 182–85;
  responses to, 185–90; workers' participation in, 196–97
Anticolonialism, 281, 283, 287, 293
Antiforeignism, 1, 13, 124, 187
Anti-Japanese boycott in 1908, 11, 295;
  boycott politics in Hong Kong, 223–
  28; and Canton Merchants' Self-
  Government Society, 214–15;

cracked down by colonial govern-
ment, 233–36; and merchants' eco-
nomic aspirations, 217–20; and riot
instigators, 232–33; and riots in
Hong Kong, 228–32; socioeconomic
background of, 208–13; touched off
by *Tatsu Maru* incident, 213–14
An-ya Pao, 279
Armentrout-Ma, Eve, 302*n*29
Arrow Incident, 52
Arrow War, 52, 57
Australia, 2, 23, 24, 27, 30, 31, 216

Bacon, Francis, 156
Balandier, George, 5, 6, 292
Bangkok, 27, 72, 73, 234
Bank of Canton, 253
Bank of Taiwan, 225
Bays, Daniel, 149
Beggars, 118, 119, 120, 122
Belilios, E. R., 139
Bentham, Jeremy, 155
Beresford, Lord Charles, 160–63
Bergere, Marie-Claire, 194, 307*n*61,
  308*nn*66 and 67
Birch, A., 4
Bird, Isabella, 70, 305*n*14
Blake, Sir Henry A., 110, 165, 166

Bonaparte, Louis Napoleon, 124
Bonham, Gov. Sir S. G., 41
Borneo, 87
Bourgeoisie, 194, 196
Bowen, Gov. G. F., 81, 84, 85, 141
Bowring, Sir John, 55
Boycott of Hongkong Tramway in
    1912–13, 11, 273–75; Canton govern-
    ment attitude toward, 279–80;
    causes of, 270–73; Chinese patrio-
    tism and anticolonialism in, 281–84;
    colonial government measures in,
    275–76, 284–86; implications of,
    286–87; letters threatening collabora-
    tors in, 276–77; promoters and their
    motivations, 277–79; workers in,
    280–81
Boycott Prevention Ordinance, 275,
    285, 286, 287
Boxer uprising, 165, 168
Bread-poisoning incident in 1857, 52–
    54
Brothels, 44
Bull, John, 167
Bunker, Gerald E., 315n13
Butterfield and Swire Company, 33,
    128, 178

Calcutta, 32
California, 24
Cambodia, 32
Cameron, Nigel, 311nn78, 79, and 82
Canada, 23, 216
Canton, 17, 18, 20, 125, 133, 164, 200,
    202, 212, 244, 250; Anglo-French oc-
    cupation of, 54; Hong Kong connec-
    tions, 31, 134, 249; independence of,
    247; turbulent situation during revo-
    lution in, 246–48; uprisings in, 238,
    241
Canton and Hong Kong Financial Co-
    operative Company, 278
Canton City Question, 41
Canton Merchants' Self-Government
    Society, 216, 218, 221, 224, 226, 232,
    233, 235; in Anti-Japanese boycott,
    214–15
Canton Sea Delicacies Guild, 226

Canton Revolutionary Government,
    270, 271, 277; attitude toward Hong
    Kong civil unrest, 261–63, 264; fi-
    nancial situation, 271, 272, 273; rela-
    tions with colonial government,
    261–63
Cargo boat people, 104; 1861 strike, 58;
    1884 strike, 126, 127, 130, 143; 1888
    strike, 170–72
Cargo coolies, 105, 106; 1872 strike,
    77–79; 1884 strike, 126, 127, 130
Chailley-Bert, Joseph, 311nn74 and 75
Chair coolies, 6, 105, 106, 108, 196,
    197, 264, 281; 1863 strike, 58, 176
Chan Chen Cheong, 191
Chan Chun-chuen, 62
Chan Hang Kiu, 233, 236
Chan Hon Tat, 277
Chan Keng Yu (Ch'en Keng-yü), 189,
    190, 250, 276
Chan Ket Chi, 220
Chan King-wah, 279
Chan Kwan I, 313n43
Chan, Kwong Tak Aaron, 318n9,
    319n15
Chan Lo Chun, 221, 233
Chan, Ming Kou, 299nn13 and 18,
    326n4
Chan Pek Chun (Ch'en Pi-ch'üan), 29
Chan Sing, 259
Chan Tai Kwong, 305n6
Chan Tin San, 305n5
Chan Tsz Tan, 305n5
Chan, Wai Kwan, 4
Chan Wai Po (Ch'en Hui-p'u), 213, 219
Chan Wan Chi, 88, 96
Chan, Wellington K. K., 308n91
Chan Wun Wing, 305n5
Chang Chih-pen, 311n80
Chang Chih-tung, 82, 125, 133, 134,
    139, 140, 169, 314n64; and *Chüan-
    hsüeh p'ien*, 158
Chang Jen-chün, 213, 218, 232
Chang Ming-ch'i, 246, 247, 248
Chang P'ei-lun, 125
Chang Sheng, 311n83
Chang Tzu-mu, 153
Chapman, Herrick, 317n62

Chau Lo, 272
Cheah Boon Kheng, 302*n*18
Chekiang, 153
Ch'en Chih, 155
Ch'en Chiung-ming, 270
Ch'en Ch'un-ch'üan, 250
Ch'en Ch'ing-ch'en, 201
Ch'en K'un-shan, 98–99
Ch'en Pao-chen, 125
Ch'en Shao-pai, 164, 165, 202, 203, 205, 241, 242
Ch'en Shu-jen, 201
Ch'en Ta, 326*n*3, 327*nn*5 and 6, 328*n*48
Ch'en Tse-hsien, 299*n*32
Cheng-hai, 28, 72, 73
Cheng Kuan-kung, 186, 187, 195, 201, 205, 206
Cheng Kuan-ying, 34, 153, 155, 158, 203
Cheng Shih-liang, 164, 241
Cheong Ah-lum, 52, 54
Cheong Sing Hong, 226
Cheong To Sang, 227
Chesneaux, Jean, 314*n*78, 330*n*122, 310*n*43
Cheung Kwong Yuen, 30
Chiang K'ung-yin, 215
China Felt Cap Factory, 252
China Sugar Refinery Company, 27–28
Chinese and Foreign Relief Society, 251
Chinese Association for the Promotion of National Products, 252
Chinese communities in America, 198
Chinese community in Hong Kong, 7, 38–39, 40, 142, 234, 289, 291; celebrates birth of Canton republic, 248–49; divided on boycott issue, 185–90, 200; formation of, 38–39, 40, 41; how it was held together, 8–10, 256; in a colonial situation, 65–102; structure of, 48–51; tensions within, 286; toward disintegration, 94, 281, 291
Chinese communities in Japan, 221
Chinese communities in Siam (Thailand), 28, 198–99
Chinese elite in Hong Kong, 7, 9, 10, 289, 290; alienation from populace,

231; conservatism of, 201; disapproval of rowdyism, 258; economic ties to foreign capitalism, 87–89, 139; harassed by rowdies, 259; in the 1884 insurrection, 135–40; loss of influence over populace, 280; mediation in social unrest, 78, 80, 81, 174; merchant elite organizations, 59–64; relations with Chinese officials, 81–84, 139–40, 175; relations with colonial government, 77, 81–84, 87, 89–94, 137–38; relations with populace, 76–77, 90–94, 137–38, 174, 175; split into factions, 99; term *elite* defined, 44
Chinese emigration, 23–26, 29
Chinese General Association for Engineering Studies, 240–41
Chinese Institute for the Study of Mechanics, 240
Chinese merchants, 6, 7, 60, 136, 271; gentrified, 71–72; in the Nam Pak Hong Guild, 61–64; in the Pacific Commercial network, 27–31
Chinese officials (mandarins), 54–55; in Canton, 1, 141; influence over Hong Kong residents, 36–37, 81–84; patriotic proclamations in 1884, 129, 131–32; and Triads, 132–35
Chiu, T. N., 298*n*3, 299*n*26
Ch'iu Chieh, 322*nn*13 and 31, 323*n*52
Chiu Hong, 226
Chiu Shiu Pok, 220, 221, 233, 236
Chiu Yue-tin, 62
Choa Chee Bee, 27, 305*n*5, 313*n*43
Choa Leep Chee, 28
Choi Atim, 114
Chow Fu, 149
Choy Fong Ginger Factory, 30
Chu Cheong Lan Cigarette Company, 195
Chu Loi, 230
Chu Shao-t'ing, 251
Chu Shih-chia, 193, 194
Chui Apo, 42–43
Chung-kuo jih-pao, 186, 224, 279, 280
Clement, C., 263
Coates, Willson H., 315*n*2

Cohen, Paul A., 8–9, 297*n*4, 298*n*12, 301*n*70, 315*n*17

Colley, Linda, 169

Colonial situation, 57, 292; defined, 5

Commercial guilds, 67, 76, 216

Compositors: guild, 260; 1911 strike, 260–61

Comprador, 26, 45, 52, 67, 87, 89, 178

Confucian patriot, 149

Confucianism: as hegemonic ideology, 75–77, 289, 290; revival of, 255–56. *See also* K'ung Meng min-tsu chu-i

Confucius, 76, 221, 243

Constitutionists, 186

Coolies, 102, 134, 141, 231, 232, 259, 293, 294; housing, 111–12; in 1894 feud, 173–75; in 1895 strike, 175–80; relations with fankwei, 120–21; and Queen Victoria's jubilees, 121–23; and tramway boycott, 281; under British justice, 114–18

Coolidge, Mary, 299*n*35

Courbet, Adm. Amede, 125, 126

Crime, 39, 41, 42, 43, 92

Cuba, 23

Cultural hegemony, 7, 9–10, 12, 63, 95, 289

Culturalism, 148–49

Da Costa, Captain, 42, 43

Dairen, 33

Dare to Die Society, 217, 225, 226, 276

Darwin, Charles, 156

Davis, Sir John, 40, 41

Denby, Charles, 25, 26

Des Vaeux, Gov. G. W., 87, 171, 172

Descartes, René, 156

Determined-to-Die Northern Expedition Troop, 251, 252

Deutsch, Karl, 148

District Watch Committee, 4, 46, 61, 69, 85, 86, 231, 259, 289, 331*n*133

East Kwangtung Red Cross Society, 250

Eastman, Lloyd, 311*nn*2 and 3, 312*n*17

Eitel, E. J., 2, 25, 45, 55, 56, 57, 87, 119; 298*n*5, 301*nn*12 and 14, 303*nn*44, 46, 48, 54, 56, and 60, 305*n*83, 310*n*47, 311*n*62

Eley, Geoff, 148, 151

Elliot, Charles, 18, 38

Endacott, G. B., 3; 298*n*6, 299*n*27, 300*nn*41 and 45, 301*n*7, 303*n*52, 307*nn*46 and 52, 311*nn*61, 63, and 68

Enlightenment Society, 201, 205

Esherick, Joseph W., 59, 63, 72, 289

European community in Hong Kong, 107, 108, 139, 177, 178, 179, 180, 274

Fairbank, John King, 300*nn*53 and 57, 329*n*88

Fankwei, 18, 39, 42, 43, 120, 122, 123, 143, 144, 146, 257, 283

Fatshan incident, 235

Faure, David, 4

Feldwick, W., 300*nn*51, 56, 59, and 60, 301*n*61, 307*n*60, 308*nn*89 and 92

Feng Hsia-wei, 183, 191, 195, 201

Feng Hui-ch'en, 191

Feng Kuei-fen, 153

Feng Shan, General, 243, 244, 246

Feng-shui, 9, 74, 75, 98, 289

Feng Tzu-yu, 201, 205, 222, 317*nn*53 and 55, 321*nn*86, 87, 97, 98, and 99

Feuerwerker, Albert, 299*n*14, 320*n*46

Field, Margaret, 196

Fieldhouse, D. K., 301*n*4

Fok, K. C., 4

Foochow, 32, 125, 141, 142

Formosa, 141, 142, 212. *See also* Taiwan

Foss, H., 139

Fox, Grace, 302*n*19

Fox, Harry H., 214

France, 161

Fuk Tak Kung, 48, 49

Fukien, 20, 24, 28, 46, 68, 153, 211

Funatsu Shinichirō, 224, 225, 229, 230, 236

Fung Sau Tin, 188, 189

Fung Wah Chuen, 85, 87, 88, 109, 187, 188, 190, 197, 199, 331*n*133

Gibb, Livingston and Co., 33

Gladstone, William, 156

Gowen, T., 164

Gramsci, Antonio, 10
Groves, R. G., 317*nn*49 and 51

Haikow, 32
Haiphong, 30, 212
Hakka, 19, 21, 39, 50, 55, 56, 59, 143
Hamberg, Theodore, 51
Hankow, 9, 10, 32, 33
Hanoi, 125, 254
Hanson, John W., 108
Hao, Yen-ping, 299*n*15, 308*n*67, 316*n*32
Hawkers, 105, 294; in the 1883 disturbances, 79–81
Hayes, Carlton, 148
Hayes, James, 4, 48, 302*nn*34, 35, and 36, 303*nn*40 and 67
Hatano Yoshihiro, 185
Hennessy, John P., 70, 84, 86, 90, 118
Hershatter, Gail, 12
Historiography: on Chinese nationalism, 148–52; on colonialism, 292; on Hong Kong studies, 2–5, 36–37, 55, 292; on labor, 7–8; Western-centric, 3
Ho Amei, 3, 82, 90, 100, 101, 136, 138, 139, 140
Ho Asik, 49
Ho Fuk (Ho Fook), 87, 331*n*133
Ho Kai, 14, 34, 85, 86, 88, 92, 97, 121, 122, 144, 152, 153, 169, 177, 179, 181, 190, 236, 248, 258, 265, 268, 313*n*43, 331*n*133; as collaborationist patriot, 160, 161, 162, 163, 271–72, 276; as spokesman for merchants, 157–60; in anti-American boycott, 199, 200, 202, 203, 204, 205; in controversy over the Light and Pass Ordinance, 99, 100, 101; in the tramway boycott, 275, 276, 280, 286; inspired by classical liberalism, 155, 157; open letter to John Bull, 166–67; reformist thought of, 154–57; and revolutionaries, 164, 166; on sanitary board, 307*n*51
Ho Kam Tong, 87, 187, 188, 231, 331*n*133
Ho, Ping-ti, 298*n*7

Ho Tso-chi, 319*nn*28 and 31, 320*n*40, 321*n*72
Ho Tso Wan, 233, 236
Ho Tung, Robert, 87, 100, 101, 165, 178, 179, 181, 305*n*6; as collaborationist patriot, 160, 161, 163, 169, 187
Ho Wyson, 97
Hobsbawm, Eric, 42, 299*n*28, 314*n*79
Hoklo (Hokkien, Fukienese), 17, 28, 30, 103, 110, 138, 143, 176, 180
Hong Kong: as a center for emigration abroad, 24–25; as a center for international trade, 26–27; as a crown colony, 38; as an entrepôt, 2, 7, 17, 23, 33, 34–35, 249, 250; as a free port, 18, 19; as a frontier settlement in the 1840s, 37–41, 288; as a refuge, 37; as a revolutionary base, 164–66; celebrates success of Chinese revolution, 248–49; Chinese commercial union in, 186, 187, 188, 189, 190, 197, 198, 204, 216, 251, 252, 275; Confucian Society in, 255; connections with Canton, 31, 36–37, 81, 134, 249; connections with Shanghai, 32, 33–34; depression in 1908, 212–13; exodus in 1858, 54, 55; labor strike in 1912, 263–65; and Nanyang trade, 29; number of Chinese importing and exporting firms in, 31–33; percentage of China's trade with, 33; police intelligence in, 132, 133, 232; politicized populace in, 243–45; population of, 18, 19, 22, 37, 39, 47, 95, 244, 299*n*24, 303*n*55, 327*n*24; rowdyism and hooliganism in, 256–60; subscriptions for the Chinese revolution in, 249–52; tensions and crises in the 1850s, 51–55
Hong Kong and Kowloon Wharf and Godown Company, 104, 108
Hong Kong and Shanghai Banking Corporation, 144, 178, 235, 271
Hong Kong Chinese Mechanics' Association, 240
Hong Kong Co-operative Financial Company, 272
Hongkong Tramway Company, 197,

Hongkong Tramway Company (*cont.*)
258, 280. *See also* boycott of Hong-
kong Tramway
Honig, Emily, 11, 13
Honolulu, 30
Hsieh-tou, 47
Hsieh, Winston, 326n1, 327nn9 and 11
Hsin-ning, 192
Hsing-Chung-hui, 152, 164–66, 170,
202
Hsü Ch'in, 201, 221, 234, 236
Hsü Hsin-wu, 299n19
Hsü Hsüeh-ch'iu, 222
Hsü I-sheng, 321n28
Hu Ch'uan-chao, 306n40, 313n49
Hu Han-min, 222, 248, 261, 270, 272,
280
Hu Li-yüan, 14, 34, 152, 153, 161, 169,
181; as spokesman for merchants,
157–60; inspired by classical liberal-
ism, 155, 156; reformist thought of,
154–57
Hu Pin, 315n16, 316nn26, and 32
Hua-an kung-so, 216
Hua-i Company, 235
Hua-yang Textile Manufacturing Com-
pany, 195, 196
Huang Chia-jen, 308n94
Huang Hsing, 243
Huang Po-yao, 204
Huang Shih-chung, 201
Huang Yung-shang, 98, 164
Hundred Days' Reform in 1898, 152,
159, 168, 169
Hung Jen-kan, 51
Hupei, 251
Huxley, Thomas, 156
Hyde, Francis E., 300nn47 and 48

Imperialism, 2, 13, 21, 140, 218, 258
India, 24, 178, 257
Indonesia, 27
Insurrection in 1884: as a turning point
in Hong Kong history, 291; and
Chinese merchant elite, 135–40;
Chinese officials' influence in, 131–
35; circumstances of, 129–30; popu-
lar patriotism in, 140–46; strike and
riots in, 126–29; Triads in, 132–35
Intelligentsia, 7, 148, 164, 170, 181,
185, 206, 241, 191
Ip of the Branch Society for Secret As-
sassination, 282
Irving, E. A., 231

Jamieson, J. W., 246, 247, 263
Japan, 2, 151, 194, 212; trade with
China, 210–11. *See also* anti-Japanese
boycott
Jardine, Matheson and Co., 33, 178
Jones, Susan, 299n16, 302n28
Java, 24, 28, 30

Kaifong, 38, 49, 50, 61, 67, 69, 86, 143
K'ai-p'ing, 44, 49, 59
Kam Shan Chung, 31, 198, 204, 216,
277, 278, 279
Kan Chiu Nam, 195
Kan Yuk Kai, 195
K'ang Yu-wei, 99, 153, 154, 157, 159,
163, 165, 169, 201, 215
Kani Hiroaki, 91, 300n37, 302nn32 and
35, 305n8, 308n69
Kant, Immanuel, 156
Kao Chen-pai, 306n20. *See also* Lin Hsi
Keelung, 125, 131
Kennedy, J. J. Stodard, 258
Keswick, J. J., 178
Kikuchi Takaharu, 185, 193–94,
320n60, 322nn8, 14, 17, and 25,
323nn38, 40, 41, 51, 53, and 59,
324nn68, 73, and 76
King, Frank H. H., 4
Ko Lo Association, 241
Ko Man Wah, 3, 29, 62, 68, 72–73, 74,
305n5
Ko Sing Tze, 74–75, 97
Ko Soon Kam, 29, 73–74, 103, 305n5
Kōbe, 142, 154, 216, 223
Kohn, Hans, 148, 159
Korea, 194
Kot Him, 241
Kōun Maru, 222
Kowloon-Canton Railway, 262

Kowloon City, 51, 98
Ku Fai Shan, 100, 199
Ku Kiu, 109
Kuang-hsü emperor, 68
Kuang-tung pang, 34
Kuhn, Philip, 10, 71
Kumano Maru, 223, 224, 226
K'ung Meng min-tsu chu-i (Confucian and Mencian nationalism), 256, 296
Kuo Sung-tao, 153
Kwan Hoi Chun, 83, 84
Kwan Sun Yin, 97
Kwan-ti, 9, 48, 49, 50
Kwang-hua-hsing Textile Company, 218
Kwangsi, 21, 215, 271
Kwangtung, 24, 28, 46, 49, 59, 131, 142, 164, 192, 210, 211, 212, 215, 217, 218, 271; 1886 flood in, 83; socioeconomic conditions in, 19–22
Kwangtung and Kwangsi Fellow-Provincials' Association (Shanghai), 213
Kwangtung Cigarette Company, 195
Kwangtung Nanyang Tobacco Company, 195, 196
Kwangtung Northern Expedition Army, 251
Kwei-chou, 59, 289
Kwok Acheong, 45, 63, 305n6
Kwok Chuen, 97
Kwok Lok, 97
Kwok Yik Chi, 220, 221, 233
Kwong Fook I-ts'z, 51, 66
Kwong Hip Lung and Company, 88, 96
Kwong On Wo, 223
Kwong Sang Hong, 196
Kwun Yum (Kuan-yin), 48

Labor, 7, 8; consciousness, 95–96; groups, 104–6; lives, 108–10; parochialism, 110–11; strikes, 95–96; wages, 106–7
Lai Wing Sheng, 116
Lau Chu Pak, 85, 87, 96, 109, 187, 199, 255, 276, 284, 285, 296, 331n133
Lau Lo-tak, 62

Lau Siu-kai, 301n1, 307nn51 and 53
Lau Tze Kai, 215, 233
Lau Wai Chuen, 85, 93–94
Lechler, Rudolph, 51
Lee Poh Ping, 300n58
Lee, S. F., 97
Lee Yuen Sugar Refineries, 176
Legge, James, 22, 51, 89, 299n23, 308n65
Legislative Council, 40, 86, 175
Leong On, 66, 136
Lethbridge, H. J., 3–4, 5, 50, 60, 304nn79 and 80, 305n8, 306n21, 307n49
Leung Chak Chau, 191
Leung Pui Chee, 88, 199
Leung Sui Hing, 220, 233, 236
Levenson, Joseph, 149
Li A-un, 133
Li Cheng-kao, 51
Li Chi-p'ei, 250
Li Chi-t'ang, 242
Li Hon Hung, 267, 268
Li Hung-chang, 85, 125, 165, 169
Li Kai Hi, 233
Li, Lillian M., 210
Li Men Hing Kwok Knitting Factory Company, 219–20, 233
Li Sing, 23
Li Ta-chao, 150
Li Tak Cheung, 3, 82, 88, 90, 136, 138, 139, 140
Li Tang, 271
Li Tsin-wei, 309n27, 316nn40 and 41
Li Tsun, 246, 247
Li Tzu-chung, 205
Li Yü-t'ang, 202, 203, 205, 250, 278
Li Yüan-hung, 245
Liang Ch'eng, 205, 213
Liang Ch'i-ch'ao, 154, 157, 159
Liang-Kuang Shipping Corporation, 218, 219
Light and Pass Ordinance 1895: protest against, 99–101
Lin Hsi, 304n78. See also Kao Chen-pai
Lin Kua-wu, 222
Linebarger, Paul, 313n56

Liu Kwang-ching, 149
Liu Yung-fu, 125
Lo Chor San, 62, 225
Lo Hok Pang, 156
Lo Koon Ting, 87
Lo Kuan She, 233
Locke, John, 155, 157
Lockhart, J. Stewart, 83, 86, 136, 173, 174
Loo Aqui, 43, 44, 49, 59, 63, 72, 288, 304n74
Lu Hao-tung, 164
Lu Lan-ch'ing, 246
Lu Yen, 302n30, 303nn46, 50, and 53, 304n72, 308n86
Lugard, Frederick, 234, 244, 248, 257, 258, 261, 265, 266
Luk Sau Theen, 313n43
Lung Chi-kwang, 246, 247, 271

Ma Ch'ao-chün, 240
Ma Chien-chung, 153
Ma Ying Piu, 219, 250
Macao, 18, 19, 41, 213
MacDonnell, Sir Richard, 67
Mai Shao-p'eng, 222
Malay, 87
Man Cheong, 49, 50
Man Mo Temple, 9, 44, 45, 49, 50, 51, 62, 66, 69, 76, 170, 173
Manchu, 152, 244, 283; dynasty, 2, 258; government, 20, 186, 222, 245
Manila, 28, 192
Mao Tse-tung, 150
Marsh, W. H., 80, 135
Mat-bag Packers' Guild, 263
May, F. Henry, 31, 93, 94, 110, 173, 174, 271, 275, 277, 279, 280, 287; assault on, 265–69; imperialist scheme, 272; being warned, 282
McCord, Edward A., 59, 304n71
Mei, June, 299nn9, 11, 20, and 30, 300n40
Meiji emperor, 231
Melbourne, 30
Mencian doctrine, 155
Merlat, Odette, 314n66
Meskill, Johanna M., 59, 304n70

Messageries Maritime Company, 144
Metal Guild, 235
Mill, John Stuart, 155, 156
Milner, A. C., 3
Miners, Norman, 329n84, 330n130
Mitsubishi Company, 225
Mitsui Bussan Company, 225, 229
Miyazaki Company, 225
Mok A Kwai, 117, 118
Mok Lai Chi, 196
Mongolia issue, 253–55
Montesquieu, 155, 156
Money Changers' Guild, 272
Moore, Barrington, 6–7
Morgan, W. P., 310n44, 312n33
Mou An-shih, 315n18
Murray, Dian H., 301n16

Nacken, J., 306nn29 and 30
Nagasaki, 197, 216, 217, 223
Nam Pak Hong Guild, 31, 46, 62–64, 128, 136, 216, 223, 224, 277, 278, 279, 289
Nan-hai, 20
Nanking, treaty of, 19, 20, 21
Nathan, Matthew, 189, 199, 200
National Disgrace Society, 232
Nationalism, 2, 14, 130, 278, 283; as a divisive force, 169; as a vehicle for sectional self-assertion, 195, 209, 219, 220, 252; bureaucratic, 149; collaborationist, 150–51, 160–63, 169, 294, 295; complexity of, 147–48, 150, 294; conservative, 148, 150; cultural, 148; defined, 13, 148; different forms of, 145, 148, 150; economic, 148; elitist, 148; historiography on, 148–52; in 1884 insurrection, 140–46; liberal, 148; and the Mongolia issue, 253–54; mystification of, 168–69; popular, 1, 13, 148, 150, 209, 293, 296; provoked by Sino-French war, 153–57; provoked by Sino-Japanese war, 153–57; socioeconomic dimension of, 14; totalitarian, 148. See also Patriotism
Native place–dialect groups, 45–48, 289
Nanyang, 17, 29

New Army, 251
New Territories, 152; British acquisition of, 163–64, 266
Newton, Isaac, 156
Ng Chin-keong, 298n2
Ng A Tong, 108
Ng Hon Chi, 331n133
Ng Li Hing, 62, 103, 305n5
Ng Sau Sang, 305n5
Ngan Wing Chi, 108, 110, 111
Ngu Ayow, 127
Ningpo pang, 34
Nip Koon Man, 233
Nippon Yūsen Kaisha, 216, 225
Noda Jitsunosuke, 300n42
Norman, Henry, 109, 123
Norton-Kyshe, James W., 2, 301nn5 and 8, 302nn20 and 21, 303nn49, 50, 55, and 64, 304n72, 309n108
Noyes, William D., 194

O Chun-chit, 68, 305n5
O Ting Sam, 305n5
On Tai Insurance Co., 139
Onogawa Hidemi, 315n16
Opium War, 18, 19, 37, 39, 43, 106
Orwell, George, 162, 178
Osaka, 142
Osaka Shōsen, 216, 225
Overseas Chinese Bomb Troop, 251
Ozawa Company, 225

Pa-tzu, 74, 75, 289
Pacific commercial network, 26–27, 62, 194
Painters' Guild, 263
Pan-yü, 20
Panama, 32
Pang, 34. *See also* Kuang-tung pang, Ningpo pang, and Teochiu pang
Pao-chia, 40
Pao-huang-hui, 165, 234, 243; versus T'ung-meng-hui, 220–23
Patriotism, 130, 253; collaborationist, 150–51, 160–63; and commercial advertisements, 195, 252; and mun-

dane interest, 281; defined, 13, 132; different forms of, 145. *See also* Nationalism
Paupers, 118–20
Pawnbrokers' strike in 1853, 57, 58
Peace Preservation Ordinance, 257, 258
Peihai, 32
Peking, 131, 141, 167, 245; 1860 convention of, 57; 1898 convention of, 163
Penang, 28, 30
P'eng Chia-li, 299nn29, 32, and 33, 300n39
P'eng Yü-lin, 125, 132
People's Army (min-chün), 250
Peru, 23, 31
Philippines, 28, 30, 182, 203, 212
Piece Goods Guild, 235
Piracy, 21, 41–42, 44, 51, 59, 132, 138, 301n16
Plague, 49, 93, 94
Po Leung Kuk, 4, 68, 69, 90, 91, 291, 305n7, 331n133
Pomerantz, Linda, 184, 300n46, 301n3. *See also* Shin, Linda Pomerantz
Pong, David, 149
Pope-Hennessy, James, 310n50, 311n70
Pottinger, Henry, 18
Prisoners, flogging of, 116–18, 257
Pugilistic clubs, 9, 47, 50, 113, 173, 174, 175
Pun Lan Sz, 220, 227, 233
Punti, 21, 39, 56, 62, 110, 111, 138, 143

Queen Victoria, 156; jubilees, 121–23
Queen's College, 98, 192
Queue, 243, 245, 258, 259
Quincy, William, 113

Racism, 2, 99–101; in America, 182–83
Rangoon, 30
Rankin, Mary B., 10, 59, 63, 70–71, 72, 149, 289, 303n41, 311n3
Reid, Thomas, 164

Reiners, William, 139
Remer, C. F., 301nn63 and 68, 308n85, 319n34
Revolutionaries, 164–66, 170, 186. See also Hsing-Chung-hui and T'ung-meng-hui
Revolution of 1911, 1, 2, 98, 102, 238, 282, 295
Rhoads, Edward J., 321n90, 323nn39 and 54, 326n137
Rice Merchants' Guild, 191
Rice trade, 27
Ricksha pullers, 6, 105, 108, 176, 196, 264, 266, 281; in 1883 disturbances, 80–81
Rights recovery movement, 185, 193, 208; and native goods promotion movement, 252–53
Robinson, William, 94, 101, 176
Roosevelt, Alice, 199, 200
Rowe, William T., 9–10
Rudé, George, 283
Russia, 161, 208, 253, 254
Russian-Mongolian Convention, 253
Russo-Japanese War, 208, 210

Saigon, 199, 221
Saiyinpun (Sei Yin Poon), 48, 49
San Francisco, 25, 30, 31, 188, 204
Sandakan, 32
Sanitary Board, 86, 307n51
Sayer, G. R., 3, 245, 327n28, 330n127
Schiffrin, Harold Z., 317nn55 and 57
Schrecker, John, 149
Schwartz, Benjamin, 149
Scott, James C., 294
Scottish Oriental Steamship Company, 29
Seikin Bank, 225, 236
Self-strengthening policy, 153, 154
Seventy-two Guilds Fishing Industry Company, 226
Seventy-two Commercial Guild, 218, 225, 246
Severn, Claud, 266
Shaffer, Lynda, 298n17
Shang-pao, 201, 221, 225, 243, 245
Shang-wu yen-chiu-she, 219

Shanghai, 11, 13, 21, 23, 28, 32, 183, 212, 244, 251, 252; Hong Kong–Shanghai corridor, 32, 33–34
Shantung, 32, 62
Sharp, Granville, 178, 179–80
Shen Pao-chen, 149
Shen-tung, 50, 71
Shih-shih hua-pao, 192, 193, 228
Shimonoseki, treaty of, 208
Shin, Linda Pomerantz, 301n3. See also Linda Pomerantz
Shuang Ai, 301nn10 and 15, 302nn20 and 21, 303n50
Shun-te, 20
Siam, 27, 29, 32, 195, 221. See also Thailand
Siemssen and Co., 33
Sin Tak Fan, 3, 88, 236
Sin Wa Fung, 197
Singapore, 23, 27, 28, 29, 32, 44, 72, 212, 221; population of, 300n58
Singh, Roor, 259
Sinn, Elizabeth, 4, 46, 49–50, 67, 69, 84, 86, 305nn4, 9, 10, and 11, 306n38, 308n83, 313n49, 314n61
Sino-British synarchy, 258
Sino-French War (1884–85), 82, 97, 102, 150, 151, 152; impact of, 124–26; nationalist response to, 153–57
Sino-Japanese War (1894–95), 150, 151, 152, 168, 181, 193; as a watershed for modern industry, 208, 210; nationalist response to, 153–57
Siu King Chung, 192
Smith, Adam, 155
Smith, Carl T., 4, 60, 298nn4 and 5, 299nn21, 22, and 25, 300n55, 301n6, 302nn22 and 24, 303nn45 and 59, 304nn74 and 75, 305nn6 and 84, 309n10, 313nn43 and 47
Smith, J. B., 139
Society of Chinese Abroad for the Promotion of Patriotic Subscriptions, 273
South Africa, 32, 267
South China, 21, 26, 28, 31, 32, 42, 212, 243
Southeast Asia, 2, 23, 27, 28, 31, 32,

62, 71, 74, 131, 191, 212, 216, 243, 251; Chinese emigration to, 29, 30

Sovereign-Rights Restoration Cigarette Factory, 195

Sparks, Douglas W., 302n33

Spencer, Herbert, 156

St. Petersburg, 254

Stanton, William, 310n37

Stearns, Peter N., 317n62

Stephen, Headley J., 301n2

Stewart, Murray, 258

Straits Settlements, 28, 195

Strand, David, 11

Strike against Registration Ordinance (1844), 40

Stubbs, Reginald E., 123

Su Chao-cheng, 239

Sugar, 27, 28

Sumatra, 24

Sun Yat-sen, 142, 164, 165, 167, 205, 221, 239, 240, 241, 242, 245, 252, 262

Swatow, 26, 28, 31, 32, 72, 110, 176, 212

Sydney, 30, 31

Sze Yap, 21, 44, 45, 49, 111, 171, 173, 174, 180; Association, 95, 242, 249, 250, 273, 277, 278, 279, 280, 281. *See also* Young China Party

Taft, William H., 197, 199, 200

Taikoo Sugar Refinery, 176

Taiping rebellion, 10, 21, 22, 51, 60, 71, 289

Taiwan, 59, 125, 131, 289. *See also* Formosa

Tam Achoy, 44, 45, 50, 59, 63, 72, 288, 304n74

Tam Chow Silver Mine, 140

Tang Lap Ting, 191

Tanka, 39, 45, 48

Tatsu Maru, 222, 232; incident, 213–14

Teng Chung-hsia, 310n32

Teng Chung-tse, 242

Teng Hua-hsi, 213

Teochiu (Ch'ao-chou), 17, 28, 29, 30, 110, 111, 176, 180, 250

Teochiu pang, 34

Thailand, 199, 254. *See also* Siam

Thompson, E. P.: on charity, 91; on class relationship, 11–12; on cultural hegemony, 10; on English gentry's hegemonic style, 64

T'ien-hou (Tin Hau), 9, 48

Tientsin, 32, 33, 56, 212

Tilly, Charles, 58, 304n73

Ting Jih-ch'ang, 68

Ting Yu, 319nn28 and 31, 320nn38, 40, and 70, 321n72

To Li Ting, 96

To Sze Tun, 305n5

Tong King-sing, 34

Tongking, 87, 125

Tōyō Kisen, 216, 225

Triad society, 9, 21, 22, 51, 56, 112–14, 240, 251; and 1884 insurrection, 132–35, 145; and revolutionaries, 241, 242

Tse Yam Luk, 215, 233

Tse Tsan Tai, 98, 164, 166, 169, 241

Ts'en Ch'un-hsüan, Gov., 200, 205

Tseng Chi-tse, 154

Tseng Kuo-ch'üan, 68

Tso Seen-wan, 88, 202, 204, 205

Tsungli Yamen, 133

Tung Kuan (Tung Kun), 111, 171, 172, 173, 174, 180

T'ung-meng-hui, 201, 202, 203, 205, 251, 278, 283; activities among workers, 239–43; and Triads, 241, 242; versus Pao-huang-hui, 220–23

Tung Tai Tseung Kee and Company, 96

Tung Wah Hospital, 4, 46, 71, 80, 82, 84, 99, 119, 127, 135, 145, 187, 206, 251, 285, 289, 290, 291, 331n133; charity and social service, 68–69; during 1894 coolie feud, 173, 175; founding of, 66–68; in the triangular government-elite-populace relationship, 90, 91, 92, 93, 94; social hegemony, 69–70

Un Li Chun, 331n133

Un Sing-ts'un, 137

Uchida Ryōhei, 221

United States, 24, 184, 216; exclusion laws, 182, 190, 198, 199, 200; exclu-

United States (*continued*)
  sion treaty with China, 185; exports
  to China, 27; trade with Hong Kong,
  26–27

Vincenot, Francis, 126

Wa Hop Telegraph Company, 90, 139,
  140
Wah On Co., 204
Waichow (Hui-chou), 167, 238, 242,
  246
Wakeman, Frederic, Jr., 298*n*8,
  299*nn*10, 12, and 17, 303*n*54
Wales, Nym, 330*n*122
Wang Ching-wei, 150–51, 162
Wang Ching-yü (Wang Jingyu), 88,
  194
Wang Hsien-ch'ien, 158, 169
Wang T'ao, 34, 69–70, 153–54
Wang Ya-fu, 201
Washermen's Guild, 263
Watanabe Tetsuhiro, 316*n*39
Weber, Max, 60, 304*n*73
Wei Piu, 97
Wei Wah On, 97
Wei Yuk, 85, 86, 87, 109, 163, 169, 177,
  181, 190, 199, 200, 247, 248, 258, 265,
  313*n*43, 331*n*133; collaborationist
  scheme, 271–72; during tramway
  boycott, 275; in controversy over the
  Light and Pass Ordinance, 99, 100,
  101; letter to Beresford, 162; receives
  threatening letters, 276–77
Wen Tzu-ts'un, 222
Weng Kat On, 223
Wesley-Smith, Peter, 317*nn*49 and 51
West Indies, 23
White, Hayden V., 315*n*2
Wing Fat Hong, 29
Wing On Company, 97
Women's Northern Expedition Troop,
  251
Wong Choi Chiu, 220
Wong Kam Fuk, 331*n*133
Wong Kwei Hung, 239
Wong See Tye, 313*n*43

Wong Shing, 85, 86, 88, 305*n*6
Wong Siu Ham, 305*n*5
Wong Ting-ming, 62
Wong-ma-kok, 42, 43
Woo, H. K. (Hu Chiung-t'ang), 88, 97
Woo, Lin Yuen, 85, 313*n*43
Wood, A. E., 96, 308*n*87
Wood, W. A., 3, 297*n*2, 309*nn*9 and 20
Worsley, Peter, 168–69, 292
Wright, Arnold, 300*nn*42, 43, 50, and
  56, 301*nn*61 and 71, 307*nn*60 and 62,
  308*n*90, 317*n*60
Wu Hsien-tzu, 221, 233, 234, 235, 236
Wu T'ing-fang, 86, 252
Wu Ting-sam, 62
Wu Tung-ch'i (Ng Tung Kai), 196, 202,
  205
Wu Yao-t'ing, 201
Wu-ch'ang uprising, 243

Yan Ping Hup, 109
Yang Hsi-yen, 250
Yang Shih-hsiang, 149
Yang Yin, 239
Yao Yü-p'ing, 251
Yeh Ming-ch'en, 52
Yeh Te-hui, 158, 169
Yen Ching-huang, 306*n*18
Yen Chung-p'ing, 298*n*8, 300*n*43,
  301*n*67, 320*n*45, 322*n*16
Yen Fu, 154, 156
Yeung Ku-wan (Yang Ch'ü-yün), 98,
  166
Yeung Wan Po, 191
Yin Wen-k'ai, 250
Yip Oi Shan (Yip Hoi Shan), 103, 190,
  305*n*5
Yip Wai Pak, 220
Yokohama, 216, 223
You Put-in, 133
Young China Party, 242, 273, 278. *See
  also* Sze Yap Association
Young, Ernest P., 150
Yu Lieh, 241
Yu Pun San, 220
Yu-so-wei, 186, 330*n*131
Yuan Heung Po, 226

Yüan Pang-chien, 303*n*57
Yüan Shih-k'ai, 149, 150, 151, 186, 252, 287
Yüeh-chih Girls' School, 250
Yuen Fat Hong, 29, 72, 73, 74, 75

Yuen Hing Shat Yip Company, 218
Yün-nan, 32, 271
Yung-hsin Li-min Machine Weaving Company, 253
Yung Wing, 34

Designer: Teresa Bonner
Text: Palatino
Compositor: Maple-Vail
Printer: Maple-Vail
Binder: Maple-Vail